D1252683

SHERINGTON

FIEFS AND FIELDS OF A
BUCKINGHAMSHIRE VILLAGE

SHERINGTON

FIEFS AND FIELDS OF A BUCKINGHAMSHIRE VILLAGE

BY

A.C.CHIBNALL

FELLOW OF CLARE COLLEGE
CAMBRIDGE

CAMBRIDGE
AT THE UNIVERSITY PRESS
1965

PUBLISHED BY
THE SYNDICS OF THE CAMBRIDGE UNIVERSITY PRESS

Bentley House, 200 Euston Road, London, N.W. 1
American Branch: 32 East 57th Street, New York, N.Y. 10022
West African Office: P.O. Box 33, Ibadan, Nigeria

Printed in Great Britain at the University Printing House, Cambridge
(Brooke Crutchley, University Printer)

LIBRARY OF CONGRESS CATALOGUE
CARD NUMBER: 66-10048

TO MARJORIE

the mother of yet another

John Chibnall

CONTENTS

APPENDICES

LIST OF ILLUSTRATIONS

PLATES

MAPS

Maps 3 and 4 were reconstructed by the author. All the maps were drawn by E. W. Tole

LIST OF TABLES

LIST OF GENEALOGICAL TABLES

ABBREVIATIONS

CLASSES OF PUBLIC RECORDS, WITH THEIR CLASS NUMBERS

CHANCERY

C 1	Proceedings, Early
C 2	Proceedings, Series I
C 3	Proceedings, Series II
C 47	Miscellanea
C 54	Close Rolls
C 60	Fine Rolls
C 66	Patent Rolls
C 72	Scutage Rolls
C 93	Charitable Uses
C 131	Extents for Debt
C 132	Inquisitions Post Mortem, Series I, Henry III
C 133	Inquisitions Post Mortem, Series I, Edward I
C 134	Inquisitions Post Mortem, Series I, Edward II
C 135	Inquisitions Post Mortem, Series I, Edward III
C 136	Inquisitions Post Mortem, Series I, Richard II
C 137	Inquisitions Post Mortem, Series I, Henry IV
C 138	Inquisitions Post Mortem, Series I, Henry V
C 139	Inquisitions Post Mortem, Series I, Henry VI
C 142	Inquisitions Post Mortem, Series II
C 143	Inquisitions ad quod damnum
C 145	Inquisitions Miscellaneous

COURT OF COMMON PLEAS

CP 25(1)	Feet of Fines, Series I
CP 25(2)	Feet of Fines, Series II
CP 40	Plea Rolls
CP 43	Recovery Rolls

ABBREVIATIONS

DUCHY OF LANCASTER

DL42	Miscellaneous Books

EXCHEQUER OF PLEAS

E13	Plea Rolls

EXCHEQUER, TREASURY OF THE RECEIPT

E36	Rentals and Surveys

EXCHEQUER, QUEEN'S REMEMBRANCER

E101	Accounts, various
E106	Extents of Alien Priories
E112	Bills and Answers
E136	Escheator's Accounts
E149	Inquisitions Post Mortem, Series I
E150	Inquisitions Post Mortem, Series II
E178	Special Commissions of Inquiry
E179	Subsidy Rolls, etc.
E199	Sheriffs' Accounts

EXCHEQUER, AUGMENTATION OFFICE

E301	Certificates of Chantries and Colleges
E314	Miscellanea
E315	Miscellaneous Books
E318	Particulars for Grants of Crown Lands
E322	Surrenders of the Monasteries

EXCHEQUER, LORD TREASURER'S REMEMBRANCER

E357	Escheator's Enrolled Accounts
E359	Enrolled Accounts, Subsidies
E368	Memoranda Rolls
E372	Pipe Rolls

EXCHEQUER OF RECEIPT

E401	Receipt Rolls
E403	Issue Rolls

JUSTICES ITINERANT

JI 1	Assize Rolls, Eyre Rolls, etc.

COURT OF QUEEN'S BENCH

KB 26	Curia Regis Rolls
KB 27	Coram Rege Rolls

COURT OF REQUESTS

Reg. 2	Proceedings

STATE PAPER OFFICE

SP 22	State Papers, Domestic

COURT OF STAR CHAMBER

St. Ch. 5	Proceedings, Elizabeth
St. Ch. 7	Proceedings, Elizabeth Adenda
St. Ch. 8	Proceedings, James I

SOCIETIES AND PUBLICATIONS

BASRB	*Buckinghamshire Archaeological Society, Records Branch*
BHRS	*Bedfordshire Historical Record Society*
BRS	*Buckinghamshire Record Society*
BSR	*Buckinghamshire Sessions Records*
CRR	*Calendar of the Curia Regis Rolls*
EHR	*English Historical Review*
LRS	*Lincoln Record Society*
NRS	*Northamptonshire Record Society*
OHS	*Oxford Historical Society*
ORS	*Oxfordshire Record Society*
PRS	*Pipe Roll Society*
RB	*Records of Buckinghamshire*
TRHS	*Transactions of the Royal Historical Society*
VCH	*Victoria County History*
YASRS	*Yorkshire Archaeological Society, Record Series*

DOCUMENTS

BUCKINGHAMSHIRE COUNTY RECORD OFFICE, AYLESBURY

D/A/GT/–	Buckinghamshire Archdeaconcy, Glebe terriers, etc.
D/A/V/–	Buckinghamshire Archdeaconcy, Visitation Books
D/A/We/–	Buckinghamshire Archdeaconcy, Registered Wills
D/A/Wf/–	Buckinghamshire Archdeaconcy, Filed Wills
D/C/–	Deeds deposited by Major Chester
D/Ch/–	Deeds deposited by the author
Tyr. D	Deeds of the Tyringham Estate, not yet (1963) calendared

BUCKINGHAMSHIRE ARCHAEOLOGICAL SOCIETY, MUSEUM, AYLESBURY

BAS	Deeds deposited

MERCERS' COMPANY, MERCERS' HALL, LONDON

ECL	Evidences of Dr Colet's lands
MAC	Court of Assistants Minute Books
MCR	Court Rolls of Mercers' manor in Sherington
MRW	Mercers' Register of Writings
RCL	Register of Company Lands
SAB	Surveyors' Account Books

NORTHAMPTONSHIRE RECORD OFFICE, DELAPRE ABBEY, NORTHAMPTON

NRO	Deeds deposited
SS	Stopford–Sackville muniments

COLLECTIONS

T	Throckmorton Muniments, Coughton Court, Warwickshire

ACKNOWLEDGEMENTS

MY early studies on Sherington owed much to the sympathetic encouragement of the late Mr Frederick William Bull, solicitor and local historian of Newport Pagnell, who stimulated my interest by letting me read the notes he had made during the course of his professional career on many important Sherington deeds. Somewhat later he allowed me to rummage freely through the contents of numerous old tin boxes left derelict in his office store-rooms; there, at my leisure, I was able to browse through a miscellany of records that revealed in an illuminating way the day to day business of a local attorney in a bygone age; there I learnt to understand and appreciate the writings with which such attornies clothed fines and recoveries, those barebones of the Public Record Office, and how they dealt with many a homely problem outside the dull routine of conveyancing. The knowledge acquired in this unconventional but happy way laid the foundation of the latter half of the present work and I recall his friendship and help with deep gratitude. I would also like to express my warm thanks to the late Professor Eilert Ekwall of Lund for his kindly collaboration in the study of the Sherington field-names. My own contribution has seldom exceeded a demonstration of the local background and the interpretations finally adopted reflect his erudition.

It is a pleasure to acknowledge the willing co-operation of those in possession of archives directly or indirectly concerned with Sherington. The Worshipful Company of Mercers have very generously allowed me the free run of their muniment room and permission to quote from their records. I would like to thank them, and also Mr Geoffrey Logsdon, Clerk of the Company, for their courtesy. The late Lady Throckmorton very kindly allowed me in 1946 to have photostat copies made of all the medieval North Buckinghamshire charters preserved at Coughton Court, a generous concession which has materially aided me in my work. I also wish to thank Mrs Gladys Chester for allowing me to inspect the Chester muniments now housed at the Old Rectory, North Crawley. The assistant keepers and staff of the Public Record Office, the County Archivists for Bedfordshire (Miss Joyce Godber), Buckinghamshire (Mr E. J. Davis) and Northamptonshire (Mr P. I. King), as well as Miss Cicely Baker of the Buckinghamshire Archaeological Museum, have all given unstinted help when needed. I am especially grateful to Miss Edith Scroggs for numerous transcripts from the Plea Rolls and to Mr E. W. Tole for so skilfully drawing all the maps.

My wife, who has shown great patience and forbearance during the time I have spent engrossed in Sherington, has been kind enough to read the whole book in penultimate draft. My friends Prof. V. H. Galbraith and Prof. C. R. Cheney have kindly read the first thirty chapters in typescript. I do indeed owe a deep debt of gratitude to these three willing helpers, who have offered constructive criticism of the text and have put me right in a number of places. None the less I alone am responsible for the errors that will almost certainly be found in a volume so full of detail.

My thanks are also due to the Syndics of the Cambridge University Press for undertaking the publication of the volume and to the staff for friendly co-operation.

Lastly, I must thank the President and Council of the British Academy for a generous grant towards the cost of publication.

INTRODUCTION

THE essays on the history of Sherington presented in this book are the outcome of sporadic work started in 1919 as a simple family inquiry which has since developed into a comprehensive study of certain aspects of the feudal and economic growth of the village. Fortunately perhaps it was not realized at the outset what a wealth of record material would ultimately be brought to light, all of which has needed detailed attention. Certain manuscript as well as printed sources of information at the Public Record Office and the British Museum had already been sifted and edited for the Victoria Country History of Buckinghamshire,[1] but the writers concerned with Sherington had not had at their disposal the title deeds and other muniments of the four main estates there. All of these were of manorial or reputed manorial status, yet the records of three of them showed without any deep study that they had been built up within the last hundred years or so by collecting farms that had once been in independent ownership, for there was a series of deeds going back to the seventeenth century for each individual farm. The fourth estate was owned by the Mercers' Company of London as trustees of the endowment provided by John Colet, Dean of St Paul's, for St Paul's School in 1509. In this case the records included a fairly complete set of Court Rolls, Account Books and various Minute Books. Other sources that have yielded valuable information include the Throckmorton muniments at Coughton Court, Warwickshire, the Buckinghamshire and Northamptonshire Record Offices and the lumber room of the late Mr F. W. Bull, solicitor of Newport Pagnell.

Examination of the deeds belonging to the owners of the four estates mentioned above gave the impression that collectively they represented the major part if not the whole of the agricultural land in Sherington during the seventeenth and eighteenth centuries, when the open-field system of tillage still prevailed. To interpret many of these old documents there was need for a contemporary map showing the lay-out of the open fields, the furlongs and the meadow lands that existed prior to 1797, in which year all the old boundaries were swept away on implementation of the Enclosure Award. No such map, unfortunately, appeared to

[1] *VCH Bucks*, IV, 451.

have survived, but as the deeds in private ownership incorporated a number of terriers in which the land was referred to in terms of fields, furlongs and strips (selions, ridges), it seemed worthwhile to attempt to reconstruct the strip map that might have been drawn by a surveyor visiting the village for that purpose a decade or so before the Enclosure Award, say around 1770.

No difficulty was experienced in showing that the three great common fields—called in the eighteenth century Dropwell or Marehill Field, Middle or Little Field and Windmill Field—comprised the major part of the land in the south, south-west and north-west sectors of the village respectively, and that the common meadow abutted on the river between Sherington bridge and the Tyringham boundary. The furlongs, however, presented a jigsaw puzzle that was only partially solved at this stage. The majority were readily allocated a position in the particular common field to which they were assigned in the terriers, but a few others seemed to belong elsewhere. It was noted at the time that in the furlongs of the former group the strips were rarely consolidated, whereas in the latter they were nearly always in compacted blocks often extending to several acres. It was a fair surmise that these consolidated furlongs were, or had once been, demesne, and that they probably belonged to the north and north-east sectors of the village, an area for which there was insufficient evidence for a full reconstruction in the terriers then under review.

An informative series of demesne terriers for the late sixteenth century was available, and as these could probably provide the missing information it was decided to start afresh and attempt to reconstruct the strip map for the year 1580. In keeping with expectation the demesne lands were found to lie exclusively in the east, north-east and south-east sectors of the village respectively, forming a quarter-circle bounded on the west by the Olney road and the south by the Bedford road. The area registered by the terriers in the form of arable land, pasture and wood amounted in all to 611 acres, whereas according to the Ordnance Survey map the sectors concerned covered 605 acres. The agreement between the two values was remarkably close and strengthened the opinion that the demesne had been correctly interpreted. The reconstruction of the rest of the map was completed without difficulty (Map 3). Fortunately the terriers covered such a large proportion of the open-field arable land and meadow that it was possible to deduce the extent of the cowpasture, an elusive item in rural topography because it is usually referred to in terms of so many 'cow-commons' instead of acres.

These studies brought to light two facts of outstanding importance. In the first place there were in Sherington at the end of the sixteenth century four manors or reputed manors called Linford, Cave, Fitz John and Mercers' respectively and the estates attached to these, together with certain small properties held freely of the Mercers' manor, accounted within a few acres for the whole of the land in the village. Early in the next century the first three of these estates were dispersed among the local farmers and it was not until comparatively recent times that economic conditions brought about a re-aggregation into three new units showing but little kinship with the old manorial estates. The deeds available enable the change-over from one set-up to the other, reflecting the interplay of economic forces during the period, to be followed in detail. Secondly, the observation that the demesne land was located exclusively in its own sector and none of it was dispersed among the strips in the great common fields suggests that piecemeal consolidation of the usual type had not occurred but that the demesne had been created 'en bloc' or in a succession of large blocks at a time when drastic and deep-seated changes were possible as, for instance, they were at the Conquest. It was anticipated, therefore, that the same distribution of the land would be found to occur at a somewhat earlier date and this was confirmed when a terrier of the Linford manor demesne for 1312 came to hand.

A detailed examination of the manorial and other relevant deeds showed that, except for a case of give and take among the open-field lands of Linford manor, all four of the Elizabethan estates had come down from about the year 1300 without significant alteration. There had, however, been a change in the meanwhile from the ancient two-field to the three-field system of tillage. It appeared probable, therefore, that the strip map of 1580 could be used as a basis for the reconstruction of one for the year 1300 and the map was drawn accordingly. The changes in the field system were incorporated and only such furlongs as had been noted in contemporary or earlier deeds were named. The gaps were surprisingly few. The map is unique for its date, and has been of great service in helping to put into the right perspective many of the disputes over land in Sherington that are recorded at length in the thirteenth-century plea rolls.

Although few title deeds for the thirteenth century have survived much information has been garnered from other sources. During this period the principal manor was still in the hands of the family named Carun who had held since the days of

Henry I, and whose last male representative Roger de Carun died in 1301 leaving an heiress Sibyl who later married Richard de Linford. At the beginning of the century only one subsidiary manor, that of Cockfield, had been sub-infeudated, but by 1300, as has already been mentioned, there were four manors or reputed manors in the village. Extents made at inquisitions, squabbles over land recorded at length in assize and plea rolls, as well as widows' claims for dower, have all helped to illustrate and integrate the diverse changes in ownership of the demesne lands between 1220 and 1300. These can, indeed, be followed with surprising exactness. The open-field lands called for a more elaborate investigation as they were often cited in terms of rent instead of acres, but the assembled data show that the whole of the acreage available in 1300 was already under tillage at a much earlier date.

To interpret the land history of Sherington beyond 1220 one is forced to depend less on factual knowledge and more on inference. The danger inherent in such a predicament is obvious and when writing the essays collected in this book the author has kept in mind an apothegm of Vinogradoff[1] which no local historian can afford to ignore.

More is known, of course, about later than about ancient times, and this will make it necessary on many occasions to turn to well ascertained later facts in order to form a judgment about ancient conditions. But it is not necessary to invert the sequence of epochs in the sketch of historical development, and by following the chronological order we may guard against carrying into the distant past conceptions of comparatively modern growth. It is not so much the fact of studying later stages before the earlier that constitutes the method of investigation from the known to the unknown, as the careful distinction between evidence and inference, and the systematic use of both.

The chapters follow a chronological order, but it is recognized that in places the reader may be left in some confusion as to the views expressed unless he has been made aware of certain unique features in the village history that do not emerge until later. This may apply especially to the early periods discussed in the first two chapters of the book, and accordingly it has been thought wise to include this short introduction, which has been limited by design to an exposition of various aspects of landholding in the village.

[1] *The Growth of the Manor*, pp. viii–ix.

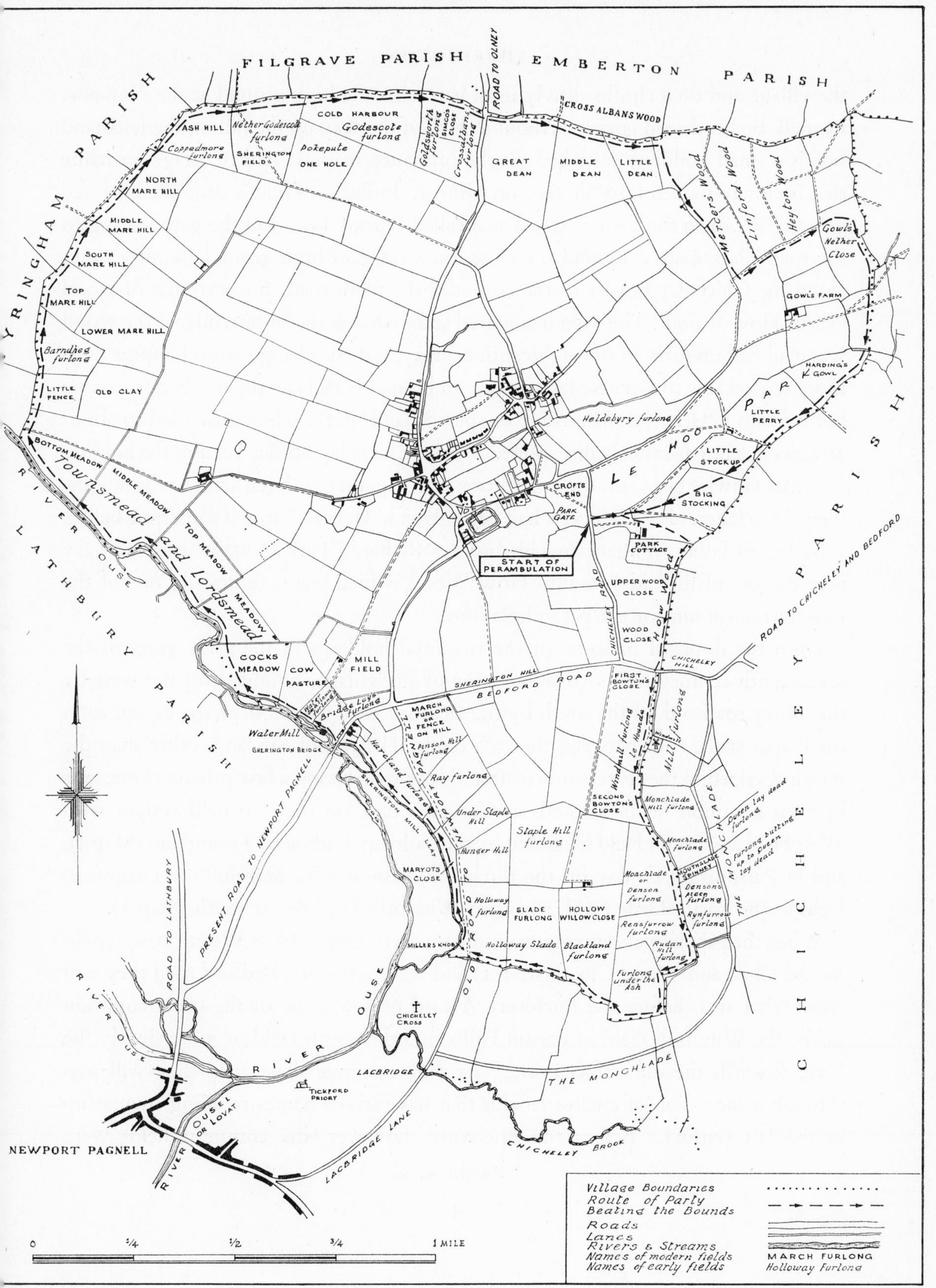

Map 1. Beating the bounds.

the village and then climbs slowly until it reaches the high ground at the Newport Pagnell–Bedford road corner. About a third of the way up the hill on the left-hand side is a small building described on the ordnance map as 'Park Cottage', a name that is closely woven into Sherington history. In Parson Fuller's time the enclosed ground on which the cottage stood was called 'Park Close' and the gate leading to the road 'Park Gate'. Behind the close, on a ridge of high ground running south along the Chicheley border to the corner at the main road, was a stretch of wood called 'How Wood'. The vista has altered somewhat in the meanwhile, as the wood was grubbed up early in the eighteenth century, but the change would appear even more remarkable to Gervase the parson. In his day Park Gate did not belie its name but led into le Hoo (OE *hōh*, ridge or spur of land) Park, which extended to about 80 acres in a north-easterly direction along the Chicheley border as far as the holding marked 'Gowles farm' on the ordnance map. Together with ten acres of the adjoining le Hoo (later, How) Wood it had been given to Gervase himself sometime before 1193 by his father William and his brother Richard. Park Cottage must be very near the site of the old gate into How Wood, which was traditionally one of the two starting-points for the perambulations.

Until the dispersal of some of the manorial holdings in the early years of the seventeenth century the north-east sector of the village, bounded on the west by the Olney road and on the south by the Bedford road was all demesne except for a small area at the fork between the two roads. The rest of the land, other than the meadows skirting the river, some scattered cow pasture and a few private closes, was in open common fields worked, in Gervase's day, on the two-field system with West Field and South Field separated by the pathway leading to Tyringham (Map 4), and in Parson Fuller's day on the three-field system with Marehill (or Dropwell) Field to the north, Little Field, and then Windmill Field to the south (Map 3).

When the parishioners emerge from the southern end of How Wood (now Upper Wood Close and Wood Close) (Map 1) and walk across the Bedford road they will enter what was, before the Enclosure Award of 1797, one of the great common fields; the Windmill Field of Parson Fuller and the South Field or more simply the 'field towards the sun' of Gervase.[1] As they continue their walk they will pass through a succession of enclosed fields that have trivial names recalling ownership in the last century. Before the Enclosure, however, the common fields were

[1] *BASRB*, IV, 74.

Map 2. Field map of Sherington, *c.* 1950.

parcelled out into furlongs, and in the present instance the first of these was called le Hoende (1313) because it extended to the end of the high ridge; the name was changed late in the thirteenth century to Windmill furlong when the prior of Tickford erected such a mill on the far side of the parish boundary with Chicheley.

The next furlong, which sloped gently downhill, is interesting for many reasons. Part of it was in Chicheley parish and the two portions were tilled from east to west across the boundary in common. Such overlapping, though unusual, explains the need to register the parish boundaries each year. The early name for the furlong was Monchlade (*c.* 1270) and in Sherington it became later (1750) Monthslade or Denson furlong. In Chicheley the name has persisted and on the ordnance map there is a wood called Mouthslade Spinney in the position occupied by the old furlong. Monch is a reduced form of minchen (OE *mynecen*, nun) and the name means nun's path. This path or track—the Monchlade—was used as a short cut by light traffic going to Newport from the east, especially when floods interfered with the river crossing at Sherington. It branched off from the main highway at the foot of Chicheley hill (Map 1) and passing south through a shallow declivity it swung round on the brook side of the parish boundary with Sherington to join Lacbridge lane a short distance north of the small bridge there. It fell into disuse when the stone bridge over the Ouse was built late in the fifteenth century but there are a few references to it under the name of Blackbird lane in the eighteenth century, a change that emphasized its passage through outlying grazing land.[1] It was closed by Act of Parliament in 1753[2] and the land taken into the Chester estate.

The Monchlade, which joined the main London road at a point close to the Newport Pagnell bridge over the Ousel, must have got its name from the nuns attached as sisters[3] to St John's Hospital for lepers there.[4] This hospital by the bridge is not recorded before 1246,[5] but there is evidence that the track itself may have been of much more remote origin.

Among the Chester muniments is a complete survey of Chicheley open fields made in 1557,[6] and from information given it can be deduced that a furlong bearing

[1] *English Place-Name Society*, XIII, 335. The ley ground under the Ash furlong (Map 3) was referred to as Blackbird grounds in 1763 (D/Ch/157/8).

[2] See p. 244.

[3] *Cal. Pat.* 3 Ed. I, p. 91.

[4] F. W. Bull, *History of Newport Pagnell*, (1900), pp. 212–33.

[5] JI 1/56, m. 12d.

[6] It was made for Anthony Cave by two professional surveyors Ambrose Saunders and Clement Vyncent. The acreage of every land (selion) and furlong is recorded: there were three open fields extending to 1360 acres, 132 furlongs and 4621 selions.

the arresting name Quene lay dead was situated alongside the Monchlade at a point close to the present-day Mouthslade Spinney. As it is referred to a century or so later in the shortened form of 'the queen furlong', one's first reaction is to wonder who the lady bearing such an august title can have been. Consideration shows that of all the consorts of post-conquest kings the only one whose body could have been in the neighbourhood for a short time after her death was Eleanor of Castile, in whose memory a number of Eleanor Crosses were erected by Edward I. She died at Harby near Lincoln on 25 November 1290 and her cortège on its way from Stony Stratford to Woburn on 11 December might well have taken the route through Newport Pagnell so as to avoid a notoriously difficult winter crossing of the Ousel at Fenny Stratford. During a halt the bier could have rested in the chapel of Tickford priory, but it would be straining credulity to argue that it might have been taken half a mile along and up the Monchlade into Chicheley field. Three other furlong names in the 1557 survey recall the queen,[1] and it is doubtful if these would all have been changed at a date as late as 1290, whatever the circumstances.

In the middle ages *quene* could indeed represent OE *cwēn*, 'a queen', but equally well OE *quean*, 'a woman', and in the present instance, where we deal with a spot so far distant from anywhere, the homely derivation is the more probable one. Quene does in fact occur as a local surname in the thirteenth century[2] and as the late Professor Ekwall has pointed out, Deadwin Clough in Lancashire was *dedequenclough* 'the clough of the dead woman' in 1324.[3] The furlong name can thus be regarded as a remarkable instance of the tenacity of tradition in England and is evidence that the border lands between Sherington and Chicheley came under tillage at an early date.

At the far end of Monchlade furlong the ground levels off and there was a small furlong, again shared between the two parishes, called Rensfurrow (1663) or Rynfurrow (1557);[4] after which the ground slopes gently down the south-eastern corner of the village on another shared furlong called Rudan hill (OE *ryden*, clearing).

Turning right at the boundary corner the parishioners will come to two large adjoining fields which have been kept as permanent pasture since the time of the Enclosure Award and are still stamped with the pattern of the pre-Enclosure furlongs

[1] Furlong buttynge up to Quene lay deade (10 acres), Dead meede furlong (6 acres) and Dead meede lees (3 acres).

[2] SS 857, undated charter of Agnes Quene de Turvey.

[3] *Oxford Dictionary of English Place-names.*

[4] No early example of the name has been found and the meaning is obscure.

shown up by relics of the old ridge and furrow tillage. Along the southern border the first of these was the furlong Under the Ash (*subtus* Eysse *c.* 1240 'under a clump of ash trees'). The original ashes must have withered and fallen more than a thousand years ago, but ashes still grow in the hedgerows of the two modern fields. Next comes Blackland furlong (Blakelond, 1238; OE *blaec*, black). The upper and higher ground of the second large field has an ancient balk running north to south down the centre, with the worn ridges and furrows of Skerdingswell furlong to the left and of the furlong on the 'Homer side of Hollow Willow Bush' on the right. The present field is called Hollow Willow, thus preserving this old and intimate furlong name. The next and last furlong on the southern boundary was Holloway furlong and slade (Holloway, 1704; nether holloway, 1623; le Nethereweye, 1316, 'sunken or lower road'), recalling the old road to Newport to be discussed later. When this fell into disuse in the seventeenth century the thin strip of land was absorbed into Upper Holloway furlong as four extra selions.[1]

Continuing on the track alongside the rivulet the parishioners will pass a number of fields that run up the hill to the right; these represent the old furlongs and retain their names: Hunger Hill (hungerhul, 1238; OE *hunger*, poor crops); Under Staple Hill (Stapulhul, 1333; OE *stapol*, hill with a post on it); Ray Furlong (Ray, 1238; probably OE *ryge*, rye); and March Furlong (March Furlong, 1763; Standhill Marsh furlong, 1628; Stanihul, 1238: OE *stan*, stone). Abutting the stream to the left there will be a small close called Millers Knob which had other names during the ages, suggesting its peculiar shape: Bacon's womb, 1575; le Toung, 1332 (OE *tunge*, tongue of land). Next comes Maryot's close[2] formerly le Elong (1322), probably an abbreviation for Elond furlong (OE *ēalond*, river land) and then Hareland, 1325, land frequented by hares. Finally, there is the present Newport road, the vicinity of which has undergone many changes over the ages.

In the days before a bridge was built on the site of the present one at Sherington the ford then in use must have been impassable at times when the Ouse was in flood. For this reason the original road between the two towns went a more indirect and slightly longer way round (Map 1). Known later as the 'old road to Newport', it was a continuation of the Olney highway in Sherington from a point where it cut the main highway from Chicheley. From there it ran almost due south and skirting

[1] D/Ch/182/15. Release 1792: '4 roods shooting to the deep slade and was the old road'.

[2] Richard Maryot was lord of Cave's manor in the fifteenth century.

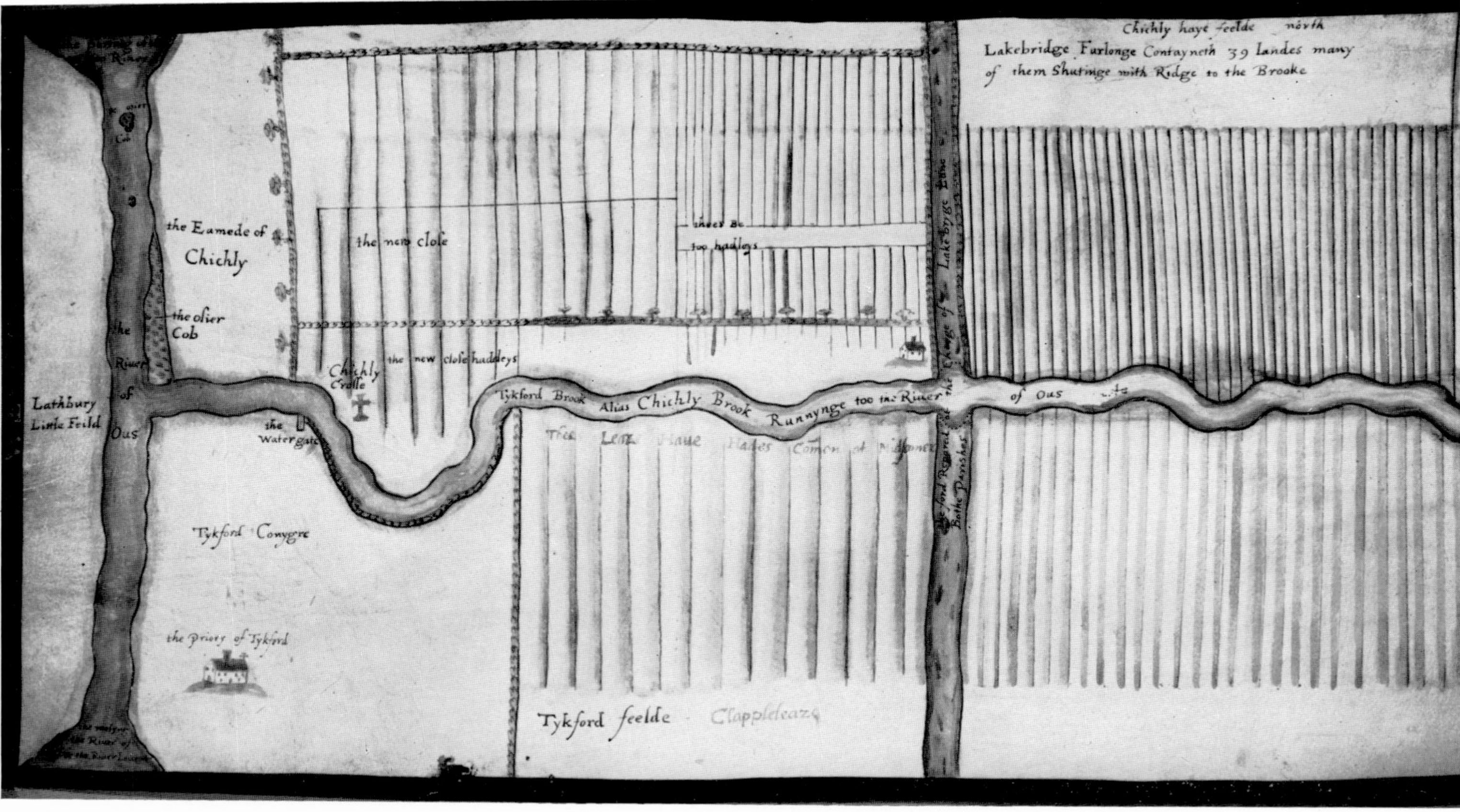

1 Chicheley Brook and Lake bryge lane *c.* 1620

II Letter of William de Sherington confirming his gift of Sherington church to Tickford priory in 1140

III Terrier of Carun manor demesne lands 1312

[illegible]

[illegible]

Terr' [illegible] Primus acr' terre arabil' in manu Petri de Dunge [illegible] J. Bicher [illegible]
[illegible]

[illegible] feld [illegible] in campo [illegible] le [illegible] acr' [illegible] rod' [illegible] apud le [illegible]
[illegible] acr' [illegible] It' apud le longe dole [illegible] acr' [illegible] It' ibidem [illegible] acr' [illegible] rod' [illegible]
[illegible] acr' [illegible] rod' [illegible] apud le [illegible] rod' [illegible] ibidem [illegible] acr' [illegible] It' apud le [illegible]
It' apud le [illegible] rod' [illegible] It' apud le [illegible] rod' [illegible] It' apud le [illegible] acr'
It' [illegible] rod' [illegible]

Summa [illegible] acr' [illegible] rod'

Est ffeld [illegible] In campo orientali [illegible] acr' [illegible] rod' [illegible] acr' [illegible]
It' ibidem [illegible] acr' It' ibidem [illegible] acr' It' apud le [illegible] It' apud le [illegible] rod' [illegible]
[illegible] acr' It' apud [illegible] acr' In le Stackinges [illegible] acr' It' [illegible]
It' ibidem [illegible] acr' It' ibid' [illegible] acr' It' in le [illegible] acr'

Summa [illegible] acr' [illegible]

[illegible] feld [illegible] In campo [illegible] apud le [illegible] acr' It' apud le [illegible] acr' [illegible]
[illegible] acr' In le [illegible] acr' [illegible] It' in [illegible] acr'

Summa [illegible] acr' [illegible] rod'

[illegible] ffeld In campo [illegible] iuxta le [illegible] rod' It' in le [illegible] In [illegible]
In [illegible] acr'

Summa [illegible] acr' [illegible] rod' [illegible]

Summa acr' [illegible] rod' It' [illegible]

IV The Old House, Sherington, in 1900

the rivulet of the Ouse on land well above flood level it entered Newport via the western end of Chicheley. As Lacbridge lane it carried on past the priory grounds and met the main London–Newport highway near the bridge over the Ousel.

The early history of the bridge at Sherington is lost, but one was in existence during the thirteenth century.[1] This would probably have had an upper fabric of wood and a stone or rubble base; even so, serious interference with the flow of traffic would have occurred when the Ouse was in flood. In medieval times the upkeep was often neglected for lack of money, and although an indulgence was occasionally granted for money contributed for the purpose[2] the only steady income, and that no more than a trickle, came from the legacies of the local inhabitants. The present stone bridge owes its completion to Richard Maryot, lord of Cave's manor and resident in the moated manor house, who bequeathed in 1491 'to the making of the arches of the brigge of Sherington now not vawted with stone with a perpoynt wall upon the seid Arches 6 marc if they will not be made for less silver'.[3] When it came into use the traveller would no longer have been inconvenienced by floods and the old road—which had carried in its day so much of the through traffic from the north—fell into disuse.

Lacbridge lane, nevertheless, comes to life again in Pl. 1, which is a reproduction of part of a curious old map preserved among the Chester muniments[4] concerning a lawsuit of 1622 over the ownership of a close called Hadleys lying north of the Chicheley Brook.[5] The evidence shows that the lacbridge (OE *lacu*, stream) had already fallen down. Somewhat later the Chicheley end of the lane was swept away in the changes which followed the establishment of the Newport Pagnell–Kettering Turnpike Trust and today only the upper end of the old road in Sherington survives.

On crossing the road that leads over the Ouse bridge, the parishioners would enter Middle Field at what was described in the Mercers' Survey of 1577[6] as 'Burge

[1] Lincoln, Reg. 5, f. 296.

[2] *Ibid.*

[3] PCC 11 Dogett.

[4] Anthony Cave, a merchant of the Staple at Calais, purchased the Chicheley estate of the dissolved priory of Tickford from Henry VIII in 1545. One of his daughters and co-heiresses brought it in marriage to Anthony Chester, in the hands of whose descendants it still remains. A noteworthy feature of the map is the Chicheley cross, which must have been destroyed when the area was fortified during the civil war. The association with Tickford priory would suggest that it had been a pilgrim cross.

[5] C2 Jas. 1, A8/25. 'At the end of the said Close standeth a newly erected tenement abutting upon the highway leading to Sherington neare a place where lately was a bridge called Larke or Lake bridge.' The map (85 in. by 13 in.) is on parchment.

[6] RCL, p. 154.

furlong which butteth the water'. It was Bridge Leys furlong to most of Parson Fuller's contemporaries, but a few of them called it Water Thorn furlong,[1] a name of much more remote origin. In Parson Gervase's day the furlong—then in South Field—was called Wartrou (OE *wearg*, felon, and *tréow*, tree), implying that it lay alongside the gallows. The village gibbet, a fairly common sight in later medieval times, was always set up in some conspicuous place like the intersection of two roads or by a bridge; it consisted of an old tree trunk with projecting branch from which the corpse of the felon executed at the local assizes, was suspended.[2] A species of thorn with a long-lasting, hardwood trunk must have been dominant in Sherington and used for the purpose, for we meet it in two other early furlong names, Threthornes (three thornes) and Scregethornhule (presumably OE *scrag*, stump). When in course of time, the gruesome custom of exhibiting on the gibbet died out, the old thorn trunk would have become of lesser interest than Squire Maryot's fine new stone bridge and the furlong name duly reflected the change. Wartrou would have become Watrou by dissimilation and in pronunciation would be readily associated with water.

Bridge Leys furlong ran down to the water edge where, in former days, there had been a millpond. While the mill was working the water cast on from the paddle wheels would have produced a whirlpool, and the furlong butting down to the river at this point was called Water Swallows in 1575 and Wateswolen in 1325 (OE *swelgend*, gulf, whirlpool). The mill could operate only when sufficient head of water was available and naturally it fell into disuse when a windmill was built by the prior of Tickford alongside the high ground of South Field during the late thirteenth century.

Further along the waterside as far as the Tyringham Fence were the two common meadows, Townsmead and Lordsmead. These names are probably as old as the feudal system but the minor divisions into the doles, poles and rods of Carun and Cockfield (Table 12), would not have come into use until Richard de Carun subinfeudated the Cockfield fee in 1189. Parson Fuller would recognize the Tyringham Fence,[3] which ran up the hill to Filgrave. In his day this was a permanent feature of the landscape, for Tyringham had been enclosed earlier in the century and it was necessary to prevent beasts and sheep from straying in and out of the Marehill

[1] The Mercers' tenants mention Water Thorn furlong in a set of terriers they drew up in 1740, while a professional surveyor refers to the same lands ten years later as lying in Bridge Leys furlong. [4/9/1386, 1388–94].

[2] For further comment, see p. 38.

[3] At the present time the property on the Tyringham side of the parish boundary is called Fence's farm.

Field in Sherington, which was still subject to all the grazing rights appurtenant to tillage under the common field system.

As the parishioners proceed up the hill they will pass over fields whose names even today recall their origin. Old Clay was Clay in 1623 and le Clay in 1295; there was a claypit at the foot of the old furlong which has since grown over and become incorporated in Barn Hole. The latter was known as Barrend Hole Hedge in 1682 and Barndheg in 1238 (OE *baerned*, 'burnt' hedge). The various Marehills were part of le Mare furlong of 1295, from OE *gemaere*, boundary, and at the top of the hill was Coppedmore furlong (1575), where OE *coppede*, peak, is coupled with 'mare' corrupted to 'more'. To the right along the Filgrave boundary comes a succession of small fields with trivial names. Before the Enclosure the first furlong was Godescote (1771, 1313), a cottage near God's ground (OE *cot*, cottage) indicative of Filgrave church and churchyard (abandoned *c.* 1500) on the other side of the boundary. Just below the position of this furlong is a field called One Hole. The 'hole' was a stonepit, now silted up, which the medieval peasant called Pokeput (1238) because he could occasionally, but only occasionally, hear an echo when he shouted in it, due, he had no doubt, to an elusive goblin who was playing him tricks (OE *pūca*, goblin, Puck, and ME *putte*, pit). Next would come Goldsworth furlong, a corruption for Goldhord (1318) meaning a place where treasure (OE *hord*) must have been found.[1] The last furlong before the Olney road was Cross Albans (1792) or Cross All bones[2] (1704). In 1313 both the furlongs flanking the Olney road were described as next to (*juxta*) le Aubeles (ME *aubel*, white poplar tree) so that there must have been at one time a wood containing such trees skirting the parish boundary on the Emberton side and *crossing* the Olney road. The wood on the east side of the road is still called Cross Albans Wood.

The area south of the Emberton boundary between the Olney road and the old Sherington wood consists of fields bearing compound names ending in dean, and the same held true in Elizabethan times. Dean (OE *denn*, woodland pasture for swine) shows that in the early middle ages the whole area was once wooded and the three small coppices that used to stand in a row near the Emberton–Chicheley corner were relics of this primeval forest. It was at the gate leading into the first of these, called Mercers' Wood, that the parishioners expected the parson to provide

[1] Cf. p. 16.

[2] There is an Allebones Spinney in the neighbouring village of Turvey (Ordnance Survey map).

drink for those beating the bounds. The little close behind the wood, recorded in 1313, was probably cleared at the same time as the Deans.

When the parishioners emerge from Heyton Wood,[1] the last of the three coppices mentioned above, and walk south they will enter a close that in medieval times was in East Field and has a history recalling Domesday. To Parson Fuller it was Gowles Nether Piece or Chicheley Meare, but to Gervase it was simply Andrewsmere (Andrew's boundary). In the Domesday Inquest Andrew held a manor in Chicheley of William, son of Ansculf, which passed later, through the Paynells, to the monks of Tickford. Their tenants in the thirteenth and fourteenth centuries were members of a family called Gold, who also farmed some of the adjoining land in the Sherington area with which we are dealing. In the middle ages various closes and furlongs along the Chicheley border had names based on 'Gowles', and 'Gowles farm' is shown on the present-day ordnance map. The parishioners will then enter the far end of le Hoo Park, known also as Le Stocking (late ME 'piece cleared of stocks or stumps') and finally pass out of Park Gate into the Chicheley road at the corner of le Hoo Wood, their starting-place.

The chief impression one draws from this inquiry is that the South Field and the West Field—the two great open common fields of the medieval period—were older than North Field and East Field, which were lords' demesne. A more detailed study of the array of furlong names given in Appendix 6 leads to a similar conclusion. The question of the age of these fields, however, is less easy to deduce with any certainty from the type of evidence under review, none of which it must be emphasized is based on documentary material earlier than about 1220. Consider first the two great open fields. Almost all of the furlong names are rooted in Old English words, yet only two of them, Ruden Hill from OE *ryden*, a clearing, and Barndheg from OE *baerned*, burnt, hedge connote a taking in of waste land or the clearing of wood; the remainder denote some characteristic of topography or tillage and imply that the land concerned had already been cleared. Tentatively therefore one may suggest that South Field and West Field were fully opened out before the time of Domesday.

Fortunately it is possible to be a little more definite about North Field and East

[1] Very close to a small settlement in Chicheley, no longer in existence, called in the middle ages 'hightown', which was part of the Tickford priory manor of Thickthorns north of the Bedford road and abutting north on Ekeney cum Petsoe.

Field. As has already been mentioned, the strip of land on the Emberton border between the Olney road and the Mercers' Wood had been cleared at a time when the Old English word *denn* was still current. The lower part of East Field, however, known in the middle ages as le Hoo Park or le Stocking was probably not cleared until early Norman times,[1] for the word stocking did not come to mean 'the clearing of stocks or stumps' until the Middle English period. We can deduce with fair certainty, therefore, that at the time of Domesday 'the Deans' had been arable land for some time but le Hoo Park had not yet been assarted from le Hoo Wood. As Andrewsmere at the far end of the demesne lands on the Chicheley border had a direct connexion with Domesday and Heldebyry alongside le Hoo Park marks the site of an Anglo-Saxon fortified manor house[2] it is probable that the rest of the demesne area in North and East Fields had been already cleared at that time.

Thus we see that by the time the companions in our fantasy have come once again to the corner of How Wood they will have had revealed to them or recalled to mind many long-forgotten items of interest about the early landscape and history of their village. And with their labour at an end it may be that Parson Fuller will unbend and 'make A drinking'. If not, Gervase the parson could honour the old custom and if so disposed give them wine instead of their usual beer, for his brother Richard the squire had a fine large vineyard attached to his manor house by the church.

[1] The whole area of 84 acres was called an assart in a fine of 1234 (*BASRB*, IV, 65).

[2] Cf. p. 17.

2

FROM ROMAN TIMES TO DOMESDAY

RECENT research has shown that the wide area through which the river Ouse meanders on its way from Stony Stratford to Olney had been settled in Roman or even earlier times, for relics of those days have been dug up in many of the present-day places concerned, including Tickford, Sherington and Emberton. There is evidence also of several primitive cross-country tracks that have long since disappeared. The main Roman military road through north Buckinghamshire was of course the Watling Street (Map 5), but some of the traffic from London to Lincolnshire and beyond left this at Fenny Stratford (*Magiovinium*) for a minor road that ran in a northerly direction along the west bank of the Ousel until it reached the neighbourhood of Caldecote Mill, when it crossed the river to the east of Newport Pagnell at Tickford. Continuing north through Sherington and Emberton it crossed the Ouse at Olney and then headed for Irchester and beyond.[1] As Roman relics have also been found at Woburn and Wavendon it is probable that another minor road or track left the Watling Street at Hockcliffe, near the Bedfordshire–Buckinghamshire border.[2]

A settlement on the site of the present town of Newport Pagnell in Roman times was probable, not only because of the north to south traffic just mentioned, but also because it was at the confluence of the Ouse and its tributary the Ousel or Lovat, waterways which would have been extensively utilized by a primitive community. The site of Sherington, flanked as it was to the north and east by gentle hills covered by primeval forest, might have been less favourable for early development, but some kind of habitation had been established within the confines of the present nucleated village in pre-Roman days, for Belgic as well as Roman relics have been found in recent diggings to the west of the old churchyard. There is no information as to the period when the area was gradually opened out, but it is probable that the flat strip of land alongside the river to the west of the Roman road

[1] The Roman roads in this region are discussed by G. W. Green, *Wolverton and District Archaeological Society News Letter*, no. 5 (Jan. 1960); see also *RB*, XVI, 99.

[2] *VCH Beds*, II, 15. *VCH Bucks*, II, 14.

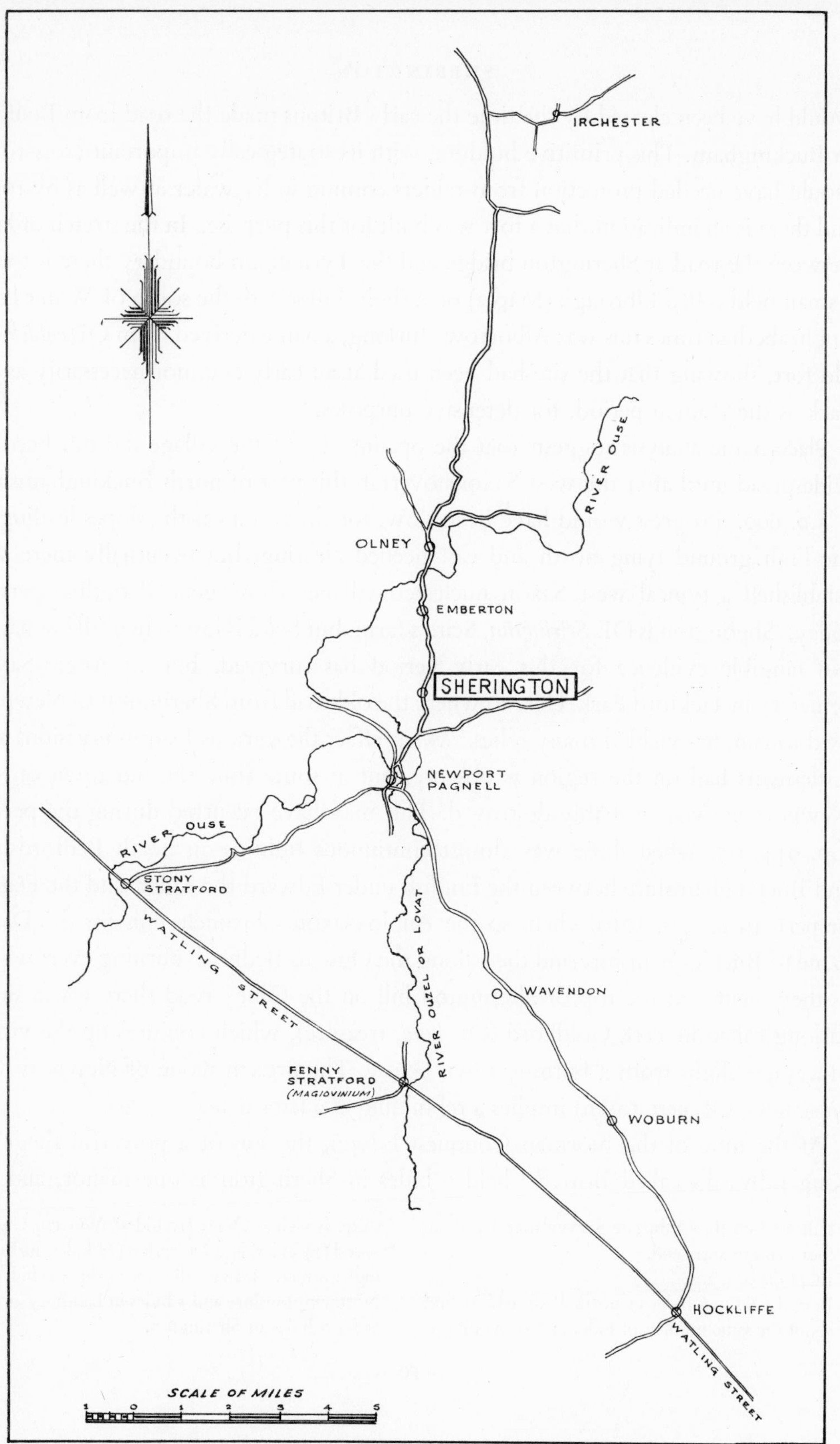

Map 5. The Roman road running north through Sherington.

would have been cleared by the time the early Britons made the road from Bedford to Buckingham. This primitive holding, with its strategically important cross-road, would have needed protection from raiders coming in by water as well as by road, and there is an indication that a fort was built for this purpose. In the stretch of land between the road at Sherington bridge and the Tyringham boundary there is today a small field called Elbrough (Map 2) on a slight hillock[1] to the south of Water lane. In Elizabethan times this was Alborrowe furlong, a name derived from OE *ealdeburg*, old fort, showing that the site had been used at an early age, not necessarily as far back as the Roman period, for defensive purposes.

Place-name analysis suggests that the opening up of the village did not become widespread until after the west Saxons overran this part of north Buckinghamshire *c.* A.D. 600. Progress would have been slow, for the forest on the slopes leading to the high ground lying north and east needed clearing, but eventually there was established a typical west Saxon nucleated village whose general outline persists today. Sherington is OE *Scīringtūn*, Scira's farm, but Scira is lost to us in all but name. No tangible evidence for this early period has survived, but an Anglo-Saxon cemetery in Tickford Park, close to where the old road from Sherington to Newport used to run, has yielded many relics.[2] What effect the various Danish invasions and settlements had on the region is obscure, but at some time the old town on the Newport site was probably destroyed. This may have occurred during the period A.D. 914–917, when there was almost continuous fighting in north Bedfordshire and Buckinghamshire between the English under Edward the Elder, and the Danes, or perhaps in A.D. 1010 when, so the Anglo-Saxon Chronicle tells us, the Danes came to Buckinghamshire and then along the Ouse to Bedford, burning everywhere as they went. At the top of Sherington hill on the Olney road there was a small furlong called in 1318 Goldhord (OE *hord*, treasure), which conjures up the vision of a tragic flight from a burning town below. The present name of Newport (OE *niwe*, new, OE *port*, town) implies a rebuilding at a later date.

At the time of the Norman Conquest Edwin, the son of a powerful thegn of King Edward's called Borred,[3] held 6 hides in Sherington as one manor, and his

[1] Indicated on the Ordnance Survey map by a 200 foot contour surround.

[2] *VCH Bucks*, I, 204.

[3] Borred held 31½ hides in north Bedfordshire and about the same number of hides in Northamptonshire, as well as Olney (10 hides), Western Underwood (7½ hides) and Lavendon (5¾ hides) in Buckinghamshire. Edwin the son held 17 hides in Northamptonshire and 5 hides in Lathbury as well as his 6 hides in Sherington.

man Alwin one hide as another. A third manor, rated at 3 hides, was held by a man of King Edward's called Osolf. As mentioned in the preceding chapter, it is almost certain that in those days the demesne sector of the village had not been fully opened out, for 'le Hoo Park' alias 'le stoking' was still primeval wood. In 1313 (Map 4) there was a long strip of land to the north of this park which was then called Heldebyry (containing OE *byrig*, dative of *burg*), suggesting that in early Norman times it still contained relics of an Anglo-Saxon fortified building—probably Edwin's devastated manor house. In Tudor times it was called Oldbery furlong (Map 3), so that the track which skirts the site of it today, called Perry lane (Map 2), has a name that unconsciously links it with the Anglo-Saxon successors of Scira himself. The old manor house of the Carun family was situated north of the church.

With the coming of Duke William from Normandy in 1066 there was of course an abrupt change of ownership. As Baring[1] has shown, we can follow his rather far-flung invasion route from Hastings to London on the reasonable assumption that in Domesday Book the depreciation in the value of a manor (or better, the summed values of every holding in the vill) when received in 1067, as compared with that recorded for the time of King Edward in 1066, is due to devastation caused by the invading army.[2] William and his forces came north through eastern Buckinghamshire and turned east at Beachampton (53).[3] They then proceeded past Loughton (47) to Bradwell (60) and Little Woolstone (56). Turning north once again their route lay through the region Great Linford (38), Gayhurst (38), Lathbury (38), Tyringham (36), Sherington (30), Emberton (45), Olney (42), Lavendon (67) and hence over the border to Turvey in Bedfordshire. As Fowler has emphasized, the army would have been living on the seed corn and plough oxen of the countryside, so that the damage inflicted would have been most severe in places where it camped for the night. Considering that Sherington was on the direct line of the invading forces the devastation seems to have been less severe than might have been expected.

After the Conquest the estates of Borred and his son Edwin were bestowed by

[1] F. W. Baring, *Domesday Tables* (St Catherine's Press, London, 1909), p. 207.

[2] G. Herbert Fowler 'Bedfordshire in 1086' quarto Mem. *BHRS*, I, 79. He calls attention to the fact that Northamptonshire and neighbouring counties had been deliberately devastated by a typical Danish raid in 1065, consequently it is hardly possible to say whether the devastations in the north of Buckinghamshire and Bedfordshire were due to the Danes or the Normans.

[3] The figures in parentheses are percentage devastation.

King William on Geoffrey de Mowbray, bishop of Coutances, who was holding the whole of Sherington in demesne at the time of the Domesday Inquest in 1086. Borred was probably dead by then and Edwin, who had been deprived of all the family wealth, was allowed to retain, as a mere undertenant of the bishop, a miserable estate rated at only 1½ virgates in what had been his own Northamptonshire village of Stanion[1]—an eloquent reminder that if the coming of the Normans meant no more than a change of overlord for the peasantry, it brought poverty and degradation to most of King Edward's nobles and thegns.

The Domesday Book return for Sherington[2] states *inter alia* 'It is assessed at 10 hides. There is land for 11 ploughs. In the demesne are 3 hides and on it are 4 ploughs. There 22 villeins with 6 bordars have 6 ploughs and there could be a seventh. There are 8 serfs and one mill worth 26 shillings, meadow sufficient for 4 plough teams and woodland to feed 100 swine. In all it is worth 10 pounds; when received 7 pounds; TRE 10 pounds.' The interpretation of this assessment given in later chapters is based on place-name analysis and evidence derived from documents illustrating the disposition of the land during the thirteenth century. The approach is novel, and even if Sherington with its complete divorce between demesne land and open common fields was not a typical village of champion country the results and conclusions may have some value in Domesday studies.

[1] *VCH Northants*, I, 290, 311.

[2] *VCH Bucks*, I, 241.

3

THE CARUN FAMILY

ON the death of the Conqueror in 1087 England and Normandy came once again under separate rule and the bishop of Coutances, like many of the Norman barons with lands in the kingdom and the duchy, were thereby forced into the anomalous position of owing allegiance to both William Rufus and Duke Robert. For a man of his autocratic and military temperament it was almost inevitable that he should be drawn into the disputes that soon arose between the two brothers, and with his nephew Robert de Mowbray, earl of Northumberland, he was active in the ill-fated movement to put the duke on the English throne in 1088. Rufus generously pardoned both of them, but the earl, who succeeded to his uncle's vast estates five years later, was in open rebellion again in 1095 and this time he was to suffer not only defeat but also long imprisonment with the loss of all his possessions.

The lands which thereby became forfeit to the Crown must have represented the major part of those assigned to the bishop in Domesday Book. Nevertheless from lack of contemporary evidence it is not known for certain how Rufus and after him his brother Henry dealt with the various properties that came into their hands. As Stenton[1] has emphasized, it was not until the new reign was well advanced that it became normal to record grants of land for military service; before then it was probable that grants of this type were made in the presence of witnesses, but without written record. Moreover when attempting to reconstruct what happened at that time from evidence of a slightly later date we must remember that the perennial troubles that beset Henry in the first few years as king had repercussions in the drastic changes that occurred in the fortunes of other Norman baronial families of great influence and power. The defeat of Duke Robert at Tinchebrai in 1106, for instance, brought disgrace and confiscation to the count of Mortain, who was another Domesday Book landowner with extensive estates in north Buckinghamshire. It is not surprising therefore that the earliest records available, most of them dated

[1] F. M. Stenton, *English Feudalism, 1066–1166*, (1932), p. 152.

between 1130 and 1160, should show that in Sherington and neighbouring villages the Domesday connexion had been in large part broken and new families were already established as feudal overlords and tenants.

The bishop's lands in the three hundreds of Newport were in scattered holdings rated at 70 hides, and in only two of the twelve places concerned, Olney and Sherington, did he own the whole village. Early in the twelfth century the holdings lying contiguous to Sherington, representing 48 of these hides, had already been parcelled out into new units. Emberton (3 hides) and Little Linford (4 hides) had become incorporated in the Paynel honour of Dudley, which derived from the extensive Domesday fief of William, son of Ansculf (de Pincquigny), with Dudley castle as its head. Fulk Paynel, who may have married one of William's daughters, founded Tickford priory in Newport Pagnell and has left his mark on the county in the name of that town. Lathbury (5 hides), Lavendon ($6\frac{1}{6}$ hides), Tyringham ($2\frac{3}{4}$ hides) and Weston Underwood ($7\frac{1}{2}$ hides) had been grouped together as part of the very small honour of Bidun, which had Lavendon castle as its head. Olney (10 hides) remained in the king's hands until the end of the twelfth century, when it was granted to the earl of Chester. Early in the reign of Stephen, Sherington (10 hides) is found vested in Ralph de Carun who held, rather unusually for such a small fief, directly of the king and not as mesne tenant of some larger fief. As will be more fully discussed later, the holding of Sherington *in capite* exposed the Carun tenants before the time of Magna Carta to the full rigour of feudal exaction and was by no means to their advantage.

The name of Carun does not figure in the Domesday return for Buckinghamshire but it does in that for north Bedfordshire. William de Carun, in addition to what he held of Nigel d'Aubigny of Cainho and of the bishop of Lincoln, was an undertenant of Eudo the Dapifer in Clifton ($6\frac{1}{2}$ hides), Tempsford ($5\frac{1}{2}$ hides) and Southill with Sandford ($4\frac{1}{4}$ hides). Eudo, who had been a boyhood companion of Duke William in Normandy and had been given the office of Dapifer around 1072, was a trusted advisor of the Conqueror and the two sons who succeeded him until incapacitated by blindness in 1105. He was thus in a position to reward a faithful retainer, and as William de Carun was his undertenant of a very substantial holding we may infer that he was one whom Eudo treated generously. Eudo's father, Hubert de Rie lived at Ryes in Calvados and Eudo would have drawn some of his following from the vicinity. Cairon, some 15 kilometres away on the river Seule, is almost certainly the place from which William de Carun took his name.[1] Eudo re-founded the great Abbey of St John the Baptist at Colchester in 1096–7 and in his declining years watched over its rise with devotion. He probably maintained also a friendly contact with the Carun family, for William's son Robert gave the Abbey a rent of 10*s.* from the mills of Tempsford in 1104 and a mill at Clifton in 1119.[2]

The relationship between the Ralph de Carun[3] who was the tenant in chief at Sherington and the Bedfordshire family living less than 25 miles away is obscure. The difficulty of tracing the descent of the lesser known people who are party to events in the first few decades after Domesday is, of course, a commonplace in genealogy and the present instance is no exception. Ralph's son and heir, William, was in possession of the village and old enough to settle the advowson of the church there on Tickford priory before about 1140.[4] His daughter Aveline had married Robert de Tinchebrai of Swanburn, and the two virgates of land in Sherington which he had given her at the time were settled by her and her husband during the reign of Stephen (i.e. after 1135) on Delapre abbey, Northampton.[5] Ralph himself therefore must have been born before 1100, have held Sherington during the latter part of the reign of Henry I and have died about the same time as that monarch.[6] He was accordingly of the same age group as the Robert de Carun who had succeeded to the Bedfordshire property before 1104 and may thus have been the person referred to under Bedfordshire in the unique Pipe Roll for 1130, which records that Robert de Carun paid into the exchequer 69*s.* for the land of his brother

[1] Lewis Loyd, *Harl. Soc. Publ.* 103, 25. I agree with him that the derivation of the name from 'le Caron' (carcase) by Fowler (*BHRC*, XIII, 304) is not borne out by the facts. But I cannot agree with his view that the statement in Domesday (*VCH Beds*, I, 210–1, 226*b*) that William de Carun's father had a small holding of 60 acres and some woodland in Easton TRE is unlikely and probably arose from a mistake. As Prof. Galbraith has pointed out to me, the statement is vouched for by the men of the hundred and must not be ignored. William's father may well have been one of the Norman coterie with whom Edward the Confessor surrounded himself before the crisis of 1051 (cf. E. A. Freeman, *Norman Conquest*, V, 755).

[2] W. Farrer, *Honors and Knights' Fees*, III (1925), pp. 3, 258.

[3] In contemporary documents Ralph is referred to by the place-name 'de Sherington' (or variants), and his son William in the same way or by the patronymic William, son of Ralph; neither of them used the family name of Carun, possibly to avoid confusion with the Bedfordshire folk. Richard the grandson (p. 36), appears to have been the first of the family to adopt this style, either because he was influenced by the prevailing social trend to exalt a Norman origin or, more likely, because a junior branch of the family settled in the neighbouring village of Filgrave were using 'de Sherington'. Except where it is necessary to quote *in extenso* from original sources the name Carun will be used throughout the text for the senior branch of the Sherington family.

[4] See pp. 26–30.

[5] *CRR*, II, 32.

[6] *Mon. Angl.* V, 212.

Ralph.[1] Without fresh evidence the suggestion, which would connect the two families in a facile way, calls for no further comment. It must, indeed, be remembered that Ralph of Sherington may have been the son or grandson of another of Eudo's faithful followers from Calvados and that the two families bore the same name merely because they had common origin in Cairon.

[1] Pipe Roll 31 Hen I, 103 (Ed. Joseph Hunter, 1833; re-issued by the Stationary Office 1929).

4

THE ANARCHY, SHERINGTON CHURCH AND TICKFORD PRIORY

THE turbulent years of the anarchy (1135–53) are difficult ones for the historian of north Buckinghamshire as the documentary evidence is so meagre. We know from the chroniclers that in the southern part of the county the region skirting the Thames valley suffered severe and repeated depredation from raids by the troops of the empress based on Wallingford castle, but they do not tell us very much about what happened further north. The war was one in which pitched battles between the supporters of King Stephen and the Empress Matilda were rare, and the fighting resolved itself into a succession of sieges during which the attacking army lived by plundering the neighbourhood and the garrison partly maintained itself by forays in which it ranged further and further afield. As Davis[1] has reminded us, every castle which had been the object of attack stood at the centre of a circle of desolate country.

Newport Pagnell has always been an important town because it lies at the intersection of two main roads and at the confluence of two rivers; it is probable therefore that a castle existed there in pre-Conquest days.[2] Strange as it may seem today, there were within a radius of 6 miles to the north and west of the town four other castles; at Wolverton,[3] Lavendon,[4] Hanslope[5] and Bradwell,[6] respectively, during

[1] H. W. C. Davis, *EHR*, XVIII (1903), 630.

[2] A mound known as 'the battery' near the confluence of the two rivers marks the site of the castle and a meadow on the opposite bank of the Lovat has been known since the twelfth century as 'castle mead'. No documentary evidence of the castle has survived. The statement that it is mentioned in the close rolls for 1224 is incorrect (cf. F. W. Bull, *History of Newport Pagnell*, 1900, p. 3). During the anarchy it belonged to Ralph Peynel as part of his barony of Dudley. Ralph held Dudley castle for the empress in 1137.

[3] Wolverton castle was the head of the barony which derived from the Domesday holding of Mano the Briton and would have been built before the war, when it was held for the king by Meinfelin.

[4] Lavendon castle was the head of the honour acquired by Halnath de Bidun from Henry I. During the war it was held by John de Bidun whose loyalty is not known.

[5] Hanslope castle was the head of the honour which represented the Domesday holding of Winemar the Fleming. During the war it was held by William Maudit for the empress.

[6] William Bayeux held land in Bradwell of the honour of Wallingford, which was in the hands of Brian Fitz Count, a great personal friend of the empress. He apparently built an 'adulterine castle' at her request.

the anarchy (Map 6) and as their owners did not all offer the same allegiance it is certain that the whole of that north Buckinghamshire area must have gone through some distressing periods during the ebb and flow of the opposing armies, for it was flanked on the east by the powerful and dominating castle at Bedford, which changed hands repeatedly during the war.

The writer of the *Gesta Stephani*[1] has left us a graphic description of conditions around Bedford at the first siege there in 1137–8. King Stephen had given his castellan Miles de Beauchamp orders to hand over the castle to Hugh de Beaumont, but he had refused on the plea that the office was hereditary in his family. Then, in the words of the writer

The king, on hearing of this was violently incensed against Miles and went to Bedford to besiege him with an army collected from the whole of England. Miles, on learning of his arrival, forcibly took from everyone and carried away with him any food on which he could lay hands, and shamelessly robbing the townsmen and their neighbours, whom hitherto he had humanely spared as his own dependants, he gathered in the castle everything that met the eye.

The garrison eventually capitulated to the king, but three years later Miles was again in possession and the area came under the domination of the empress. In 1146 the earl of Chester recaptured it for the king,[2] in whose possession it remained until towards the end of the anarchy when, in 1153, it fell to Duke Henry (afterwards Henry II) as he swept south with his forces from Tutbury castle to relieve Wallingford castle. The account in the *Gesta Stephani* of this last operation illustrates the ruthless character of these internecine wars. 'At the same time he (Duke Henry) suddenly arrived at the town of Bedford, where the King's supporters had taken refuge in a very strong castle, and after heavily plundering the town delivered it to the flames.'[3]

None of the five castles in the Newport Pagnell area could have withstood such treatment. Except that of Lavendon, which had fortifications of masonry, all were of the mound and bailey type with, presumably, wooden structures that could be built quickly to meet an emergency and as readily destroyed. Their history during the war is not known, but three of them, at Newport Pagnell, Wolverton and Bradwell respectively, seem to have been completely destroyed. Hanslope castle, perhaps renovated, continued until the next century, when it was destroyed by

[1] *Gesta Stephani*, ed. K. R. Potter, 1955, pp. 31–3.

[2] *Gesta Stephani*, p. 122.

[3] *Ibid.* pp. xxvii, 155. Duke Henry later made reparation for the damage he had done to St Paul's Church, Bedford.

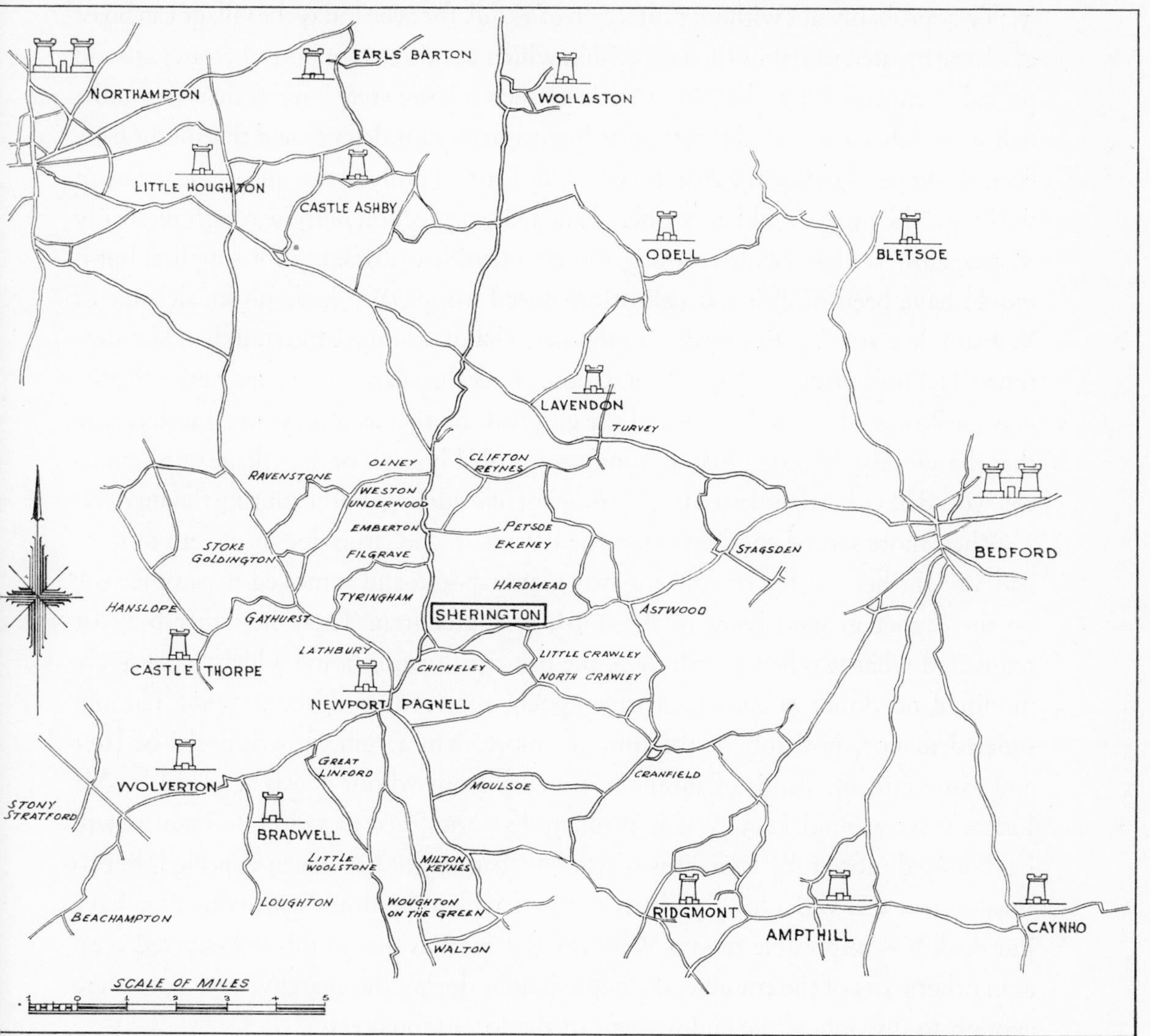

Map 6. Castles within 12 miles of Sherington during the period of the anarchy in Stephen's reign.

Faukes de Breauté in 1215; Lavendon was still used as a castle at the end of the century,[1] but fell into disuse soon after.

The looting of the troops employed must have led to much devastation and misery in north Buckinghamshire, especially in the neighbourhood of Sherington, which was within 5–6 miles of all five local castles. At the start of the war Sherington

[1] *PRS*, NS, 3, 93.

itself was probably not without protection of a kind, for even today the village can boast of a large moated site (Frontispiece) within which stood a manor house before 1250 and probably much earlier. The moat encloses such a large area[1]—more than one and a half acres—that it was almost certainly dug originally for defence and this might have been many years before the anarchy when the Carun family first acquired the fief from the king. The moat would have offered adequate protection in those rough and ready days against lawless bands roaming the countryside or foraging for supplies, but it would have been of little use against organized troops. We have no knowledge of William de Carun's activities during this period, but as he gave the church of Sherington to Tickford priory, a Peynel foundation, about the year 1140 we may infer that he was a follower of Ralph Peynel and the empress. Be that as it may, one can feel sure that the weakly defended manor house and probably most of the village of Sherington would have been molested by the troops of one side or the other during the anarchy.

When more settled conditions returned William de Carun does not seem to have had any further use for the old moated manor house and removed to another site on the higher ground lying to the north of the church. There he either built or renovated what was henceforth to be the principal manor house which, extensively modified no doubt at each successive epoch, survived until about 1780. The old moated manor, probably at the time no more than a ruin, was disposed of later and came into the hands of Emma le Vineter, from whom it was acquired by Mr Justice Cave around 1253. When William de Carun died in 1180 his estate, as will be discussed more fully later, was worth less than might have been expected, but to what extent this was a hang-over from the troublesome times with which we have just dealt it is impossible to say. What we do know is that in this war-scarred area, as in other parts of the country, the depredations during the anarchy were not severe enough to discourage the endowment of the local monastery.

The alien priory of Tickford, dedicated to St Mary, was a daughter cell of the great French abbey of Marmoutier or 'Maius Monasterium' at Tours. It was a small but complete monastic house for Cluniac monks, with hall, cloister, dorter and church, which had been founded by Fulk Peynel early in the twelfth century and further endowed by his son Ralph and grandson Gervase. None of the original documents recording their gifts during the first half of the century have survived,

[1] The only other well-preserved moat of comparable size in north Bedfordshire and Buckinghamshire is at Marston Moretaine (*VCH Beds*, III, 308).

but we know from a general confirmation charter of the bishop of Lincoln in 1151–4[1] that their main endowment was represented by the churches of Newport and Chicheley, and the chapels of Linford, Little Crawley, Petsoe and Astwood. Once the priory had become firmly established the owners of local estates rallied to its support, and one of the first was William de Carun who, at the height of the anarchy around 1140, gave the monks his church at Sherington. He was followed a few years later by Robert de Bradwell and Ralph his son—the owners of Bradwell—who with the consent of William de Bayeux the feudal overlord, gave the chapel there with half a hide of land.[2] When William formally handed over the church at Sherington in the presence of the ecclesiastical authorities concerned he appears to have done so without providing any written instrument of transfer. Thirty years later it was probably the then prior of Tickford who warned him that the monks might find it difficult to sustain their title to the church in the absence of a deed.[3] William accordingly seems to have arranged with their mutual friend and patron Gervase Peynel for a formal written transfer in the presence of the heir-apparent King Henry, son of King Henry, and must in due course have received a request to wait upon the officials of the latter's chancery to discuss details of the proposed deed. For some reason, however, he was unable to attend and sent a letter of apology

[1] *Cal. Doc. France*, 444.

[2] Archives du Dept. Indre et Loire, Série H, Liasse 362. The charter (1140–54) is covered by the bishop of Lincoln's confirmation of 1151–4 and was witnessed, *inter alia*, by David, archdeacon of Buckinghamshire (1140–77). 'Notum sit omnibus tam presentibus quam futuris quod Robertus de Bradeuuella concessione Radulfi filii sui & heredis dedit Deo & ecclesie beate Marie de Neuport monachisque sancti Martini maioris monasterii ibidem Deo servientibus in puram elemosinam capellam de Bradeuuella cum dimidia hida terre & viginti acras in uno campo & totidem in alio, unam virgatam solutam & quietam & alteram similiter excepto servicio Regis. Hanc donacionem concessit Willelmus de Baews capitalis dominus eorum pro salute anime sue & fraternitate ecclesie maioris monasterii in elemosinam perpetuam & posuit super altare sancte Marie per unum cultellum. Hanc donationem & concessionem viderunt & audierunt testes idonei clerici & laici: Willelmus capellamus de Neuport Willelmus sacerdos de Scrintonia Petrus clericus Baldeuuinus clericus archidiaconi de Buncberi Herueus canonicus Lincolnie Willelmus de Scrintone Radulfus filius Walteri Willelmus filius Lamberti Willelmus Malclere Warinus famulus Ricardus scoland Sered de Harolmed. Teste David archidiaconus & omne capitulum Neuportie Galfridus filius Willelmi Jordanus lathebrie Johannes Maldut Hugo de foraco Bertram de Luch.' The charter would appear to be the earliest extant for the Newport Pagnell area. It will be noted that the donors 'put the land upon the altar by a knife' as a symbol of transfer.

[3] 'Under Henry II's possessory assize of *ultima praesentatione* appointments to benifices made in Stephen's time could not be used as evidence of the possession of the right of presentation. It was quite possible that in the stress of civil war enfeoffments had been made under duress. At any rate it is clear that in the early years of Henry II's reign both king and barons considered the time of King Henry I as the most recent normal period' (S. Painter, *Studies in the History of the English Feudal Barony*, 1943, p. 35).

(Pl. III), pointing out that thirty years ago he had given the monks of Tickford the church of Sherington, to which they had been duly instituted on his presentation and with the authority of the church of Lincoln by David the archdeacon of Buckinghamshire.[1] The heir-apparent, King Henry, son of King Henry,[2] was holding court at the royal manor of Woodstock in December 1170 and there, in his presence and in that of his barons, including Gervase Peynel, William's gift of Sherington church to the monks of Tickford was duly confirmed.[3]

Before the time with which we are dealing, the early twelfth century, the right of patronage to a church was parcel of the ownership of land and lords of manors

[1] Archives du Dept. Indre et Loire, Série H, Liasse 362. 'Venerandis dominis suis N archidiacono et priori de Huntendone Willelmus de Syrentona Salutem. Quod ad presens lingua non possumus literis explicamus. Noverit discretio vestra me ecclesiam de Sirentone tempore bone memorie Alexandri Lincolniensis episcopi monachis de Tichefort pro animabus anticessorum meorum in perpetuam elemosinam dedisse. Et David archidiaconum ad meam presentationem auctoritate Lincolniensis ecclesie eos in eadem instituisse quam donacionem et concessionem a XXX annis retro factam ratam et firmam habemus quod et literis sigilli nostri impressione signatis protestamor. Valete.'

N[icholas] may have been the archdeacon of Bedfordshire (1145–70) who became a monk at St Neots, but more likely Nicholas de Sygillo (*c.* 1165–89), archdeacon of Huntingdonshire. David succeeded Rich. de Wiville as archdeacon of Buckinghamshire in or after 1140. The letter must have been written prior to the drawing up of the confirmation charter of 1170–1 (note 3). Although the 30 years mentioned in the letter must not be interpreted too literally, the evidence suggests that the Church was given to the monks in or soon after 1140.

[2] Henry, the eldest son of King Henry II was crowned in his father's lifetime on 14 June 1170 and died some 6 years before his father on 11 June 1183.

[3] Archives du Dept. Indre et Loire, Série H, Liasse 362. Fowler (*RB*, XI, 225) gives the full latin text and an English translation which is reproduced below. He also gives reasons for assigning the charter to 1170–1.

'William son of Ralph to all his men and friends, French and English, both present and to come, greeting. Know ye that I have given and by this my charter have confirmed to God and the church of the Blessed Mary of Tickford and to the monks of Marmoutier there serving God, the church of Sherington with all its appurtenances for a pure and perpetual arms free and quit of all worldly service and custom, for the salvation of my soul and the souls of my antesessors. And the said monks have granted the aforesaid church of Sherington to Gervase my son, to be held during his whole life from the said monks by rendering to them therefor twenty shillings yearly. And the said monks then received two virgates of land arable which belong to the said church, namely one virgate free and quit of every worldly service and custom, but the other virgate free and quit of every earthly service and exaction so far as to me belong, saving service to the king. But to Gervase aforesaid remained the house and croft with buildings for his whole life. This gift have I made in the presence of King Henry son of King Henry and his barons at Woodstock. Witnesses: Richard archdeacon of Poitiers, Earl William of Manderville, Earl Simon, Earl William de Ferrers, William de St. John, Gervase Peynel, William son of Aldelin, Fulk Peynel, Thomas de Almari, Godwin the clerk of Newport, William de Blossomville' (endorsed, notification of William de Sherington concerning Tickford or Newport). Another charter was executed immediately before the one just given, the witnesses being the same in each case. The slight differences in wording were probably intentional to prevent any weakness of title. In the first charter the land conveyed to the monks was stated to be half a hide, showing that at that date the local hide contained four virgates.

presented as a matter of course. By giving his family church[1] in frankalmoin to a local monastery William de Carun nevertheless was but following the fashion of the time in which a growing number of landed folk, with an eye to their own salvation, were willing to help the newer foundations like Tickford, even at some sacrifice of their rights. William had, indeed, to strike a hard bargain with the monks before they would present his nominee to what he undoubtedly still looked upon as his 'family living'. It would seem that sometime in 1170, probably when he wrote the letter to the heir-apparent's officials, he arranged with the monks to grant the church at Sherington to his son Gervase for life, in return for which he ceded to them in his charter at Woodstock the two virgates of land which belonged to it.

Neither party to this transaction was in the least bit concerned with the spiritual welfare of the parishioners. The bargain was just a part of William's efforts to secure for Gervase, then a youth in his early teens, a livelihood suitable for the younger son of the local squire. Within a year or two William was to settle on him the rich and compact holding of about 80 acres in the demesne sector of Sherington, called in those days le Hoo Park, which was by far the largest piece of enclosed land in the village. Gervase was thus to be endowed with means sufficient to absolve him, if he so wished, from the drudgery of parish duties and to maintain him as a member of the knightly circle into which he had been born.

It is not to be wondered at, therefore, that the monks should seek then and there to safeguard their own and their church's interest by requiring Gervase himself to become party to an agreement in which the conditions of their grant were amplified.[2]

[1] The church is dedicated in memory of St Laud (bishop of Coutances from 528 to 568) and so must have been built or rededicated by Geoffrey, bishop of Coutances, some time between 1066 and 1093.

[2] Archives du Dept. Indre et Loire, Série H, Liasse 362. Fowler (*RB*, XI, p. 232) gives the full latin text and the English translation reproduced below.

'This agreement made between the monks of Marmoutier dwelling at Newport and Gervase son of William de Sherington, namely, that the said Gervase shall hold the church of Sherington from the monks abovesaid, so long as he shall live in the dress of a secular clerk, by rendering to the same monks yearly twenty shillings from the farm. But the said monks [shall have] three crops of the church [land] with all appurtenances, namely, in the three years from Easter next after the death of Thomas, Archbishop of Canterbury, and a half hide of the church land shall remain to them for ever. But if perchance (may it not be so!) it shall happen that the said monks bring a plea for the aforesaid church elsewhere than in the Court of the Archdeacon of Buckingham, the monks and Gervase shall jointly find the costs out of the estate of the said church. Witnesses to this agreement are: Ralph, priest of Linford, Master Geoffrey, Jordan de [Stokes?], William Dorenge, Godwin the clerk, Herman, John Chamberlain, William Brito, William son of Ansculf, Hugh the writer of this agreement and many others.' The agreement seems to have been made within a few months of the murder of Archbishop Thomas Becket (29 Dec. 1170) and therefore in 1171. All witnesses appear to be local men.

In the first place he was to hold the church only so long as he should live in the dress of a secular priest. Later in life Gervase might choose to become a monk, and if he retired to a powerful monastery the prior and monks of Tickford foresaw that they might find it difficult to insist on his forfeiture of the church unless he were bound specifically to this effect. Secondly, the monks were to have the whole profit from the church lands for the first three years. There were probably two reasons for this. Gervase was still very young, and although he must have been already in minor orders the monks might have hoped that he would undertake further study before assuming full office at Sherington. In addition, the clause would provide them, as in fact it did in 1201 and again in 1229,[1] with indisputable evidence of seisin of the church lands. These consisted of 2 virgates, one of which was free from all earthly service and the other free from all service except that due to the king. The former was frankalmoin of the church[2] and was the glebe,[3] while the latter was retained by the prior and monks as a lay fee.[4]

The most striking feature of the whole transaction, however, was the leasing of the church to Gervase for life at a yearly rent of 20*s*. He was to hold the church at farm, as *firmarius*, and not as rector, a situation more akin to a vicarage than a parsonage. Hugh, bishop of Lincoln (1186–1200), did in fact give the monks leave to appropriate when Gervase should cease to be possessed,[5] but they took no action and the incumbents that followed in succession after Gervase were all duly instituted as rectors. The curious position of Gervase in the clerical hierarchy of the day, as lessee of the church, arose because the canon law at the time, like the common law, still regarded the church as so much material property that could be dealt with as though it were a lay fee provided that someone was made responsible for the cure of souls.[6]

[1] *CRR*, II, no. 32; XIII, no. 2228. The jurors state that William, son of Ralph, gave the church to the prior of Newport who was in seisin for three years and received all fruits.

[2] *Jurata Utrum* in 1227: whether the 2 virgates were in frankalmoin appertaning to the church of Gervase, parson of Sheirinton or a lay fee of William, prior of Neweport; the jury state that one virgate was held by Robt. de Aqua (presumably as lessee of the prior) and that the other virgate was frankalmoin of Gervase (*BASRB*, VI, 12), KB26/28 m. 25; 92 m. 19.

[3] no terrier of the glebe earlier than 1637 has been Noted: with appurtenant toft and croft it extended to 21¼ acres of which 14 acres were dispersed in the common fields (Cole Ad. MSS 5839).

[4] Confirming charter to Tickford Priory, the original muniments having been destroyed by fire (*Cal. Pat.* 1307–13, p. 393). The land is given as 7 acres and 10*d*. rent arising from a messuage which Ralph Machin held and 1 messuage and 14 acres land which Sampson the clerk held at a rent of 9*s*. The same holding was returned at the dissolution (E36/165/98).

[5] *CRR*, XIII, no. 2228.

[6] Cf. C. R. Cheney, *From Becket to Langton*, 1956, p. 123.

5

RICHARD DE CARUN AS A WARD OF THE KING

THE death of Stephen and the arrival from Normandy of Henry II led first of all to some desultory fighting, but after this a new era opened for the country as firm government replaced vacillating policy. Buckinghamshire, like many another shire, was still carrying some of the scars of its past sufferings, and in the Danegeld return for the new king's second year Buckinghamshire and Bedfordshire (they were administered jointly by one sheriff) received the large allowance of £107 14*s*. 3*d*. for 'waste' out of a total assessment of £315 16*s*. 8*d*.[1] How much, if any, of this (so-called) 'waste' represents conditions in the Newport Pagnell area we cannot say, for the destruction in the various parts of the two counties would have been committed at different periods and the rate of recovery would have varied from place to place. It is, however, pertinent to remember that within a radius of 11 miles of Sherington as many as sixteen castles had been operative at some time or other during the anarchy, and of these eleven were in north Buckinghamshire and north Bedfordshire (Map 5). The allowance of course can be no more than a rough and ready measure of the extent of past devastation, nevertheless we do know that Henry's own troops had dealt harshly with Bedford and its neighbourhood but three years before.

There is little evidence of William de Carun's activities during the early years of the new king's reign, other than his payment of scutage on two knights' fees in 1161,

[1] See H. W. C. Davis (*The Anarchy of Stephen's Reign*, *EHR*, XVIII, 1903, 630), who has assessed the extent of destruction by comparing the proportion which the amount deducted for 'waste' from the Danegeld of each shire bears to the total amount of Danegeld which it owes (cf. H. A. Cronne, *TRHS*, 1937, 130). The procedure has been criticized by A. L. Poole (*Domesday Book to Magna Carta*, 1951, pp. 151–2), who maintains that the relative degree of destruction thereby exhibited is in many instances quite unrealistic. On the assumption that the sum of money allowed as 'waste' is in some way a measure of what this term presumably implies, and not merely an arbitrary fraction of the total Danegeld owed, it would seem that the magnitude of this sum for any particular shire is the best rough guide to the disabilities under which it was suffering in 1156. 'Bucks and Beds' heads the list, and the amounts allowed the other shires tail off slowly without showing any of the extravagant differences to which Poole objects. The allowance to towns was small, and irrelevant because their recovery would have been far quicker than that of the countryside.

1162 and 1165, showing that he did not attend in person the feudal levies to which these referred. In 1166, when Henry II asked his tenants in chief to send him information about the knights they had enfeoffed, William, in his *carta*[1] stated that he owed the service of two knights and had not enfeoffed anyone. His fief consisted of the village of Sherington with no outside members whatever and its rating at two whole knights' fees raises an interesting point in feudal tenure which will be more profitably discussed later after presentation of evidence relating to other feudal incidents that stem from the same anomaly.

William again paid scutage in 1168 and 1172. On his death in 1180 his land was taken into the king's hand by the sheriff, where it remained for the next eight years or so, the profit being duly recorded in the Pipe Rolls.

Pipe Roll	Date	Farm	Perquisites and crops sold	Total paid into exchequer
		£ s. d.	£ s. d.	£ s. d.
26 Hen. II	1180[a]	4 7 6	3 0 0	7 7 6
27 Hen. II	1181	7 1 0	15 2	7 16 2
28 Hen. II	1182	6 11 6	10 0	7 1 2
29 Hen. II	1183	6 8 0	1 14 9	8 2 9
30 Hen. II	1184	6 1 8	9 0	6 10 8
31 Hen. II	1185	6 14 6	1 0 7	7 15 1
32 Hen. II	1186	6 16 6	1 3 0	7 19 6
33 Hen. II	1187	6 18 0	1 19 6	8 17 6
34 Hen. II	1188[b]	3 8 11	2 5 6	5 14 8
	1180–8	54 7 7	12 17 9	67 5 4

[a] Less than a full year. [b] Half year.

One would normally infer from this that the heir was under age and the king had retained the wardship in his own hand. We learn, however, from the record of an inquiry made by the itinerant justices in 1185[2] that this was not so in the present

[1] *Red Book of the Exchequer*, ed. Hubert Hall, vol. 1, p. 314.

[2] *Rot. de Dominabus*, *PRS*, 35, 42.

'Ida, que fuit uxor Willelmi de Schirinton, et filia Hugonis de Bulli, est de donatione Domini Regis, et est .lx annorum, et habet .iij. filios et .iij. filias; primogenitus est .xxx. annorum. Postquam Willelmus obiit, cepit Dominus Rex terram suam in Muleshoe [Moulsoe Hundred], et tenuit in manu sua jam .v. annis; et valet annuatim .vj l. et .iij.s. et .vj.d. et .ij. anseres et .iiij capones; et si apponerentur .ij. carruce et dimidia et .c. oves et .v. vacce et v. sues, valeret .X.l. Pars Domine, qui est sexta pars, valet .XXX.s.; et si apponeretur dimidia carruce, valeret .xl.s. Preter redditum, cepit vicecomes de dicta villa .lxij. s et .vij.d.'

Marginal note: Hoc est, de custodis.

The editor of the text (J. H. Round) noted that

case, which has unusual features. The justices were required to ascertain the rights of the Crown over widows, minors and heiresses, and whether these had been infringed. The entry for William de Carun's family is more informative than most, because the justices wanted information that would enable them to certify the full value of the king's wardship. In addition therefore to the usual particulars about the widow's dower and the number and age of the children, an account is given of the sources of profit from the estate.

Ida the widow was said to be sixty and to have three sons and three daughters. That the eldest son was already thirty is not surprising, for his youngest brother Gervase was old enough to be in minor orders when given the farm of Sherington church in 1170, but it is not immediately apparent why the estate should have passed into the king's hands on William's death in 1180, for Richard the heir was even then of full age and presumably eligible to sue out his livery without delay. Circumstantial evidence discussed below suggests that he was on crusade at the time.

Gervase Peynel, the owner of Newport Pagnell and feudal overlord of much land in the vicinity was a friend of William de Carun, whose charter to the monks of Tickford he had witnessed before the young King Henry, son of King Henry, at Woodstock in 1170 and whose youngest son, another Gervase, had been given on his recommendation the church of Sherington by the monks of Tickford.[1] At the time Gervase Peynel was a member of the young King Henry's court, and five years later he joined him and Queen Eleanor in the abortive rebellion against Henry II, who subsequently retaliated by ordering the dismantling of his castle at Dudley and forcing him to pay a very heavy fine.[2] As is well known, Henry II did not readily forgive those who had taken up arms against him in this revolt: he kept his queen, for instance, in detention for the rest of his life except when he needed her presence on state occasions, and the lands returned to Gervase Peynel did not include the extensive liberties that had been appurtenant in the past to the borough of Newport Pagnell.[3]

There is no evidence of William de Carun's activities during this period but from the heartless way that Henry II treated his widow Ida, who was assigned as dower only one-half of the normal one-third part of his estate, we may infer that he followed Gervase Peynel. The heir Richard, of the same age as the young king, was

the value of the farm given in the roll (£6 3*s.* 6*d.*) was intermediate between that of 1184 (£6 1*s.* 8*d.*) and that of 1185 (£6 14*s.* 6*d.*), confirming his view that the roll was drawn up between these two dates.

[1] See p. 48, n. 1.

[2] 500 marks *pro habendo benevolentie regis* (*PRS*, 25, 166).

[3] *CRR*, IX, 330.

Carun of Sherington

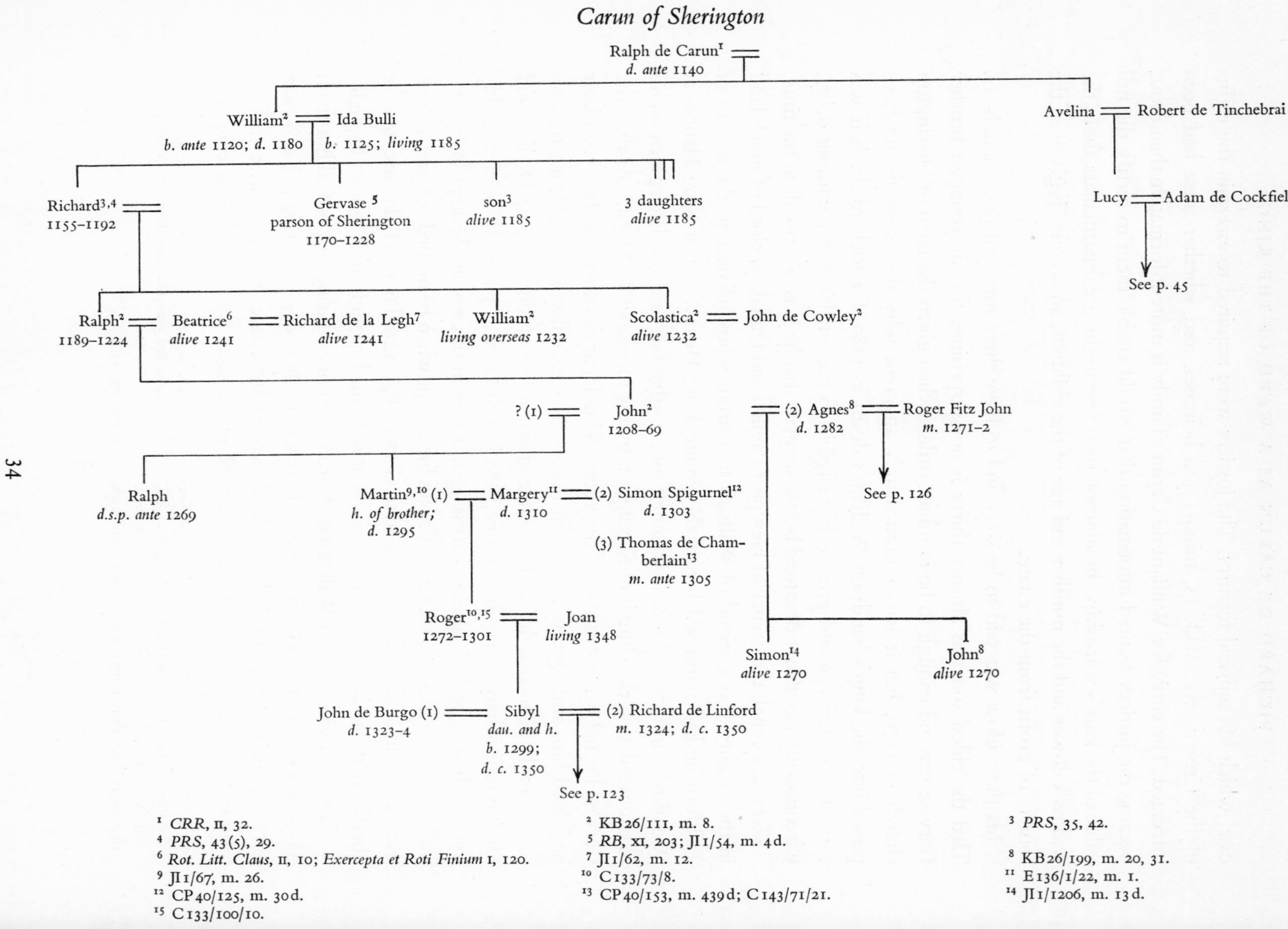

[1] *CRR*, II, 32.
[2] KB 26/111, m. 8.
[3] *PRS*, 35, 42.
[4] *PRS*, 43 (5), 29.
[5] *RB*, XI, 203; JI 1/54, m. 4d.
[6] *Rot. Litt. Claus*, II, 10; *Exercepta et Roti Finium* I, 120.
[7] JI 1/62, m. 12.
[8] KB 26/199, m. 20, 31.
[9] JI 1/67, m. 26.
[10] C 133/73/8.
[11] E 136/1/22, m. 1.
[12] CP 40/125, m. 30d.
[13] CP 40/153, m. 439d; C 143/71/21.
[14] JI 1/1206, m. 13d.
[15] C 133/100/10.

as likely as not a page or an esquire in Gervase's service and so would have incurred in his turn the elder king's displeasure.[1] This may have spurred him on to take the Cross and go east with the expedition organized in 1177 by Henry's first cousin the count of Flanders. Being abroad at the time of his father's death he was in no position to sue out his livery[2] and the estate would thus have passed into the king's hand until his return early in 1188, a few months after the fall of Jerusalem.[3] This account is, of course, a speculative reconstruction of what must have been the most critical period of Richard's life, but it provides a satisfactory explanation of the several unusual features mentioned above and as a corollary would suggest that he would not have married until his return to England, in keeping with the birth of his heir, Ralph, in 1190. Whatever the true facts of the case King Henry II did not return Richard's lands until he had paid a very heavy fine for them.

The payment due to the Crown from an heir holding a small tenancy in chief before the time of Magna Carta has been the subject of disagreement among authorities in recent years[4] and to appraise the treatment that Richard de Carun received at the hands of Henry II it is necessary to state briefly the general principles which seemed to guide the action of the Crown in his reign. It was mentioned in the *Dialogus* that the heir of a greater or lesser barony held in chief, if of full age, must pay an amount which could be fixed only at the king's pleasure, whereas if he were a minor he could, on coming of age, receive his land either freely of the king's grace or, like an heir of full age, on payment at the king's pleasure. The treatise does not specifically mention a very small fief of one or more knights' fees held in chief, but one is led to infer that the tenant of such was to be treated as a baron.[5] This last point is important because mesne tenants paid only a relatively small 'relief' of £5 per knight's fee and, as we shall see later, this rating was sometimes applied to small tenancies in chief.

In the case of the Sherington fief the heir Richard was not a minor and it was only

[1] It is possible that he was imprisoned and so remained until 1188, but there is no mention of this on the justices' roll, which is in most cases informative about the circumstances of an heir who was over the normal age, e.g. the heir of Peter de Peleuill was a leper aged 24 years in the custody of the king, who allowed him his maintenance in hospital (*Rot. de Dominabus*, 53).

[2] Fealty to the king could not be sworn *in absentia*.

[3] Vicomes rend. comp. de lxiij.s. xj.d. de exitu de Schirinton de dimidio anno antequam rex redderet eam Ricardo de Schirinton (*PRS*, 38, 121).

[4] A full discussion is given by I. J. Sanders, *Feudal Military Service in England*, 1956, pp. 98–106.

[5] *Dialogus de Scaccario*, ed. C. Johnson (London, 1950), pp. lxi, 94–6. On p. 95 the editor says in a footnote 'The Dialogus makes no clear distinction between an honour and a group of manors, though it equates honour and barony. But even the tenant of a single knight's fee must be regarded as *baro minor*, since the distinction in the rate of relief depends on the immediacy or otherwise of the tenure.'

because of unusual circumstances that his land had passed into the king's wardship. For eight years King Henry had taken the whole profit from the estate except a pittance set aside for the widow. Richard, therefore, on his return to England, might well have expected to receive his patrimony without any further payment to the king or—in the words of the *Dialogus*—freely of the king's grace, for when a wardship had brought profit for a number of years it would seem only fair that the sum paid for relief should be correspondingly lessened. This was indeed conceded to mesne tenants. King Henry, however, ruled otherwise, and he exacted his feudal dues to the last farthing. During the wardship he had netted a total sum of £67 5*s*. 4*d*. and in spite of this he called upon Richard to pay a fine[1] of 100 marks before he would give him his livery.[2] As in the last decade of the twelfth century it was becoming customary for the heir of a barony to pay £100—a sum the barons considered an onerous burden—the exorbitant level at which Richard's fine was assessed needs no emphasis. To raise the money he was forced to dispose of part of his estate to his cousin Lucy de Cockfield.[3]

It will be seen that in 1188 Richard was definitely regarded by the officers of the royal exchequer as a baron and had to pay a fine fixed at the arbitrary will of the king in accord with the *Dialogus*. As his father's *carta* of 1166 made no mention of baronial tenure it is pertinent to inquire why he had to submit to a treatment so different from that meted out to certain other tenants in chief with very small fiefs. Round cites cases where the holding was one fee or less, and where the holding was not part of an escheated honour but could be clearly identified among those held *in capite* in 1166, which were uniformly rated at £5 per knight's fee.[4] Sanders[5] has recently sifted what little evidence is available on fiefs held by barony and by military service in the first hundred years after the conquest and shows how

[1] The subtle difference between 'fine' and 'relief' in connexion with these payments is discussed by I. J. Sanders, *Feudal Military Service in England*, p. 98.

[2] Ricardus de Carun redd. comp. Cm. pro fine terre de Schirintone (*PRS*, 38, 127). The abrupt change of name from 'de Schirinton' (p. 21, n. 3) to 'de Carun' should be noted. Richard and his descendants appear to have used the new variety exclusively after this date.

[3] See p. 44.

[4] J. H. Round, *Family Origins*, 1930, pp. 234–6. A. L. Poole (*Obligations of Society*, 1946, p. 95) quotes four cases from the Pipe Roll of 1185 and says they 'prove conclusively that relief of tenants holding of the Crown by knights service were charged at the rate of £5 per fee'. The conclusion is unwarranted: Hugh Burdet held two fees of the honour of Huntingdon and Brian son of Ralph five fees of the honour of Peverel of London. Miles of Beauchamp's half a fee in Lavendon was his wife's one fifth share of the honour of Bidun (W. Farrer, *Honors and Knights Fees*, II, 329; III, 21; I, 3).

[5] Sanders, *loc. cit. passim.*

difficult it may often be to draw a clear distinction between one tenure and the other. His discussion is of necessity based on data culled from the *cartae* of 1166 and the Pipe Rolls for, as he points out, there is a great dearth of evidence of the terms upon which estates were held of the Crown because the first grants of land to tenants in chief do not appear to have been written in any documents. A probe of the present incident has indeed revealed some indirect but none the less interesting cases of enfeoffment during the period just before or after 1100, and poses the intriguing question of how these could have come to the attention of the exchequer officials in the thirteenth century if early written record had not existed. One is driven to the conclusion that pride of descent had kept alive details of tenure that in the early days had been handed down by word of mouth.

The Sherington fief, like that known later as the honour of Lavendon, had been part of the extensive Domesday holding of the bishop of Coutances. Henry I (presumably) enfeoffed Ralph de Carun or a forebear of his early in the twelfth century, and the fief had descended to his grandson Richard, with whom we are concerned. In turn it was to pass to Richard's son, Ralph, and his grandson, John, who succeeded in 1229. As the descent was an unbroken one from father to son the only title deed to the fief that John would have been likely to possess was the original charter of enfeoffment of Henry I or a confirmation of it from a later king. In 1250 John was heavily in debt to one of the jews from whom Henry III was extorting a large sum of money and the royal officials, as they had done in his grandfather's day, were determined to squeeze him to the last farthing. His land was duly valued by inquisition and the jury declared *inter alia* that John held in chief by the fee of the hauberk and that the value of the service could not be fixed save at the king's will.[1] Feudal tenure in such terms does not belong to the mid-thirteenth century; it is an echo from Norman times.

The *fief del haubert*, according to Stenton,[2] was a Norman phrase implying that the owner of the fief was a knight of the higher class who had what was regarded as a full provision for war, including a hauberk of mail, and not of the lower class with more limited equipment. In England it soon became customary for the knights enfeoffed for the king's service to go to war with full equipment and the phrase

[1] 'et dicunt tenet terram suam in capite domini Regis per feodum halberkii unde nesciverunt illud servicium extendi nisi ad voluntatem domini' (*Cal. Inq. Misc.* I, no. 82; C145/4/3).

[2] F. M. Stenton, *English Feudalism*, 1932, 14–15.

ceased to be current during the reign of Henry I. The present writer is aware of only two other instances where a fief is so described. The first was mentioned by Stenton himself, who had noted that in 1261 the abbot of Tavistock held $15\frac{1}{2}$ fees 'in fee de Haubergh'. This fief, of pre-Conquest origin, had been organized as a barony of 15 knights' fees by Geoffrey, the Norman abbot in the period 1082–8.[1] The second concerns the barony of Caynho, Bedfordshire (Map 6) which originally contained 25 knights' fees derived from the Domesday holding of Nigel d'Albini. Early in the thirteenth century this fief, which had been already largely denuded by grants of fees elsewhere, devolved upon three co-heiresses and on the death in 1272 of Simon Daubeny, a grandson of one of them, *inquisitiones post mortem* were held within a week of each other at Bedford and Derby respectively. Both dealt with Caynho. The jury at Bedford certified that the manor (head of the moiety of the barony) was held of the king in chief for a moiety of a barony, Simon finding $1\frac{1}{2}$ knights at his own cost when the king goes with the army in England, while that at Derby found that it was held in chief by service of the hauberk fee.[2]

It will be seen that all the three fiefs reputed to be held in chief of the hauberk fee are of early Norman origin, when baronial tenure had not become precisely defined. Those of Tavistock and Caynho were clearly of the class referred to in the *Dialogus* as major baronies, even though by 1272 the latter had become dispersed and—like the grinning Cheshire cat—was left with no more than its head.

The medieval furlong called Wartrou (felon's tree)[3] implies that the Anglo-Saxon or early Norman owners of Sherington had their own gallows, but no claim to more than the right of holding a view of frankpledge was made by later members of the Carun family.[4] If the fief granted by Henry I was indeed a small barony—with perhaps outside members that had become dispersed before William, son of Ralph, made his return in 1166—then all superior rights must have been withdrawn during the twelfth century when the jurisdiction of the royal courts was being made exclusive. The Sherington property would have remained, nevertheless, the *caput* of a barony and the exchequer officials would have considered they had the right to demand relief at the king's pleasure in 1188. If such a view be accepted then further comment on the small fiefs cited by Round must await the outcome of research into their origin.

[1] H. P. R. Finberg, 1951, *Tavistock Abbey*, p. 9.

[2] *Cal. Inq.* II, 11.

[3] Cf. p. 10.

[4] Neither Martin nor Roger de Carum claimed exalted jurisdiction before the Edwardian justices (Placito de Quo Warranto, Rec. Con.).

6

THE LAST SEIGE OF BEDFORD IN 1224

RICHARD DE CARUN died between 1191 and 1193, so that he enjoyed his hard-earned patrimony for only a brief spell. Information about his life at Sherington is meagre,[1] but he confirmed his father's gift of le Hoo Park to his brother Gervase the parson and gave the yearly rent of 8*d.* arising from it to Sherington church in perpetuity for the maintenance of an altar light.[2]

Ralph, the son and heir, born in 1190, was an infant at his father's death and the estate, in consequence, once more passed into the king's hands. This time it was let to farm at a fixed rent of £4 per annum, a sum that reflects the loss of the Cockfield fee. Francis de Bohun of Midhurst, Sussex, had possession for the first two years, and at his death the assize judge and later justiciar Geoffrey Fitz Peter took over and retained it until 1201.[3] In that year Robert de Vipont, a great friend and supporter of King John, with whom he was then serving in Normandy, offered 20 marks and a palfrey for the lands and custody of the heir.[4] There was a family connexion between Robert and his young ward,[5] and one can imagine that Ralph, then 12 years of age, was received into the Vipont household as a young squire for training in the arms and graces of knighthood. Three years later King John gave Robert the wardship,[6] so that for the rest of the term no payment became due to the Exchequer except for scutage.[7]

[1] He paid scutage in 1190 and so did not accompany King Richard on the third crusade (*PRS*, NS, 1, 142).

[2] KB26/111, m. 8. The rent, then worth 11*d.* per annum, was still being paid at the time of the dissolution in 1525 (Chantry Certificates, Augmentation Office, Bdl. 5, no. 31).

[3] *PRS*, NS, 5 and *passim*. During both tenancies the undertenant was a William de Sherington who had a small estate at Leckhamstead and held the bailiwick of Buckingham (see pp. 68–8). William paid scutage for the 2 knights' fees in 1193–4 (Redemption of King Richard), 1195–6 and 1198–9 (Coronation of John). His arrearages were not finally paid off until 1212 (*PRS*, NS, 5–28, *passim*).

[4] *Rot. de Ob.* 106; *PRS*, NS, 14, 170. As the king was always on the move the need for horses was great; in the present case the palfrey went to the queen.

[5] Ralph's grandmother was Ida d. of Hugh de Bulli and Robert's wife was Idonea d. and heiress of John de Bulli, a cadet of the Tickhill family (*Rot. de Dominabus*, 12, 42).

[6] *Rot. Chart.* (Rec. Com.), 120.

[7] Robert owed the 'scutage of Scotland' levied in 1209; it was remitted by letter from the king (*PRS*, NS, 28, 145).

The feudal system might have been suitable for its age, but its application in the case of the Carun fee was extremely harsh. Fate had decreed that the estate should become a Crown wardship for a total of 24 years out of the 30 covering the death of William in 1180 and the coming of age of his grandson Ralph in 1210, so that the family had direct control over its own affairs for no more than six years during this long period. It might be argued that feudal rights had not been exacted with any greater severity than the system demanded or allowed, and that Richard de Carun was merely unfortunate in that his time of trouble happened to coincide with one in which the Crown—faced with a continuous rise in the cost of living—was exacting its feudal dues without scruple even to the point of abuse. Be this as it may, it was Henry or his agents who drained the fief of all its available assets and forced the sale of the subsidiary manor—to leave an attenuated estate over which a mantle of poverty had already descended and was to remain with it until the final break up some four hundred years later in the time of Elizabeth.

When Ralph came of age in 1210 his estate had been a Crown wardship for seventeen years. According to the *Dialogus* no relief should have been demanded in such a case and none was paid,[1] but whether this can be ascribed to the conscientious ruling of the 'king's will' or the personal influence of Robert de Vipont we cannot say. The case is of interest because it illustrates so well a point first emphasized by Round,[2] that the feudal abuses remedied by Magna Carta were not introduced by John but were in full existence under Henry II.

The first few years after Ralph's succession to Sherington saw a slow worsening of the relations between King John and his barons. Ralph was young, and although he might have played some minor role in the stirring events of the day we have nothing but factual knowledge about him: that he owed the service of two knights' fees in 1210–12[3] and paid the scutage of Poitou in 1212–13.[4] When the revolt was coming to a head in 1215 Bedford castle was occupied by the barons at the invitation of its castellan William de Beauchamp and it remained in their hands during the parleys at Runnymede. On the outbreak of civil war a few months later the king, in order to control the activities of the barons centred on London, put part of his forces under the control of the earl of Salisbury and Falkes de Breauté. A few weeks later Falkes made an expedition through Bedfordshire and on 25 November invested

[1] No entry in relevant Pipe Rolls.

[2] J. H. Round, *Family Origins*, p. 233.

[3] *Red Book of the Exchequer*, p. 536.

[4] E372/60. Ralph paid 25*s.* 5*d.* and owed 54*s.* 7*d.*

Bedford castle; the castellan was away and as he sent no help the garrison surrendered in seven days. Meanwhile Falkes attacked and destroyed the small castle at Hanslope owned by William Maudit, who was with the barons.[1] At the end of the year John himself set out with his main force—which included a large proportion of foreign mercenaries—to subdue the north. The chroniclers[2] have left us a harrowing account of the devastation and plundering, especially of the barons' estates, as John's army swept through to the Midlands and then on to Berwick, returning via Lincolnshire and East Anglia. He left St Albans on 19 December and two days later passed through Newport Pagnell[3] *en route* for Northampton. It is unlikely, however, that much damage was done in the neighbourhood of Newport and Sherington by the king's or Falkes de Breauté's troops, for the Honour of Dudley, which included Newport and many villages in the area, was in the hands of the earl of Salisbury and Ralph de Carun was a protégé of Robert de Vipont, one of John's stoutest adherents.

Peace soon followed the death of John and the council acting for the boy King Henry III agreed that Falkes should retain Bedford castle. During the next few years little is recorded about Ralph: he paid the first scutage of the new reign[4] and at times was one of the four knights called upon to choose the twelve others needed for a local grand assize.[5] Meanwhile Falkes, an ambitious foreigner who had dealt harshly in the past with those who opposed King John, became increasingly unpopular as the new régime established itself. The climax came in June 1224, when he was arraigned before the justices in eyre at Dunstable on many counts connected with his past actions. He was found guilty, heavily fined and summoned to appear at the Shire Court at Bedford to be outlawed. When the justices left Dunstable on 17 June one of them, Henry de Braybrook, an old enemy of Falkes's, was kidnapped by Falkes's brother William, his castellan at Bedford, and imprisoned in the castle there. Henry III and his council, who were then at Northampton, could not afford to ignore this affront to the administration of justice: the feudal host was summoned and the royal party moved out of Northampton for Bedford on 19 June. The king was at Newport Pagnell the next day, and from there issued six mandates concerning munitions for the forthcoming siege and the forwarding of four casks of wine from

[1] Mathew Paris, *Chron. Majora*, II, 636.

[2] R. Wendover, III, 348; see also Kate Norgate, *John Lackland*, p. 256, C. F. Farrar, *Old Bedford*, p. 41.

[3] *Itin. John*, a. 17.

[4] E372/62: He paid 51*s*. 5*d*. and owed 23*d*.; he also paid 54*s*. 7*d*. arrears for the scutage of Poitou.

[5] *CRR*, IX, 330; XI, 24.

his cellars in Northampton castle.[1] Ralph de Carun obeyed the summons and joined the forces investing Bedford castle. The siege was protracted and the garrison did not surrender until 15 August when all but three were hanged. Henry's losses were fairly heavy and Ralph was one of the six knights who, with two hundred men-at-arms, were killed.[2]

As John the heir was only 16 years old in 1224 the Sherington estate passed for the third time in 44 years into the king's wardship. When the fighting was over Henry spent a few days at the nearby Elstow nunnery and it was presumably while he was there that Beatrice the widow offered 80 marks for the custody of the lands and the wardship and marriage of the heir, for an agreement to this effect was enrolled in London on 9 September.[3] As the wardship was for no more than five years the bargain was a hard one, but in effect only £44 was paid.[4] Beatrice, in virtue of her husband's attendance at the siege, was excused one but not both of the fees liable for the scutage of Bedford as she could recover a part payment of the second from her mesne tenant Robert de Cockfield.[5]

Before his return to London Henry decreed the total demolition of Bedford castle and gave Henry de Braybrook the task—no doubt a congenial one after his recent experience—of seeing that his orders were carried out. None of the local people except perhaps the Beauchamp family, its hereditary castellans, would have regretted its passing, for on at least six occasions during the preceding century it had been the centre of warlike activity and each time the towns and villages in the vicinity had been subject to some degree of devastation. These depredations would now cease and never again would this particular part of the country be overrun by troops accustomed to live on the land over which they marched and fought.

[1] *Rot. Lit. Claus.* I, 605.

[2] C. F. Farrer, *Old Bedford*, gives a full account of the siege.

[3] *Excerpta et Rotulis Finium* (Roberts), I, 120.

[4] Beatrice was to pay £10 at St Hilary and at Easter in each year until the debt was settled. Actually she paid £30 in 1224–5 and £14 in the year following, when the remainder of the debt was excused (E 372/68, 69, 70).

[5] *Rot. Lit. Claus.* II, 10. The widow Denise de Cockfield was then holding the mesne fee of her brother-in-law, Robert, in dower.

7

THE COCKFIELD FAMILY

THE Lucy de Cockfield to whom Richard de Carun had sub-infeudated a subsidiary manor in Sherington was a grand-daughter of the first Ralph de Carun and a representative of the old feudal families of Tinchebrai and Cockfield whose lands, though more extensive than Richard's, were not compact and held in chief like his but were scattered among various counties in small parcels held as mesne tenancies. Sometime before 1140 Ralph de Carun had given his daughter Aveline in marriage with Robert de Tinchebrai,[1] a cadet of the Peverel family[2] with lands in Oxfordshire (Swanbourne, Stoke Lyne), Northamptonshire (Guilsborough, Little Oakley, Charwelton) and Nottinghamshire (Nuthall). The marriage settlement included two virgates of land in Sherington, and Robert and Aveline gave these during the reign of Stephen to the abbess and nuns of St Mary, Northampton (Delapre abbey).[3] On Robert's death in 1190[4] all his lands with the exception of half a fee in Swanbourne passed to his daughter and heiress Lucy, who had married Adam de Cockfield of Feltwell, Suffolk.

Incidents in the early history of the Cockfield family are mentioned in the annals of St Edmund's abbey,[5] under whom the senior branch held lands in Suffolk (Lindsey and its castle, Cockfield, Groton and Semer). Adam de Cockfield, son of Lemmer who was holding in the eleventh century, married Adeliza Crichetot who, in her own right, held lands of the honour of Warenne in Feltwell, Norfolk, and in Hangleton, Sussex. With the consent of her younger son Adam who according to

[1] *CRR*, II, 32. A branch of the family had land at Harlestone, Northamptonshire, and a contemporary pedigree is given in Henry de Bray's Estate Book (*RHS*, Camden series, XXVII). The name, taken from the Norman town made famous by Henry I's victory over Duke Robert in 1106, occurs in many queer forms: Thenerchebrai, Tenerchebray, Tenethebrai, etc.

[2] *Rot. Cur. Reg.* I, 46. On Robert's death his lands were claimed by Hugh Peverel of Sampford Peverel, Somerset, on the plea that his father William Peverel and Robert's father were brothers and that he was heir male because Lucy was born out of wedlock. The court judgement is not recorded, but Lucy retained all the lands except Swanbourne which, by agreement with Hugh Peverel, was given to Henry de Clinton (*PRS*, NS, 6, 123–4, 201).

[3] *Dugdale Monast.* V, 212.

[4] *PRS*, NS, I, 145.

[5] Camden 3rd series, LXXXIV.

her will was to inherit Feltwell after her death, she settled, sometime between 1156 and 1162, land worth 7*s.* yearly on Castle Acre Priory for the souls of the earl of Warenne, her lord Adam de Cokefield, her brother William de Crichetot and her son Alan, all no doubt then deceased.[1] Later, sometime before 1185, Adam the son gave a toft and land in his demesne at Feltwell to the same priory for the souls of his parents, his wife Lucy and her mother Aveline.[2] With his wife Lucy he also confirmed the Tinchebrai gift of land in Sherington to Delapre abbey.[3]

It was this Lucy—widowed before 1185[4]—who acquired the subsidiary fee in Sherington from her cousin Richard in 1189.[5] She died about 1202 and her son Adam inherited a valuable estate[6] for which, on his death in 1211, the justiciar Geoffrey Fitz Peter paid £400 to have custody of the land and heir as well as the marriage of the widow Agatha.[7] The heir, another Adam, succeeded in 1219 but died two years later, so that when the estate came to his brother Robert it was saddled with the provision of dower for two young widows. The elder, Agatha, was given Nuthall, Nottinghamshire,[8] while the younger, Denise, who was shortly to marry Robert d'Eyvill of Egmanton, Nottinghamshire, received the manors of Stoke Lyne in Oxfordshire and Sherington in Buckinghamshire, which she retained for just on 40 years. To Lucy and her Cockfield descendants the manor of Sherington was of no interest other than as one of the numerous small properties from which they drew an income: they never resided, and their personal contact with the village must have been of the slightest. It is the irony of fate, therefore, that their name and not that of Carun is still on record in the village, for among the meadow

1 W. Farrer, *Honors and Knights' Fees*, III, 360–1.

2 *Ibid.* p. 364.

3 *Dugdale Monast.* v, 145.

4 *Rot. de Dominabus*, 56, where her name seems to supply the missing words.

5 No deed for the transfer has survived, and it is assigned to 1189 for the following reasons: (*a*) William de Carun had made no sub-infeudation before 1166. (*b*) The distribution of the demesne lands in 1185 suggests that the estate was still intact (see Table 4). (*c*) The Pipe Roll accounts from 1180 to 1188 show no change in net income. (*d*) In a lawsuit of 1201 Lucy de Cockfield declared that she owned property in Sherington in the time of King Henry father of King John: 1189 was the last year of Henry II. (*e*) 1189 was the year when Richard de Carun was hard pressed for money.

6 From his father: Norfolk (1 fee in Feltwell, ½ fee Sniterle, ½ fee East Tudenham); Suffolk (½ fee Little Waldingfield, ½ fee Wileby and Helaby, 1 fee Moulton); Sussex (1 fee Hangleton and Ardington). From his mother: Oxfordshire (½ fee Stoke Lyne); Northamptonshire (1 fee Little Oakley and Charwelton); Nottinghamshire (½ fee Nuthall). A total of 7 fees.

7 *PRS*, NS, 28, 122. On the justiciar's death in 1213 Geoffrey de Mandeville acquired the rights for £300 but at the king's request transferred them within a few days to Thomas de Erdington (*Rot. Lit. Claus.* I, 140, 159, 272).

8 *Book of Fees*, 287, 532, 556. She was holding in 1235–6.

Cockfield of Cockfield, Nuthall and Sherington

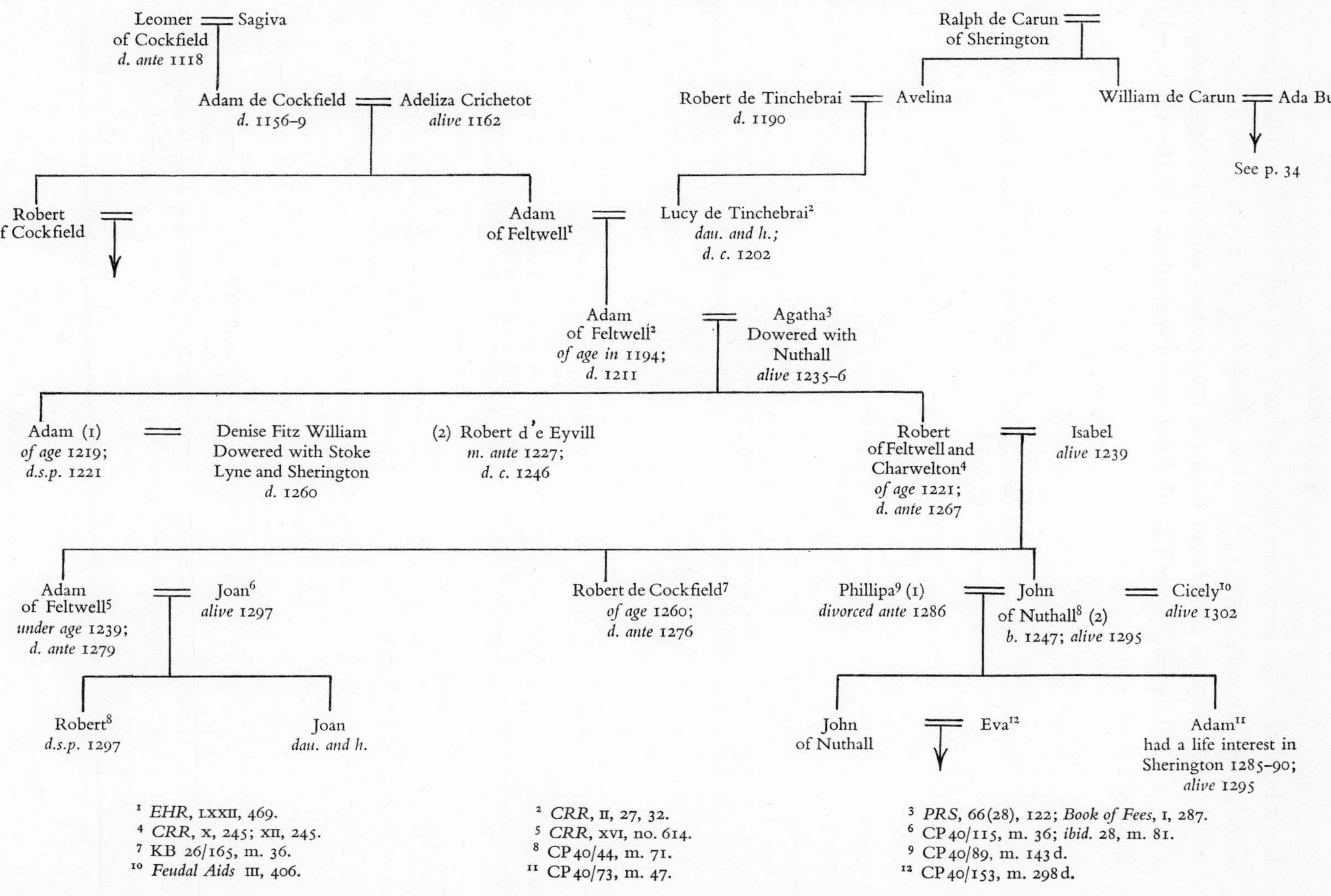

[1] *EHR*, LXXII, 469.
[2] *CRR*, II, 27, 32.
[3] *PRS*, 66(28), 122; *Book of Fees*, I, 287.
[4] *CRR*, X, 245; XII, 245.
[5] *CRR*, XVI, no. 614.
[6] CP 40/115, m. 36; *ibid.* 28, m. 81.
[7] KB 26/165, m. 36.
[8] CP 40/44, m. 71.
[9] CP 40/89, m. 143 d.
[10] *Feudal Aids* III, 406.
[11] CP 40/73, m. 47.
[12] CP 40/153, m. 298 d.

lands bordering the river opposite Lathbury is a field called 'Cock's Meadow' which takes its name, as we shall see more clearly later[1] from the 'doles of Cockfield' which were brought into being with the companion 'doles of Carun' when the original meadow lands were parcelled out on sub-infeudation of the Cockfield fee in 1189.

[1] See p. 112.

8

JOHN DE CARUN AND ELIAS THE JEW

JOHN DE CARUN was the same age as the young King Henry and like him was inclined to chafe at the tutelage to which he was subjected during his minority. Both were headstrong and anxious to get their own way, but whereas Henry as king could free himself from all restraint in 1227, when 19 years old, by declaring that he was of full age, John had perforce to curb his patience for another two years. Nevertheless, he seems to have been already conscious that the feudal obligations to which he would be committed on coming of age were as onerous as those carried by his great-grandfather William and that he would have for the purpose an income that for one reason or other was not likely to be much more than half what William had enjoyed. He was aggrieved, moreover, because he felt that during his minority various people were taking a mean advantage and doing their best to whittle down the value of his already attenuated inheritance: his mother for instance was taking far more than her fair share as dower; the prior of Tickford was trying to steal his right of presentation to the family living; his great-uncle Gervase's bastards had obtained possession of valuable land that should be his escheat; while some of his neighbours were even beginning to assert that they had right of common over part of his own demesne land. On occasion his pent-up feelings found forceful expression and eventually he found himself with much to answer for when the assize justices came to Wycombe in 1232.

Meanwhile, without waiting for his coming of age,[1] he had brought an assize of darrein presentment in 1229 against the prior of Tickford to declare the right of presentation to the church of Sherington, which was opportunely vacant on the death of his great-uncle Gervase.[2] He claimed as heir of his great-grandfather William, who had made the last presentation. The prior in evidence stated that William had given the church to the monks in pure and perpetual arms and asserted that Gervase was never parson on William's presentation but only a lessee of the

[1] Selden Society, 62, 256.

[2] KB 26/102, m. 16.

church under the monks.[1] The jury agreed and found in the prior's favour.[2] John's action was typical of the numerous suits in the twelfth and thirteenth centuries brought by children or successors of men who had given their local church to a monastery, and shows how difficult it must have been for the latter to accept that their elders had irrevocably given away what had always seemed to be part and parcel of the family domain.

According to the custom of the time Ralph de Carun's widow Beatrice could not be endowed with the capital messuage, which was the manor house,[3] but with John's permission she could be and was assigned part of the garden therein on which to build a house for herself. There she lived with her second husband Richard de la Leigh, a cadet of a family seated at Thurleigh, a village 5 miles north of Bedford. John soon found himself at loggerheads with them for, in his own words, 'they had taken in dower all that they could lay their hands on'. He sought a writ to measure dower, a remedy occasionally used by a guardian against a mother who had received more than her proper share, but he seems to have got no satisfaction. In defiance he took the law into his own hands and turned them out of the house and grounds. They countered by bringing an assize of novel disseisin in 1232 and the jury found in their favour.[4]

It was during this assize at Wycombe in 1232 that John instituted legal proceedings to recover the land that had been in the occupation of his great-uncle Gervase the parson. His youth does not obtrude in this instance and he must have sought good legal advice for his case was well presented.[5] As has already been mentioned[6] Gervase's father, William de Carun, had given him some time before 1180 property in Sherington which subsequent lawsuits show was the compact holding of 80 acres called in those days le Hoo Park (Map 4). William's grandson and heir Ralph, who

[1] He exhibited William's charter (see p. 28) as well as confirming charters of John's father, Ralph, and of Hugh, bishop of Lincoln. Also Letters Patent of David, archdeacon of Buckinghamshire, instituting the monks.

[2] The jurors stated that William had given the church to the prior and monks, who had had seisin for three years and received all fruits. The prior, on the advice of his friend and patron Gervase Peynel, had then granted it to Gervase, clerk, to farm for 20*s.* per annum, so that Gervase held the church all his life as farmer and not rector. Attention has already been called (p. 30) to the astute move of the monks in 1180–1 whereby they obtained clear evidence of seisin of the church.

[3] Pollock and Maitland, II, 419, quoting Bracton.

[4] JI 1/62, m. 12. Damages of 40*s.* were awarded. One has to remember that Beatrice had paid dearly for the wardship.

[5] *Ibid.* m. 32d. It is probable that his attorney was the William de St Edmund to whom he made over the property soon after he had recovered it.

[6] See p. 29.

was Gervase's nephew, had given in addition 6 acres of the contiguous le Hoo Wood. Gervase died in 1227 and by the time John was of age, and in a position to present his case, the property had become vested in approximately equal portions in Simon, son of Gervase, Richard, son of Gervase, John, son of Hawise, and Scolastica, the wife of John de Cowley. The first two were Gervase's bastards, and had obtained their share through Scolastica, who was his niece. John, who proceeded on a writ of right, claimed that Gervase had died seised of the property, and that as he was a clerk with no legal heirs of his body it should escheat to him as heir of his great-grandfather William.[1] The case was adjourned by the local justices to the king's bench at Westminster and on 3 November 1232 John, son of Hawise and Scolastica de Cowley, to whom the whole property had gone in the first instance, put in an appearance.[2]

No written evidence of William's original gift to Gervase, or confirmation by his son Richard was produced, but they did exhibit a charter of Richard's whereby he gave to God and the church of Sherington for the maintenance of a light before the altar there the service of 8*d.* yearly owed by Gervase for the land which he had of the gift of his father William. They also showed the charter of Ralph the plaintiff's father by which he confirmed the gifts of the above-mentioned William and Richard, and enfeoffed Gervase to himself, his heirs and assigns. John, son of Hawise, claimed as an assign and Scolastica as next heir through her father Richard for, she stated in her evidence, John could not be both lord and heir.[3] John declared that Ralph his father had never been seised of the property in question so that his charter of enfeoffment was invalid. He reiterated his claim that Gervase had made no assignment in his lifetime and had died seised. There was an adjournment for a year, when a jury of twelve was to inquire if Gervase had died seised: if he had, then John's claim was valid and he should be re-seised; if not, then the others were

[1] KB 26/111, m. 6d. He claimed that William had had seisin as of fee and of right by the taking of explees to the value of half a mark (cf. Pollock and Maitland, II, 605).

[2] John's claim was for 1 messuage, 80 acres land and 6 acres wood measured by a perch of 18 feet in suits as follows: 1 messuage and 20 acres land against John de Lathbury and Amphelis his wife, who called to warrant John, son of Hawise; 20 acres land and 2 acres wood against the same John and Amphelis, who called to warrant John de Cowley and Scolastica, his wife; 20 acres land and 2 acres wood against Simon, son of Gervase, and a like amount against Richard, son of Gervase, both of whom called to warrant the same John and Scolastica (JI 1/62, m. 32d; KB 26/111, m. 6d, 8; KB 26/113, m. 6d).

[3] The doctrine that the same man could not be lord and heir was held to be valid in an assize of mort d'ancestor, but it could not affect proceedings under a writ of right (cf. Flower, Selden Society, 62, 154).

to hold in peace. In those days 'a right in land rested on seisin, and seisin alone; a deed that was not followed by seisin was worthless'.[1] The verdict was in John's favour and he was awarded damages of 40*s.*[2]

The ultimate settlement was partly collusive and by no means vindictive.[3] The chief sufferers were Simon and Richard, the parson's sons, for whom John made reasonably generous provision from among his other holdings in Sherington and its open common fields. On the whole, therefore, John's youthful efforts to retrieve his family fortune had been by no means unsuccessful, even though the church was lost for all time and his mother's inflated dower was to remain an unfair burden for many years to come.[4] In spite of all this, however, John was a poor man compared with his great-grandfather, for about one-third of the whole estate had gone to form the Cockfield fee and Beatrice's dower was taking more than a third of what was left. Small wonder therefore that in 1234 he was short of money and obliged to sell the le Hoo Park estate to William de St Edmund a few months after he had recovered it.[5]

Shortage of money was still dogging him when he joined King Henry's ill-fated expedition to Gascony in 1242. The campaign did not meet with the approval of the magnates and when the military tenants were summoned to meet at Winchester on 27 April many were reluctant to serve. John, however, attended, and after being knighted by the king he sailed from Southampton[6] for France on 17 May.[7] He served throughout the action and on his return was given the usual writ authorizing him to collect scutage of 40*s.* on the knight's fee[8] from his tenants. While these formal records illustrate John's feudal obligations they do not bring out the crucial point that to play the part assigned to him he had to live beyond his means. While

[1] Plucknett, *TRHS* 4th series, XXXII, 145.

[2] KB26/113, m. 6d.

[3] It was, in part, embodied in a series of fines, two of which are very informative topographically and contain illuminating clauses that would not be readily understood without a knowledge of the story just revealed (*BASRB*, IV, 63, 65, 72, 74).

[4] Both Beatrice and her husband were still alive and quarrelling with him over common of pasture in 1242 (JI1/55, m. 7d). The fines covering 2 virgates of land in Sherington suffered by John against Eustace le Mordaunt of Turvey in 1237 seem to have been concerned with Beatrice's dower (*BASRB*, IV, 73).

[5] Part of the estate, amounting to 44 acres, and described as the whole moiety of the assart that was of Gervase the parson, was conveyed by fine. It was to be held of John for a yearly payment of 2*s.* or one sore sparrowhawk (*BASRB*, IV, 65).

[6] He received there an advance of pay of 1 mark Pipe Roll 26 Hen III, p. 262, ed. H. L. Cannon, Yale University Press, 1918.

[7] Letters of protection were issued on that day (*Cal. Pat.* 1232–47, 336).

[8] *Book of Fees*, II, 896. At the inquest of fees held that year John was stated to hold 2 fees in Sherington of which Robert de Cockfield held 1.

at Winchester he would have been drawn into the festivities that attended the conferment of knighthood, besides having to make sure that his military equipment was in the proper condition for service overseas. To pay for these activities he was obliged to borrow money and he went to Elias le Eveske, one of the most influential Jews in the country. The debt was to remain a mill-stone round his neck for the rest of his life.[1] Two years later, however, he was again in arms and took part in the short but bitter campaign of Gannoc in Wales.[2]

During the period with which we are dealing King Henry was also in trouble over money. This was partly because the council disagreed with much of his policy and had been reluctant to vote more than trifling additions to his regular income. He had thus been forced to raise money by the most profitable of the other means at his disposal and this meant tallaging the Jews. It was, indeed, the great tallage of 60,000 marks laid on them in 1245 and spread over several years which brought John de Carun into conflict with the justices who dealt with the king's Jewish affairs. Henry was particularly pressed for money in 1250 and as Elias le Eveske, like the others, was being squeezed to the utmost limit John's debt to him was called to account. On 14 January of that year writs were issued to the sheriffs of Buckinghamshire and Surrey requiring them to send in a return before 10 February of the yearly value of his lands. The necessary inquisitions were duly held[3] and on 21 February the justices decided that as his lands were returned at £7 15*s.* 5*d.* per annum John should repay the debt (total not stated) by yearly instalments of 6 marks.[4] Elias objected to the valuation, which should have been in his opinion £20 or more per annum. To obtain further information the justices apparently called John to London for personal interview, and on examination he must have been shown to have influenced the jury in his own favour, for he was amerced the very large sum of 10 marks *pro stultiloquio*.[5] Be that as it may, the justices were satisfied that they had been misled and on 8 April the two sheriffs were ordered to empanel new juries of reliable men who could certify the true value of John's estate in demesne, rents,

[1] *Cal. Inq. Misc.* I, 25.

[2] C47/5/1. There is a list of those serving with the army in Wales (29 Hen. III). It includes 'Sir John de Carun serving for himself—recognized service of 2 knights'.

[3] *Chan. Inq. Misc.* I, 25. The Sherington extent, details of which are discussed elsewhere (p. 101) gave a total of £7 7*s.* 6*d.* The one for Surrey is mutilated; it concerned a small property in Oxted which was presumably rated at 7*s.* 11*d.*

[4] *Cal. Close* 1247–51, 266.

[5] Madox, *History of the Exchequer*, I, 564. Several examples of fines *pro stultiloquo* (foolish talk) are quoted, but none other exceeds 1 mark. Compare Flower (Selden Society), 62, 428. The Pipe Rolls show that it took John many years to pay off this fine.

villeinages and all issues.[1] The outcome is not recorded, but there was certainly cause for complaint, for the value of John's estate at the time is computed to be about £15 4*s.* 7*d.* per annum without perquisites.[2]

In 1253 Henry once more summoned the host for service in Gascony and John attended. It may be that as he was so deeply in debt he welcomed the opportunity of taking paid service abroad,[3] for in the same year he had to find £4 as his contribution to the aid for knighting the king's eldest son Edward.[4]

Towards the end of his life John was required to attend a general eyre at Newport Pagnell, and as these judicial visitations are reputed to have been dreaded by the local population on account of the severity of the treatment often meted out, it is interesting to note that in 1262 his case appears to have been dealt with by all concerned in the spirit of a happy family party. He was in trouble over le Hoo Park, which he had sold to William de St Edmund in 1234.[5] The property consisted of a messuage and 26 acres of land held of John in knight's service, and 58 acres held of him in socage.[6] Sometime before 1255 William had died leaving a son of the same name who, in due course, inherited the land held in socage at the normal age of fourteen. William the son now complained that John was holding back the messuage and 12 acres of the land held in knight's service which should have come to him at the age of 21. The case is set out briefly and with clarity in the eyre roll.[7] In the first place John admitted openly in court that William was the legitimate son and heir of his father and should inherit. The point is of unusual interest because John's son Martin successfully claimed the whole le Hoo Park estate some 25 years later on a plea that William the son was a bastard.[8] Secondly, John had been found guilty of

[1] *Cal. Close* 1247–51, 355.

[2] See p. 101.

[3] *Cal. Pat.* 1247–53, 232: letters of protection dated 30 May 1253.

[4] E372/98, Bucks. The rate was 3 marks per fee: John would be able to recover *pro rata* from his tenants.

[5] See p. 50.

[6] JI1/67, m. 26; JI1/1247, m. 15d. (See p. 49, n. 2.)

[7] JI1/58, m. 15d. The roll contains two entries relating to William de St Edmund, junior. The first deals with the leasing at an annual rent of 35*s.* to Richard the servant of Lawrence de Saunford of the 58 acres held in socage. An abbreviated translation of the second is as follows: Whether William de St Edmund, father of William de St Edmund, was seised in demesne of a messuage and 12 acres land in Sherington, whereof John de Carun is tenant. John appears and admits that William, father of William, died seised of property, and said William is next heir; but says that William held of him in knight's service, and he makes no claim except as guardian of William the son, under age: freely grants that as soon as latter attains majority he shall have seisin. William, seen in court, is of full age and so has seisin. John in mercy for unjust detention beyond age, pardoned because he is poor; William remits damages.

[8] JI1/67, m. 26; KB27/121, m. 48d; see p. 63.

retaining for his own benefit a small part of the estate and should therefore have been fined. The justices, nevertheless, pardoned him because of his poverty and the young ward—not to be outdone—forgave him the damages to which he was entitled. How far the remission by the justices was 'human kindness' and how far feudal custom of not ruining a tenant who did his duty we cannot say. John was still heavily burdoned with jewry and during 1262, in the thick of the trouble with de Montford, Henry needed the loyalty of his knights. The justices as a body, nevertheless, were not always as humane as this. In the very same year, 1262, John obtained judgement at Bedford against a certain Ralph de Lymore for having taken his crops, and the jury awarded him damages of 5*s*. It was the custom then for the justices to allocate part, but generally only a small part, of the damages by way of remuneration to their own clerks, and in this particular case it comes as a shock to read that they were given the whole sum and John got nothing for his trouble.[1]

All these observations on contemporary feudal tenure and legal practice make dry enough reading, yet they illustrate in a unique way the life of a small military tenant of the period who was too undistinguished to have been thought worthy of mention by the local chroniclers but who could be called upon to assume obligations which might weigh heavily on one whose inheritance, like his, was not large enough to support the way of living thereby incurred.

[1] Selden Society, 60, 137; compare Flower, *ibid.* 62, 463.

9

MR JUSTICE CAVE ACQUIRES PROPERTY IN SHERINGTON

AT the time that John de Carun was in trouble with the exchequer of the Jews another John, whose star was on the ascent, had recently taken a lease of the moated manor house in Sherington. The newcomer, John de Cave, from South Cave in Yorkshire,[1] was the eldest of five brothers, all of whom were connected in some way with the church or the law and were, indeed, a good example of the professional family that the increasing centralization of government around the king and council was calling into being. Although John became a justice in November 1254 and was thus a man of some note in his generation, very little is known about his early life. As we shall see later, his professional career seems to have been linked with that of another Yorkshireman, the learned justice Roger de Thurkelby, and it is possible that before he left his native county he had had some connexion with Fountains abbey. Nevertheless, we do not know for certain when he migrated south, and can only conjecture that the choice of Sherington as his headquarters in the strenuous life that befell him as a justice itinerant was influenced—perhaps quite fortuitously—by the money-lending activities that he and his colleagues indulged in as a side-line to their professional work.

It has been shown recently that a few of the clerical justices of the first half of the thirteenth century received their early training as clerks to older justices[2] and there is evidence, circumstantial but none the less convincing, that John de Cave served Roger de Thurkelby in this capacity. In the first place John was party to eight fines dealing with tenements that he purchased between 1245 and 1254, and all of these were levied in Thurkelby's court.[3] In no single instance, however, does the relevant court roll record the usual payment to the king for license to concord. Secondly,

[1] He inherited a small estate in Drewton, a hamlet lying between North and South Cave. A dispute that he had with the Knights Templars about a house in South Cave gives his family history (KB26/154, m. 21d; *Mon. Angl.* IV, 962).

[2] Meekings, *Bull. Inst. Hist. Res.* XXVI (1953), 172; Pegus, *EHR*, LXXI (1956), 529.

[3] *CRR*, XV, no. 483. JI1/1046, m. 76d. *BASRB*, IV, 97, 98, 100(2). CP25(1) 173, 41, no. 691. *JASRS*, LXVII, 153; LXXXII, 10, 87–8.

John was a creditor in nine recognizances of various types which were enrolled between 1250 and 1254 on the rolls of Thurkelby's court.[1] In all these cases, of course, other justices sat with him, but their attendance was not regular.[2] Finally, during the eyre held by Thurkelby and the bishop of Carlisle at York in Hilary Term 1252 a covenant between Denise d'Eyvill and John concerning a lease of Sherington manor was enrolled on the court roll for safe keeping.[3] A fee would normally have been charged for this privilege, but the detailed account of the money collected by the justices at this eyre does not record any such payment.[4] These observations seem to admit of only one reasonable explanation, to the effect that John was one of Thurkelby's clerks and that the normal payments for business transacted on his behalf were remitted as part of his salary, which would have been paid out of the profits of the court.

John must have been born about 1220, and as he had a close association with the Cistercian abbey of Woburn during his working life, it may be suggested that his move to the south as a young man was due to an early connexion with the mother house of Fountains in Yorkshire. In 1234 Woburn was reduced to poverty through the mismanagement of Abbot Richard, who was accordingly deposed and his monks dispersed among other houses of the order. Roger, the new abbot, was a monk from Fountains, and probably took from there a small team which must have included one or two with business ability, for the house was financially in a flourishing condition again within a few years.[5] It seems likely that John de Cave was concerned with these matters, for it was not long before he had a local attachment as rector of Battlesden,[6] a village 2 miles south of Woburn near the Hockcliffe junction of the Watling Street and the Woburn–Newport Pagnell road.

Meanwhile, as has already been suggested, he probably joined the entourage of Roger de Thurkelby, who had become a judge in 1240. John was certainly making money soon after that date, for he took a lease of the moated manor house in Sherington in return for a loan of 18 marks[7] and acquired some additional property in South Cave.[8] Moreover, it was not long before he was loaning money, a sure

[1] KB26/143, m. 14, 23; 148, m. 7, 45d; 154, m. 9d, 12d. *CRR*, XV, no. 143; XX, no. 1297.

[2] Of a maximum attendance of 17, the score was: Thurkelby 17, Wassand 10, Cobham 7, Erdington 5, Preston 5, Trussell 4, Wauton 4, bishop of Carlisle 3, Hilton 1.

[3] JI1/1046, m. 59d.

[4] JI1/1047.

[5] *VCH Beds*, I, 366.

[6] The date of his institution is not known, but his death was recorded when his successor was instituted in 1261–2 (*LRS*, XX, 190, 322).

[7] KB26/154, m. 21d.

[8] *YASRS*, LXVII, 153; LXXXII, 10, 87–8.

sign of accumulating wealth, as shown by the fact that seven recognizances for a total of 62 marks were recorded in his favour on the plea rolls of 1250–1, including, significantly, one of £3 from the parson of Mursley,[1] wherein Woburn owned most of the land, and another of 13 marks from the prior of Wing, who had instructions that if John were not available, repayment should be made to the cellarer of Woburn in his name.[2]

It was during this latter period that John acquired an interest in the Cockfield fee in Sherington. As was mentioned in an earlier chapter,[3] this was part of the dower assigned in 1220 to Denise, Adam de Cockfield's widow, who had married sometime before 1227 Robert d'Eyvill of Egmanton, Nottinghamshire, and various places in Yorkshire. A cadet of this family, Roger d'Eyvill, was a landowner in South Cave and John had had dealings with him. Hence when Denise, once again a widow, was fined 35 marks by the justice of forest pleas for Yorkshire in or before 1250,[4] John was known to her as someone from whom she could raise money. It was on 25 November 1251 that she assigned to him her life interest in the Sherington fee for a rent of 17 marks per annum, John to pay the first three years rent forthwith.[5]

When the lease of the moated house expired in 1254, John acquired the freehold from William le Vineter of Stony Stratford and Emma his wife, together with all Emma's inheritance in Sherington, for 60 marks.[6] During the next few years he gathered in several small parcels of land dispersed in the open common fields[7] and the estate thus collected, excluding the Cockfield fee, which reverted to John de Cockfield on Denises's death in 1260–1, became known eventually as Cave's manor. There is no evidence that in the time of Emma's predecessors this estate had been sub-infeudated, but the moated house was referred to as a 'capital messuage'. Other property acquired about this time included a small freehold in Wolverton[8] and about 4 carucates of leasehold land, mostly held for the term of his life, under Ramsey abbey.[9]

[1] KB26/143, m. 23.

[2] *Ibid.* m. 14.

[3] P. 44.

[4] E372/96, Yorks. Her relatives Henry and Jocelin, as well as her late husband, had also been heavily fined.

[5] JI1/1046, m. 59d. The covenant stated that she had already demised the fee to Ralph le Franceys of Sherington for the term of her life for 20 marks per annum, which John was henceforth to receive. The 51 marks John had paid out at once were repaid within three years, and in addition he received 3 marks per annum until Denise's death in 1260–1. In the circumstances the rate of interest, 6 per cent, was very reasonable for the period.

[6] CP25(1), 16/33/26.

[7] *BRS*, IV, 100(2), 106; CP25(1), 16/36/9, 33.

[8] *BRS*, IV, 97, 98.

[9] 1 carucate in Bythorne, Huntingdonshire, from Wm. de Wyston, steward of Ramsay abbey (*CRR*, XV, no. 483); 1 virgate in Denton, Northampton-

Promotion to the bench came in October 1254 when he was appointed one of the justices in eyre for the counties of Buckingham and Bedford. Assizes were held at Newport Pagnell, Bedford and Dunstable, the prior complaining bitterly of the cost of entertaining them at the latter place.[1] During the next few years he was employed more or less continuously as a justice itinerant in all parts of the country and on local Bedfordshire–Buckinghamshire commissions. For such work the moated manor house at Sherington would undoubtedly have been a convenient centre as well as a safe haven for his official rolls; nevertheless, the life must have been an exacting one and early in 1261 he had become a sick man. In June of that year he was commissioned with Peter de Perci to hold assizes in Lancashire and Cheshire, Peter receiving orders to proceed alone if John had not joined him by 1 August.[2] John in fact died within a few weeks of that date.

John held high office for only a short time and so did not amass as large a fortune as some of his contemporary clerical justices. Unusually, also, he held only one benefice and that of no great value,[3] which may reflect no more than his diocesan Grosseteste's strong views on pluralism and especially on the employment of ecclesiastics in secular office. His heir was his brother Simon, who came south from their native Yorkshire within a few weeks to settle various disputes about John's land in Sherington,[4] Denton[5] and Wolverton.[6]

Master Simon de Cave had been instituted vicar of Carnaby, Yorkshire, when in minor orders. As the years passed he seems to have drifted from clerical to secular activities, including money lending, for he sued several people for the recovery of debts to a total of 28 marks at the Yorkshire assizes in 1260. After he had inherited his brother's fairly ample fortune he seems to have made Sherington his main residence, and his clerical life would thus have become even less diligent than before. It is probable that this would have caused but little comment if he had not come up against a reforming archbishop. When Walter Giffard was translated to York late in 1266 he gave particular attention to certain clerical disciplines, among them the

shire, from the same (CP 40 (1), 173/41/691); 2 virgates in Westcote in Tyso, Warwickshire (Dugdale Society, XI, no. 781); 9 virgates in Denton of Ramsay abbey (*Cart. Mon. Rams.* Rolls Series, p. 246); 10 acres land and 15 acres wood in Suthwode in Emberton, CP25(1), 16/36/4.

[1] *Ann. de Dunstaplia*, p. 192.

[2] *Lanc. and Ches. Rec. Soc.* XLIX, 234.

[3] In 1291 (Nicholas Taxation) the rectory of Battlesden was worth only £5 6*s*. 8*d*. per annum.

[4] JI1/58, m. 6, 8d.

[5] JI1/5, m. 23; CP25(1), 174/47.

[6] JI1/58, m. 16; CP25(1), 16/37/1.

order of Cardinal Otto, the legate in England in 1237, requiring all vicars to proceed to the priesthood within one year after their institution. Simon, although repeatedly warned and cited, treated the order with contempt. The archbishop acted promptly and Simon was deprived.[1]

Walter Giffard, while still bishop of Bath and Wells, had been active in the barons' war of 1263–6 and had helped to draw up the Dictum of Kenilworth. There is no record of anyone in Sherington being connected with the fighting, but when it was all over and efforts were being made to rectify some of the unlawful acts of the period, Simon de Cave—who claimed to have been loyal to the king—complained in 1268 that Ellis de Tingewick, the keeper of Salsay and Whittlewood forests, had seized property in Wolverton that had belonged to him before the war. Ellis in evidence stated that he also was loyal and had obtained the land from William de la Mare, the rector of Sherington.[2] The case was adjourned and as Simon died early in the following year, Ellis no doubt retained possession.

Simon was succeeded by his brother Robert, who had hitherto run the small ancestral estate at Drewton. As John's executor he was still trying to collect as late as 1286–7[3] the 6½ marks owed by Richard, son of John of Walrington.

[1] Surtees Society, 109, 209.

[2] KB26/185, m. 14d; 191, m. 5; 193, m. 3.

[3] CP40/31, m. 123; 69, m. 94.

10

MARTIN DE CARUN AND THE LAW

JOHN DE CARUN did not long survive the barons' war and as his eldest son Ralph died without issue within a year or so the estate devolved on the second son Martin, who was dealing with the widow's dower in 1270. He inherited, of course, all John's financial embarrassments including the debt to Elias le Eveske, and one of his first acts was to sell a virgate and 6 acres of land to Master William de la Mare, the rector of Sherington,[1] on condition that he acquit him of jewry.[2] William at the time was also tenant for life of the 84 acres of land in le Hoo Park by demise of his brother Richard de la Mare, who in turn held for life by grant of William de St Edmund, junior.[3] The question of whether this latter William before his death had, in effect, put Richard in seisin of the property was not raised by Martin until some fourteen years later.[4]

The widow Agnes sought dower on the basis of land held by John at the time of her marriage; it included, therefore, le Hoo Park and gifts made by him to younger sons.[5] Martin objected on the plea that she was never legally married to John and an official of the diocese of London was thereupon directed to make the necessary inquiries. In due course she received her dower. Agnes was presumably John's second wife and Martin must have been the issue of his first marriage, otherwise his declaration would have been tantamount to an admission of bastardy which could have barred his own inheritance from John. Her claims to dower on gifts made by John *inter vivos* of two virgates of land to their son Simon and a rent of 10*s*. a year to their son John[6] were allowed.[7] While these actions were pending Agnes took as her second husband Roger, a younger brother of John Fitz John of Hanslope, who

[1] Presented by the prior and monks of Tickford on the death of Master Thomas de Shireford in 1259.

[2] JI1/1281B, m. 5d.

[3] JI1/67, m. 26.

[4] See p. 62.

[5] KB26/199, m. 31d (for extent see pp. 100–101).

[6] *Hundred Rolls* (Rec. Com.), I, 41.

[7] Simon had already disposed of part of his holding: the claim was for 31 acres land and 1 acre meadow against Simon, 15 acres land against Robert de Clifton, clerk, and 3 acres land against Martin de Carun, a total of 50 acres or 25 acres to the virgate (JI1/60, m. 12; JI1/1206, m. 13; KB26/199, m. 20).

was to acquire within a few years an estate in Sherington that became known later as Fitz John's manor.

Edward I was on crusade when his father died in November 1272 and his return to England was delayed for nearly two years. In the meanwhile all judicial eyres appointed by the old king had been suspended and there were complaints of misgovernment and crime. On 10 October 1274 Edward accordingly issued commissions to hold inquests into various grievances as a practical demonstration of his 'desire to redress the state of the realm'.[1] The articles of the inquest, covering a wide field,[2] were put as questions to a jury drawn from the hundred concerned, and some of the replies reveal interesting side-lights on conditions in Sherington at the time.[3]

To the inquiry about the lord king's fees and services it was returned, *inter alia*, that Martin de Carun held one knight's fee *in capite* for the service of one knight twice yearly at Northampton castle and twice yearly at the Hundred Court. The other fee was stated (incorrectly) to be held by John de Cockfield *in capite* (instead of as mesne tenancy of Martin), the abbess of Fontevrault taking the service due, worth 32*s*. a year, by gift of the king's ancestors.[4] Martin also gave 10*s*. yearly for hidage as well as 40*d*. for the ward of Northampton castle and for the ward of le Hoo. This last service was to the Hundred Court of Bunsty,[5] for in later years Cockfield manor owed suit of court[6] and an annual payment of 4*d*. there.[7]

There were various complaints against the king's officials. The men of the hundred were having to pay the sheriff fifteen marks a year, whereas in the time of Simon de Eltesden (1252–5) they had been called upon for only five. In recent years the bailiff of the hundred was retaining for his own use 6*s*. yearly paid by Sherington for hidage and half a mark (*sic*) for the ward of le Hoo. The present sheriff, Thomas de Bray, had accepted a bribe of half a mark to relax his distraint of Robert de Cave for knighthood. These grievances follow the pattern of those aired by other hundreds and we do not know what action, if any, the king took to remedy them.

1 Powicke, *The Thirteenth Century*, p. 358.

2 See Helen M. Cam, *The Hundred Rolls*, pp. 248–59.

3 *Hundred Rolls* (Rec. Com.), I, 41–2.

4 The residents of the village owed 'cert' or 'certainty' money to the king as chief lord of the fee for the keeping of the leet or view of frankpledge. There is no record of the gift to the abbess. The only other mention of the service is in the certificate of Musters for 1522 (p. 168 and Table 25), where it is stated to be worth 33*s*.

5 T, 244 (cf. p. 70). Le Hoo, meaning a ridge or promontory, is not uncommon as a place-name, and there was a le Hoo wood and park at Bunsty, an outlying portion of Lathbury now incorporated in Gayhurst. (*Hundred Rolls*, Rec. Com. I, 39.) The wood there is still called Hoo Wood.

6 E150/6/17.

7 See p. 168, n. 3.

It was also alleged that during the king's absence abroad Roger Fitz John of Hanslope, his brother Ralph and other local people had taken Martin de Carun's crops to the value of one mark each year. They had also robbed his servant William Daunsel when he tried to protect his master's property and had raided Martin's wood almost daily, cutting down his trees and removing them for their own benefit. The observations suggest that during the two years concerned Martin had been away from home—probably in the king's service—for remedial action was not taken until 1277–8.[1] We know that he was indeed on active service in the Welsh wars a little later, for with one 'serviens' he attended the muster at Worcester in 1277 and at Rhuddlan castle in 1282.[2] Martin, like his father John before him, might have welcomed a spell of paid military service because of straitened circumstances.[3] Like his father also, and probably for the same sentimental reasons, he sought in 1281 to present a suitable person to Sherington church, which was then vacant and—he claimed—in his gift. The prior of Tickford objected and won the day.[4]

It was not until about 1282 that Martin's estate became free from dower on the death of his step-mother Agnes. In the same year his near neighbour Robert de Cave went into partnership with other members of the Cave family as attorneys at the king's bench, and it is surely no mere coincidence that Martin forthwith should have embarked on a series of cunningly devised legal proceedings which led eventually to the recovery of the portions of the original Sherington estate that had been lost by his immediate forebears. Martin sued in the Court of Common Pleas, where the Caves did not practice, and employed a local Newport attorney, Ralph Sampson. The advice that Martin received, nevertheless, was expert, whoever gave it, and we find him using all the tricks and chicanery that the law tolerated in those days to gain his own ends.

He dealt first of all with le Hoo Park, taking forcible possession of it on the death of Master William de la Mare in 1280. This set in motion a series of court actions which necessitated the assembling at long intervals during the next nine years of local Sherington juries at places as far away as Edlesborough, Wycombe and Westminster.

[1] An assize of novel disseisin was arraigned by Martin against Roger and the others in that year (47th Report, Dep. Keeper Publ. Rec. p. 344).

[2] *Parl. Writs*, I, 234, 521; II, 208, 521.

[3] As late as 1285 he had not assumed the obligation of knighthood (Lipscomb, *History of the County of Buckingham*, IV, 112).

[4] CP 40/38, m. 53. William de la Mare died in 1280 and the prior presented John de Luca (see p. 120).

Martin claimed that Master William, who had held the property of him, had died seised and that as he was a bastard without heirs it should revert to him as an escheat. William's brother Richard de la Mare contested this in 1282[1] and after the usual delays the case was heard at the Edlesborough assizes in 1285.[2] Richard stated that he himself originally owned the property and that he had demised it to William for life. Shortly before William died, however, he had brought an assize of novel disseisin against him[3] and obtained a writ whereby the sheriff gave him full seisin once more. Martin had therefore unlawfully disseised him. The jury found in Richard's favour with damages of 50*s*.

Martin next sought to upset this verdict by taking the case back a whole generation to the family of St Edmund, from whom Richard had acquired his title. At the Wycombe assizes in Easter Term 1286[4] he claimed that the property had once been held of his father John de Carun by William de St Edmund for homage and a rent of 2*s*. or a sore sparrowhawk.[5] William, who was a bastard, had died in John's homage without an heir, and John's right of escheat should descend to him, Martin, because his elder brother Ralph had died without heirs of his body. Richard denied these allegations. He stated that he himself held the property of William de St Edmund to farm, with liberty to sell and doing forensic service to the king as pertaining to one virgate of the land. After William's death John had quit-claimed the property to him, and he exhibited John's charter. Martin countered by declaring that the deed was executed in William's lifetime and was therefore of no avail as William had died seised; Richard, in other words, had not been given seisin and the charter was worthless. The jury found in Martin's favour and he was to recover his seisin.

Richard was dissatisfied with the verdict and arranged for a record of the case to

[1] CP40/45, m. 79; 47, m. 87.

[2] JI1/1247, m. 15d, 18d. These are two complementary entries on the roll. In the first the claim is for 1 messuage, 58 acres land, 1 virgate land and 4 acres meadow in one place and 1 messuage, 6 acres land and 1 virgate land in another place. In the second the claim is for 2 messuages, 116 acres land and 2¾ acres meadow, from which one can deduce that the local virgate was then about 26 acres. The first portion, in the demesne sector of the village, was le Hoo Park, consisting of 58 acres land held in socage and 1 virgate (26 acres) land held in knight service (cf. p. 52), a total of 84 acres. Although this acreage is quoted in later disputes, a round number, 80 or 100 acres, is occasionally used. The second portion, in the open common fields, was the tenement given to Master William by Martin about 1270 to acquit him of jewry (cf. p. 59). Martin now disclaimed any interest and it was dismissed from the suit.

[3] 48th Report, Dep. Keeper Publ. Rec. p. 166, no. 1.

[4] JI1/67, m. 26.

[5] Cf. fine of 1234, *BASRB*, IV, 65.

be forwarded to the king's bench so that the jury could be asked 'to certify to the judges' as to the oath they had made at Wycombe.[1] The case was heard in Michaelmas Term 1289,[2] when Richard alleged that the jury had not sufficiently studied the evidence. There were two Williams de St Edmund, William senior, who was a bastard and William his son, who was legitimate. When, therefore, Martin claimed from William de St Edmund, if William senior was meant there was no escheat as William had a son who inherited; if William the son was meant, again there was no escheat as he was legitimate. He asked for a further examination of the evidence. Martin conceded that there were two Williams, father and son, but said that he claimed escheat from the son, who was a bastard. He agreed to a further examination. The jury duly considered the evidence and expressed the opinion that the former verdict referred to William the son, who was a bastard. Martin, therefore, was entitled to his escheat and should remain quit with seisin.

The proceedings of these three courts, as written into the rolls, give the firm impression that the verdicts returned were in accord with the evidence presented. Yet there can be no doubt that in the last case there had been a grave miscarriage of justice. The judges at Westminster, unfortunately, did not have before them the roll of the eyre held at Wycombe in 1262, which records the actual testimony of Martin's father John that William de St Edmund, junior, was the lawful son and heir of William senior and entitled to inherit the very same plot of land that they had been asked to deal with.[3] It is inconceivable that Martin was not aware of the true position, and as well as giving false evidence on his own behalf he must have packed the jury, which was drawn largely from local men old enough to recall what had happened more than a quarter of a century earlier. Such men would be well known to Martin, but not necessarily so to Richard who, at the time, was in the service of the Sanford family in south Buckinghamshire.

The justices having given him legal possession of le Hoo Park in 1286, Martin turned his attention to the Cockfield fee, which was held of him by John de Cockfield of Nuthall, Nottinghamshire. John had demised it for life to Adam de Cockfield, who in turn had given a similar lease to Martin.

[1] KB27/106, m. 31. The jury were summoned to Westminster in Michaelmas Term 1286, and the members were all fined for non-compliance, the amounts being entered against their names on the roll. The fines were remitted when they attended three years later. Fifteen jurymen were listed and of these at least nine were local squires like Martin.

[2] KB27/121, m. 48d.

[3] See p. 52.

To understand the legal trick played by Martin, with Adam's connivance, to recover the reversion of the fee it must be remembered that in those days the tenant for life, for the purpose of public law, was a freeholder with full rights of seisin. In litigation he represented the land, and all that this meant in the lawsuit about to be discussed will be made very much clearer if, as a preamble, the hypothetical case sketched by Maitland to illustrate the matter[1] be quoted *in extenso* under the names of the present litigants.

Suppose for example Adam de Cockfield is holding the land as tenant for life by some title under which on his death the land will revert or remain to John de Cockfield in fee. Now if Martin de Carun sets up an adverse title, it is Adam, not John, whom he must attack. When Adam is sued, it will be his duty to 'pray aid' of John, to get John made a party to the action, and John in his own interest will take upon himself the defence of his rights. Indeed if John hears of the action he can intervene of his own motion. But Adam had it in his power to neglect this duty, and to defend the action without aid, to make default, or to put himself upon battle or the grand assize, and thus to lose the land by judgment.

The last sentence makes it clear that collusive action between Martin and Adam could deprive John of his remainder in fee.

After various preliminaries during 1287 Martin, in Trinity Term 1288, claimed the fee against Adam as his right of inheritance.[2] Adam, instead of 'praying the aid' of John to defend his title, called upon him to warrant—in other words to provide him with an alternative property of equal value.[3] The request for warranty caused delay, and Martin's case did not come up for hearing again until Easter Term 1290,[4] when Adam was essoined by his attorney as on the king's service. John's attorney, however, attended and after pointing out to the justices that Adam held only for life he asked to be admitted in John's defence. The justices suspected collusion and directed the sheriff to take the property into the king's hands. In the following term Adam again attempted to essoin himself as on the king's service, but a writ from the king denied this and declared that justice to Martin was being maliciously delayed. John's attorney reiterated that Adam had no interest in the property—

[1] Pollock and Maitland, *History of English Law*, II, 9–11.

[2] CP 40/67, m. 79; 69, m. 165, 74d.

[3] Adam's claim for warranty was heard in Easter Term 1289 and the sheriff was instructed to extend and value the property (*Cal. Inq. Misc.* I, 413). Adam objected to the valuation submitted, £4 3*s.* 0*d.* and after much delay the sheriff in 1294 revalued at £6 8*s.* 0*d.* Adam complained that this was still too low. The case dragged on for another eighteen months and then petered out (CP 40/78, m. 53; 104, m. 104; 108, m. 52; 110, m. 55d).

[4] CP 40/82, m. 51d.

which was John's inheritance—save for life and begged to be allowed to answer in John's name so that the property be not lost by default. The justices, however, ruled that as John had not been called to witness by Adam he could not be admitted for defence, and Martin must recover his seisin against Adam.[1]

It will be seen that Martin's two incursions into the law, using tactics that we should brand today as barefaced even if legal robbery, had been successful; yet they brought him less immediate pecuniary benefit than might have been anticipated. The Cockfield fee that came to him, for instance, did not represent the whole estate that Denise d'Eyvill had held in dower since 1221 and was letting to farm for twenty marks a year in 1250. On her death in 1260–1 it had reverted to Robert de Cockfield, and sometime between then and 1280 either he or John, his third son who succeeded him by arrangement, had disposed of rents to the yearly value of 38*s*. Martin,[2] as described above, had been the life tenant of this attenuated estate for many years before securing the fee simple and had, indeed, sub-let part of it to his step-father Roger Fitz John about 1284[3] for the term of the latter's life. From Martin's point of view, therefore, the change was one of status of ownership with Roger retaining his position as sitting tenant. Like his father John before him, Martin found it difficult to get on with a step-father, and in 1292 he was suing him for wasting the estate.[4]

Within a few months of the final judgement on le Hoo Park in 1289 Martin entailed it, with certain other lands, by a grant to William, son of Roger de la Mare,[5] who made a joint enfeoffment on Martin and his wife Margery with remainder to their heirs.[6] Such an enfeoffment was probably inspired by the desire to avoid payment of relief on Martin's death (as it did),[7] but it saddled the family estate with

1 CP40/83, m. 128d. As a middleman between the sitting tenant and the reversioner Adam's financial loss would have been fairly small.

2 See p. 63.

3 *Cal. Close*, 1279–88, 375. Martin seems to have made the grant soon after the death of his step-mother Agnes about 1282.

4 CP40/92, m. 162d, m. 210; 93, m. 114. The tenement demised for the term of Roger's life was 1 messuage, 1 carucate land and 16 acres wood. Martin alleged that Roger had sold the wood, pulled down a residence worth 30*s*. and a kitchen worth 20*s*., and had cut down 7 fruit trees, worth 2*s*. each in the garden of the residence, also 7 ashes worth 8*d*. each, 4 willows worth 2*s*. each and 80 young oaks worth 2*d*. each. Roger denied all destruction except in repair of houses.

5 CP25(1) 17/51/9. Fine between Martin and William for 1 messuage and 140 acres land.

6 On 29 Nov. 1290 Martin acknowledged a debt of 16 marks to William (*Cal. Close*, 1288–96, 111). The debt had not been fully paid off in 1294 (KB27/141, m. 22; 142, m. 15) and William acquitted Margery and her son Roger by charter on 5 Dec. 1295 (T, 37).

7 Sanders, *Feudal Military Service in England*, p. 105.

a widow who had a life control over more than her fair share, to the detriment of the heir Roger.

The acquisition of this small enclosed park would have enhanced the value of the demesne estate, but the financial gain to Martin must have been largely offset by the abnormally high cost of the litigation concerned. Three independent lawsuits had had to be fought in succession during the nine years to 1289, necessitating payments to attorneys and court officials in almost every legal term over that period. The Cockfield fee had been an additional expense, and although Martin secured the reversion of his step-mother Agnes's dower on her death in 1283 he became more and more deeply involved. At the time of his death in November 1295[1] the sheriff was distraining his goods and chattels for non-payment of various debts acknowledged in the Common Pleas.[2]

[1] *Cal. Inq.* III, 191. Extent: 1 cap. messuage worth 26*s.* 8*d.*; in demesne 160 acres land (incorrectly given as 80 acres in printed text) worth 6*d.* an acre; 8 acres meadow worth 3*s.* an acre; a separate pasture worth 1*s.*; rents of assize and customers 60*s.*, customers do no work; grove worth 1*s.* Total £6 12*s.* 8*d.*

[2] £6 3*s.* 4*d.* to Robert de Fraunces, a Sherington farmer; acknowledged Nov. 1292 (CP40/103, m. 5, *passim* to 118, m. 120). 46*s.* 8*d.* to the prior of St John of Jerusalem in England; acknowledged 1291 (CP40/90, m. 62; 98, m. 98d).

11

THE LAST OF THE CARUNS

WHEN Roger de Carun succeeded to Sherington at the age of 23 he was far worse off financially than his father had been, for Roger Fitz John still retained the Cockfield fee and his mother Margery had the settled lands in addition to her third of the residual estate as tenant in dower. Early in the following year Margery gave the park, as she was entitled to do under the settlement, to a Master Henry de Lisle, who was not unlearned in the law.[1] Roger very naturally objected to being deprived of his reversion in this way, and collecting a crowd of local people, including Robert de Cave, William Daunsel and Robert Cous of Sherington, Hugh Ardres of Turvey and William de la Mare, he forcibly ejected Henry from the property. Henry countered with an assize of novel disseisin at the Wycombe assizes in Easter term 1296.

In the meanwhile Margery had taken as her second husband one Simon Spigurnel, a local attorney who would have known that in any action over land in those days proof of seisin was decisive, and that there could be no more effective evidence of this than an *ad hoc* entry in a plea roll. Sir Henry Spigurnel, a close relative of his, was one of the justices at Wycombe, and between them they probably arranged with the clerk writing the roll to report the case in full. The following extract recalls the words of Maitland 'we see once more that deep reverence for seisin which characterizes medieval law'.[2]

Roger claimed the land by inheritance as heir of Martin; Henry by enfeoffment of Margery.

The jury declare on oath that Martin did at one time hold the said property, which was an entire tillage completely enclosed, as his right. He made a charter of enfeoffment to William de la Mare and sent one Walter de la Burne as his attorney to put William in

[1] He was made a sub-deacon on 13 Dec. 1295 and presented to the rectory of Boddington, Northamptonshire, by the prior and monks of Tickford on 17 Jan. 1296. An escapade while acting as assistant to the archdeacon of Buckinghamshire in 1292 is recorded elsewhere (p. 119).

[2] Pollock and Maitland, *History of English Law*, II, 443.

seisin for himself and heirs in perpetuity. This Walter, on the second day before the Purification of the Blessed Virgin in the eighteenth year of the present king [31 January 1290], led William to the property, called neighbours together and in their presence and in Martin's name as his attorney delivered seisin to him to hold as aforesaid, and afterwards left. After his departure William remained on the property *trium levatarum* [three sun-rises ?] by way of taking seisin, and then left, appointing Jordan le Prevost to keep seisin in his name. William remained seised continuously until the end of three weeks after the Nativity of St John Baptist [15 July 1290], but in meanwhile did not take any esplees or do any handy work there, neither did Martin, nor did he make any claim, but ratified the act of Walter his attorney and accepted William's seisin. But the jury say that sheep of Martin's shepherd agisted in his fold outside the property at various times within that period consumed pasture growing on property, though this was by evasion.[1] And they say that at the Quindene of St John [8 July] in the same year a fine was levied in the King's Court at Westminster between Martin and William whereby Martin agreed that property was William's by right. At the end of three weeks William gave it to Martin and Margery, who by said gift held it for Martin's life. He died about Martinmass last [11 November 1295], she survived him and held property in peace, maintaining her estate therein until Friday a month ago, early on which day she herself took Master Henry to property and gave it to him to hold to himself and heirs and delivered full seisin. He remained peacefully seised therein until the following Saturday at first hour, when Roger and the others except Robert Cous and William Daunsel ejected him unlawfully by force of arms. The jury, when asked whether the property was held of the Crown and had been seised into the king's hand after Martin's death said no.

It was decided that Master Henry should recover his seisin, damages being taxed at half a mark. Roger and William, having been committed to gaol, were allowed to make fine later for 40*s*. each.[2]

Margery, as we have seen, had been generously dealt with by her husband and it is perhaps symptomatic of the chronic condition of poverty in which the Carun family were then living that, like her husband and son, she seemed to have been unable to keep out of debt. Within a few weeks of Martin's death she gave Thomas de Bray of Wollaston, Northamptonshire, a pledge for £14 10*s*., and when summoned to court for non-repayment seven years later put forward the dishonest plea that the recognizance, being made in her name, was void as at the time of

[1] If this had not been admitted at the time it could have formed the basis of a future action to upset the settlement.

[2] JI1/1309, m. 28d. The justices noted that the property was held *in capite* (this was incorrect) and had been originally alienated without license; also that Master Henry had entered into possession without leave

writing she had already married Simon Spigurnel. The jury would have none of it and declared that she was then *soli*, not in any marriage tie, and that Thomas should recover his debt with £5 damages.[1] Later, when married to Thomas Chamberlain, she employed Thomas de Bray as bailiff of the Sherington property: he was soon being called to account.[2]

Not all the land settled by William de la Mare on Martin and Margery was at her disposal when widowed, for Martin had himself sold 40 acres to John de Grey and others.[3] Margery, as we have just seen, settled the whole of the park, the 'tillage completely enclosed' on Master Henry, leaving but 16 acres (actually 12½ acres) unallocated. Roger the son and heir, whose ultimate inheritance of the park had been filched from him by his mother, was naturally apprehensive that she would treat this residuum in the same way. Perhaps as the only course that seemed open to him he took forcible possession of it a few months before his death in 1301, but when called to book at the assizes he was ordered, as he had been in the earlier case, to return the property to Margery.[4]

Early in 1303 Master Henry regranted 50 acres of the park to Margery and her then husband Simon Spigurnel.[5] Five years later, when she was the wife of Thomas Chamberlain, she settled this, with the above-mentioned 12½ acres on herself and her husband with remainder to their heirs.[6] In 1310 Thomas and Margery sold the 50 acres of park to Ralph Basset of Drayton and Joan his wife.[7] Margery died on 29 September 1310[8] and on 1 August 1312 the king's escheator seised the 50 acres into the king's hands on the pretext that it was held *in capite* and had been alienated without permission.[9] It was placed to farm with John de Burgh and remained there until 1323, when an inquisition declared that the land was held of the principal manor and not of the king.[10] In 1312 the principal manor itself was also held at

[1] CP40/126, m. 185; 145, m. 121. He had given her £10 in money and had sold to her wheat, barley and rye to the value of £4 10*s*. 0*d*. The judge gave Thomas the option of waiting for her money or seizing her goods and chattels with a moiety of her lands: he chose the latter alternative.

[2] CP40/153, m. 439d.

[3] See p. 75, n. 2. In 1310 Margery the widow of William de la Mare claimed her dower in 1 messuage and 40 acres land of Ralph Basset and Joan his wife: there can be no doubt therefore that the tenement had been part of the settled estate (CP40/180, m. 112, 173; 187, m. 210d).

[4] JI1/1311, m. 77, 79d. The property was described as 12½ acres land, 2 acres pasture and 3 roods meadow.

[5] *Cal. Inq.* IV, 86; *Cal. Close*, 1302–7, 24. The extent was erroneously given at 42 acres unless a further regrant was made later.

[6] C143/71/21.

[7] *Cal. Inq. Misc.* II, 147.

[8] E136/1/22, m. 1.

[9] E136/1/23, m. 5.

[10] *Cal. Inq. Misc.* II, 147.

farm by John de Burgh and a terrier of the arable lands in his charge made on 29 September of that year mentions 'In le Stockyng L acr'. The entry is underlined, and the bailiff making the survey hesitated whether to include it in the final summation. The escheator was clearly uncertain whether the seizure at the time had been justified.[1]

In the reconstructed map of 1580 (Map 3) Great Stockings Close, Little Stockings Close and Park Close lie alongside or near le Hoo Wood and abut on the Chicheley road opposite Park Gate Leys. The 50-acre 'Stockyng' was part of le Hoo Park, and in retrospect it had also been part of Martin de Carun's 84-acre 'tillage completely enclosed' which in turn derived from a holding of like dimension wherein 42 acres were described in a fine of 1234 as 'the whole moiety of the assart that was of Gervase the parson'. The chain of evidence to connect Gervase's assart with the place marked as le Hoo Park[2] on the reconstructed map of 1300 (Map 4) is thus complete.

Early in 1296 Roger de Carun demised his manor for a term of years to David le Gaunt, one of the king's clerks, and his efforts to prevent his mother from alienating the park estate having come to naught he returned to London. There he was already in debt to a taverner,[3] Robert de Wodeham, and for reasons that are obscure his total indebtedness increased markedly during the next year or so. In 1297 he sold the freehold of the Cockfield fee to the sitting tenant Roger Fitz John and soon afterwards disposed of all that was left of the Sherington estate except the demesne and some freehold rents to Reynold, Lord Grey de Wilton. These two transactions are treated at length in the next chapter. In 1298 David le Gaunt complained that while overseas in Flanders and under the king's special protection Roger and many others had ejected his men from the manor and carried off his corn and crops.[4] Roger, indeed, seems to have led an unsettled life and was only 29 when he died in June 1301, leaving a daughter and heiress Sibyl one year old.

[1] NRO *Ecton*, 1190, m. 1. Cf. p. 274, Table 53.

[2] T, 244. Quit-claim by Richard de Cave of Shirington to John de Burgo of Shiringtone and Sibyl his wife and their heirs of all rights, etc., in part of wood and pasture which Margery widow of Martin de Carun and Joan, widow of Roger Carun held in dower in le Hoo and le Hoo Park in Shiringtone of the inheritance of the said Sibyl — (Shiringtone 21 Aug. 1323). The use of the term park in this context probably indicates no more than an enclosure or paddock. Ralph Basset appears to have used it as a preserve for beasts of the chase a little later (*Cal. Pat.* 1324–7, 292).

[3] CP40/116, m. 17; 121, m. 26d; 222, m. 2d. The debt was still being carried on the plea rolls seventeen years after Roger's death. Roger also owed 6 marks 10*s*. to Robert de Shirewode, apparently a clerk to John de Langeton, the Chanceller (*Cal. Close*, 1296–1302, 115; KB27/160, m. 48).

[4] *Cal. Pat.* 1292–1301, 379.

As sixth in direct descent from the first Ralph de Carun, Roger must have felt pride in his Norman ancestry; yet at a period in history when, by custom, marriage was essentially a business transaction, the family had never been rated high enough by the governing and landowning hierarchy for any member of it to have obtained in marriage an heiress with land that would have enriched their estate. Holding directly from the Crown, it may be that in such affairs they were too much under the dead hand of the exchequer—especially in a period when the heir was a minor—and missed the personal connexion that was so mutually advantageous to the mesne tenant and his superior overlord. Right from the start the family seems to have been unable to hold its own and the one dominant theme that emerges from these studies is a slow but unremitting impoverishment. As characters in history they were of no importance and none of them found a place in the annals of the chroniclers. We can be grateful therefore that so much of interest about Roger and his immediate forebears has been recorded in the contemporary plea rolls. With material culled from a few other sources they do indeed give us a glimpse of their characters and idiosyncrasies. John was essentially a man of his generation and station. Being under obligation to serve his king he followed him both abroad and in the Marches: improvident and like all headstrong warriors he was hot-tempered and ever ready with sword and club:[1] yet without guile. Of all the characters with whom we deal in this medieval period he seems the most natural and the most lovable. Martin, on the other hand, like his wife Margery, was cast in a harder mould. Shrewd, calculating and with a true appreciation of the legal reforms introduced by Edward I, he seems in some queer way to have overreached himself in his desperate efforts to rebuild the ancestral estate. Roger, who inherited the aftermath of his forebears' inability to maintain themselves in contemporary society, was to be pitied. His means were too slender for the role he might have been expected to play and he found exile in London preferable to poverty at home. The decline of the family fortune may have been due largely to faults and follies, yet we must remember that the Caruns, in their relation to Sherington, were essentially part of the feudal system and perhaps in spite of themselves they were decaying with it.

No single observation could emphasize this more effectively than the verdict of the jury at the inquisition *post mortem* on Roger in 1301. 'They say on oath that

[1] JI 1/56, m. 37d. In 1240 John was kept in custody and fined 20*s*. for an assault with sword and club in Sherington fields.

Roger Karoun held of the king in chief the manor of Shirinton for the service of two knights' fees.'[1] All the trappings of feudalism are there, but what a hollow mockery! The statement is word for word what William de Carun returned in his *carta* of 1166, yet whereas William in his day had the whole village of Sherington behind him and could certify that he had not sub-infeudated anyone, Roger bequeathed to his daughter and heiress Sibyl the torn shreds of an estate.[2] The young widow Joan was assigned the usual third part as dower and she retained it for a long time[3] but its value was so small that she had to pay no more than one mark for permission to marry whomsoever she would in the king's fealty.[4]

The king gave the wardship and marriage of the infant Sibyl to his cousin Edward, earl of Cornwall, and his executors, who sold it at once to Richard Golde the farmer of part of the Tickford priory manor in Chicheley. After six years he sold it to his brother Thomas, from whom it was acquired in 1311 by Roger de Pateshalle, rector of Bletsoe, Bedfordshire. Roger complained that after he had held it no more than a month John de Burgh with a crowd of armed supporters had broken the doors, windows and hearthstone of the manor house, and had carried off goods and chattels to the value of 20 marks. A little later he had carried off Sibyl and married her against her guardian's will.[5] At an inquiry held on 14 February 1313 it was stated that John de Burgh, who was a local official of the escheator, had acted with the king's connivance, but Sibyl, symbolizing we may feel the decay of her race, was unable to hear or give evidence about all these violent proceedings as she was deaf and dumb.[6]

[1] C133/100/10.

[2] C133/100/10. The extent was 145 acres land, 6 acres pasture and 3 roods meadow in demesne, with freehold rents amounting to 20*s.* 5¼*d.* The poverty of the estate was overemphasized because a third part was still held by Margery as tenant in dower.

[3] *Cal. Pat.* 1348–1350, 99. A settlement of the manor in 1348 was to include a third part expectant on her death.

[4] *Cal. Fine*, 1319–27, 35.

[5] *Cal. Inq. Misc.* II, 37; C143/73/14.

[6] *Cal. Pat.* 1313–17, 252. John le Barker of Olney was one of the supporters.

12

THE FITZJOHN AND RE-ARRANGED COCKFIELD MANORS

AT the turn of the century the feudal obligations attached to the manors in Sherington become somewhat confused. The Cockfield fee, held as a mesne tenancy for the service of one knight, seems to disappear, while a new fee, that of Fitz John, comes in to share with the principal manor the service of two knights *in capite*. As a result of these and other changes the new century opened with four manors operative in Sherington, two of them, Cave's and Cockfield's under no feudal obligation.

Roger Fitz John, who remained in Sherington after the death of his wife Agnes about 1282, was the life tenant of what has been referred to in the previous chapter as the attenuated Cockfield fee.[1] He had also become tenant under Martin de Carun of the small property that Martin's brother Simon had once held by gift of their father John.[2] Martin's son Roger quit-claimed these two holdings to him in 1297, the estate to be held of the king for one-third of the two knights fees owed by the principal manor.[3] Roger's charter is preserved among the Throckmorton muniments at Coughton Court and carries his armorial seal.[4] The property was known

[1] See p. 65. The estate recovered by Martin from Adam de Cockfield was 1 messuage and 1 carucate land, 7 acres meadow, 12 acres wood and 8 marks rent. Allowing for the freehold rents (10*s.*) the customary rents were £4 16*s.* 8*d.* The history of the fee after it became vested in the Fitz Johns shows that the customary lands were about 150 acres or 6 virgates, suggesting that the rent of a virgate was 16*s.* 1½*d.*, in reasonable agreement with other authentic contemporary values for land in the region. The sheriff's extent, 1 messuage and 105 acres land, 2 acres meadow, 30 acres wood, 10*s.* freehold rents and 30*s.* customary rents (*Cal. Inq. Misc.* I, 413) was made in connexion with John de Cockfield's warranty, and Adam complained bitterly that the valuation was far too low (cf. p. 64, n. 3). The sheriff's officials used the extent when called to the inquisition *post mortem* on Roger de Carun in 1301 and on Roger Fitz John in 1313: such practice was not uncommon.

[2] Described as 31 acres land, together with a garden of 2 acres, a dovecote, and 1 acre meadow (JI 1/60, m. 12; 1206, m. 13).

[3] *Cal. Inq.* v, 207. The inquisition *post mortem* on Roger Fitz John states that he made fine for £10 before the barons of the exchequer at York in 26 Ed. I (1297–8).

[4] T, 41. Quit-claim, Roger, son and heir of Martin de Carun of Schringtone, to Roger, son of John of Schringtone, of all property which he held for life of himself or his father in town and territory of Shrington, namely in houses, curtilages, gardens, stew-ponds, hedges, quick-sets, ditches, lands, meadows, feedings, pastures, ways, paths, waters, fisheries, woods, rents, homages, fealties, wards, reliefs, socages, tallages, free customs, aids, with

henceforth as Fitz John's manor, and later deeds show that it was Simon's messuage—to the south of the church at the junction of the roads now called School lane and Church lane—that became the Fitz John manor house. As late as mid-Victorian times the farm on the site was known as Fitz John's manor farm.

The Grey fee was a collection of tenements purchased at various times from Martin and Roger de Carun by John de Grey and his father Reynold, first Lord Grey de Wilton, who had his Buckinghamshire seat at Water Eaton, near Bletchley.

None of the original documents dealing with the acquisition have survived, but fortunately much of the individual detail can be culled from the contemporary plea rolls, on which are entered claims for dower by the two widows Margery and Joan de Carun.[1] The immense value of such records, unfortunately so inaccessible, is illustrated by the present case. The Grey estate passed eventually in 1505 from Edmond, Lord Grey of Wilton, to Sir Henry Colet, whose son John Colet gave it four years later to the Mercers' Company in trust for the benefit of St Paul's School. When comparison is made between the original estate computed from the dower claims *c.* 1300 and the survey made for the Mercers in 1577, the agreement, item by item, is excellent, showing that the customary lands and rents, as well as the freehold rents, had remained unchanged over the intervening two hundred and seventy odd years.

In 1286 John de Grey purchased by fine from William le Porter of Tilbrook Bedfordshire, and Agnes his wife a parcel of rent in Sherington of the annual value of 38*s*. There are grounds for believing that these rents, which would carry manorial rights, were formerly part of the original Cockfield fee, the major part of which, as we have just seen, passed to Roger Fitz John and became known later as Fitz John's manor. The name Cockfield was apparently carried with the rents to the

villeins and their families and chattels and all other appurtenances belonging or likely to belong thereunto; also the tenement which he had from Simon de Carun in the same town, namely messuage with garden, stew-pond, quick-hedges and ditches, with a virgate of land, saving one penny yearly for customs, suits of court, etc. Warrantry. Witnesses: Sir Edmond de Wedone, Sir Roger de Tyringham and Sir Almaric de Nodariis, knights; John de Pateshalle and many others (named). 15 Aug. 1297. Seal on tag.

[1] Dower could be claimed on all land held by the husband at the time of marriage unless the parties had made other arrangements. If, subsequently, a part of the land was alienated a separate claim for dower was made against the purchaser, who generally called to warrant the heir of the seller. This is what happened in the instances cited below (cf. Flower, Selden Society, 62, 237–40).

Greys and was applied by them to the new fee they were assembling.[1] John de Grey also acquired from Martin de Carun a freehold rent of 10*s*. a year arising out of a virgate of land that had once belonged to his brother John.[2] After Martin's death John de Grey and his father Reynold purchased from Roger de Carun for the use of John the rest of his customary lands and most of his wood.[3] On the marriage in 1304 of John de Grey's daughter Joan with Ralph Basset of Drayton, John settled the consolidated estate,[4] referred to later as Cockfield manor, on them and their issue, with remainder to his own right heirs.[5] As we shall see later,[6] the Basset family failed in the third generation and the manor reverted under the entail to John's great-grandson Henry de Grey in 1391.

1 CP25(1) 17/49/36. The fine specifically bars the heirs of Agnes, so the rents were probably an inheritance from her family. Their earlier history is not known, but it is very probable that the original Cockfield fee had lost rents to the annual value of at least 38*s*. between 1260 and 1285 (p. 65). The transfer of the name Cockfield to the new Grey fee is good circumstantial proof that the 38*s*. rents came from this source.

2 In 1278 John de Carun owned a rent of 10*s*. given him by his father John (*Hundred Rolls*, Rec. Com. I, 41): claim in 1271 by Agnes, widow of John de Carun against her son John for dower in 1 virgate of land (KB26/199, m. 20); claim in 1298 by Margery, widow of Martin de Carun, against John de Grey, for dower in 1 messuage and 40 acres land: John admitted liability only for such land as had been obtained by Martin from his brother John, i.e. in 10*s*. rent from 1 virgate (CP40/125, m. 30d; 135, m. 127).

3 Claim in 1302 by Joan, widow of Roger de Carun, against Reynold de Grey for dower in 8 acres meadow, 6 marks rent, 40 acres wood; Reynold exhibits three charters of enfeoffment by Roger covering only 31*s*. 1½*d*. customary rents; Joan again claims 6 marks. Joan claims against Henry son of William son of John of Sherington dower in 1 messuage, 1 virgate and 4 acres of land and ½ acre pasture. Joan claims against Roger Gerbray dower in 6½ acres land (CP40/142, m. 126d). After various delays, during which time Roger Gerbray and Henry call to warrant John de Grey, Joan claims dower in 6 messuages and 2½ virgates land, 8 acres meadow, 40 acres wood and 36*s*. 1½*d*. rent against Reynold; 1 messuage, 1 virgate and 6½ acres land against John; and 4 acres land and ½ acre meadow against Roger Gerbray. All defendants call to warrant Sibyl, daughter of Roger de Carun and a ward of Richard Golde. Reynold is without a day: Joan to have her third part out of lands in custody of Richard (CP40/145, m. 194, 333d; 155, m. 66d).

4 It was shown in note 3 that 2½ virgates of Reynold de Grey's customary land was rated at 6 marks (80*s*.) less 36*s*. 1½*d*. or 43*s*. 10½*d*., so that the virgate was worth 17*s*. 6⅗*d*. If it be assumed that the virgate contained ½ acre meadow rated at 8*d*. as well as 26 acres arable land, the latter will be worth 8*d*. per acre. The rent of 36*s*. 1½*d*. was thus equivalent to 53½ acres arable land and about 1¼ acres meadow, so that the total customary arable land was $(4+6\frac{1}{2}+53\frac{1}{2}+91)=155$ acres and the meadow $(1\frac{1}{4}+1\frac{3}{4}+\frac{1}{2}+8)=11\frac{1}{2}$ acres. The extent of the new manor was accordingly 7 messuages, 6 virgate (155 acres arable land and 3½ acres meadow) of customary land rented at 8 marks (£5 6*s*. 8*d*.), 48*s*. freehold rents, 8 acres meadow and 40 acres wood (cf. Table 10).

5 CP40/521, m. 441, no. 6 (see p. 129). The marriage settlement is enrolled. Dated at Ruthin 27 March 1304. The property mentioned is in Olney, Clifton Reynes, and 'all the tenements which I have in Shyrington, in demesnes, homages, rents of free tenants and customers, all serfs and their broods... 40a. wood, 8a. meadow and pasture in the same town'.

6 P. 129.

A property extending to about 100 acres was brought together at the turn of the century by Roger de Tyringham, whose family had long held the neighbouring village of that name, with most of Filgrave and Astwood, as a member of the honour of Dudley. He did not inherit any land in Sherington,[1] but he had acquired 2 virgates of land in the open fields there[2] as well as 4 acres of pasture and 8 acres of wood[3] before 1301. Soon after, presumably by grant from Master Henry de Lisle, he obtained the distal (eastern) portion of le Hoo Park, a property extending to 26 acres.[4] Although his descendants acquired a little more land and some rents of assize later in the century the estate, having originated subsequent to *Quia Emptores*, had no manorial status.

[1] The inquisition *post mortem* on John de Tyringham, Roger's father, includes a very complete inventory of his lands.

[2] Held of Roger de Carun for the service of 3*s.* per annum (C133/100/10).

[3] Claim for dower by Joan, widow of Roger de Carun (CP40/141, m. 210d).

[4] Described in 1577 as a 'sisters part' held of the Mercers' (earlier, Grey de Wilton) manor for 2½*d.* per annum (Table 6).

13

THE CAVE FAMILY AS LAWYERS

WHEN he inherited his brother Simon's estate in 1270 Robert de Cave, whose older sons John and Hugh were already in minor orders and destined for the law, gave the old family holding at Drewton to his third son Nicholas.[1] The move south was a home-coming for Robert's wife Sibyl, for she was the third of five daughters and eventual co-heiresses of Hugh de Verly of Woughton-on-the-Green (Woketon), a village on the Ousel 4 miles south of Newport Pagnell.[2] Their first few years at Sherington were uneventful and only trivial matters are recorded.[3]

It was about 1279 that various members of the Cave family became associated in what we should describe today as a firm of attorneys or professional pleaders at the king's bench. The original partners were Robert of Sherington, Thomas[4] his son and William his brother.[5] As these retired or died they were replaced by Robert's son Robert, occasionally distinguished by the appellation Master,[6] another William[7] and a Geoffrey de Cave,[8] the last two carrying on together until the firm

[1] Robert reserved a rent of £3 per annum from the property (4 bovates land and 31*s.* rent). Some time before 1280 he foreclosed for alleged non-payment but was found guilty of disseisin (JI 1/1062, m. 30d).

[2] CP 40/64, m. 103d; 65, m. 2. Hugh de Verly the father died *c.* 1243; his issue is described in the account of a dispute over the presentation to Woughton Church, which was vacant in 1286. It was agreed that Robert and Sibyl should present for that turn. They introduced William de Thorntoft, who is mentioned later (p. 78). The account given in *VCH Bucks*, IV, 516, based on the second reference only, is inaccurate.

[3] A dispute with the rector over a local stone quarry (JI 1/60, m. 6); an unsuccessful attempt to secure the presentation to Filgrave Church (JI 1/1221, m. 3d); settlement of a dispute over land at Denton, Northamptonshire, with Belle, widow of Pictavin, one of the much persecuted Jews in the ghetto at Bedford (Plea Rolls, Exch. Jews (J. M. Rigg), II, 237; III, 4, 14).

[4] He succeeded his brother Hugh as rector of Plumpton, Northamptonshire, in 1287 (*LRS*, XXXIX, 48).

[5] William was connected with the wardrobe in 1257 (*Cal. Close*, 1256–9, 172) and was presented to the church of Wickenby, co. Lincoln, in 1265 as William 'Camerarius' (*LRS*, XI, 81). He was attorney to his brother Simon in 1262 (JI 1/58, m. 29) and executor to his brother Roger, canon of Lincoln in 1280 (*LRS*, XLVIII, 151). The bishop announced his discharge in 1291.

[6] As Master Robert he appears as alternate with Geoffrey in 1293 (KB 27/136, roll of attorneys). He became a king's clerk later (*Cal. Pat.* 1327–30, 337).

[7] He occurs as alternate with the other William in 1285 (KB 27/90, roll of attorneys).

[8] He became rector of North Cave in 1311 (Surtees Society, 151, 198) and was an assize judge in that year and in 1324. His relationship to the other Caves is not known; there were so many with the surname in the vicinity of North and South Cave during the thirteenth century.

disbanded in 1311. The clients were drawn largely from the counties in the eastern half of England, especially Yorkshire, but at times from Devon and Wales. The development of such business connexions was fostered by the growing amount of litigation which followed in the wake of Edward I's early legislation and the Caves were not the only family to seize the opportunity for profit. Conditions of travel for the partners and their clerks nevertheless were not good in those days and Sherington, on one of the better roads running from Westminster to the north, could have been a convenient stopping place. Robert and William it is to be remembered were both middle aged before they entered upon this strenuous life.

The Cave fraternity at Westminster must have been a prominent one in the lesser hierarchy serving the king's bench at this time, but it is uncertain whether any of them, except John and Hugh mentioned below, had any official position there. Sayles, however, has given cogent reasons for believing that Geoffrey was one of the 'examiners' of the rolls of court from 1285 onwards.[1]

All of Robert's seven sons except Nicholas, who was already provided for in Yorkshire, were in professional employment and as Robert himself spent much of his time on travel he seems to have found it advantageous to let other people run his landed property.[2] Some time after 1280 he demised his Sherington manor for ten years to his brother William, who in his turn demised it to John de Thorntoft, a member of a family prominent, like the Caves, in official circles.[3] John died about 1289, bequeathing the profits of the manor for the payment of his debts and for alms. His executors were William de Thorntoft and Robert his brother, who complained that as soon as John was dead, Robert de Cave, with John and Nicholas his sons, Roger Fitz John and other local men entered the manor, carried away his corn and ejected them.[4] This occurred late in 1290, when the Cave family, short of

[1] Selden Society, 55, lxxxiii. A branch based on Middleton-in-the-Wold supplied several assize judges around the turn of the century. The Cave pedigree in Burke's Peerage under Cave-Brown-Cave, attributed to Sir William Segar, is a fabrication.

[2] The small estate in Denton, Northamptonshire, was demised for ten years in 1285 at 40*s*. a year (KB27/127, m. 27).

[3] The Thorntofts, like the Caves, were minor gentlefolk from Yorkshire; William, who had land at Catton and North Cave as well as Thorntoft itself (Surtees Society, 49, 254), took service with Edward I some time before 1290 and was made clerk of the hanaper in 1298. A pluralist, one of his first livings was Woughton-on-the-Green, to which he was appointed by Robert and Sibyl de Cave in 1287. He retained a pension from it on his resignation in 1301 in favour of Thomas de Thorntoft (*Cal. Papal Letters*, II, 34).

[4] *Cal. Pat.* 1281–92, 411.

Cave of South Cave and Sherington

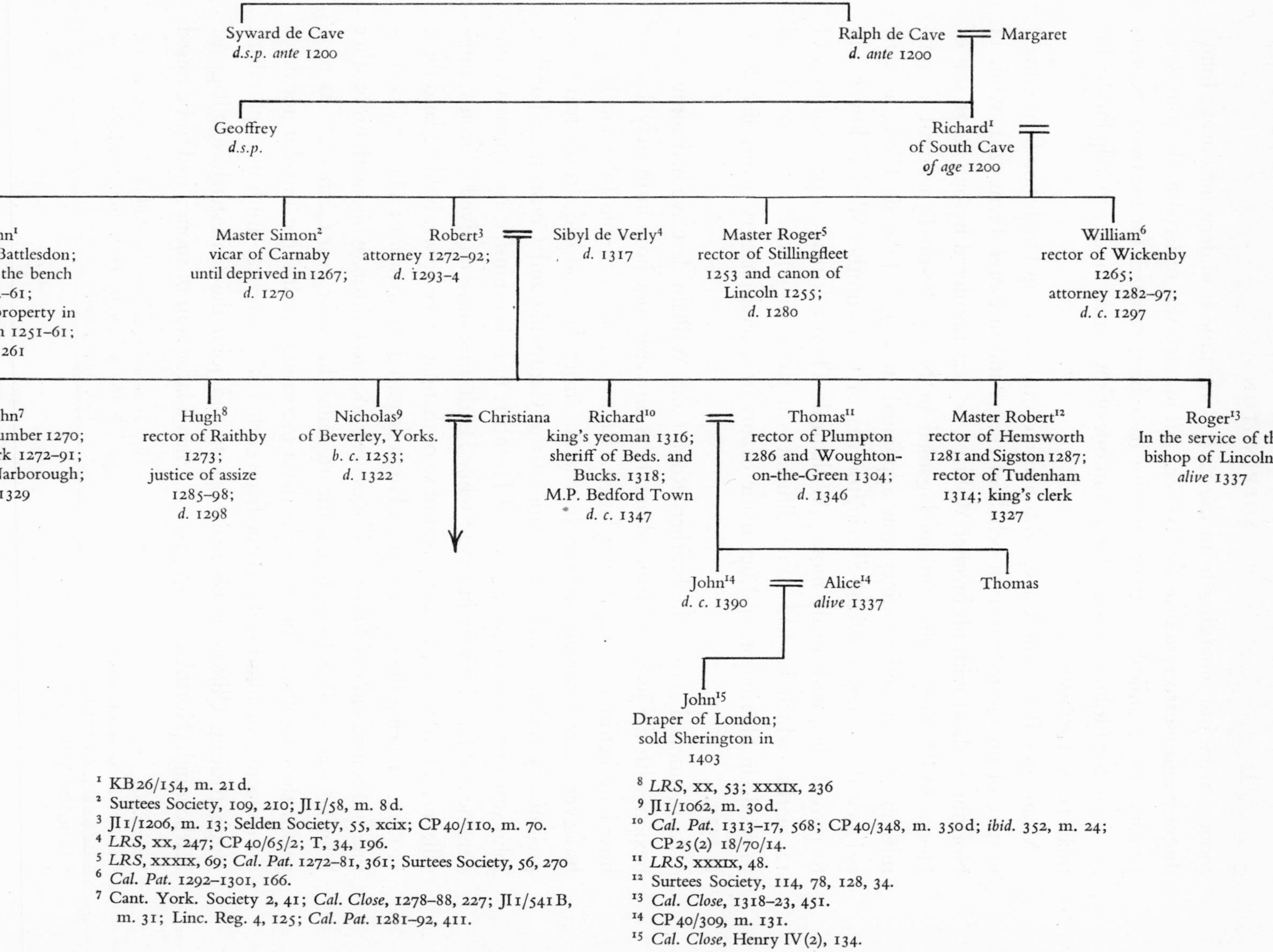

[1] KB 26/154, m. 21 d.
[2] Surtees Society, 109, 210; JI 1/58, m. 8 d.
[3] JI 1/1206, m. 13; Selden Society, 55, xcix; CP 40/110, m. 70.
[4] *LRS*, xx, 247; CP 40/65/2; T, 34, 196.
[5] *LRS*, xxxix, 69; *Cal. Pat.* 1272–81, 361; Surtees Society, 56, 270
[6] *Cal. Pat.* 1292–1301, 166.
[7] Cant. York. Society 2, 41; *Cal. Close*, 1278–88, 227; JI 1/541 B, m. 31; Linc. Reg. 4, 125; *Cal. Pat.* 1281–92, 411.
[8] *LRS*, xx, 53; xxxix, 236
[9] JI 1/1062, m. 30d.
[10] *Cal. Pat.* 1313–17, 568; CP 40/348, m. 350d; *ibid.* 352, m. 24; CP 25(2) 18/70/14.
[11] *LRS*, xxxix, 48.
[12] Surtees Society, 114, 78, 128, 34.
[13] *Cal. Close*, 1318–23, 451.
[14] CP 40/309, m. 131.
[15] *Cal. Close*, Henry IV (2), 134.

money, were just emerging from the harrowing time it underwent during John's disgrace and incarceration in the Tower. An inquiry was ordered in the following January and an amicable settlement must have been reached, for the two executors agreed to loan John de Cave a large sum out of their trust money to help him in his financial embarrassment.[1]

Meanwhile Robert de Cave, who had recently taken up knighthood, continued in spite of his age to travel on behalf of clients and in Easter Term 1291, while in Northumberland with his brother William, he was murdered by one Hugh son of Henry Middleburg, who remained gaoled in Newcastle-on-Tyne until a commission of oyer and terminer was appointed in 1295.[2] John de Cave, as heir, assigned the reversion of the Sherington manor to his mother Sibyl as dower, and to provide her with ready money William de Thorntoft made a personal loan of 12 marks—which he had some difficulty in recovering later.[3] Sibyl continued to reside in Sherington and her name occurs in several charters before her death in 1317.

As mentioned above, the brothers Robert and William de Cave had some connexion with the judiciary from about 1278 onwards, but how intimately and for how long before then we do not know. Robert's two older sons John and Hugh, however, were definitely serving there at an earlier date and had already had some preliminary training under the aegis of the Campville and Constantine families. John was presented to the rectory of Humber, near Leominster, by Thomas Constantine and Joan his wife in 1270,[4] while Hugh must have received Clifton Campville, near Tamworth, within a year or so of that date since he was holding land there in 1272.[5] During the next ten years Hugh acquired the manor of Thorpe Constantine and some land in Chilcote, villages next door to Clifton, while with his brother John he was holding Essington, some 16 miles due west near Cannock.[6] As time passed their legal activities brought them increasing wealth, but this did not deter the collecting of additional revenue from ecclesiastical sources. Both were pluralists, Hugh treating Clifton as his main centre and John the Leicestershire village of Narborough (Northburg). In 1290–1, when a large sum of money had to be raised

[1] See p. 84.

[2] *Cal. Pat.* 1292–1301, 166.

[3] CP40/115, m. 115d.

[4] Cant. and York Society, II, 41, 303.

[5] *Historical Collections for Staffordshire*, IV, 254, 258.

[6] *Feudal Aids*, V, 9. *Derb. Arch. Soc. J.* NS, XII, 19. *Cal. Inq.* II, 496.

to appease the king's wrath with John, Hugh's clerical revenue was at least £90 a year[1] much more than that of John himself.[2]

It is not as clerics, however, but as lawyers that the brothers have claim to be remembered. Hugh was clerk to Chief Justice Hengham in 1277[3] and probably retained the office until 1285, when the king first employed him as an assize judge. From then on, until his death in 1298, he continued to serve as a judge, and some of his utterances have come down to us *verbatim* in the first of the famous Year Books.[4] John was acting as an attorney at the king's bench in 1279[5] and was chief clerk there in 1283.[6] From evidence given at his state trial discussed below it would seem that he succeeded his brother Hugh as Hengham's clerk in 1285. Like all those employed in such favoured positions he had the right to act as an attorney and to engage in private practice. During 1285–6, for instance, he acted as attorney to Hengham himself in another court, as clerk to the prior of Lapley and as clerk to the rector of Godmanchester. It was for corrupt practice while serving as clerk to his old patron Geoffrey de Campville in 1287 that he fell foul of the king and ruined his career at the bench.

After more than three years continuous absence in Gascony Edward I returned to England in August 1289 to find that discontent with those left to administer justice at home was fairly widespread. During the ten years immediately preceding his departure abroad his legislation, through the possessory assizes, had been largely directed towards the speeding up of justice, and while, in practice, this had meant increased work for the lawyers it had not led to the smooth progress that the orderly minded king had looked for. The clamour, which implicated many of his leading justices as well as some of his most trusted court officials, caused him deep concern and of necessity called for extraordinary measures outside the normal judicial routine. Accordingly he issued in October 1289 a proclamation appointing his chancellor Robert Burnell and six other men who had been with him in Gascony as auditors to receive complaints from all who felt they had been aggrieved by his officials, both high and low, while he was abroad.

1 Clifton Campville, £16 13*s*. 4*d*.; Adbaston, Staffordshire, £13 6*s*. 8*d*.; Raithby, Northamptonshire, £8 13*s*. 4*d*.; Keyingham, Yorkshire, £17 6*s*. 8*d*.; Gargrave, Yorkshire, £33 6*s*. 8*d*.; prebend of Tamworth, 13*s*.4*d*.(Nicholas Taxation, 1291, Rec. Com.).

2 Humber, £5; Narborough, £16; Barby, Northamptonshire (deprived before institution) £13 6*s*. 8*d*.; prebend of Lincoln, (?); prebend of St Probrus, Cornwall, £3 10*s*. 0*d*. (Nicholas Taxation, 1291, Rec. Com.).

3 Dugdale, *Origines Juridiciales*, p. 94.

4 Year Book XX and XXI Edward I (Rolls Series).

5 KB27/45, m. 8d.

6 *Cal. Close*, 1279–88, 227.

The proceedings before the auditors at Westminster led to the disgrace of many judges, including the chief justices of the two benches, all of whom were sent to the Tower and pardoned only on payment of very heavy fines. Those of lesser rank who received similar treatment were Adam de Stratton, chamberlain of the exchequer, Henry de Bray, sometime king's clerk and escheator this side of Trent, and Robert de Littlebury, clerk of the rolls, all of whom ultimately received pardon on payment of a fine of 400 or 500 marks. A fourth official, John de Cave, was found guilty of a flagrant offence under the Statute of Maintenance, and was also committed to the Tower. Partly by inadvertance the importance with which the king and auditors viewed his case has been overlooked, so that it is dealt with here more fully than would otherwise have been justified.

Chief Justice Hengham, who was fined the enormous sum of 7000 marks, was convicted on only one of the nine charges that are known to have been proffered against him.[1] In this particular one, which concerned the issuing of a defective (vicious) writ in Michaelmas Term 1287, he was associated with two other judges, including William de Saham. All three came before the auditors in Easter Term 1290, when Hengham maintained that the irregularity was due to nothing more than the carelessness of the clerk who wrote the writ.[2] Saham was more outspoken and alleged the malicious deception of the clerk responsible for the scrutiny and sealing of it, and himself brought an action against John de Cave, whom he named as the culprit. But the sharp-witted clerk, displaying considerable forensic skill, bullied the judge into the damaging admission that he had in fact sealed the writ himself,[3] and on further cross-examination got him so confused that he was reduced to pleading again and again to be allowed to withdraw his plaint. The discomforted Saham was sent to the Tower and fined 2000 marks; John on this particular score went free and the fortress did not claim him until the next term.

Llanstephan with its castle standing on the southern shore of Carmarthenshire overlooking the Tovey estuary was owned in 1287 by John de Cave's patron Sir Geoffrey de Campville, and the living there, a valuable one worth 60 marks a year, had become vacant that October. In December Geoffrey brought an assize of

1 Selden Society, 55, lxviii, n. 6.

2 *State Trials* (Camden Society, 1906), p. 35.

3 John's heated and triumphant reply to this admission so excited the clerk who was writing the roll that he set down the exact words: the accused had made a statement 'before you, the auditors, who have record and who represent the person of the king'. He then falls once more into the third person (quoted, with minor alteration, from *State Trials*, p. xiv).

darrien presentment at Carmarthen against the prior of the Hospital of St John of Jerusalem in England and Brother Gilbert de St Augustine the master of its preceptory at Slebech. Both parties claimed the advowson through Geoffrey de Marmyon, who had owned the church and estate in the time of Henry II; Geoffrey de Campville by descent, because his great-grandfather William had married the daughter and heiress Albreda, the prior and his colleague in virtue of a charter to the brethren at Slebech which had been confirmed by the daughter and her husband. The case presented many difficult legal points and was in part thrashed out at the king's bench, the verdict of the jury being given at Carmarthen in Hilary Term 1289 to the effect that the advowson had always gone with the property. The justiciar for south Wales thereupon directed that a letter be sent to the bishop of St Davids requiring him to admit Geoffrey's nominee.

From what transpired at the state trial held later it is clear that John de Cave was Geoffrey's candidate and had acted as his attorney at Carmarthen. Alas! having heard the verdict it was John's mortifying duty to read to the justiciar a letter that both Geoffrey and the prior had received from the bishop, in which he informed them that the church had remained vacant for so long beyond the statutory time that he had exercised his right as diocesan and collated Thomas de Colach.[1] Geoffrey, therefore, had recovered the presentation—if not for that turn at least for the succeeding ones—while the fat living had gone to the bishop's nominee. All that could come to John was a possible share in the damages awarded his patron for the two years that the dispute had been *sub judice*, namely 120 marks. Presumably Geoffrey allowed him to keep the whole or part of this—a fatal step as we shall see later.

When the airing of grievances was encouraged by the king, Brother Gilbert, the preceptor of Slebech, complained in Trinity Term 1290 against John on the plea that contrary to the statute which forbade the clerk of a justice receiving the presentation of a church through litigation he had, while clerk to Hengham, procured

[1] The prior claimed that this order could only be impleaded before the king or his chief justice: the case was therefore remitted to the king's bench and heard first in Hilary Term 1288 (KB27/108, m. 8), when Robert and William de Cave were two of the three alternate attorneys engaged by Geoffrey. The entry on the roll recites the earlier proceedings at Carmarthen and then becomes involved in technicalities; it is transcribed in full by Sayles (Selden Society, 55, 172–6). The case came up again in the following Michaelmas Term (KB27/114, m. 23), when William de Cave was one of four alternate attorneys. The entry is informative, reciting the history of the advowson, the verdict at Carmarthen in Hilary Term 1289 and the letter from the bishop of St Davids.

Llanstephan for himself by helping Geoffrey de Campville to sue out a writ that had led to a false assize. John replied that in the octave of Michaelmas 1287 he was not a clerk at the king's bench or to Hengham and had surrendered all his rolls, etc., to John de Chester. He was at the time in Gloucestershire on business for the abbot of Fécamp and the presentation came to him 'as a stranger and clerk to Geoffrey de Campville' and not as an official; had he refused the offer he would have lost the pension! John's evidence was palpably false, for the Saham case shows that he was in the bench at that particular time and there can be no doubt that while he was with Hengham he had a lucrative private practice. The auditors found him guilty and he was committed to the Tower by the king's will.[1]

John was allowed later to make fine for 500 marks,[2] his brother Hugh and many others standing surety.[3] The large sum demanded was in keeping with the contemporary opinion that the king was out for money and related the fine more to the defaulter's ability to pay than to the magnitude of the offence. Presumably by episcopal sequestration John was deprived of all his spiritualities except the rectory of Narborough and early in July letters were sent to the bishops of Lincoln, Hereford and Exeter, the dean of Lincoln and the sheriff of Staffordshire foreclosing on all assets pertaining to his rectories, prebends and lay fees respectively. For other, unrecorded, offences[4] he was fined an additional 100 marks and very fortunately for him the king assigned the whole amount to his consort Queen Eleanor, who died a few months later (28 November). Her chief executor Robert Burnell forgave him 300 marks, leaving him to find no more than a similar sum, which he seems to have done without difficulty in under two years.[5] William de Thorntoft and his brother Robert loaned him 70 marks of their trust money[6] and he took action to recover debts to the value of at least 55 marks.[7]

Robert de Cave died soon after John regained his freedom and his widow Sibyl,

[1] JI1/541B, m. 31. The membrane is mutilated and part of John's evidence is unreadable or missing. The date is assumed to be Trinity Term 1290 because John's conviction led to action being taken early in July of that year. The brethren of Slebech recovered the advowson of Llanstephan.

[2] In *State Trials*, p. 220, the fine is given in error as 10 marks.

[3] E368/62, m. 32d; the names of the twelve other pledges are given.

[4] Cf. *State Trials*, p. 222.

[5] E372/138 membrane Gloucester and residue Stafford.

[6] Recognizances for £40 (KB27/126, m. 8) and 10 marks (CP40/87, m. 14) out of the trust funds of John de Thorntoft, notification going to the sheriffs of Buckinghamshire, Northamptonshire and Yorkshire.

[7] CP40/87, m. 11; 89, m. 56. KB27/126, m. 46d.

by agreement, was left in possession of the Sherington estate as her dower. Financially John's position righted itself very quickly, for he inherited his brother Hugh's lands in 1298 and within a year or so had acquired a small estate in North Cave and the neighbouring village of Hotham.[1] He still retained the Denton property in Northamptonshire[2] and did his best—including a direct appeal to the king—to recover the property in Wolverton, Buckinghamshire, that his uncle Simon had lost to Newton Longville priory.[3] In 1316, when well over 60, he went on a pilgrimage to Santiago, to find on his return that his mother was dead and the Sherington estate once more on his hands. John himself was not a Buckinghamshire man and preferred his rectory at Narborough, while his eldest surviving brother Nicholas was already well established in Yorkshire.[4] His next brother Richard, a king's yeoman, had always lived in the vicinity of Sherington and John settled the manor on him forthwith. The wily old clerk remembered the dangers inherent in serving the king and he took care to give Richard no more than a life interest in the estate.[5] As we shall see later, Richard's son and heir John must have blessed the prescience of his uncle when the exchequer sleuthhounds in 1353 got on his track about irregularities connected with his father's dealings as sheriff of Bedfordshire and Buckinghamshire in 1318–19, nearly 35 years before.

[1] KB27/155, m. 36. *YASRS*, LXXI, 152.

[2] In a restraint for knighthood it was reputed (falsely) to be worth £20 a year (cf. p. 56, n. 9; 78, n. 2).

[3] CP40/161; m. 225d, 292d; 173, m. 41; 174, m. 2d. *Cal. Close*, 1307–13, 135, 354.

[4] *Cal. Inq.* VI, 221.

[5] The fine accompanying the settlement gives for the first time the extent of the Cave property, namely 1 messuage and 180 acres land, 8 acres meadow, 12 acres wood and 10*s.* 8*d.* rent. The entail was to Richard and his heirs, then, in succession, to his younger brothers Thomas, Robert and Roger for life with remainder to his own right heirs (CP25(2) 181/70/14).

14

THE LAND IN MEDIEVAL SHERINGTON

Here as elsewhere we shall not obtain the best insight into things until we actually see them growing from the beginning.

LITTLE is known about the distribution of the land in Sherington before the early thirteenth century, but from then on the amount of information increases decade by decade until by 1312, as shown in Table 1, it is as complete as one can reasonably expect for a village wherein the original feudal fief had undergone fragmentation into so many bits and pieces. To throw light on the evolution of the estates that had come into existence by then the distribution for that year has been used as a base-line for exploring, step by step in reversed chronological sequence, the position as it was from time to time back to the twelfth century. The series of extents thereby obtained are set out in graphic form in Tables 2 and 3: these give the descent of all holdings of more than about 10 acres and reveal at a glance the early history of certain minor estates such as those that came into the possession of John de Cave[1] and William son of Alexander de Sherington.[2] Before describing in detail the changes in

[1] The land held in dower by Sibyl de Cave in 1312 (Table 1) was an inheritance of her husband Robert from his brother John, who had purchased the moated manor house and the two closes south of it from Emma the wife of William le Vineter in 1255. John had also acquired 125 acres of arable land in the open fields, of which 30 acres had originally been settled by John de Carun on Simon and John, two of the bastard sons of his great-uncle Gervase the parson (p. 50), 24 acres had come from various smallholders who were called upon to warrant in 1260 (KB 26/169, m. 13), and 20 acres had been acquired from Felicia the wife of John le Blake, one of the daughters and co-heiresses of William son of Alexander de Sherington (*BASRB*, IV, 106). The remainder of the holding, about 50 acres, in the open fields, came presumably from Emma le Vineter, who assigned to John not only the residue of all her lands in Sherington, but also 'all the land that Sarah, widow of William le Franceis and Olive, widow of Ralph le Franceis held of her there in dower' (CP 25(1) 16/33/26). It was presumably the same Emma who, as Emma de St Mark, was a party in 1194 to an assize of 1 hide of land in Sherington (*PRS*. 14, 23). The St Mark family owned an estate in Lavendon (*VCH Bucks*, IV, 382) and it is significant that the conveyance of a small plot of land in Sherington by William le Franceis in 1227–35 was witnessed by John de St Mark (T, 80).

[2] Known also as William de Sherington. He was of Filgrave, where he held half a fee of the honour of Chaworth (*Book of Fees*, II, 893), and had land in Leckhamsted (*BASRB*, IV, 37). On his death in 1256–7 his estate was divided among four daughter co-heiresses (see p. 93). He held at least 73 acres in the open fields of Sherington and 20 acres of this went to Felicia le Blake, who sold to John de

TABLE I

Holders of land in Sherington c. 1312

Owner	Messuages	Demesne: Pasture (acres)	Demesne: Arable (acres)	Open fields: Non-demesne pasture and home closes (acres)	Open fields: Arable (acres)	Meadow (acres)	Wood (acres)
Sibyl de Cave[a]	4	41	—	8	125	8	—
Roger Fitz John[b]	2	—	136	—	156	8	30
Ralph Basset (Grey de Wilton manor)[c]	7	20	19	5	112	11½	40
Ralph Basset (le Hoo Park)[d]	—	50	—	—	—	—	—
Sibyl de Carun[e]	1	20	148	—	31	8	—
Joan de Carun (dower)[f]	1	18	32	—	—	—	—
Roger de Tyringham	1	26[g]	—	—	52[h]	2	8
Henry de Shirford[i]	1	—	—	2	41	1½	—
Ellot Holdings[j]	1	—	—	1	8[o]	1	—
Delapre abbey[k]	1	—	—	8	40	2	—
Tickford priory[l]	2	—	12	—	10	—	—
Glebe[m]	1	4	—	—	15	2	—
Ralph Basset (Grey de Wilton) freeholds (Table 6)	4	—	—	—	176[o]	3	—
Carun freeholds (Table 7)	7	—	—	—	61[o]	2½	—
Nicholas de Kenet[n]	—	—	—	—	24	½	—
	31	183	347	24	850	50	78

[a] See p. 85. The two 20 acre closes south of the manor house are the 'sisters parts' paying a rent of 5½*d.* to the Grey de Wilton (Mercers' manor, Table 6). Sturmurs Close (4 acres) paying a rent of 8*d.* and Marryot's Close (4 acres) are not in the demesne area.

[b] See p. 73 n. 1.

[c] See p. 75 n. 4.

[d] See p. 69

[e] Table 53. The demesne pasture includes the home closes (8 acres), Bury close (5½ acres), Jaggins close (2 acres), Mowell's close (3 acres) and 20 acres of pasture and meadow called 'le Pittel' (Gore Leys in 1580).

[f] See p. 72.

[g] The eastern end of le Hoo Park: it was the 'sisters part' paying a rent of 2½*d.* to the Mercers' manor (Table 6).

[h] Paying a rent of 3*s.* to Carun manor (Table 7).

[i] Inherited from his mother Hawysa daughter of William son of Alexander alias de Sherington (JI1/1303, m. 25).

[j] Representing 35 small peasant holdings, see p. 132, n. 2.

[k] E318/755.

[l] E106/2/1; Bull, *History of Newport Pagnell*, p. 72.

[m] Lincoln Terrier, 1707.

[n] *Cal. Close*, 1256–9, 371.

[o] There is overlap between these items.

landownership during the period under review attention must be drawn to the division of the village territory in 1312 (Table 4). The data are taken from various surveys discussed in Appendix 1 and as the whole of the village is accounted for the acreages assigned to the open common fields and the demesne could not have been exceeded at the time of the Domesday Inquest.

As mentioned before[1] field-name analysis has led to the tentative conclusion that in 1086 the common fields and all the demesne except le Hoo Park had already been fully opened out. To reconcile this view with the number of ploughs returned at the inquest it is necessary to be able to judge the value at the time of what Maitland has called the teamland, that is, the amount of land cultivated by one plough in one year. This is a problem that has been frequently discussed in Domesday studies, for *inter alia* the factor must clearly vary from place to place according to the nature of the soil.[2] Fortunately in the present instance a fiscal return of 1185, to which reference is made later, gives us good grounds for believing that the teamland in Sherington at that date was about 120 acres, in good agreement with the value assigned to this region of Bedfordshire and Buckinghamshire by those who have dealt exclusively with Domesday material.

The inquest jury returned that there was sufficient land in the open fields for seven ploughs, but that only six were present. Seven ploughs, each tilling some 120 acres

Cave, 42 acres descended to Henry de Shirford and 11 acres to Nicholas de Kenet. William inherited from his uncle, another William son of Alexander or de Sherington, who had farmed the principal manor from 1194 to 1200 during the minority of the heir Ralph (p. 39, n. 3). His relationship, if any, to the Carun family is not known. According to a much later inquisition of 1335 his land in Sherington was held *in capite* for a quarter of a knight's fee (C143/318/1).

[1] See p. 12.

[2] The present position in Domesday studies has been cogently put by G. Herbert Fowler, who agreed with Maitland that in this part of England the teamland is best represented by 120 acres with a rather elastic boundary capable of some expansion or contraction as needed ('Bedfordshire in 1086', Quarto Mem. *BHRS*, I, 61).

---

[a] *VCH Bucks*, IV, 241.

[b] *Red Book of the Exchequer*, 314.

[c] *Rot. de Dom.* 42.

[d] JI 1/62, m. 23 d. KB 26/111, m. 2 d, 8; 113, m. 6 d.

[e] *PRS*, XIV, 23.

[f] JI 1/1046, m. 59 d.

[g] CP 25(1) 16/33/26.

[h] JI 1/58, m. 15 d; 67, m. 26. KB 27/121, m. 48 d.

[i] *Cal. Inq. Misc.* I, 25; KB 26/199, m. 31 d; see also p. 100, n. 2.

[j] *Hundred Rolls*, I, 41; JI 1/60, m. 6; 1206, m. 13.

[k] KB 26/165, m. 36; JI 1/1046, m. 59 d.

[l] CP 25(1) 16/33/26; KB 26/154, m. 21 d.

[m] JI 1/1309, m. 28 d; 1311, m. 79 d.

[n] C133/73/8; *Cal. Inq.* III, 191 gives in error 80 acres of demesne arable.

[o] CP 40/125, m. 30 d.

[p] T, 41; *Cal. Inq.* I, 413; CP 40/83, m. 128 d.

[q] JI 1/58, m. 8 d.; 1206, m. 13.

[r] JI 1/1309, m. 28 d.

[s] JI 1/1311, m. 79 d.

[t] *Cal. Inq.* IV, 15.

[u] JI 1/1311, m. 79 d.

[v] See Table 1.

TABLE 2

Descent of the demesne arable and pasture lands

The acreage (a.) quoted includes all the pasture except the 'meadow and pasture' (m. and p.) called 'le Pittel' (see text).

Date	Holdings								Total acreage
1088	84 a. most of it not yet assarted	Domesday Inquest: 4 ploughs on the demesne (4 × 120)[a]							480+
1166	William de Carun has not yet subinfeudated[b]							16 a.	
1185	Gervase de Carun[d] 84 a.	Richard de Carun in king's wardship[c] 3 ploughs on the demesne 365 a.					47 a.		512
1194	Gervase de Carun 84 a.	Richard de Carun 240 a. + 20 a. m. and p.				Lucy de Cockfield 105 a.	Emma de St Mark 47 a.[e]		512
1220	Gervase de Carun 84 a.	Ralph de Carun 240 a. + 20 a. m. and p.				Adam de Cockfield[f] 105 a.			512
1234	John de Carun 324 a. + 20 a. m. and p.[i]					Denise d'Eyvill in dower 105 a.	Emma de Vineter 47 a.		512
1250	William de St Edmund[h] 84 a.	John de Carun[i] 190 a. + 20 a. m. and p.			Simon de Carun[j] 50 a.	Denise d'Eyvill in dower 105 a	Emma le Vineter[g] 47 a.		512
1260	William de St Edmund 84 a.	John de Carun 190 a. + 20 a. m. and p.			Simon de Carun 50 a.	Robert de Cockfield[k] 105 a.	John de Cave[l] 47 a.		512
1295	Martin and Margery de Carun[m] (settlement) 84 a. + 12 a. m. and p.	Martin de Carun[n] 160 a. + 8 a. m. and p.		John de Grey 39 a.	Simon de Carun[t] 18 a.	Roger Fitz John[p] 136 a.	Sibyl de Cave[q] 47 a.	Tickford priory, 12 a.; Glebe, 4 a. = 16 a.	520
1301	Henry de Insula[r] 84 a.	Margery de Carun[s] settlement and dower 47 a. + 12 a. m. and p.	Roger de Carun[t] 145 a. + 6 a. m. and p.		John de Grey[o] 39 a.	Roger Fitz John 136 a.	Sibyl de Cave[u] 47 a.		532
1312[v]	Roger de Tyringham 24 a.	Ralph Basset 50 a.	Sibyl de Carun 148 a. + 20 a. m. and p.	Joan de Carun in dower 50 a.	Ralph Basset 39 a.	Roger Fitz John 136 a.	Sibyl de Cave 47 a.		530

FOR NOTES RELATING TO TABLE 2 SEE PAGE 88

a year, would thus cover about 840 acres, a value very close indeed to the 858 acres based on the later surveys (Table 4). This would be in keeping with the deduction from field-name analysis that by 1086 the South Field and the West Field had been fully opened out so that the area contained very little if any land that had not at some time been cultivated. The jury also returned that there were four ploughs on the demesne and these would have been equivalent to about 480 acres, in reasonable agreement with the surmise that in 1086 le Hoo Park was still woodland but that the rest of the demesne, amounting to 467 acres (Table 4) was already under tillage. On the assumption, therefore, that the value of the teamland did not change appreciably between 1086 and 1185 the acreages that have been assigned to the Domesday demesne and open fields respectively are reasonably correct.

Ralph de Carun acquired the Sherington fief soon after Domesday and was succeeded by his son William, who died in 1180. Unfortunately no record that can throw light on the value and disposition of the property during this long span has survived and the earliest information that we have belongs to the year 1185. As discussed in Ch. 5, William's son and heir Richard was apparently abroad at the time of his father's death and the estate remained in the king's hands from 1180 until 1188 (p. 32). In 1185 the justices itinerant were asked to ascertain the full value of the wardship and their return,[1] if examined in light of the contemporary situation revealed in Tables 2 and 3 is more illuminating than the bare details would lead one to expect.

In 1166 William the father had certified that none of the fief had been subinfeudated and as far as is known it was still intact in 1185. Nevertheless, sometime before the latter date a sizeable portion of the land had already passed into other hands[2] and what remained in 1185 could not have extended to more than 365 acres in demesne and 609 acres in the open fields, the assumption being made (immaterial

[1] *Rot. de Dominabus*, *PRS*, 35, 42 (cf. p. 32).

[2] Tables 2 and 3: Tickford priory, 2 virgates; Delapre abbey, 2 virgates; Gervase the parson, 84 acres (le Hoo Park); Emma de St Mark, 1 hide (p. 86, n. 1); William, son of Alexander, 73 acres (p. 86, n. 2); various smallholders, 40 acres: a total of 145 acres in demesne and 235 acres in the open fields.

---

[a] See Table 2.

[b] See p. 56.

[c] See Table 7.

[d] *BASRB*, IV, 7.

[e] *Cal. Inq. Misc.* I, 25.

[f] CP25(1) 16/33/26.

[g] See p. 86, n. 1.

[h] See p. 86, n. 1.

[i] JI1/1303, m. 25.

[j] *Cal. Close*, 1256–9, 371.

[k] See p. 132, n. 2.

[l] See Table 1.

[m] All the freeholds had been created before 1250 and the assignment to 1220 is arbitrary.

[n] The change reflects the sale by Martin de Carun to John de Grey of 10*s.* rent from 20 acres land formerly owned by John de Carun, junior.

[o] *BASRB*, IV, 100; CP25(1) 16/36/9.

TABLE 3

Descent of the open-field arable and pasture lands

Date	Holdings												Total acreage
1086	Domesday Inquest: 7 potential ploughs (7 × 120)												840
1166	Ecclesiastical holdings: Delapre abbey, 48 a.; Tickford priory, 10 a.; glebe, 15 a.	William de Carun has not subinfeudated											
1185		Richard de Carun in king's wardship 609 a.									William son of Alexander 73 a.	15a.	844
1194		Lucy de Cockfield 312 a.		Richard de Carun 297 a.					Emma de St Mark 50 a.		William son of Alexander 73 a.		844
1220[m]		Cockfield freeholds[a] 156 a.	Adam de Cockfield[b] 156 a.	Carun[c] freeholds 81 a.	Ralph de Carun 216 a.					24 a.			
1235		Cockfield freeholds 156 a.	Denise d'Eyvill in dower 156 a.	Carun freeholds 81 a.	John de Carun[e] 175 a.		Richard son of Gervase[d] 11 a.	Simon son of Gervase and Amphelis his wife[o] 30 a	Emma le Vineter 50 a.	Various small holdings[g] 24 a.	William son of Alexander 73 a.		844
1250		Cockfield freeholds 156 a.	Denise d'Eyvill in dower 156 a.	Carun freeholds 81 a.	John de Carun 175 a.				Emma[f] le Vineter 50 a.		William son of Alexander 73 a.		844
1260		Cockfield freeholds 156 a.	Robert de Cockfield 156 a.	Carun freeholds 81 a.	John de Carun 175 a.			(30 a → John de Cave)	John de Cave[h] 125 a.	Hawysa de Sherington 41 a.	Thomas de Kenet 11 a.[j]		844
1295		John de Grey freeholds 156 a.	Roger Fitz John 156 a.	Carun freeholds 81 a.	Martin de Carun 134 a.		(11 a. → 52 a.) 52 a.		Sibyl de Cave in dower 125 a.				844
1301		John de Grey[n] freeholds 176 a.	Roger Fitz John 156 a.	Carun[n] freeholds 61 a.	31 a. Margery de Carun	John de Grey 111 a.	Roger de Tyringham		Sibyl de Cave in dower 125 a.	Henry de Shirford[i]	Nicholas de Kenet	Various small freeholders[k]	852
1312[l]	73 a.	Ralph Basset freeholds 176 a.	Roger Fitz John 156 a.	Carun freeholds 61 a.	Sibyl de Carun 31 a.	Ralph Basset 111 a.	52 a.		Sibyl de Cave in dower 125 a.	41 a.	11a.	15 a.	852

FOR NOTES RELATING TO TABLE 3 SEE PAGE 90

TABLE 4

Division of the village territory in 1312

Items marked * are taken unchanged from the corresponding division in 1580 (Table 30)

	Acres	Acres
Common fields		
West Field	423	
South Field	427	
	——	850
*Non-demesne closes		23
Demesne		
North Field, arable and pasture	214½	
East Field, arable and pasture	138	
East Field, le Hoo Park	84	
South Field, arable and pasture	91½	
West Field, Willowmed	23	
	——	551
Woods		78
*Cowpasture		97
*Meadow		54
*Farms and home closes		64
*Cottages		9
*Roads		22
		1748

The area recorded on the map accompanying the Enclosure Award of 1797 is 1763½ acres.

to the following argument) that the open-field freeholds that are found appurtenant to the various manors at a later date had not yet been created. In their valuation of the demesne stock the justices included three *carruce*, and if these are indicative of three plough-teams[1] calculation shows that on a demesne of 365 acres the teamland would be 121–122 acres a first approximation that is close to the conventional 120 acres mentioned above. The justices valued the land, including that held as dower, at £7 15*s*. 0*d*. and the stock carried on the demesne, stated to be three *carruce*, 100 sheep, five cows and five swine, at about £4 5*s*. 0*d*. If the land and the demesne stock of the sub-tenants be arbitrarily assessed *pro rata* the former would be worth

[1] It will be noted that the justices' return indicates three potential ploughs on the demesne whereas Domesday shows four. The interpretation given above, that alienation occurred without sub-infeudation, may explain some of the anomalies to which Round drew attention, e.g. in his discussion of the Blund manors in Suffolk (*Rot. de Dominabus, PRS*, 35, xxxi).

Sherington of Filgrave and Leckhamsted

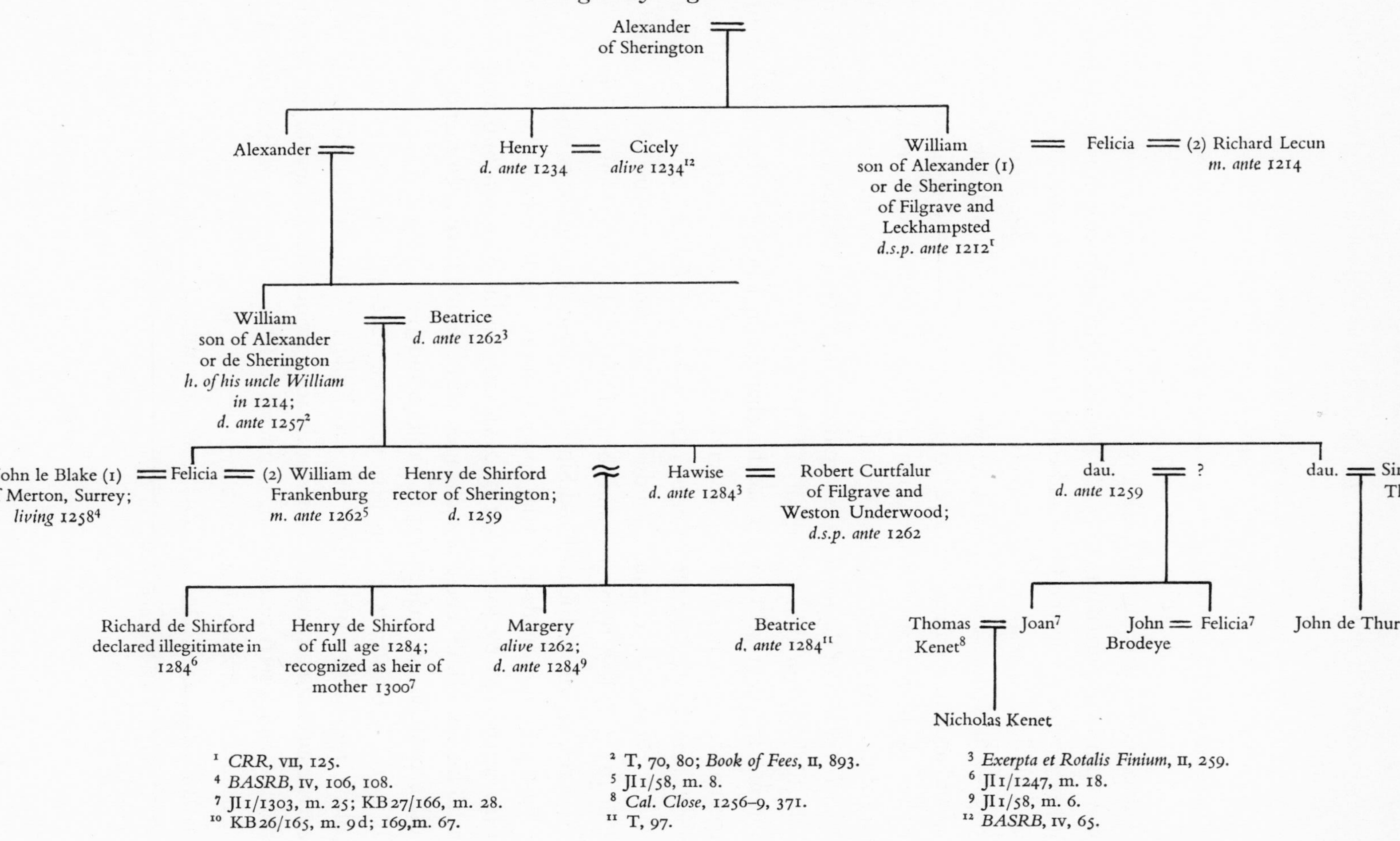

[1] *CRR*, VII, 125.
[2] T, 70, 80; *Book of Fees*, II, 893.
[3] *Exerpta et Rotalis Finium*, II, 259.
[4] *BASRB*, IV, 106, 108.
[5] JI 1/58, m. 8.
[6] JI 1/1247, m. 18.
[7] JI 1/1303, m. 25; KB 27/166, m. 28.
[8] *Cal. Close*, 1256–9, 371.
[9] JI 1/58, m. 6.
[10] KB 26/165, m. 9d; 169, m. 67.
[11] T, 97.
[12] *BASRB*, IV, 65.

about £3 12*s.* 0*d.* and the latter £1 8*s.* 0*d.*: Sherington in 1185 would thus have been worth about £17 when stocked, a rise in value from £7 in 1066 and £10 in 1086 that seems reasonable enough considering the lean time that the whole countryside must have gone through during the anarchy.

It was some four years later, in 1189, that Richard de Carun was obliged to subinfeudate nearly half of his fief to his cousin Lucy de Cockfield. Her share comprised 105 acres of the demesne (table 4), a rent of 3*s.* 1½*d.* issuing from the moated manor house with its appurtenant closes,[1] 312 acres in the open common fields (table 3), a third of the fishery in the Ouse and one half of the water-mill. How much of the open-field land was already held freely by the tenants is not known. The farm and cottages that went to make the new fee were scattered alongside the Newport–Olney road and around the manor 'waste' to the north of the moat, an area of rough grazing that has been treated as common throughout the ages and today goes by the name of Calves End Green. In a few of the early deeds the fee is referred to simply as 'the lower half of the town' in contradistinction to the Carun estate which clustered on the higher ground in the vicinity of the church.

During the next 50 years or so the changes in landownership were of minor importance. The Cockfield fee descended in turn to Lucy's grandsons Adam and Robert, being settled by the latter in 1220 on Denise, Adam's widow, as part of her dower.[2] Richard de Carun's grandson John inherited the main fief on coming of age in 1230; he first recovered and then disposed of his great-uncle Gervase's park of 84 acres, giving to Richard and Simon, Gervase's bastard sons, about 30 acres in the open common fields as partial compensation.[3] A little later the estate became further attenuated by John's gift of 2 virgates to his own son Simon and of 10*s.* rent to his son John.[4] These few changes, all of which have been mentioned before in other contexts, are made clear in Tables 2 and 3.

It is from documents of this period, about 1220–40, that information becomes available for the first time about the actual tillers of the soil, the husbandmen who were the successors by descent or by infiltration from other villages of the 22 villeins, 6 bordars and 8 serfs recorded in Domesday. Two deeds especially, a fine of 1238 and an undated charter of somewhat earlier date, are very informative and provide much of the data collected in Table 5. As one might have expected, the Old English

[1] Table 6, under William Mountgomery.

[2] P. 44.

[3] P. 50.

[4] P. 59, n. 6.

TABLE 5

Smallholders in Sherington between 1220 and 1240

Ref.	Name of freeholder	Minimum freehold land acres (a.) or selions (s.)	Ref.	Name of freeholder	Minimum freehold land acres (a.) or selions (s.)
1	William le Franceis (Frenchman)	1¼ a.	1	Adam le Blungere	1 s.
4	Ralph le Franceis (Frenchman)	2 s.	1	Simon, son of Rose	1 s.
4	Richard, son of Gervase	11 a.	4	Simon le Grey (grey-haired)	1 s.
6, 11	Simon, son of Gervase	25 a. + ½ a. meadow	4	William de Clopeham (Clapham, Beds.)	1 s.
1	Henry le Poure (the poor or from Picardy)	3½ a.	4	Clement Largus (broad)	1 s.
8	Wybert	2 a.	4	Simon Godemanne (good man)	1 s.
1, 4	Michael, son of Wybert	3 s.	4	Simon Damisel (young squire or page)	3 s.
4	Simon, son of Michael	1 s.	4	Reginald Damisel	1 s.
7	Robert, son of Simon son of Michael	7½ a.	4	Bartholomew Thoromod (son of Thormond)	1 s.
4	Adam le Smith	1 s.	3, 1	Hugh le Russ (the red)	1¼ a.
10	William, son of Adam	5 a.			
4	Gilbert, son of Adam le Smith	1 s.	9	Gilbert le Russ	8¼ a.
3, 5	Simon, son of Adam le Smith	5 a.	9	Simon, son of Richard	1 a.
1	Bartholomew le Blund (fair-haired)	3 s.	9	William, son of Martin	1 a.
1	Richer (dweller by the stream)	1 s.	9	Adam, son of Stephen	¼ a.
4	Bollus (round)	1 s.	2	Henry Sweyn (servant)	½ a.
10	Eustace le Carpenter	2 a.			

References: (1) T, A3. (2) T, 80. (3) T, 94. (4) *BASRB*, IV, 74. (5) CP25(1) 14/14/14. (6) JI1/58, m. 12. (7) JI1/62, m. 15. (8) JI1/62, m. 26. (9) JI1/696, m. 14d. (10) KB26/169, m. 13. (11) CP25(1) 16/36/9.

personal names must have given place some time previously to the Christian names introduced by the Normans and it is interesting to note that while these simple village folk of low social status had already adopted quite a wide variety of them, that of John, so popular in later generations, had not yet come into favour.[1] The surnames call for no particular comment; ten derive from family relationships, five

[1] Cf. P. H. Reaney, *A Dictionary of British Surnames*, p. xxix.

TABLE 6

Mercers' manor freehold rents in 1577[a]

The items listed above the line form part of larger estates and are not included in the total acreage. Numbers shown thus, 63*, are not included in the area shown on Map 8; the direction in which they lie is indicated on the map.

No. on Map 8			£	s.	d.	Acreage
89	William Mountgomery	Chief messuage called Yettes or Marryots		2	0	—
	William Mountgomery	2 'sisters partes'			5½	—
	William Mountgomery	Land called Sturmanns			8	—
139	Katherine Ardes widow	Messuage called Williamson			1	—
	Thomas Turringham esquire	One 'sisters parte'			2½	—
		Certain lands late Thomas Course the son of Henry Course			6	—
	Edward Chibnall	4 a. land; 7½ a. land late Thomas Hooton			2½	11½
	Edward Chibnall	18 a. land, 3 a. meadow, late Alice Barker's			8	18
157	Edward Chibnall	House wherein he dwelleth and 100 a. land held in knight's service	1	9	6	100
40	Robert Mathew	20 a. land		10	0	20
198	Anthonie Smyth	1 messuage, 7 a. land		3	6	8
	Anthonie Smyth	Certain lands late Richard Grendon's and sometime John Younge's			1	—
	Anthonie Smyth	1 acre of ley by the bridge			3	—
53	Tho. Orpen, late Tho. Course	1 messuage, 10 a. land			7	10
63*	John Springnell	1 messuage, 7 a. land			1½	7
46	Tho. Maunsell	1¼ a. land			1½	1¼
			2	8	11½	175¾

[a] RCL, 193, cf. p. 172, n. 1.

denote occupation or office, two denote nationality, another two are place-names and the rest emphasize some personal characteristic. Viewed as a whole they suggest a self-contained and rather inbred community.

The amount of land held by these folk, 74½ acres and 24 selions, is large and from the limited evidence that has been used to compile Table 5 the list of holders cannot be complete. An unidentified but by no means a small proportion of the land concerned will have been held freely under one or other manor (Tables 6 and 7)

TABLE 7

Carun manor freehold rents in 1301[a]

The items listed above the line form parts of larger estates and are not included in the total acreage.

Owner	Holding	Service	Rent per annum s.	d.	Acreage
Lord John de Grey	1 mess., 1 virgate	1 lb. cummin priced 1½*d.*		1½	—
Lord John de Grey	1 mess., 32 a.	—		13	—
Roger de Tyringham	1 mess., 2 virgate	—	3	0	—
Roger, son of John	1 mess., 100 a. land; 30 a. wood, 40*s.* rent	—		1	—
Sibillia de Cave	1 mess., 14 a.	1*d.* and one pair of gloves priced 1*d.*		2	—
Henry, son of Simon	1 virgate	Per scuta et in quando currit		—	—
Robert Cous	1 mess., ½ virgate	—		1	13
Ralph Eustace	1 mess., ½ virgate	suit of court		—	13
John le Parmer	1 mess., ½ virgate	suit of court		—	13
Nicholas Kenet	⅙ virgate	—		4½	4⅓
Ralph Ellot	4 a.	—		2	4
Gilbert, son of Richard	4 a. land, one piece pasture	—	2	0	4
Henry, son of Simon	3½ a.	—		1¾	3½
Gilbert, son of Simon	2 a.	—		2	2
Geoffrey, son of Gille	2 a.	—		¼	2
Roger Hodelin	1 a.	—		½	1
William Bouchmaler	1 a.	—		2	1
Simon Godknave	½ a.	—		¼	½
Richard Herman	⅔ fishery in Ouse while it lasts	—	8	0	—
Joan Gurveys	1 watercourse (*Cursum unius aqua*)	—		1	—
Thomas Golde	1 mess., 1 croft	—		1	—
Nicholas de Stachedene	1 toft	—		½	—
Henry le Bret	1 piece of land	1 capon priced 2*d.*		2	—
Beatrice Annslice	⅔ toft	—	1	6	—
Augustus, son of Margaret	1 mess.	—	2	0	—
Petronilla, daughter of William	1 cottage	—		8	—
Richard de Shirford	1 mess.	—		2	—
			20	5½	61⅓

[a] C133/100/10.

and so allowed for in Table 3. Simon the parson's son seems to have owned more than some of his fellows with their solitary selion or so, but it is a mistake to judge the standing of these people solely on the extent of their freeholds, for Ralph the Frenchman and probably also his father William before him was the farmer in the early 1240's of the Cockfield fee under the widow Denise d'Eyvill, and many of the others must have held customary land under one or other of the large estates.

Most of the freeholders mentioned in the Throckmorton charters owed no more than suit of court to the lord but a few held by knight's service and the list, probably incomplete as before, includes three holders of 1 virgate and another of one half of a virgate respectively. Some tenants in both categories had, in addition, to render forensic service, which included attendance at the Shire and Hundred Courts. 'Peter le Somenour did his fealty and acknowledged that he held of the lord one half virgate of land for homage, scutage and other forensic services.'[1] Peter did not have to pay a money rent, but he had to find his quota of scutage when it was levied and to attend the Shire Court at Buckingham as well as the Hundred Court at Moulsoe. Both lords and tenants found it advantageous to be represented at these courts, but the obligation to attend was an onerous one.[2]

[1] NRO *Ecton*, 1190, m. 1.

[2] Cf. J. A. Raftis, *The Estates of Ramsey Abbey*, pp. 47–8.

15

THE VALUE OF LAND IN MEDIEVAL SHERINGTON

THE forces that were helping to shape the economic history of Sherington during the thirteenth century become progressively clearer from about 1235 when, for the first time, information about the rate at which land was being rented can be gathered from contemporary leases and other relevant documents. The evidence collected in Table 8, representing both large and small holdings, shows that during the century the annual rent of the demesne and open-field land rose to between $7\frac{1}{2}$*d.* and 8*d.* per acre. This estimate, nevertheless, needs qualifying. In the first place the common device of demanding a fine for entry and then allowing a proportionately cheaper rent does not seem to have been applied in these cases. Secondly, it is on record that the tenants of the Carun fee did not provide any work service[1] and the same must have been true for the Cockfield fee, for both sets of tenants paid the same rate of money rent. The only exception was in a lease for life made by the prior of Tickford in 1272,[2] in which the lessee of a virgate was to procure the labour of two men for one day in autumn, the prior finding their food. This is presumably a carry-over from the previous century and represents conditions that might have been general when William de Carun gave the virgate to the monks in 1170. Thirdly, the estimate is in keeping with those prevailing in the neighbourhood villages of Chicheley[3] and Tyringham,[4] where no work service was demanded.

A series of computed valuations of the Carun estate is given in Table 9. In no instance can the total sum deduced represent the full annual income, for details of such extras as the issues of court and from the woods are not available.[5] Attention

[1] *Cal. Inq.* 3, 191.

[2] See Table 8, n. f.

[3] E 106/2/1. Inventory of Tickford lands made when Edward I seized the alien priories in 1294. Tickthorne's manor in Chicheley, lying to the east of the Sherington demesne, contained $415\frac{1}{2}$ acres rated at 8*d.* per acre.

[4] C 133/7/6. Extent of John de Tyringham's lands made in 1274; 204 acres in demesne at 8*d.* per acre and 19 virgates in villeinage held by custom at 18*s.* per virgate. The virgate in Sherington was rated at 17*s.* $6\frac{3}{4}$*d.* in 1300 (see p. 75, n. 4).

[5] The half interest in the water-mill that was part of the estate in 1185 went with the Cockfield lands. The two thirds fishery in the Ouse had already been commuted for a freehold rent (Table 7).

TABLE 8

Annual value of land in Sherington during the twelfth and thirteenth centuries

Date	Property	Acreage in demesne (D) or open fields (OF)	Annual value in pence (per acre)	English wheat prices[i] (20 years' means): Period	Wheat price in shillings per qr.
c. 1140	Delapre abbey[a]	48 a. OF	1·75	1160–79	1·89
1185	Carun manor[b]	375 a. D, 609 a. OF	1·89[j]	1180–99	2·60
c 1234	Carun manor[c]	186 a. OF	5·15[j]	1220–39	4·19
c. 1255	Le Hoo Park (Wm. de St Edmund)[d]	58 a. D	7·25	1240–59	4·58
c. 1260	Cockfield manor[e]	156 a. OF	7·5		
1272	Tickford priory[f]	7 a. D, 7 a. OF	7·7	1260–79	5·62
1294	Tickford priory[g]	6½ a. OF	8·0	1280–99	5·97
1300	Grey de Wilton manor[h]	155 a. D and OF	8·0	1300–20	7·01

[a] *Dugdale Mon.* v, 212; *Nich. Tax* (Rec. Com.), p. 47, a rent of 10*s.* covered 2 virgates of land and a house rented at 3*s.*

[b] Tables 2 and 3, assuming that no freehold rents had been created.

[c] Claim for dower by Agnes, widow of John de Carun, who was married *c.* 1235. A rent of £3 19*s.* 0*d.* covered 186 acres; see Table 2 and 3, also Table 9, n. c.

[d] See p. 52, n. 7; 58 acres demised for a term at 35*s.* per annum.

[e] See p. 73, n. 1; the widow Denise d'Eyvill died in 1260.

[f] T, 5, 311, A47, A87: lease for life, the tenant owing the service of two men for one day a year in autumn, the prior finding their food.

[g] E106/2/1. Inventory of alien priory made in 1293–4.

[h] See p. 75, n. 4.

[i] *Cambridge Economic History of Europe*, II, 166.

[j] Labour services may not have been commuted.

must also be drawn to the fact that as all the pasture except a few acres in the demesne was subject in varying degree to right of common it was worth but little more than the arable land: to simplify the presentation therefore it has been treated as belonging to the latter category. The valuation for 1185 is taken from the justices' inquiry for that year,[1] while the one for 1234 is based on a claim for dower by Agnes, widow of John de Carun.[2] The remainder are computed from the data in Tables 2 and 3, and some of them call for brief comment.

[1] See p. 32. The widow's dower is allowed for. It is clear from the entries in the contemporary Pipe Roll that perquisites of court were not included.

[2] KB26/199, m. 31d. Claim for dower in 3 carucates land, 20 acres pasture, 24 acres meadow, 40 acres wood and 100*s.* rent. This would be the property owned by John at the time of the

The years 1250–1 witnessed two events which indirectly illuminate some of the basic assumptions underlying the approach to the problem of land value in the period under review; these were John de Carun's unfortunate clash with the justices of the Jews over the repayment of his debt to Elias the moneylender, and the leasing by Denise d'Eyvill to John de Cave of the Cockfield estate which she held in dower. In the first of these cases the dispute, as already mentioned,[1] was about the value of John's lands; a local jury had certified that these were worth only £7 7*s*. 6*d*. per annum whereas Elias was adamant that a more realistic sum would be nearer £20. The computed valuation in Table 9, amounting to £15 14*s*. 7*d*. without perquisites, is strongly in favour of the Jew's contention and if John had spoken evasively in court, as was probably the case, his fine of 10 marks *pro stultiloquio* was not necessarily excessive. In Tables 2 and 3 the extents for the year 1250 have been elaborated from those of 1312 by working back through the maze of changes during the intervening years, and for the Carun estate they show 210 acres (including 20 acres meadow and pasture) in demesne and 175 acres or 7 virgates in the open fields. The local jury returned 2 carucates in demesne and 7 virgates in villeinage,[2] as close an agreement as one could expect in view of the assumptions on which the computed values are based. It is when we turn to the inquest valuation that the great discrepancy occurs. The jury returned £4 for the demesne or only 4*s*. 8*d*. per acre, and half a mark for the virgate in villeinage, or but 3*s*. 1*d*. per acre. Whether the omission of the meadowland by the jury was deliberate or not we cannot say; it may have been on lease, or the jury may have been acting under John's influence. That the much larger total sum arrived at by computation is indeed valid follows from the second event mentioned above. The widow Denise's covenant with John de Cave mentions, *inter alia* that the Cockfield fee was then demised to farm (i.e. at full rent) for the term of her life to Ralph le Franceis of Sherington for twenty marks (£13 6*s*. 8*d*.) per year.[3] Allowing a reasonable sum for perquisites and wood, this is very close to the computed annual value.[4]

marriage and as it includes 3 carucates in demesne the year must have been about 1234, when le Hoo Park was for a short period in John's hands. As the freehold rents were £1 0*s*. 10*d*. the customary rents must have been £3 19*s*. 2*d*. Hence, on the assumption that the customary land was 186 acres (Table 3), the rate per annum was 5*s*. 15*d*. per acre. In light of later findings it is assumed that the demesne and open-field arable land had approximately the same annual value.

[1] See pp. 51–2.

[2] *Chan. Inq. Misc.* I, 25. The rent of the free tenants and cottars was 20*s*. 10*d*.

[3] See p. 56, n. 5.

[4] See p. 73, n. 1. The claim in 1286 was for 1 messuage and 1 carucate land (£3 4*s*. 9*d*.), 7 acres

At the inquest on the death of Martin de Carun in 1295[1] the extent of his lands was in good agreement with those given in Tables 2 and 3 but the fiscal valuation at 6*d*. per acre for arable land was a little low. The same applies to the attenuated estate left by his son Roger in 1301.[2]

As has been mentioned above, the valuations set out in Table 9 are lacking in certain items, but as they are all alike in this respect the totals for the various years are comparable. In spite of the rise in the value of land the slow attrition of the estate stands out only too clearly and we have but to compare what was left to the young heiress Sibyl with the two new manors of Grey de Wilton and Fitz John (Table 10) to appreciate how much had been lost. Richard de Carun's fee in 1185, representing practically all of the village except the few holdings that eventually became consolidated as the Cave manor estate, was worth about £8, an unrealistic figure perhaps since it was, in effect, the amount handed over to the exchequer and takes no account of the sheriff's costs and perquisites. Had his estate remained intact it would have been worth about £28 in 1250 and £35 in 1312 (Table 10), a fourfold increase in a little over a century. Although there is no necessary correlation between them it is interesting to note that the price of grain during this period had kept pace with that of land (Table 8).

meadow (8*s*. 9*d*.), 40 acres wood and 8 marks rent. 38*s*. rent of free tenants had already passed to John de Grey. The issue of one half of the water-mill, based on that of Tyringham in 1274 (C133/7/6) was £1 13*s*. 4*d*. The total is £12 11*s*. 6*d*.

[1] C133/73/8. The extent included 160 acres arable land in demesne at 6*d*. per acre, 8 acres meadow at 3*s*. per acre, a several pasture at 1*s*. per acre and 60*s*. rent (of which the free tenants paid 20*s*. 4*d*.). The open-field land (Table 3) was 134 acres. 56 acres of this, however, represents the de la Mare settlement on Martin and his wife Margery (140 acres less 84 acres in le Hoo Park) and was not extended (p. 65), hence 78 acres was rented at 39*s*. 8*d*. or 6·1*d*. per acre.

[2] C133/100/10. The extent included 145 acres land at 6*d*. per acre, 3 roods meadow worth 1*s*. and 6 acres pasture at 2*s*. per acre.

TABLE 9

Annual value of the Carun estate during the twelfth and thirteenth centuries

		Demesne lands			Customary lands				Demesne meadow and pasture in le Pittel			Meadow in Lordsmead			
Date	Owner	Number of acres[a]	Annual value in pence per acre[b]	Total value £ s. d.	Number of acres[c]	Annual value in pence per acre[b]	Total value £ s. d.	Free-hold rents £ s. d.	Number of acres	Annual value in pence per acre	Total value £ s. d.	Number of acres	Annual value in pence per acre	Total value £ s. d.	Total annual value £ s. d.
1185	Richard, as a ward of the King	365	1·89	2 17 6[d]	609	1·89	4 15 11[d]	—	—	—	—	—	—	—	7 13 5
c. 1234	John[e]	324	5·15	6 19 1	175	5·15	3 15 1	1 0 10	20	23[f]	1 18 4	7	10[f]	5 10	13 19 2
1250	John	190	7·4	5 17 1	175	7·4	5 7 11	1 0 10	20	30[f]	2 10 0	7	15[f]	8 9	15 4 7
1295	Martin	160	8·0	5 6 8	134	8·0	4 9 4	1 0 4	8	36[g]	1 4 0	—	—	—	12 0 4
1301	Roger	145	8·0	4 16 8	—	—	—	1 0 4	6	36	18 0	¾	16[i]	1 0	6 16 0
1301	Joan, widow of Roger; dower[j]	50	8·0	1 13 4	—	—	—	6 10	—	—	—	—	—	—	2 0 2
1310	Margery, widow of Martin; settlement and dower[h]	47	8·0	1 11 4	31	8·0	1 0 8	—	12	36	1 16 0	8	16	10 8	4 18 8
1312	Sibyl, as a ward of the King	148	8·0	4 18 8	31	8·0	1 0 8	13 6	20	36	3 0 0	7½	16	10 0	10 2 10

[a] From Table 2. [b] From Table 8. [c] From Table 3.

[d] Token figures, see Table 8, n. b. [e] See p. 100, n. 2.

[f] In the absence of direct information the demesne meadow is assumed to be worth 4½ times and the river meadow twice the value of arable land.

[g] C133/73/8.

[h] The extent is deduced from the Terrier and Court Roll of 1312 (NRO *Ecton*, 1190, m. 1).

[i] C133/100/10.

[j] Taken as one-third of her husband's estate (*Cal. Pat.* 1348–50, p. 99).

TABLE 10

Annual value of the various estates in Sherington c. 1312

Owner of property[a]	Demesne lands[b]		Customary lands[b]		Freehold rents	Meadow[c]		Total annual value
	Number of acres	£ s. d.	Number of acres	£ s. d.	£ s. d.	Number of acres	£ s. d.	£ s. d.
Sibyl de Cave	47	1 11 4	133	4 8 8	10 8	8	10 8	7 1 4
Roger Fitz John	136	4 10 8	156	5 4 0	10 0	8	10 8	10 15 4
Ralph Basset (Grey de Wilton Manor)	—	—	156	4 0 4	2 8 0	11½	15 4	8 7 4
Ralph Basset	50	1 13 4	—	—	—	—	—	1 13 4
Sibyl de Carun	148	4 18 8	31	1 0 8	13 6	7½	10 0	10 2 10
	—	—	—	—	—	20[d]	3 0 0	—
Joan de Carun (dower)[e]	50	1 13 4	—	—	6 10	—	—	2 0 2
Roger de Tyringham	26	17 4	52	1 14 8	—	2	2 8	2 14 8
								42 15 0

[a] From Table 1. [b] Valued at 8*d.* per acre. [c] River meadow valued at 16*d.* per acre.
[d] Demesne meadow in 'le Pittel' valued at 3*s.* per acre. [e] See Table 9, n. j.

16

THE TWO-COURSE SYSTEM OF HUSBANDRY IN MEDIEVAL SHERINGTON

WHEN Sherington was settled in the earliest Anglo-Saxon times the settlers taking in new ground remote from the river would have found that their two main assarting areas, the one running north from the river towards Filgrave and the other on the spur of land shooting south beyond the eastern bend in the river, were separated by a very small stream that drained the higher ground to the north-east of the settlement. As more and more land came under cultivation the less there was left within the settlement boundary for further assarting, and to maintain the fertility of the soil a two-course system of husbandry must have been established at an early date. Topographically it is obvious that the two common fields thereby required would lie one each side of the stream, called in the later middle ages the 'town ditch', and one can appreciate that the villagers of the day would have referred to them in their simple language as 'the field towards Filgrave' and 'the field towards the sun' respectively, expressions actually used in a fine as late as 1238.[1] Nevertheless, when it became customary at the turn of the twelfth century for the free peasant to acquire and dispose of land by written deed a more precise designation seems to have been called for and in the long series of Sherington charters ranging in date from *c.* 1220 to 1350 preserved among the Throckmorton muniments, the furlongs concerned, if assigned to a field at all, were invariably mentioned as lying in either North Field or South Field respectively.

At the time of the Domesday Inquest it was returned that the open fields were assessed at 7 fiscal hides and that they had on them 6 ploughs instead of a possible 7, reflecting perhaps the unsettled conditions of the neighbourhood either at the time of the Danish invasion of 1065 or of the Conqueror's own triumphant march on London the following year. Presumably, therefore, land equivalent to only 6 of the fiscal hides or 24 fiscal virgates was under cultivation in 1086. If the villein holding

[1] *BASRB*, IV, 74.

be taken as 1 virgate and that of a bordar as one-quarter of a virgate the total holding of 22 villeins and 6 bordars would have been $23\frac{1}{2}$ virgates, showing a good correspondence between the fiscal and tenurial units. When the attempt is made, however, to translate the Domesday figures into measured acres the correlation becomes somewhat less exact. With 6 ploughs at work and a teamland of 120 acres the amount of land in cultivation would have been about 720 acres, and if this represented 24 fiscal or tenurial virgates then each virgate was equal to about 30 acres. This is more than the value current in Sherington during the twelfth and thirteenth centuries (Table 11), but the discrepancy is not large and may mean that the more prosperous villeins were tenants of more than one measured virgate. The bordars, having less land of their own to cultivate could have hired themselves out as labourers or taken on some specific occupation: Eustace the carpenter, Adam the smith and Henry Sweyn, all of whom come to our notice later in the thirteenth century, were probably their descendants.

TABLE 11

The virgate in Sherington during the twelfth and thirteenth centuries

Date	Owner	Number of virgates concerned	Arable and pasture land in acres per virgate	Meadow in acres per virgate
c. 1140	Delapre abbey[a]	2	23	1
1170	Tickford priory[b]	1	21	—
1170	Tickford priory (Glebe)[b]	1	19	2
c. 1250	Simon de Carun[c]	2	$24\frac{1}{2}$	$\frac{1}{2}$
1300	Grey de Wilton[d]	6	26	$\frac{1}{2}$

[a] *Dugdale Mon.* v, 212; E318/755 giving extent at dissolution in 1544. [b] Table, 1.
[c] P. 59, n. 7. [d] P. 75, n. 4.

The work services required of those who held in villeinage at Domesday are not known, and the one glimpse we have of conditions in the next century (p. 99) suggests no more than boon work during harvest. If, as mentioned below, the slave labour available at the time of Domesday, with some small help from the villeins and bordars, was sufficient for the cultivation of the lord's demesne, it may well be that with few exceptions[1] the freehold rents that were appurtenant to the two

[1] Table 6. The rent of 10*s.* represents John de Carun's gift to his son John *c.* 1240–50; the rent of £1 9*s.* 6*d.* must be of about the same date.

manors towards the end of the thirteenth century (Tables 6 and 7) originated at an earlier epoch and do not necessarily represent the commutation of work services. One cannot be dogmatic, but the Throckmorton charters for the period *c.* 1220 to 1270, dealing with quite small holdings of a few selions or an acre or two, do not give the impression that the land concerned had only recently become freehold. On the contrary they suggest a free peasantry of considerable antiquity, for the scattered strips are nearly always stated to be lying next to those of other peasants and not those of the principal landowners.[1]

The arable lands to the north-east of the village are probably not as ancient as the open common fields just discussed, but field-name analysis has indicated that all except the assart le Hoo Park belong to the Anglo-Saxon period (Ch. 1). When first opened out the area may not have been used exclusively as demesne, but it must have become so fairly early because Heldebyry, the name given to one of the furlongs in 1312, probably marks the site of an old Anglo-Saxon fortified manor house. At the Domesday Inquest the demesne was rated at 3 hides and on it were 4 ploughs, suggesting that new land had come under cultivation since the last (Anglo-Saxon) assessment of gelding hides.[2]

Although no medieval account rolls have survived sufficient evidence has leaked through to show that the demesne was eventually subject to the same system of husbandry as the open common fields, but that its development came later and for various reasons was on somewhat different lines. At the time of the great inquest of 1086 the bishop's demesne would have been cultivated by his slaves, of whom there were two per plough,[3] with the help of the virgaters and bordars if any supplementary work were required. None of them would have had right of common unless by special grant, because much later, when some of the virgaters had become small freeholders, they did not thereby acquire any herbage rights in the demesne. *A priori*, therefore, there would have been no need for husbandry practiced by the bishop's officials to have conformed to any recognized system. Even during the mid-twelfth century, when le Hoo Park and the moated manor holding had become detached from the main Carun estate any pasture rights could have been settled by private agreement and no fundamental change in husbandry would have been

[1] Cf. G. C. Homans, *English Villagers of the Thirteenth Century*, pp. 91–101.

[2] Cf. Maitland, *Domesday Book and Beyond*, p. 450.

[3] Regarded as in general sufficient for the purpose; cf. M. M. Postan, 'The Famulus', *Ec. Hist. R.*, supplements, 2.

necessarily called for until the Cockfield fee was sub-infeudated in 1189. Many of the demesne furlongs then passed into divided ownership, making it imperative to regulate pasture rights.

As the great open common fields were already under a two-course system of husbandry its extension to the demesne area under such conditions was a logical development. It may not have meant any great break with what had been practised in the past, but it would have called for the parcelling out of the demesne into two large common fields. The village would then have possessed two sets of paired fields, or four fields in all, and as the demesne lay to the north-east it would have been natural to call the pair there the North Field and East Field respectively. This is indeed the nomenclature used by the bailiff John Richer when he drew up a terrier of the Carun lands in 1312,[1] the two great open common fields being referred to as the South Field and West Field respectively.

Nevertheless, it is clear from the Throckmorton charters, as mentioned above, that for at least a century before this date the free peasantry had always referred to their two ancient common fields as South Field and North Field respectively, the latter lying north of the town ditch and under the shadow of Tyringham and Filgrave. They were still referring to their North Field as late as 1330. Yet John Richer would not have used the same expression for any other area unless some fairly recent and fundamental re-organization of the local agricultural economy had led to the view that revision of some of the older customs was needed. The break with the past came when the demesne ceased to be run as a private concern in 1189, and this eventually necessitated not only the naming of the two new fields just mentioned, but also of demesne furlongs that had hitherto not required a name at all.[2] John Richer's classification eventually prevailed, and as late as 1580, under the three-course system of husbandry, the field against Tyringham and Filgrave was still being called the West Field.

The throwing open of the demesne to champion husbandry, however, did not mean that all those entitled to common of pasture in the great open fields thereby acquired similar rights over the demesne. The herbage rights there would have remained the incorporeal hereditament of the freeholders concerned, who would have dealt with them by enclosure or otherwise to their own mutual advantage.

Several incidents in the thirteenth century illustrate the provisions of some such

[1] See Table 53 (p. 274).

[2] E.g. le Tenacres.

agreement. In 1231 John de Carun claimed to have the exclusive right of pasture in a plot of land near the Olney road because, he alleged, it was his demesne.[1] He had, however, been dealing with common of pasture in at least two of his own demesne furlongs, for in 1234 the right was returned to him as part of a settlement of other property.[2] Much later, in 1312, Gilbert son of Richard the parson, a freeholder in the open common fields, claimed right of common in all the Carun demesne lands by demise of Roger de Carun.[3] When herbage rights were granted in this way it was usual to specify the period of the year during which they could be taken, and in the case of John de Carun's two furlongs it was for such time as they were sown or in fallow. In general, however, the right was more restricted than this. The rector, Master William de la Mare, for instance, complained in 1271–2 that Martin de Carun and others had disseised him of his common of pasture in 50 acres where he used to common in time of fallow, in 100 acres (le Hoo Park) where he used to common from the time that corn was cut until the new grain was sown, and in a tillage called Toftes wherein he had common every third year in time of fallow.[4] This last claim is of special interest as it shows that when Martin de Carun, the freeholder, had the right to restrict the number of those entitled to pasturage it was possible for him to work this small enclosed tillage of 2½ acres on a three-course system of husbandry.

There is thus abundant evidence that during the thirteenth century common of pasture in the demesne was open only to those with severalty interest. In the great open common fields, on the contrary, where the normal champion husbandry was

[1] William, son of Alexander de Sherington (p. 86, n. 2), a freeholder in the open fields, complained that John had disseised him of his common of pasture in land alongside the Olney road by building a great bank and blocking his ingress. John argued that no one commoned with him there as the land was his demesne and he could do what he liked with it. The jury declared that the land was not demesne as it had never been sown or ploughed. William was to recover his seisin and the bank was to be demolished.

[2] John de Carun recovered le Hoo Park in 1233 (p. 50). He conveyed half of this to William de St Edmund early in 1234 with, presumably, right of common over some of his demesne furlongs. In Trinity Term of that year William levied a fine against him for the other half of the property, and quit-claimed back to him the rights mentioned in the text. John granted that William should have all the common easements in all places as other knights and freeholders had in the vill; William to have his free chase and free ingress and egress, etc. (*BASRB*, IV, 65).

[3] Court Roll, 21 Sept. 1312 (NRO *Ecton*, 1190, m. 1 d).

[4] Master William also claimed that he had been disseised of his common of pasture from ladyday to lammas on the roads leading to Bedford and Olney—a very lean privilege that emphasizes the great dearth of pasturage in Sherington. He recovered his seisin in all cases (JI 1/60, m. 7).

practised, the free and customary tenants had equal rights with the lord and like him they were stinted.[1] During the next two centuries the demesne lost much of its exclusiveness, due probably to the indiscriminate granting of pasture rights and when, in Tudor times, the pasturing of sheep became a fashionable as well as profitable investment the attempt by the freeholders in the demesne to assert their ancient right of enclosure caused much resentment.[2] The prime reason for these developments was a general shortage of meadow and pasture, a condition that dates back to Domesday and continued to dog the fortunes of the village until well into the eighteenth century, when improvements in agricultural practice and the enclosure of the common fields in 1797 brought about a radical change for the better.

[1] See p. 231, n. 2.

[2] See pp. 169–170.

17

THE MEADOWS, WOOD AND WATER-MILL IN MEDIEVAL SHERINGTON

THE RIVER MEADOWS

THERE is good evidence that in 1470,[1] and more especially in 1580,[2] the river meadow extended to 54 acres. As was usual in champion country its management was governed by custom, and to appreciate what this meant in medieval Sherington it is necessary to consider first the various subdivisions into which the meadow land was parcelled out. The prime unit, as in the common fields, was the strip, which ran at right angles to the river and was bounded on the north by the cowpasture. Called in Sherington a rood, it was a furlong or so long but much narrower than usual, containing on an average only 28–29 instead of the conventional 40 perches of land. There were about 290 of these strips, which lay in two meadows, one called Lordsmead where they had (presumably) once been reserved for the lord, and the other called Townsmead, in which all the tenants had rights. These two meadows in their turn were subdivided into doles and other small parcels (Table 12), the names of which proclaim convincingly the complete break with the old agricultural economy that must have occurred when the Cockfield fee was carved out of the main estate in 1189. The significance of Wolasale dole is not known and its name is elusive.[3] Lordsmead, as its name implies, may have been the lords' exclusive holding

[1] Table 19.

[2] Table 30. A terrier of the Mercers' estate drawn up in 1750 by a professional surveyor endorses the estimate. He gave consecutive numbers to the roods in each meadow and described those belonging to the Mercers. In Lordsmead they owned 32, representing 5 acres 3 roods 13 poles, the highest number listed being the 128th. The mean area per rood was 29 poles and the minimum total area of the meadow, assuming at least 130 roods or strips was 23·5 acres. In Townsmead the Mercers owned 22 strips for 3 acres 3 roods 24 poles, the highest number being the 156th. The mean area of the rood was 28 poles, and the total area of the meadow, assuming 160 roods or strips was 28 acres. The two meadows would have contained between them about 52·5 acres, of which the Mercers held 9 acres 2 roods 27 poles as against the 11·5 acres given in various medieval and Elizabethan extents.

[3] T 124, dated *c.* 1260, ½ acre meadow in Wollamshawe; T 90, dated 1312, 1 rood in first 20 poles of Cockfield in Woolstone in Townsmead; *BAS*, 413/44, dated 1628, in the 20 poles and in the 10 rods of Carun in Wollesale.

TABLE 12

The river meadows

Lordsmead (about 130 strips for 23½ a.)[a]	Townsmead (about 160 strips for 30½ a.)
First dole of Cockfield or le Put dole[b]	Wolasale Dole
First dole of Carun	First 20 poles of Cockfield
Second dole of Cockfield	20 poles of Carun
Second dole of Carun	Second 20 poles of Cockfield
First 10 rods of Carun	10 rods of Carun
First 10 rods of Cockfield	First dole of Carun
Second 10 rods of Carun	First dole of Cockfield
Second 10 rods of Cockfield	Second dole of Carun
	Second dole of Cockfield
	10 rods of Carun

[a] If the dole contained the normal 20 strips there must have been a third 10 rods of either Carun or Cockfield.

[b] The dole was to the far west against the Tyringham fence, and lay south of the clay pit (T, 73, 88).

in the earlier middle ages, but by the time the Carun–Cockfield assembly (Table 12) had come into being the peasantry were establishing themselves as freeholders there and also in Townsmead. The system of annual re-allocation of strips by lot, which was extensively practised in parts of both meadows in more recent times, is probably an old one, but the earliest reference to it is dated 1443.[1] In the thirteenth century the strips in the first dole of Carun and the first dole of Cockfield in Lordsmead, as well as the first dole of Carun in Townsmead, must have been under continuous occupation, for in all the existing charters they are identified by quoting the two neighbouring owners.[2] In accordance with normal champion procedure both river meadows would have been open to those with common rights for pasturing as soon as hay was mown, i.e. at opentide. This was claimed by the rector in 1271–2 and allowed by the assize judge.[3]

[1] C139/146/12.

[2] T 83: 1 rood in the first dole of the demesne meadow of the fee of Kokfeld, between the meadow of William son of Adam son of Stephen and that late of Eustace the carpenter (*c.* 1260).

[3] JI 1/60, m. 7.

MEADOW IN THE DEMESNE

In 1580 (Map 3) there was a roughly triangular plot of about 20 acres lying to the south-west of Mercers' Wood and abutting south on the track then called Mill Lane End (now Perry Lane). The small stream that drained the high ground beyond the wood passed east to west through this plot on its way down to the village, where it became the Town Ditch. In those days it was valued as ley ground and was appropriately called Gore (a triangular piece) Leys,[1] but at an earlier date, possibly because the water supply was then more abundant, it was known as 'the meadow and pasture in le Pittel'. Thus described it was let on a four-year lease in 1312 for a yearly rent of about 4*s.* per acre nearly six times what arable land was fetching and thrice that of river meadow.[2] It was demesne of the principal manor and lay to the east of an arable piece called in those days Heldebyry, a name that connotes, as mentioned before, the site of an Anglo-Saxon fortified manor house. Le Pittel is probably an early form of pightle, a word whose origin is obscure[3] and which has been used in more recent years—like toft and croft—for a smallish piece of land attached to a house.[4] A characteristic of tofts and crofts was that they were managed by their holders as they thought fit and were not subject to village custom like the open fields. Le Pittel was in the same category. In 1271–2 the rector, when claiming common in all the meadows and pastures at opentide and in fallow, specifically excluded 'a place called Pitles'.[5] Le Pittel must have been the pightle of the Anglo-Saxon manor house.

THE COWPASTURE

The cowpasture was a somewhat scattered area of ley and grassland extending to about 100 acres[6] over which the lord and his tenants, both free and customary, had pasture rights. The only evidence for it in the medieval period is in a court roll of 1312, which records the leasing of one piece and three pieces of pasture in le Coumedewe for 21*d.* and 5*s.* respectively.[7] No information about pasture rights in that

[1] The northern half of the plot is still called Gower Leys.

[2] NRO *Ecton*, 1190, m. 1. In 1312 it was let off in two pieces of very dissimilar size, one at 3*s.* 6*d.*, the other—previously held by Margery de Carun—at 6 marks.

[3] *OED.*

[4] In 1185 Roger de Asterly held a toft and a croft of 21 acres at Saltfleetly (*British Acad. Records of Social and Economic History*, IX, 107).

[5] JI 1/60, m. 7.

[6] See p. 271.

[7] NRO *Ecton*, 1190, m. 1d.

period has come down to us, but in Elizabethan days two beasts could be pastured for each acre of pasture held or, in contemporary legal terms, the acre carried a double cow-common.[1]

THE MEADOW IN DOMESDAY

The observations given above on the meadows and cowpasture in medieval Sherington help to explain the Domesday return, which mentioned that although ten and potentially eleven plough-teams were at work the meadow would support only four of them. At first sight the discrepancy is striking and could indicate an acute shortage of fodder, but a more detailed examination shows that the position was not as unsatisfactory as might have been expected. Ideally, of course, each plough-team should have had its quota of meadow and the disproportion for Sherington with a ratio of 11:4 or 2·75 is greater than for any other village in north Buckinghamshire or north Bedfordshire.[2] Yet in the hilly south and in certain parts of the chalk region the disproportion was sometimes very much greater than this, showing that land graded as meadow was not essential for the local agricultural practice of the period.

If the Domesday return referred only to the river meadow (54 acres) the four plough-teams concerned had a quota per ox of 1·6 acres, raised to 2·2 acres if le Pittel (20 acres) be included. These values are within the limits set by Maitland (1 acre) on the one hand[3] and Fowler (3 acres) on the other.[4] Such theorizing, however, is largely beside the point, for what we have to explain is not how four but how eleven plough-teams would have fared under such conditions. The cowpasture was, of course, available, and the extent to which the three different grades of feed could have contributed is set out in Table 13. The quota for the lord's teams seems reasonable. The 22 villeins at Domesday had between them 6 plough-teams or 48 oxen, an average of about 2 oxen per head. The quota of Townsmead for these would have been about 1 acre, an amount that could well have formed part of the virgate of the day. The argument, however, is a little one-sided, because additional supplies

[1] One must distinguish between a cow-common in the cowpasture and common of pasture in the open fields, as the pasture rights were different, see pp. 230–2.

[2] Only 3 out of the other 35 villages in the Three Hundreds of Newport had a ratio of 2 or more: Hanslape (2·36), Wolverton (2·22) and Calverton (2·0). Eleven villages, 9 of them with long frontages to the Ouse, had the ideal ratio of 1:1.

[3] Maitland, *Domesday Book and Beyond*, p. 443.

[4] Fowler was quoting the views of Walter of Henley and other thirteenth-century writers ('Bedfordshire in 1086', Quarto Mem. *BHRS*, I, 61).

TABLE 13

Meadow and pasture for cattle

The Lord's demesne		Tenants' holdings	
Number of plough-teams	4	Number of plough-teams	7
Number of oxen	32	Number of oxen	56
Acres in Lordsmead (M)	23½	Acres in Townsmead (T)	30½
Acres in le Pittel (P)	*c.* 20	Acres in tenants' share of cowpasture (TC)	77
Acres in Lord's share of cowpasture (DC)	20		
M, acres per ox	0·73	T, acres per ox	0·5
M + P, acres per ox	1·36	T + TC, acres per ox	2·0
M + P + DC, acres per ox	2·0		

of feed could be got from the open fields and home closes, while there were other farm animals besides oxen to be catered for. On this latter point we have but one scrap of information, which comes from the justices valuation of the Carun estate in 1185. On a demesne of about 375 acres there were 24 oxen, 5 cows, 100 sheep and 5 pigs. Compared with the livestock density that called for stinting in 1682, admittedly under a three-course system of husbandry,[1] the extra burden in 1185 seems very light, suggesting that in the early middle ages it was a scarcity of livestock and not of food that held back the economy in Sherington.

THE WOODS

The woods in 1312 extended to 78 acres and were all in the demesne area. The evidence that le Hoo Park was assarted some time after Domesday has already been discussed, so that the total wood at the time of the inquest must have been at least 162 acres. As this provided panage for 100 swine the mean acreage per swine was 1·62 acres, in reasonable agreement with the 1·5 acres Fowler concluded was sufficient for one pig.[2]

THE WATER-MILL

Most of the villages in Bedfordshire and Buckinghamshire with direct access to the river Ouse had a mill at the time of Domesday. These river mills in their heyday before the coming of the windmills were a source of profit to the owners especially

[1] See pp. 230–2.

[2] Fowler, 'Bedfordshire in 1086', Quarto Mem. *BHRS*, I, 62–3. His estimate was based on statements made in a fine dated 1244, from which one can conclude that a pig needs an acre for common of pasture.

where, in addition to the normal revenue derived in grist and money from local inhabitants who owed socage to the mill or used it voluntarily, it could cater for those less favourably placed elsewhere. Sited as it was on the road coming in from Bedford to Newport Pagnell, the Sherington mill could have tapped much of the custom of those farming in the upland regions towards the Bedfordshire border. Neither Astwood nor Ekeney, for instance, had a stream, while Chicheley brook, which meanders through Hardmead before entering Chicheley itself, could have provided water for a very small mill only occasionally in the winter.

Although the Ousel or Lovat flows into the Ouse at Newport Pagnell the river below is sluggish and there would have been insufficient head of water at the Sherington mill for an overshot wheel, that is, one where the stream of water strikes it from above. The mill was undoubtedly undershot and was equipped with a battery of three paddle-wheels,[1] each of which would have had its lower part immersed in the water pouring from the mill pond. The heavy demand from customers outside the village must have led to this unusual development, which explains why the mill was rated in Domesday at 26*s*., a higher figure than for any other single mill in the county. It is probable that the rivulet which branches off just below the Chicheley brook and skirts what used to be the South Field of Sherington was the leat which fed water to the mill pond.

The history of the mill during the twelfth century still awaits full elucidation. The ownership of one half passed with the Cockfield fee in 1189, but at what time William son of Alexander or perhaps Alexander himself (see p. 91) became possessed of the other half is not known. It was William's nephew, also called William, son of Alexander, who was jointly concerned with Robert de Cockfield in 1241 about strengthening the mill pond.[2] When this latter William died in 1257 the subdivision of his half share among his four daughters and their heirs created many fractional holdings and Robert found it difficult to collect his numerous

[1] Evidence read in isolation might suggest that there had been three mills displayed along the river bank among the meadow lands. It is certain, however, that there was but one mill with three wheels, as the following references show (1) T. A47 (1252–60): ½ acre *ultra viam molendinorum*. (2) JI1/58, m. 6: Robert de Cockfield in 1262 summoned the heirs of William son of Alexander as his partners to repair the mills. (3) *BASRB*, IV, 106: one of William son of Alexander's heirs sells to John de Cave quarter of half of 3 mills. These observations are explicable only on the assumption that the word *molendinum* or *molinum* meant the wheel rather than the buildings, machinery and staff, as Fowler has pointed out in another context (*ibid.* I, 72).

[2] *BASRB*, IV, 79.

partners' share of the cost of repairs. The mill was still running in 1261–2[1] but within a decade or so the competition of new windmills in the vicinity[2] must have led to its being shut down, for in 1284–5 William's grandson, Richard de Shirford, was claiming a sixth part of the site of the mill in Sherington.[3] No trace of the mill or mill pond now remains, and for lack of evidence the small islands shown in Maps 2, 3 and 4 have been reproduced unchanged from the Enclosure map of 1797. It will be obvious, of course, that erosion and silting up must have brought about profound changes during the course of centuries.

[1] JI 1/58, m. 6; KB 26/165, m. 9d.

[2] The Tickford priory manor of Thickthorns in Chicheley included a windmill worth 21*s.* per annum in 1324–5; the water-mill at Tickford was then also in disrepair (*Dugdale Mon.* v, 203).

[3] JI 1/1247, m. 18d. It will be noticed that when the paddle-wheels have been removed the mill is referred to in the singular instead of the plural.

18

THE CHURCH AND ITS CLERGY IN THE THIRTEENTH CENTURY

WHEN the prior of Tickford won his case against John de Carun in 1229 he presented Master Thomas de Shirford, who was already in deacon's orders. Like his predecessor in office Thomas found it difficult to conform to the then prevailing rules about marriage of the clergy, a matter on which his diocesan the great Grossteste held very strong views. The rather sordid story is well described some years later when Henry de Shirford, his son by Hawisa the daughter of a Sherington land-owner William son of Alexander,[1] claimed the inheritance of his mother's freehold land.

The jury say on oath that the property was once in seisin of Hawisa, and later one Robert Curtfalur married her; further, she deserted her husband and followed one Master Thomas de Shirford, parson of the church of Sherinton, who kept her for a long time as his concubine and begot on her one Richard. Later, he married her in the chapel of St Martin at Ekeney (Hygeneye) and thereafter begot the Henry who now claims. But they say that at the time of the marriage Master Thomas had been promoted to the office of deacon. Also, Robert Grostest, then Bishop of Lincoln, had them both called before him and proceeded against Thomas *ex officio* on account of the marriage. Master Thomas solemnly purged himself of the charge brought against him by the bishop, and after such purgation kept her all his life. Asked whether Robert Curtfalur approached Hawisa during the time that Master Thomas kept her, they say no; and Henry, asked whose son he claimed to be, said he was son of Master Thomas.[2]

It is interesting to note that in spite of Grossteste's reprimand, and Thomas's light-hearted treatment of it, Henry was successful in his claim. Thomas died in 1259 and without any further protest from John de Carun the prior presented Master William de la Mare, whose various lawsuits over land in Sherington have already been discussed.[3]

[1] See p. 93.

[2] In 1294 Henry claimed 1 messuage and 41½ acres land, 1½ acres meadow and 2 acres pasture in Sherington as inheritance from his mother. (JI 1/1303, m. 25; Abbrev. Plac. Hil. 30 Ed. I: see also Table 3.) A prior claim by the elder son Richard in 1284 failed on the score of illegitimacy (JI 1/1247, m. 18d).

[3] See pp. 61–3.

On the death of Master William in 1281 Martin de Carun revived the old family claim to the right of presentation, but eventually let the case go by default and the prior nominated John de Luca in the usual way.[1] Nevertheless, Tickford was not to be concerned with the advowson for very much longer. Throughout the period in question the state of the priory was causing Sutton, the bishop of Lincoln, grave concern, largely because the prior Simon de Reda[2] was quite unfitted for his post and the monks were both unruly and lax in the keeping of their office. By custom the right of visitation and correction belonged to the abbot of Marmoutier, but in 1290 conditions at Tickford had become so notorious that Sutton as diocesan felt compelled to visit the place in person. He found it in a state of turmoil and on bidding the brethren meet him in the chapter-house the prior submitted, but three of his monks, including the subprior, insulted the bishop to his face and flatley refused to obey his orders or those of their own prior. Sutton accordingly ordered his registrar to excommunicate them on the spot.[3] His action, of course, was contrary to the privileges of the Cluniac order and the abbot complained to the pope. Delegates to inquire into the matter were duly appointed, who first removed Simon de Reda for incompetence and evil living and then arranged for the abbot and bishop to discuss their respective rights before appointing his successor. The two met in London during February 1291, when Sutton agreed that in future he would acknowledge the privileges of the abbot's order,[4] in return for which the abbot granted him the advowson of Sherington.[5]

In July of the same year Sutton commissioned Master Richard de Frideswide, the archdeacon of Buckinghamshire, to visit the priory with one of the canons of Lincoln and make certain that the necessary reforms were being introduced.[6] Richard, who had a house in Sherington[7] and must have known the neighbourhood well, seems to have treated the new prior Geoffrey Villicus with but scant courtesy if we may judge by the following incident. During or soon after his visit the prior

1 CP 40/38, m. 53.

2 Appointed 1270 (Archive du Depart. Indre et Loire, Série H, liasse 362).

3 *LRS*, xx, lxiii, 6.

4 *VCH Bucks*, IV, 362.

5 Grant by Bro. Geoffrey, prior of Tickford, with the consent of Dom Robert, abbot of the greater monastery of Tours, to Dom Oliver, bishop of Lincoln; advowson and presentation to church of Schrintone, with all rights in perpetuity; confirmed by abbot: London Feb. 1291 (Archive du Depart. Indre et Loire, Série H, liasse 362). In 1314–15 the bishop paid a fine of £10 to Edward II for confirmation of the grant (Abbrev. Rot. Originalia, I, 213).

6 *LRS*, XLVIII, 122, 125, 142.

7 He was licensed to have a private chapel in his house at Sherington (*LRS*, XLVIII, 71).

and monks impleaded him together with his assistant, Master Henry de Lisle, first in the court Christian and then in that of the Common Pleas at Westminster, for having committed some trespass.[1] He ignored the charge and the sheriff William de Turville was ordered to attach him. As he refused the service the sheriff, according to custom, ordered his bailiffs Walter Russel of Hoggeston and David de Hoggeston to distrain him by his beasts in the lay fee of Martin de Carun. These were returned to him later when he agreed to be attached, whereupon 'he publicly excommunicated the servants of the king of whatever rank and estate throughout the whole of Bucks who had been concerned with the seizure'. The sheriff, who himself came under the ban, addressed a pathetic appeal to the Council pointing out that he had done no more than carry out the king's orders, and begging the lord king to find a remedy.[2] The matter was referred to the king's bench, where the justices decided that business could not be determined without the presence of the archdeacon. It was thus once more the duty of the sheriff to attach the haughty churchman. What transpired this time is not recorded but the case illustrates the cumbrous and highly formalized legal procedure of the day.

John de Luca, the last of the rectors appointed by the priors of Tickford, was a privileged absentee who served as procurator to Percival de Lavagna, the archdeacon of Buckinghamshire, until the latter died in 1290, and then as a canon of London.[3] John himself died in 1301, and the bishop collated another absentee pluralist Adam de Ludford S.T.P.[4] who was succeeded in 1303 by Thomas de Luda, sometime treasurer of Lincoln.[5] The living was then worth 20 marks.[6]

[1] The action before the Common Pleas was filed in the name of the prior's attorney William de Tudenham (CP 40/91, m. 266).

[2] Selden Society, 57, 80.

[3] *LRS*, xx, 258, 262; xxxix, 167. Percival was the brother of Pope Adrian V and spent all his time in Rome. John de Luca's name suggests that he was of Roman origin.

[4] He had been rector of Aswardby, co. Lincoln, since 1273 (*LRS*, xx, 56).

[5] Linc. Reg. 2, m. 174.

[6] Nicholas Taxation, p. 34. It was worth only 10 marks in 1252 (W. E. Lunt, *Valuation of Norwich*).

19

SHERINGTON IN THE FOURTEENTH CENTURY

THE surviving evidence for the fourteenth century is adequate enough to indicate the main changes that occurred among the landowners and other people concerned, but is by no means as extensive as that for certain of the early periods discussed at length in previous chapters. It is, moreover, rather unevenly distributed throughout the years in question so that unless a careful balance is maintained minor events may receive undue emphasis: in Sherington, for instance, the dearth and pestilence of 1315–21 seems on first consideration to have had a more profound effect than that of the better known and much more destructive Black Death of 1349–50. Only minor changes, if any, occurred in the larger estates during the century under review, but the smallholders with their scattered strips were badly hit by both the calamities just mentioned and most of them lost what little land they possessed.

Sibyl, the deaf and dumb heiress of Roger de Carun, had married John de Burgh with the king's permission and he was given seisin of her father's lands when she came of age in 1313.[1] On his death without issue she took as her second husband Richard de Linford,[2] a member of a family from Great Linford that had gained knightly rank during the reign of Edward I.[3] The estate on which Richard and Sibyl lived uneventfully[4] was a small one for the squire of the principal manor, and for the rest of their lives it was burdened by the dower of one-third allotted to the widow Joan de Carun, who caused great trouble by wanton destruction of property.[5] She

[1] *Cal. Close*, 1313–18, 37.

[2] John witnessed a charter as lord of Sherington on 10 March 1323 (T A70) and Richard did likewise on 18 Oct. 1324 (T 248).

[3] Lawrence the son of Peter de Linford was page and later chamberlain to Sir Ralph Pipard of Great Linford, who had extensive estates elsewhere. Ralph settled on him the manor of East Harnham, Wiltshire, and various holdings in Derbyshire (*Tropenell Cart.* ed. Davies, II, *passim*; Jeayes, *Derbyshire Charters, passim*). His relationship to the Richard of Sherington, who had a younger brother of the same name, is unknown.

[4] Richard was a witness to thirteen Sherington charters dated between Oct. 1324 and May 1349. In 1343 he had licence to celebrate in the oratory of his mansion because of infirmity (Linc. Reg. 7, m. 174).

[5] In 1333 Richard and Sibyl impleaded her for wanton destruction; *inter alia* a byre had been

was still alive when they made a settlement of the manor in 1348,[1] but all three seem to have perished in the Black Death.

John de Linford the heir was able to take advantage of the havoc wrought among the smallholders during this time of pestilence. Various parcels of land seem to have been first acquired—probably with John's connivance—by Thomas de Reynes of Clifton Reynes and the collected property, described as a carucate of land held *in capite* for one-quarter of a knight's fee,[2] was then settled on John, royal permission being obtained for him to entail on himself and his heirs.[3] The enhanced size of the estate is reflected in the extent made at the inquisition held on John's death in 1360.[4]

The next heir, another John, was but 9 years old at the time of his father's death and thus became a ward of the king, who granted the wardship and marriage to one of his yeomen, Roger Grote of Calverton. Roger, although a friend of the Linford family, treated his perquisite of office—as was customary in those days—on a purely business basis and sold it at once to Henry Sterky, who in his turn assigned a rent charge of 18 marks per annum first to John Fitz Richard, the resident squire of Olney, and then to Ralph Basset of Drayton, who already owned the Grey–Cockfield manor in Sherington. The gross annual income of the estate could not have been much more than this, so that if Henry had retained—as was probable—

damaged to the value of 13*s.* 4*d.*, while ash trees worth 6*d.* each and apple trees worth 2*s.* each had been felled and sold. They were awarded £7 8*s.* 0*d.* damages, of which only £1 was recovered (CP 40/303, m. 80). Joan and her son Richard were also accused of forcibly taking away wheat, barley, oats, peas, beans, linen and woollen clothes to the value of 100*s.* (CP 40/305, m. 257).

[1] *Cal. Pat.* 1348–50, 99.

[2] C 143/318/1. By elimination one can deduce that the carucate was made up of the small properties listed below, totalling at least 93 acres land and 2 acres meadow, the owners of which were mentioned by name a few years before 1350 and never once after that date. As Henry de Shirford's and part of John Kenet's land derived directly from the small fee owned by William son of Alexander in the twelfth century (Table 3, see also p. 86, n. 2) the carucate could have been regarded as held *in capite*. John Kenet owned 24 acres land and ½ acre meadow in 1346–7 (*Cal. Close*, 1256–9, 371. CP 40/346/m. 108; 352, m. 419). Henry de Shirford owned 41½ acres land, 1½ acres meadow and 2 acres pasture in 1334, (Abb. Plac. Hil. 30 Ed. I; T 306). William Carpenter owned half a virgate in 1333 (T 305 and Table 7). John Palmer owned half a virgate in 1336 (T 312 and Table 7). Kenet, Carpenter and Palmer were the last representatives of old peasant families: Henry was the bastard son of a former parson of Sherington.

[3] *Cal. Pat.* 1354–8, 201. John had enfeoffed Hugh de Shirford, from whom he afterwards re-acquired it.

[4] C 135/149/12. Arable land in the demesne was rated at 6*d.* per acre. The rents of assize were returned as worth £4 10*s.* 0*d.* and deducting the value of the freehold rents (£1) the customary land must have been worth 70*s.* per annum, equivalent to 140 acres or almost 100 acres more than Sibyl de Carun owned in 1312. The total value of the estate was returned as £12 9*s.* 4*d.* (cf. Tables 9 and 10).

Linford of Sherington

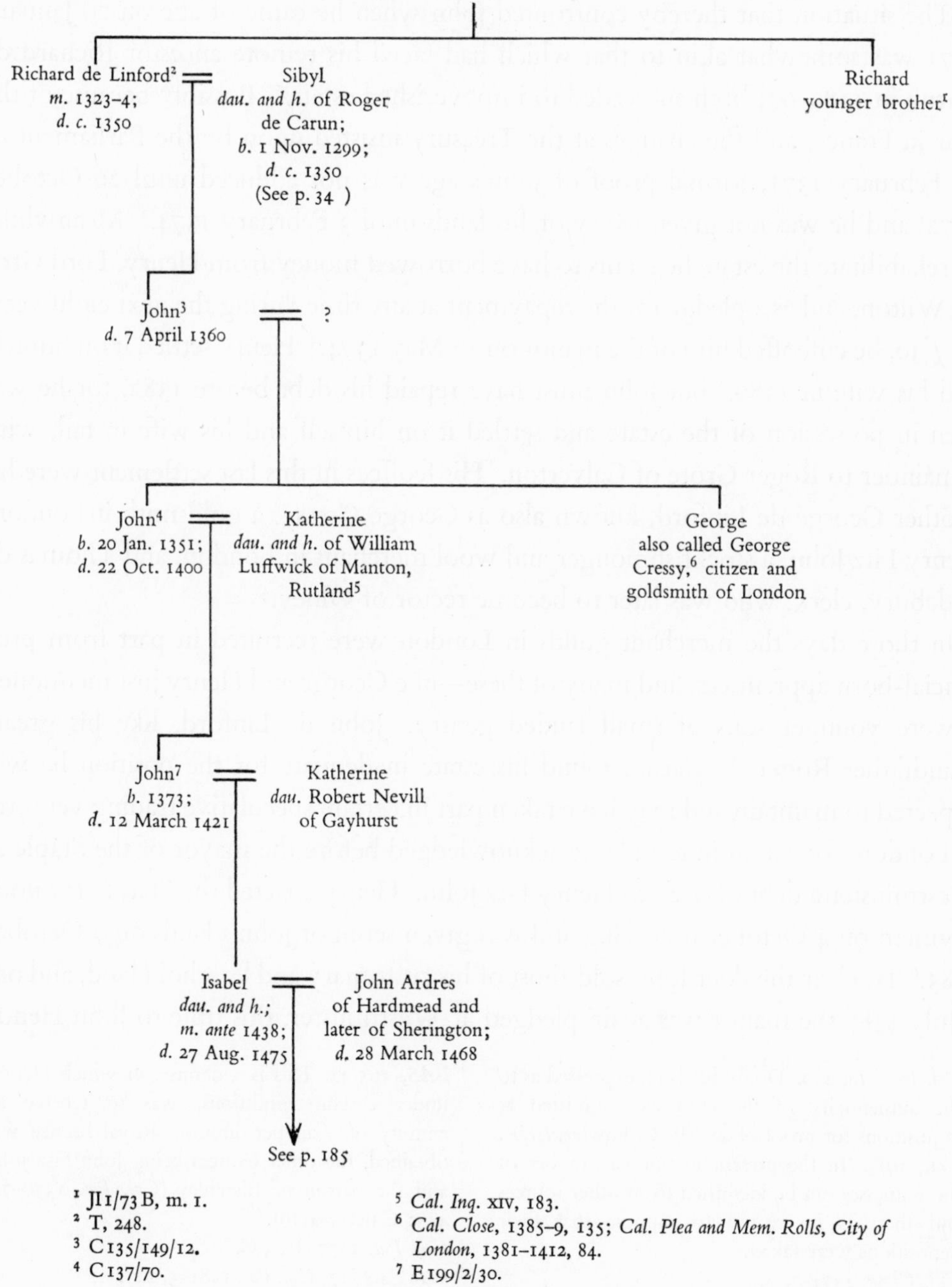

[1] JI1/73B, m. 1.
[2] T, 248.
[3] C135/149/12.
[4] C137/70.
[5] *Cal. Inq.* XIV, 183.
[6] *Cal. Close*, 1385–9, 135; *Cal. Plea and Mem. Rolls, City of London*, 1381–1412, 84.
[7] E199/2/30.

some small financial benefit to himself, the property, during the course of the twelve years minority, must have become badly denuded of most of its realizable assets.

The situation that thereby confronted John when he came of age on 20 January 1371 was somewhat akin to that which had faced his remote ancestor Richard de Carun in 1189–90; both succeeded to impoverished estates. Possibly because of the war in France, and the changes at the Treasury insisted upon by the Parliament of 27 February 1371, formal proof of John's age was not adduced until 26 October 1372[1] and he was not given livery of his lands until 3 February 1374.[2] Meanwhile, to rehabilitate the estate he seems to have borrowed money from Henry, Lord Grey de Wilton, and as a pledge for the repayment at any time during the next eight years of £40, he enfeoffed him of the manor on 12 May 1374.[3] Henry settled it on himself and his wife in 1380,[4] but John must have repaid his debt before 1382, for he was then in possession of the estate and settled it on himself and his wife in tail, with remainder to Roger Grote of Calverton. His feoffees in this last settlement were his brother George de Linford, known also as George Cressy, a goldsmith in London, Henry Fitz John, a stockfishmonger and wool merchant in London, and Thomas de Aldebury, clerk, who was later to become rector of Olney.[5]

In those days the merchant guilds in London were recruited in part from provincial-born apprentices, and many of these—like George and Henry just mentioned—were younger sons of small landed gentry. John de Linford, like his great-grandfather Roger de Carun, found his estate inadequate for the position he was expected to maintain and may have taken part in certain speculative trading ventures in London, for on 28 June 1382 he acknowledged before the mayor of the Staple at Westminster a debt of £21 to Henry Fitz John. Henry enacted the Statute for non-payment on 4 October following and was given seisin of John's lands on 7 October 1383.[6] To clear the debt John sold most of his customary and leasehold land, and on, 6 July 1387 the manor was again pledged at Westminster, this time to John Hende

[1] *Cal. Inq.* XIII, 210. Doubt has been expressed as to the authenticity of the evidence submitted at inquisitions for proof of age (R. C. Fowler, *EHR*, XXII, 101). In the present instance a number of the witnesses can be identified from other sources and there is no reason to suppose that their depositions were faked.

[2] *Cal. Close*, 1374–7, 8.

[3] *BAS*, 365/44. This is a demise, in which Henry, under certain conditions, was to receive an annuity of £20 per annum. Royal licence was obtained, the other feoffees being John Fitz John and the parson of Bletchley (*Cal. Pat.* 1370–74, 445; C143/384/19).

[4] *Cal. Pat.* 1377–81, 426.

[5] C143/400/17; *Cal. Pat.* 1381–5, 227.

[6] C131/29/3.

one of the leading citizens and drapers of London, who received seisin for non-payment a year later.[1] After judgement had been given against John in both of these pleas for debt his lands were extended, and the extents form the basis of the data collected in Table 14, which show how much of the rented land must have been sold between the two dates concerned. John de Linford and his brother George, with Roger Grote and Thomas de Aldebury, re-entered the manor in 1389 and ejected Hende, who thereupon sued them at the Newport Pagnell assizes and obtained a verdict in his favour.[2] The debt must have been paid off within a few years, for John died seised of the manor in 1401;[3] yet four years before this he had acknowledged a further debt of £16 to his neighbour John de Cave,[4] who had already become a citizen and draper of London.[5]

TABLE 14

Assize and farm rents in Linford manor

Date	Extent made for (1) Inquisition *post mortem*; (2) debt	Total value of estate £ *s.* *d.*	Rents of assize (A) or rents of assize and farm (F) £ *s.* *d.*
20 May 1360	(1)	12 9 4[a]	(A) 4 10 0
4 July 1383	(2)	10 0 7[b]	(F) 6 0 0
29 June 1388	(2)	5 6 8[c]	—
17 Oct. 1401	(1)	5 0 0[c]	—

[a] Demesne arable rated at 6*d.* per acre.
[b] Demesne arable rated at 2¾*d.* per acre.
[c] Total value given, no details.

The Linfords' distant cousins the Fitz Johns had a much less eventful life during the century under discussion. Roger, the first of the line, who died in 1313, was always described as Roger, son of John. His son Robert was likewise Robert, son of Roger, until 1340, when he adopted the surname le Fitz John.[6] As simple country

[1] C131/35/1.

[2] JI1/1505, m. 2.

[3] E149/78/1. The manor was valued at £5, but no details were given. In right of his wife, John also held the manor of Luffwick in Manton, Rutland, together with rents totalling 4 marks issuing from certain villages in the vicinity.

[4] *Cal. Close*, 1396–9, 87.

[5] CP40/539, m. 148d.

[6] As Robert son of Roger he was a witness to 50 Sherington charters dated between *c.* 1295 and 1340; he occurred once, in 1323, as Robert le Fitz Roger (T 244).

Fitz John of Hanslope and Sherington

John son of John of Hanslope *occ.* 1246–7[1] = Joan[2]

- John son of John of Hanslope[2] *occ.* 1271 = Isabel[3]
  - John son of John of Hanslope *occ.* 1280–1306 = Beatrice[3]
  - Agnes (1) widow of John de Carun *m. c.* 1272[5]; *d.* 1282 = Roger son of John of Hanslope and later of Sherington[4] *d.* 1313 = (2) Sibyl[6] *m. c.* 1282
    - Robert Fitz John[7] of Sherington *b.* 1287; *d. ante* 1351 = ?
      - John[11] *occ.* 1349; *d. ante* 1362 = Isabel[12] *alive* 1362
        - John[14] *d.* 1413 =
          - John[15] *b.* 1383; sold manor 1440 = Amicia[16] *alive* 1420
            - John[17] chaplain; *alive* 1479
      - Emma =
        - Isabel =
          - John Houghton = Joan[13] *d.s.p.* 1428
    - John[10]
    - Margery (1)[9] *alive* 1317 = Thomas[8] *d.s.p.* 1368 = (2) Joan *alive* 1346–7
  - Ralph son of John[18] *occ.* 1281

[1] JI 1/56, m. 37d.
[2] *ORS*, III, 17.
[3] CP 40/32, m. 14; *ibid.* 50, m. 6.
[4] T, 15; *Cal. Inq.* v, 207.
[5] JI 1/60, m. 12.
[6] JI 1/1303, m. 25.
[7] T, 78–366 *passim.*
[8] CP 40/346, m. 108, 148.
[9] T, 196.
[10] KB 27/282, m. 36.
[11] Add. 59280.
[12] CP 40/411, m. 310.
[13] CP 40/669, m. 437.
[14] CP 40/435, m. 387d; C 138/1/5.
[15] *Cal. Pat.* 1436–41, 367.
[16] CP 25(1) 22/117/7, 44.
[17] D/Ch/89/1.
[18] CP 40/41, m. 33.

gentlemen of very small estate the various members of the family come to notice only occasionally as mainpernors, feoffees, alnagers and collectors of taxes. Henry Fitz John, the stockfishmonger of London, belonged to the senior branch of the family settled in Hanslope.[1]

The Cave family, who inhabited the moated manor house, maintained for the first few decades of the fourteenth century the tradition of service to the state set by its forebears. From 1292 onwards the property had been held in dower by Dame Sibyl de Cave, and at her death the eldest son John, rector of Narborough, settled it in 1318 on his third brother Richard, who had probably been born in the manor house soon after his parents migrated south from Yorkshire in 1270.[2] At the time this occurred Richard held office as king's yeoman, and ten years before that he had been given the custody of the lands of his neighbour Robert Dakeney of Lathbury, Buckinghamshire, and Cainho, Bedfordshire,[3] which he treated in the same ruthless way as had Roger Grote in the instance cited above.[4] On succeeding to the Sherington estate Richard was nominated sheriff of Bedfordshire and Buckinghamshire for 1319–20,[5] and in the autumn Parliament of 1320 he became one of the two burgesses for Bedford borough.[6]

The war that broke out in the following year led to much confusion, and both Richard and his brother Roger of Chicheley had to petition the king for restitution of their lands, which had been seized on information that they were with his contrarients at Kingston.[7] In due course the sheriff certified that Richard had been with the bishop of Ely for the defence of the isle of Ely and that Roger had worn the robes of the bishop of Lincoln.[8] Richard next attended the Parliament at York in November 1322,[9] wherein it was agreed that every township should furnish for the prosecution of the war one man at arms to serve for 40 days. The commissioners appointed for Buckinghamshire returned that Richard himself was an esquire accustomed to arms, but that his lands in the county were worth no more than 100*s*. per annum.[10]

1 C47/2/41.

2 See p. 85.

3 *Cal. Fine*, 1307–19, 294. The widow took one-third of the value of the land in dower and Richard was given the other two-thirds—extending to £9 15*s*. 8*d*.—until the full age of the heir Roger, at a rent of £12 per year.

4 Robert Dakeney's executors were claiming £14 illegally detained (CP 40/300, m. 355d; 304, m. 222d; 306, m. 278d).

5 *Cal. Fine*, 1307–19, m. 398.

6 *Parl. Writs*, II(3), 652.

7 *Cal. Fine*, 1317–27, 82. *Rot. Parl.* I, 398, 414.

8 *Cal. Close*, 1318–23, 451.

9 *Parl. Writs*, I, 221. His wages were 2*s*. per day.

10 *Parl. Writs*, II(3), 652. This was substantially true, see Table 10.

He was, accordingly, not liable for distraint for knighthood. He represented the borough once again at the Parliament of March 1329 held at Winchester[1] and a few months later went abroad with the king.[2] On his return he was granted the usual reward for good service over a number of years, namely exemption from being put on assizes, juries, etc., and from being appointed sheriff, coroner, etc.[3] He was back in Parliament again between 1333 and 1335[4] and during these years the manor was let to the bishop of Lincoln.[5]

Richard's son, John, like his contemporary neighbour the first John de Linford, seems to have led the quiet uneventful life of a small country squire, but there is record of one incident that must have caused him grave concern at the time. The date was 1353, when the exchequer was still experiencing the dire effects of the Black Death, but the story goes back many years before then and shows that Richard, the father, had been guilty of an opportune yet none the less scandalous fraud during the very critical period of February 1327 when Edward II was still alive and his son had just been chosen king.

Before he was made sheriff in 1318 Richard had been for some years the collector of the tenth when this was granted to Edward II, and in 1327 the exchequer claimed of him £48 for arrears. Richard successfully petitioned the new king to be allowed to offset this sum against a bill on the wardrobe for the financial year 1317–18 amounting to £70 14*s.* 4½*d.* and certified by the keeper, the bishop of Coventry and Lichfield. The bill covered his wages and robes as a king's yeoman, his expenses outside the court and the cost of two horses that died while he was using them in the king's service.[6] It was not until some years later that the exchequer became aware that Richard's bill was a fabrication[7] and in Trinity Term 1333 the king recovered the full sum against him.

For some reason the claim was not pressed during Richard's lifetime, and it was not until October 1352, when the exchequer was driven by its needs to rake up all possible dormant claims that any action was taken. John, the son, then attended before the barons of the exchequer to complain that he was being sorely distrained by the sheriff of Buckinghamshire for £43 13*s.* 4*d.* in land and tenements that had

[1] *Cal. Close*, 1330–3, 138.

[2] *Cal. Pat.* 1327–30, 388.

[3] *Cal. Pat.* 1327–30, 470.

[4] *Return: Members of Parliament*, I, 102, 104, 106.

[5] CP40/303, m. 122d; 304, m. 34d; 305, m. 16d.

[6] *Rot. Parl.* II, 434–5; *Cal. Close*, 1327–30, 9.

[7] G. Herbert Fowler, *Rolls of the Office of Sheriff of Beds and Bucks*, 1332–4 (County Museum, Aylesbury, 1929), p. 35, no. 53.

belonged to his father.[1] In defence he stated that when his father incurred the debt in 1327 he did not own any land except in fee tail and in support he showed John de Cave's fine of 1318, by which the Sherington estate was settled on Richard and his issue and in default to Richard's brothers Thomas, Robert and Roger for life, with remainder to the heirs of John. Richard was thus seised during his lifetime; John had inherited and held in tail. No land or goods had come into his hands as executor and he begged that the distraint against him might be lifted. An inquisition held on 16 July 1353 confirmed that Richard held only in tail and judgement was accordingly given in John's favour.[2] As mentioned earlier,[3] John must have been grateful to his uncle for having arranged that his father should never become possessed of the fee simple.

John de Cave, the grandson—like so many of his contemporaries—was attracted to commerce in London and became a draper there. He did not return to Sherington on succeeding to the family estate and the manor house was let to Richard Buckingham, the farmer of the subsidy on cloth for the county of Northampton.[4]

The small manor obtained by John de Grey and settled on his daughter Joan when she married Ralph Basset of Drayton in 1304 passed to the grandson, another Ralph, on whose death without issue in 1390 it reverted under the terms of the settlement to John's great-grandson Henry Grey de Wilton.[5] Ralph's property was extensive and much of it entailed by settlement in favour of Thomas, earl of Stafford, and Thomas de Beauchamp, earl of Warwick. A sealed chest containing all the evidences of his estate had been deposited with the abbot of Lavendon by Ralph on 1 October 1386, and after his death in 1390 the abbot refused to allow any one of the three beneficiaries to open it. They accordingly summoned him to show cause before the justices of the Common Pleas in Easter Term 1391. The abbot's attorney attended on his behalf and with some display of ceremony had the chest brought into court and placed before the justices. He first drew their attention to the seals, which were unbroken, and then begged that the chest might be opened in their presence so that if debate or controversy arose as to its contents they could make a decision forthwith. After an adjournment till the following Easter Term, so as to allow all interested parties to be represented, the chest was duly opened in court and its contents

[1] It must have been agreed at the exchequer in 1327 that Richard owed £43 13*s.* 4*d.* and that he was owed £68 (see p. 128, n. 7).

[2] E13/78, m. 26, 37d.

[3] See p. 85.

[4] *Cal. Close*, 1385–9, p. 602. E199/2/1.

[5] See p. 75.

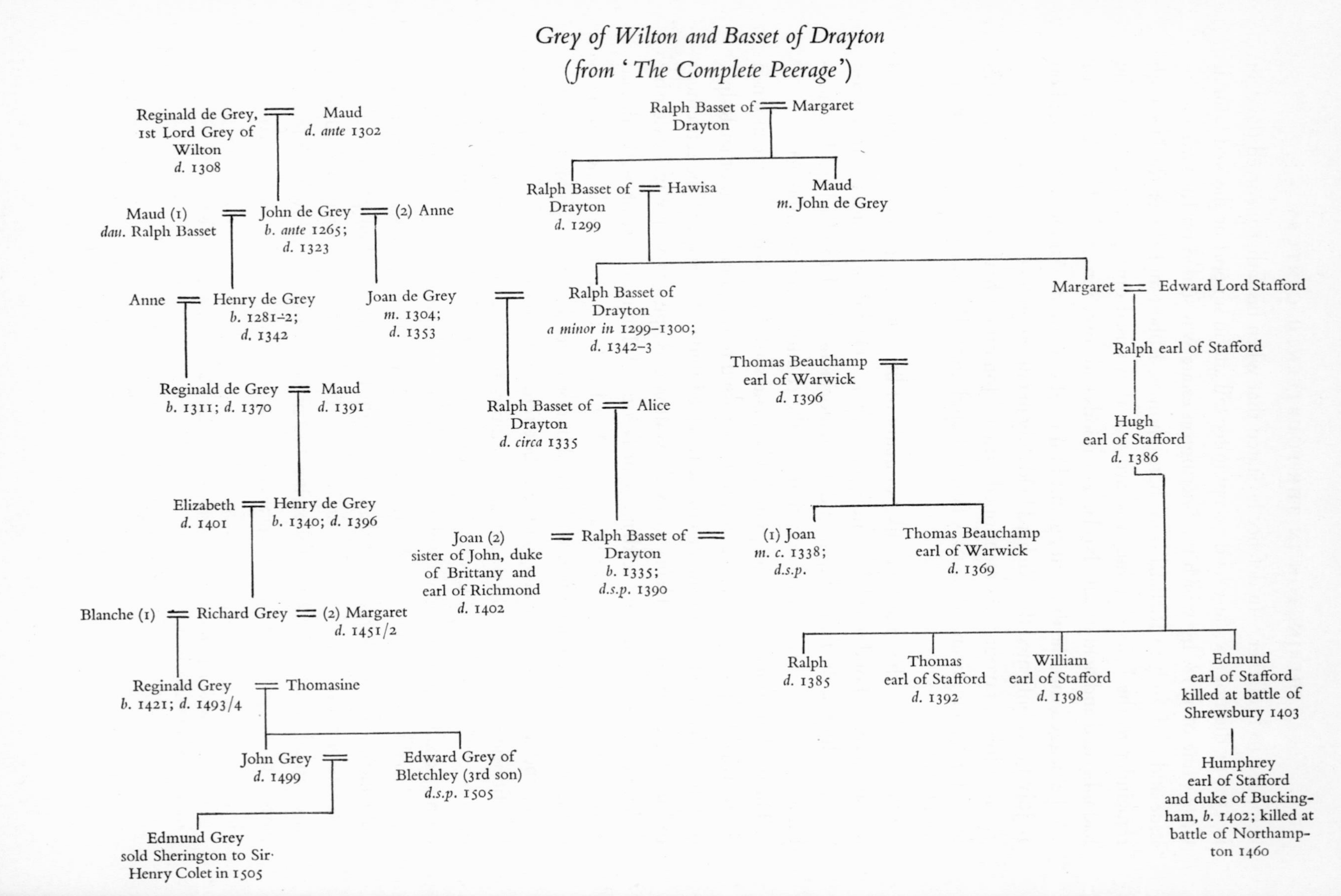
Grey of Wilton and Basset of Drayton
(from 'The Complete Peerage')
Reginald de Grey, 1st Lord Grey of Wilton d. 1308
Maud d. ante 1302
Ralph Basset of Drayton
Margaret
Maud (1) dau. Ralph Basset
John de Grey b. ante 1265; d. 1323
(2) Anne
Ralph Basset of Drayton d. 1299
Hawisa
Maud m. John de Grey
Anne
Henry de Grey b. 1281–2; d. 1342
Joan de Grey m. 1304; d. 1353
Ralph Basset of Drayton a minor in 1299–1300; d. 1342–3
Margaret
Edward Lord Stafford
Ralph earl of Stafford
Thomas Beauchamp earl of Warwick d. 1396
Reginald de Grey b. 1311; d. 1370
Maud d. 1391
Ralph Basset of Drayton d. circa 1335
Alice
Hugh earl of Stafford d. 1386
Elizabeth d. 1401
Henry de Grey b. 1340; d. 1396
Joan (2) sister of John, duke of Brittany and earl of Richmond d. 1402
Ralph Basset of Drayton b. 1335; d.s.p. 1390
(1) Joan m. c. 1338; d.s.p.
Thomas Beauchamp earl of Warwick d. 1369
Blanche (1)
Richard Grey
(2) Margaret d. 1451/2
Ralph d. 1385
Thomas earl of Stafford d. 1392
William earl of Stafford d. 1398
Edmund earl of Stafford killed at battle of Shrewsbury 1403
Reginald Grey b. 1421; d. 1493/4
Thomasine
John Grey d. 1499
Edward Grey of Bletchley (3rd son) d.s.p. 1505
Humphrey earl of Stafford and duke of Buckingham, b. 1402; killed at battle of Northampton 1460
Edmund Grey sold Sherington to Sir Henry Colet in 1505

distributed—but not before a copy of every charter in it had been engrossed on the plea roll.[1] Henry recovered the Sherington manor, one-third of which he allowed Ralph's widow to retain as dower.[2] On his own death in 1396 the other two-thirds went to his widow Elizabeth,[3] who died at Lavendon abbey in 1401. The Basset holding of 50 acres in le Hoo Park, which was part of the settlement on the earl of Stafford, together with 10*s.* rent from the Grey manor, had already been granted for life to John Billing.[4]

TABLE 15

Chronological distribution of Throckmorton charters

	Sherington	Weston Underwood	Olney
Undated or before 1295	27	47	13
1295–1304	10	7	1
1305–14	12	6	5
1315–24	39	18	21
1325–34	7	13	5
1335–44	5	14	3
1345–54	3	23	1
1355–64	1	7	1
1365–74	1	8	—
1375–84	4	5	—
1385–94	—	2	—

It will be clear from all that has been said above that in spite of the various changes in ownership the larger estates in Sherington remained more or less intact throughout the whole of the fourteenth century. The smaller holdings, however, suffered in some cases severe depredation, for the peasant owners were less able to withstand the impact of the famine years 1315–21 and of the Black Death in 1349–50. The Throckmorton charters for Sherington, Olney and Weston Underwood provide indirect yet none the less convincing evidence for the unhappy effect of the dearth and pestilence in the first of these periods. With but few exceptions they deal with the sale or exchange by local peasants of a few strips in the open fields, and their

[1] CP40/521, m. 441. Henry de Grey claimed 10 messuages, 3 tofts and 6 virgates land, 8 acres meadow, 6 acres pasture, 40 acres wood and 40*s.* rent with appurtenances in Sherington (cf. p. 75, n. 4). The chest contained the marriage settlement of 1304 (*ibid*, n. 5).

[2] CP40/538, m. 285d. E149/80/1.

[3] E136/18/12. Essex County Records D/DVo/13.

[4] E149/56/2. C136/107/46. C137/38/41. E136/18/8.

chronological distribution (Table 15) shows that in all three villages, especially Sherington, there was great activity in the decade 1315–24. The first two of these years, with 1321, were famine years and the price of wheat rose to an unprecedented height. In addition, there was a heavy loss of cattle from a virulent murrain, so that the peasant who relied exclusively on agrarian toil for his livelihood was hard hit and many were forced to sell out to those more favourably placed. Thirty-nine Sherington charters for this critical period have survived, and as the data set out in Table 16 show, they are concerned very largely with the two local families of Smith and Brittain.

TABLE 16

Throckmorton charters for Sherington

Classification of charters	1315–19 No. of charters	1315–19 Total acreage	1320–24 No. of charters	1320–24 Total acreage
Smith alias Ellot family	6	2½	6	2½
Brittain family	9	5	8	4¾
All charters	21	9⅓	18	8¼

Every village had its smithy, consequently when surnames first came into general use one or more families in each place could have adopted that of Smith. This seems to have been the case in Sherington where, by the end of the thirteenth century, there were many bearing that surname who were not necessarily blood relatives. Ralph, son of Simon le Smith (p. 134), possibly to avoid confusion with others of the same name in the vicinity, was often referred to as Ralph Ellot, and it was his son, described before 1322 as John, son of Ralph le Smith, and afterwards as John Ellot who was buying land in Sherington during the decade 1315–24.[1] Of typical peasant stock, John had inherited about 8 acres in the open fields, and it was probably the additional support of his smithy that enabled him to hold his own in the crisis years and acquire land from his less fortunate neighbours. He purchased another acre in one rood lots between 1330 and 1333 and the whole property[2] passed to his son John Ellot about

[1] The donors were Henry Dayrel, Nicholas Coyt, Ralph Cous, Roger le Brit and John Gille, all members of peasant or smallholder families.

[2] The 35 Smith–Ellot charters preserved at Coughton make a cartulary of the property (14½ acres land, ½ acre pasture and ½ acre meadow), which consisted of 38 strips scattered among 24 furlongs.

1346, who conveyed it on 26 May 1349, at the height of the Black Death, to Roger Tyringham of Tyringham.[1]

The Brittain family (le Bretun, Brittoun, le Brit, Brut)[2] held a few strips of land at the end of the thirteenth century and during the years 1315–24 various members of it acquired between them about 10 acres.[3] The holding[4] of a branch using the spelling le Brut was inherited later by Margery the sister of Henry Brut, who conveyed it in 1365 to Thomas de Reynes[5] and others as feoffees for Roger de Tyringham. In all, therefore, some 23–24 acres of land that had been in peasant ownership for generations became part of the Tyringham estate, which was thereby increased to about 100 acres of land.[6]

The Black Death in its turn seems to have been primarily responsible for the creation by consolidation of one other medium sized property besides the Linford carucate mentioned above. During 1350 and the years following John de Cave acquired from various sources about 23–25 acres of land which was largely of peasant origin. He transferred these in 1381 to John Olney of Weston Underwood.[7]

Directly or indirectly the Black Death was thus responsible for the transfer of some 120–130 acres of land from peasant ownership to one or other of the existing larger estates. Internal consolidation, nevertheless, was not the only process that was changing the land distribution in the village as the century progressed: new men with money available from commerce were buying their way in.

Sherington was close to the market town of Newport Pagnell and not very far away from the more important one of Stony Stratford. Both boroughs would have acted as exchange centres for the surrounding villages and as they were on roads

[1] T 363, 364, 365.

[2] It has not been possible to construct a complete pedigree of this family.

[3] Geoffrey le Brittoun, 4 acres; John and Nicholas his sons, 3¾ acres; John son of Ralph le Brut, 1½ acres; Simon le Brut, ½ acre. The donors were Tho. Richer, Nicholas Coyt, John Cous, William Bouchmaler, Alice Mason, Ralph Dayrel, Richard Richer and Peter le Somenour, all smallholders.

[4] The Throckmorton muniments contain 41 charters of this family. Margery's holding would appear to have been about 8 acres land and ½ acre meadow (cf. JI 1/1477, m. 47).

[5] T A 114, 412.

[6] In 1405 Alice, widow of John Tyringham, claimed dower in 1 carucate of land in Sherington (CP 40/578, m. 362 d).

[7] The property consisted of 4 acres from John Trop, which had been purchased during 1315–25 by Richard Trop and Alice his wife from Ralph le Smith, Alice's father and John, son of Alexander, son of Adam; 7 acres from William le Eyr, who had acquired them from John Stachedone; 2–3 acres from John Jory and all the land that John de Cave had inherited in 1346 on the death of his uncle Thomas de Cave, rector of Woughton-on-the Green (T 464; CP 25(1) 29/94/5). Trop, Jory and Stachedone represent old smallholder families that do not seem to have survived the Black Death.

Smallholders in Sherington

(From Throckmorton Charters and various Plea Rolls; dates denote occurrence)

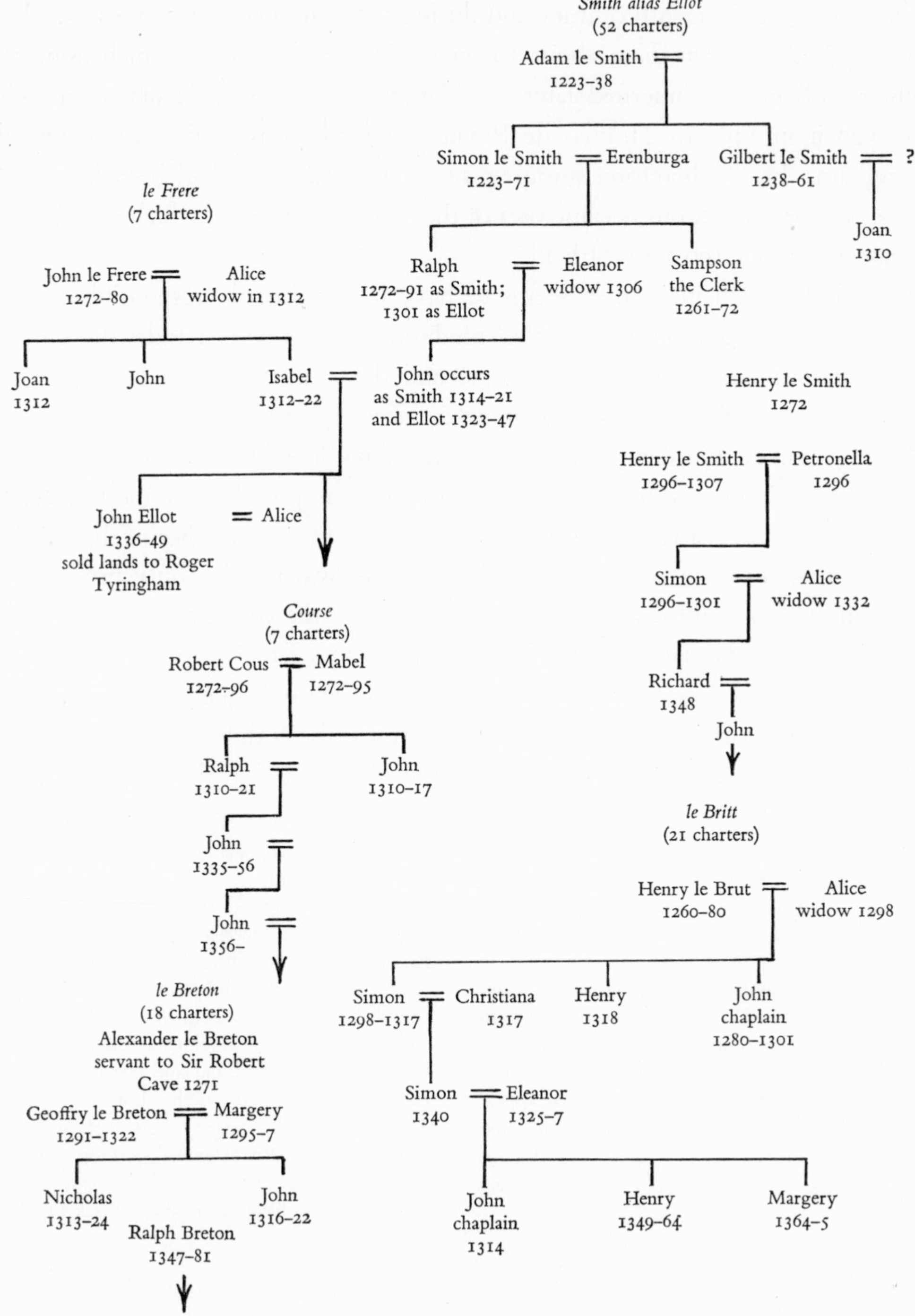

leading from London to the north as well as on a route from the west Midlands to Norwich and the East Anglian ports, they would have been convenient stopping places not only for itinerant traders but also for the middlemen who linked the village producer with the merchant in the city or port. Two of these middlemen, who were active for two or three decades after 1340, eventually became established in Weston Underwood and Sherington respectively.

John le Barker of Olney,[1] a merchant dealing chiefly in wool, amassed a considerable fortune with which he acquired the Nowers manor in Weston Underwood. Sometime between 1364 and 1368 he changed his name to John Olney of Weston Underwood,[2] and as such both he, his son, another John, and his grandson Robert were parties to various transactions concerning the Cave and Fitz John land in Sherington.[3]

John de Chebenhale[4] was a middleman merchant who dealt at Newport Pagnell and Stony Stratford on a smaller scale than John Barker, with whom he was in some form of partnership in 1351–3.[5] He is first mentioned in connexion with Sherington in 1339,[6] and from then until 1366 he comes to notice from time to time when he sues or is being sued for trade debts.[7] The Plea Roll entries concerning these complaints seldom mention more than that money was owing to the plaintiff, but occasionally the case is quoted at some length and we are given a glimpse of the matter in dispute. In 1358, for instance, Robert Baronn called upon John de Chobenhale to account for monies received during the year ending Michaelmas 1357, the amount being quoted as £40 for merchandise and profit and 100 marks in money

[1] A John le Barker of Weston Underwood occurs in 1315 (see p. 72, n. 6) so that the name had become hereditary and did not imply that the holder followed the trade of a tanner.

[2] See *VCH Bucks*, IV, 498. The change of name suggested there is amply supported by evidence from the Throckmorton muniments.

[3] Margaret, the daughter and heiress of Robert Olney the grandson, married Thomas Throckmorton of Coughton, Warwick, and it is through this connexion that such a fine collection of early charters for Weston Underwood and Sherington is now preserved at Coughton Court.

[4] The name is taken from a hamlet within the parish of Fressingfield, Suffolk. The first syllable was usually written with an 'o' in lawsuits at Westminster and with a 'u' in local Buckinghamshire affairs. Contraction to the disyllabic Chibnall occurred around 1400, the first syllable being written indiscriminately with i, u or y respectively.

[5] John de Chobenhale of Shrynton and John Barker of Olney, by their attorney, put themselves the fourth day against Thomas Shepeherde of Shrynton and John Frere of Shrynton in a plea that each of them render their account for the time they received the monies of the said John de Chobenhale and John Barker (CP 40/367/m. 157; 370, m. 81d; 375, m. 146).

[6] In 1339 Ralph Basset of Drayton sued John for trespass in the court of common pleas (CP 40/320, m. 339) as well as the king's bench (KB 27/319, m. 73d, *passim* to 325, m. 101).

[7] CP 40/342, m. 348d; 343, m. 332d; 345, m. 173; 371, m. 4, 237; 395, m. 214; 396, m. 270; 399, m. 200; 402, m. 202; 419, m. 7d; 425, m. 219; 421, m. 321.

due from John Barbour of Stony Stratford.[1] Likewise in 1364 Alice, widow of John Stretche, sued John de Chubbenhale of Shryngton for £60 damages arising out of a transaction in which, at the request of John de Newport, clerk, he had invested £50 for him in cloth of gold, garments and six sacks of wool.[2] As a side-line John acted as parson's bailiff to the absentee rector, John de Wye,[3] during 1343–6.[4] He is first described as of Sherington in 1351, and in 1364 he purchased a small estate of 100 acres held in knight's service under the Grey–Cockfield manor[5]—a typical franklin's holding that was to be retained by his descendants for several hundred years.

The dispersal of the Linford open-field arable lands[6] in the period 1383–88 brought

[1] CP 40/394, m. 155, 395, m. 29d; 396, m. 146; 398, m. 43, 94; 396, m. 17; 400, m. 21d.

[2] CP 40/417, m. 149d; 418, m. 222; 419, m. 47; 421, m. 267; 424, m. 205.

[3] The sequence of rectors was as follows: Thomas de Luda (p. 120) resigned in 1309 and William de Beby was collated on 1 Jan. 1310 (Linc. Reg. 2, 183). Sometime before 1326 he was replaced by Master Walter de Staurence (Linc. Reg. 4, 336d), a prebendary and later archdeacon of Stow. He resigned during 1329 and the bishop collated John de Wye (Linc. Reg. 4, m. 336d), who was given leave to lease the church in 1332 and to be absent for 3 years in 1343 during which time William Cranfield, Chaplain, was in charge (Linc. Reg. 5, 131; 7, 100, 137d). Walter de Farndale, who succeeded John on 18 Nov. 1361, exchanged benefices in 1379 with William atte Crosse, who remained rector until 1401 (Linc. Reg. 9, m. 321d; 10, m. 445d).

[4] As such he claimed £7 10*s*. 0*d*. from three residents in Filgrave and two in Tyringham during 1343 (CP 40/335, m. 195d). Presumably they were farming the glebe or had refused to pay tythe arising from holdings in Sherington.

[5] 'John de Chubbenhale of Schryngton gave the king half a mark for licence to concord with Richard Goneyre and Margery his wife concerning a plea of covenant of tenements in Shryngton' (CP 40/417, m. 228). The fine is not preserved at the PRO. As the name Goneyre is otherwise unrecorded in Sherington the land was probably an inheritance of the wife Margery. No account rolls of the Basset of Drayton property have come to light, but as mentioned earlier (p. 74) the freehold rents totalling 38*s*. acquired by John de Grey in 1286 were worth the same sum when they came into the possession of the Mercers' Company in 1509 (Table 6). The 100 acres held by the Chibnalls in knight's service paid 29*s*. 6*d*. per annum to the Mercers and ½*d*. per annum to the lord of the principal manor. The holding must therefore have included the virgate described as follows in the Carun Court Roll of 1312 'Gilbertus filius Ricardi tenet unam virgatam terre per homagium et scutagium et servicium libre unius cumini et reddit per annum domino Radulfo Basset 20*s*.'. The individual rents and services of the other three virgates are not known: their total rent must have been 9*s*. 6*d*.

[6] These consisted of 31 acres (Table 1) and the carucate (93 acres land, 2 acres meadow) acquired in 1353. No details of Tho. Grendon's purchase have survived and the acreage listed below is the one his descendants disposed of in 1549.

Holding	Land (acres)	Pasture (acres)	Meadow (acres)	Reference
Tho. Grendon	81	6	2½	Chester deed dated 7 March 1588
Predecessor of Tho. Colyns	26	6	2	Recovery 1 Hen. 7.
Roger Brown	15	2	1	C 143/387/9 *Cal. Pat.* 1374–7, 197
Total	122	14	5½	

TABLE 17

Holders of land in Sherington c. 1400

Numbers shown thus, 40*, are not included in the area shown on Map 8; the direction in which they lie is indicated on the map.

			Demesne		Open fields			
No. on Map 8	Owner	Messuages	Pasture (a.)	Arable (a.)	Non-demesne and home closes (a.)	Arable (a.)	Meadow (a.)	Wood (a.)
188	John Linford	1	38	180	—	—	8	—
	John Billing (for life)	—	50	—	—	—	—	—
127	Thomas Grendon	4	—	—	6	81	2¼	—
89	John Cave	4	47	—	8	125	8	—
	John Olney	—	—	—	—	23	—	—
	John Colyns	—	6	—	—	26	2	—
	William Huet	1	2	—	—	15	1	—
182	John Fitz John	2	—	136	—	156	8	40
161	Richard Grey of Wilton	7	20	19	5	112	11½	40
	John Tyringham	3	26	—	½	76	4	8
157	John Chibnall	1	—	—	5	104	3	—
40*	John Coyt	—	—	—	—	20	—	—
	— Barker, late James de La Mote	—	—	—	—	18	3	—
	Remainder of Grey manor freeholds	3	—	—	—	38[a]	—	—
	Remainder of Linford manor freeholds	4	—	—	—	14[a]	—	—
138	Delapre abbey	1	—	—	8	40	2	—
	Tickford priory	2	—	12	—	10	—	—
179	Rector's glebe and rectory	1	4½	—	—	15	1¾	—
		34	191½	347	32½	897	54¾	88

[a] These may duplicate other items.

three newcomers to the village: Thomas Grendon, whose descendants were leading yeomen during the next 150 years; Roger Brown, whose holding passed to William Huet; and the predecessor of the Thomas Colyns who sold his land to Richard Maryot in 1486. Table 17 lists the holders of land about the year 1400.

TABLE 18

Lay subsidy return for Sherington in 1332[a]

	s. d.		s. d.
de Ricardo Lymford	2 10	de Nicholea Stagedon	18
de Ricardo de Cave	3 4	de Juliana Herman	11
de Roberti filio Rogeri	2 10	de Alicia uxore Simonis le Smyth	18
de Johanne de Dounton	2 0	de Johanne Trop	12
de Emme Jory	3 0	de Johanne Longe	14
de Thoma filio Rogeri	2 0	de Simone Britt	12
de Willelmo Golde	2 4	de Johanne Masoun	20
de Willelmo le Carter		de Andrea C...	8½
de Rogero Britt	13½	de Willelmo Rycher	8½
de Thoma filio Katrine	10	de Johanne Palmer	2 0
de Willelmo Gerveys	10	de Johanne Frere	11
de Gervasio Stouton	12	de Radolfi Gunnyld	10
de Alicia Trop	10	de Johanne filio Rad...	16
de Alicia uxore Gilberti	20	de Simone Jones	8½
de Margeria Corage	10	[4 names undecipherable]	
de Johanne Stagedon	20		

[a] E 179/242/84/5.

There is no information about the variation in land values during the century under review: such data as we have was compiled for fiscal purposes and followed a stock pattern.[1] It is to be noted, however, that following the general trend in the country the Linford demesne lands were being leased.[2] Farm rents first appear in 1383 (Table 14), when John de Linford was engaged on business in London and was probably spending much of his time away from home. Of the 180 acres he is recorded as holding in demesne only 38 acres were sown with spring and winter corn.[3] On a two-field system of cropping an equal area would be lying fallow; one can thus deduce that the other 100 acres or so had been leased.

Most of the changes discussed in the present chapter emphasize the slow worsening

[1] In inquisitions *post mortem* the demesne lands were rated at 6*d*. per acre and meadow between 1*s*. 4*d*. and 3*s*. 4*d*. per acre. In extents for debt much lower values were quoted.

[2] Leasing of the open-field arable land was not unknown at an earlier date. In the Carun Court Roll for 1312 two of the four small parcels of land dealt with were leased for five years: the other two were let for the same short period but at will. The manor was then in the king's hand and short terms were understandable.

[3] Sixteen acres of arable land sown with corn, worth 2*s*. per acre; 20 acres of arable land sown with barley, worth 2*s*. per acre and 2 acres peas worth 12*d*. per acre (C 143/29/3).

of the position of the free peasants as the century progressed. Many of the older families listed in Table 7—Sweyn, Ruffus, Damisel, Gray, Blund and Franceis—had moved off elsewhere or had died out before the dearth and pestilence of 1315–21. They had been replaced by others, but not all the additions in Table 18 represent new families, for many of those in the earlier list had been using at that time a name denoting nothing more than a family relationship, e.g. Richard, son of Gervase, would have become Richard Gerveys. The decade 1315–24 was a hard one, but the peasants survived and it was the Black Death of 1349–50 which took such a heavy toll of them. At least twelve families seem to have been affected.[1] The land of these and many other peasants passed into the hands of those with larger estates, but there is no reason to suspect that as a class the peasants thereby became unduly impoverished. The Subsidy Roll for 1332 (Table 18) may be useless as a guide to individual wealth, but the sums paid by the peasants show that however unrealistic the incidence of the tax they were able to bear an impost of the same order as that of the local lords of the manor. They must have come to rely more and more on the produce and profit of their tenant lands or on additional money earned by some form of local trade. It is certain that by the turn of the century they had but little land of their own—no more than we shall find their descendants possessed during the reign of Henry VIII, when detailed records once more become available.

[1] Last date noted in brackets: Adam (1349), Bouchmaler (1340), Carpenter (1333), Copshot (1335), Courage (1342), Dayrel (1349), Gerveys (1336), Gunyld (1333), Jory (1346), Kenet (1345–7), Long (1346) and Palmer (1336).

20

SHERINGTON IN THE FIFTEENTH CENTURY

THE unsettled conditions which characterized the reign of Henry IV and the upheaval due to the Wars of the Roses had but little direct effect on Sherington where, as in certain other villages in the neighbourhood and indeed in many parts of the country, the main difficulties of the period may be ascribed to a slow decline in population. As we saw in the last chapter, the Black Death took its toll of the inhabitants of Sherington, and from that time there had been a small but continuous loss due to recurrent pestilence and migration of the younger people to places where living conditions might be more favourable. In 1446–7 the village could qualify for a substantial tax remission on account of 'decay', but under Henry VII the situation took a turn for the better, due it is clear to the fortunate circumstance that a large part of the open common-field land came under the direct control of a shrewd and prosperous London lawyer Richard Maryot.

Throughout the whole period under review the land distribution remained essentially as it was at the end of the previous century (Table 19) and in the earlier years a resident squire with little or no outside property continued to find it hard to live without running into debt. It is not surprising, therefore, that we find him exploiting, as John de Linford had done before, the then fashionable enfeoffment to uses, a devise which enabled a small landowner to place his estate under the protection of a more powerful neighbour who would probably be acting in association with men learned in the law or connected with trade. Such groups of financiers—for this is what they really were—employed trained clerks to help in the administration of their affairs, and many of these held as absentees one or more livings in the neighbourhood of the principal partner. Provided that the feoffees acted in the true interests of those who appointed them such an arrangement seems in some cases to have freed a heavily encumbered estate from debt within a very few years.

The Linford manor is a case in point. The estate inherited by John Linford in 1402 was burdened with debt and in 1415 he settled it on five feoffees—his neighbours

TABLE 19

Holders of land in Sherington c. 1460

Numbers shown thus, 63*, are not included on the area shown in Map 8; the direction in which they lie is indicated on the map.

			Demesne		Open fields			
No. on Map 8	Owner	Messuages	Pasture (a.)	Arable (a.)	Non-demesne pasture and home closes (a.)	Arable (a.)	Meadow (a.)	Wood (a.)
188	Isobel Ardes	5	72	180	—	—	8	20
177, 63*	Henry Grendon	3	—	—	6	81	2¼	—
89	Richard Maryot (Cave)	1	47	—	8	148	9½	12
	Thomas Colyns	—	6	—	—	26	2	—
	William Huet	1	2	—	—	15	1	—
182	John Fitz John	5	—	136	—	156	8	24
161	Lord Grey de Wilton	7	20	20	5	111	11½	20
120*	Duke of Buckingham	1	18	—	—	—	—	—
	John Tyringham	3	26	—	½	76	2½	8
157, 41	William Chibnall	3	—	—	10	104	3	—
40	John Coyte	1	—	—	—	20	—	—
53	Henry Course	1	—	—	—	10	—	—
198	John Smith	1	—	—	—	8	—	—
	Alice Barker	—	—	—	—	18	3	—
	Thomas Hooton	—	—	—	—	7½	—	—
138	Delapre abbey	1	—	—	8	40	2	—
	Tickford priory	1	—	12	—	10	—	—
179	Rector's Glebe and Rectory	1	4½	—	—	15	1¾	—
		35	195½	348	37½	853½	54½	84

John Olney of Weston Underwood, Robert Gifford of Whaddon and Walter Fitz Richard of Olney, together with William Campion, clerk, the rector of King's Cliffe, Northants and John Stouton, a citizen and clothier of London who was of Sherington stock.[1] The terms of the settlement are not known, but in 1449 Walter

[1] As the fee was held *in capite* royal license should have been obtained. The surviving feoffees had to pay £9 into the hanaper for pardon in 1429 (*Cal. Pat.* 1422–9, 532).

Fitz Richard, the only surviving feoffee, conveyed the estate to John's daughter and heiress Isobel, then the wife of John Ardes of Sherington,[1] with remainder to her right heirs.[2]

John Ardes was a scion of the old feudal family of Ardres settled in Turvey, Bedfordshire,[3] (p. 185). His grandfather Thomas de Ardres was a younger son and had become possessed of a small estate in Hardmead on marriage sometime before 1360 with Alice, the daughter and heiress of William Botiler of that place.[4]

The estate settled on John and Isobel Ardes in 1449, augmented a little later by purchase from Humphrey Stafford, duke of Buckingham, of the Basset 23 acres (Great Stocking Close) in le Hoo Park,[5] passed to their son Michael on his mother's death in 1475. He remained, apparently, in undisturbed possession until a few weeks before his own death in 1503 when, as a tenant *in capite*, he was the subject of a claim under the royal prerogative. Henry VII, who gave close personal attention to his chamber administration, set out to increase his prerogative revenue by a more rigid exaction of his legitimate feudal dues and feudal incidents, many of which in the course of time had tended to lapse. In August 1486 commissioners were sent into the various counties to review possible sources of revenue, including *inter alia* land *in capite* which had been purchased, alienated or entered without license. The commissioners for Buckinghamshire were Richard Empson, Edmund Hampden and Richard Maryot,[6] and their return gave Henry an up-to-date record of tenants

[1] He was described as of Hardmead, gentleman, in 1422 and of Sherington, esquire, in 1438 (KB27/642, m. 22; *Close Rolls*, 1447–54, 232).

[2] 20*s*. was paid into the hanaper for royal license (*Cal. Pat.* 1446–52, 336).

[3] The Stopford-Sackville MSS on loan at the Northants Record Office include upwards of 40 charters of the Ardres family of Turvey, ranging in date from the early thirteenth century to 1440. The second r in the name was lost by dissimilation soon after the latter date.

[4] Thomas was also tenant of an estate in Hardmead owned by William Taylor. With his brother John he was party to a lawsuit about this in 1360. John opened his evidence with what would seem today a trivial plaint 'whereas William in his writ names him as John de Ardres his right name is John Dardres and not John de Ardres, which he is prepared to verify, and asks judgment on the writ' (JI1/1458, m. 12). The judges ignored the plaint, but Flower has cited many instances from the Curia Regis Rolls which show that accuracy in the naming of parties was regarded as essential for a good writ (Selden Society, 62, 341).

[5] On Ralph Basset's death in 1390 these 50 acres land, together with 8 acres meadow and 10*s*. rent from the Grey de Wilton estate, were on lease for life to John Billing (see p. 131, n. 4). Under Ralph's will the reversion to the 50 acres passed to Thomas, earl of Stafford, who granted it for life to Elizabeth Beauchamp. On John Billing's death she leased it for life to Nicholas Bradshaw, a squire to Edmond, earl of Stafford, and on Nicholas's death in 1416 the reversion passed to Edmond's son Humphrey, later duke of Buckingham (C139/10/20).

[6] *Cal. Pat.* 1485–94, 133.

holding *in capite* which was used so effectively a little later in connexion with the so-called Empson and Dudley extortions.

It was presumably because of this survey that the sheriff of Buckinghamshire received a writ in 1502 ordering him to report on the land once held *in capite* by John Linford the son. An inquisition was duly held at Newport Pagnell on 18 September of that year, when the jury were shown a series of charters depicting the fate of the property from the time of John Linford's settlement on trustees in 1414 until the issue of Letters Patent of Richard III in 1484 giving a general protection for all acts performed under the suzerainty of Henry VI and Edward IV.[1] Michael, having been mulcted by Richard III for entry into his mother's fee[2] would presumably have resented as an unjust extortion any claim put forward by Henry VII for the same feudal incident. He died, however, before any action could be taken and nothing further transpired until Anthony, the son and heir, paid £5 to the treasurer of the chamber[3] to have livery of his father's lands.[4] As Anthony was also called upon to pay £1 12*s.* 8*d.* or twice the usual amount into the hanaper for the necessary charter[5] it may well be that Henry was treating the incident as covering the entry of both father and son, but be that as it may the sum demanded, under whatever pretext, was not extortionate.

The Fitz John family history continued to be uneventful. John Fitz John, the penultimate member of the line, succeeded his father in 1413[6] and a year later he settled the manor house and the attached farm, then in the occupation of Thomas Grendon, on Robert Olney of Weston Underwood and other feoffees.[7] Besides his Sherington property John had land in Chicheley[8] and he successfully acquired in

[1] The inquisition recites full details of the following deeds: (*a*) Charter of enfeoffment by John Linford dated 1 May 1414; (*b*) Letters Patent of Henry VI dated 1 April 1429; (*c*) Charter of Walter Fitz Richard dated 20 Nov. 1449 conveying the estate to John and Isobel Ardes, with companion Letters Patent of Henry VI; (*d*) Letters Patent of Richard III dated 23 June 1484 giving a general pardon for all acts performed before 21 Feb. 1484 and any profits received since 29 Sept. 1482 (E 199/2/30).

[2] The sum paid is not known because the hanaper accounts of Richard III are not preserved.

[3] E 101/413/2(3). 'A receipt book of John Heron, treasurer of the chamber', p. 103, 25 Nov. anno 19 (1503): 'Item receved of Antony Ardys upon an obligation 50*s*.': repeated on p. 154 under date 8 July anno 19 (1504).

[4] *Cal. Pat.* 1494–1509, 312: licence of entry dated 20 June 1503.

[5] E 101/219/4: particulars of Hugh Oldom, keeper of the hanaper, 18–19 Hen. 7.

[6] C 138/1/5. The extent was 1 messuage and 100 acres land, 5 acres meadow, 20 acres wood and 20*s*. rent. This was held *in capite* for three quarters of a knight's fee and was rated at 5 marks.

[7] T 544. *Cal. Close*, 1413–19, 181. The 2 messuages and 40 acres land and 4 acres pasture were settled on feoffees in 1420.

[8] CP 25(1) 22/117/7, 44.

1428 a half share of an estate in Moulsoe which he claimed as an inheritance from his distant cousin Joan Houghton.[1] John was thus not entirely dependant on his Sherington rents, but he was often in debt,[2] and when Robert Olney's feoffees returned the manor farm to him in 1436[3] he granted one moiety of the estate to John Chamberlain and Margaret his wife for life[4] and a little later settled the other moiety, with reversion to the whole, on a new set of feoffees for the use of Robert Olney.[5] Shortly before his death the latter placed all his property in the hands of a powerful group of London lawyers and merchants who, as feoffees, conveyed the Sherington estate to Richard Maryot in 1479.[6] It is not known whether John Fitz John the son, a chaplain who was for a time rector of Gayhurst, inherited any contingent interest in the estate, but in view of the many settlements to which it had been subjected in the past Richard Maryot, as a good lawyer, was probably justified in requiring John to suffer a recovery of his father's and grandfather's lands in Sherington.[7]

Very few deeds of Cave's manor for the period under review have survived, but there is evidence that between 1449 and 1455 it was acquired by Richard Maryot. When John Cave the London citizen and draper inherited about 1390 the property was on lease to Richard Bukingham (Bekingham) (see p. 129) and at the turn of

[1] CP 40/669, m. 437.

[2] *Cal. Pat.* 1422–9, 250, 312.

[3] T 590. The other feoffees were Walter Fitz Richard of Olney and Robert Mouter, rector of Sherington, who was to become clerk to the hanaper from 1439 to 1449.

[4] *Cal. Pat.* 1429–36, 595.

[5] *Cal. Pat.* 1436–41, 367. CP 25(1) 22/121/3. T 605. The principal feoffee was Nicholas Wymbish, rector of Olney and Hanslape as well as a well-known clerk in Chancery, who was then managing most of Robert's property. The estate was stated to be 2 messuages and 143 acres land, 5 acres meadow, 24 acres pasture, 40 acres wood, 20*s.* rent and a third of the fishery in the Ouse.

[6] *Cal. Close*, 1476–85, 174. *BRS*, 121/36–122/36. The feoffees included John Tate, mercer and son of John Tate sometime mayor of London, John son of Thomas Tate, Robert Tate, William Catesby, John Catesby, sergeant-at-law, William, Lord Hastings, and Ralph Hastings, knight of the king's body.

[7] D/Ch/89/1: exemplification of a recovery made 29 Feb. 1479 against John Fitz John chaplain for 5 messuages, 5 tofts and 300 acres land, 20 acres meadow, 12 acres pasture, 24 acres wood, 14*s.* rent and the rent of 6 capons in Sherington. The copyhold rents have been extended. It was but seven years before, in 1472–3, that the effectiveness of the recovery for evasion was confirmed by the courts and the wording of the present instrument is less formal and more informative than in the stereotyped version that became current later. The present instrument, moreover, carries two valuable additions. On dorse: Shiryngton, attorns as well of the fee tenants as tenants at will made by John Fitz John chaplain 24 Nov. 19 Edward IV, to wit—Thomas Underwoode, then former of the capital messuage, Richard Dedipas, Henry Grendon, Thomas Grendon, Thomas Smyth, Henry Frere, Richard Haryes, John Brytte senr., John Britte junr., all of whom attorn, etc. Endorsed: Recovery against John Fitz John chaplain of all land and tenements which were his father's and grandfather's in Shiryngton, 19 Ed. IV.

the century it was the subject of two fines suggesting that a settlement of some sort had already been made.[1] Thomas Bekyngham was the owner or tenant in 1429, in which year William Barrow, bishop of Carlisle and a former rector of Sherington, left tenements held of him there to his nephew Hugh.[2] One Hugh Horsington, possibly the same Hugh, was in possession in 1443[3] and six years later he released all claims on the estate to Humphrey duke of Buckingham, John Heton, Robert Olney and other co-feoffees including John Maryot, all of whom were stated to be already seised of it as of fee.[4] In virtue of another settlement—which seems to have included the 23 acres acquired earlier by John Olney—the property passed some time before 1455 to Richard Maryot,[5] who died seised of it in 1491.[6] In 1479, therefore, Cave's and Fitz John's manors became merged into one property, to which Richard added within a few years the holdings of William Huet[7] and Thomas Colyns[8] (Table 19).

Richard Maryot's antecedents are not known. A lawyer with a large practice he occurs repeatedly as a co-feoffee with many wealthy London merchants, including a John Maryot described in 1450 as a citizen and salter.[9] He settled in Sherington as early as 1455, in which year he agreed to keep watch over his neighbour John Tyringham's interest for a retaining fee of one mark per annum.[10] He had presumably acquired the Cave moated manor house by then but throughout his life he kept a house or chambers near Fleet Street in London.[11] A justice of the peace for Buckinghamshire he died in 1491[12] and was buried in Sherington church.[13] In his will he bequeathed money for the rebuilding of Sherington bridge[14] and directed

[1] *Cal. Close*, 1402–5, 134, 146: charter and warrantry of John Cave to John Layot, clerk (sometime rector of Clipston, Northants), of 1 messuage and 180 acres land, 8 acres meadow, 12 acres wood and 10*s*. 8*d*. rent in Sherington (23 Jan. 1403). *Ibid*. 173: quit-claim with warrantry of Thomas Stokkynge, clerk (sometime rector of Gayhurst) to John Layot, clerk, of the same tenements (3 June 1403).

[2] Surtees Society, 116, 39–40; see also pp. 177–8.

[3] C 139/146/12. He paid a quit-rent of 2*s*. per annum for the manor house (cf. Table 6).

[4] *Cal. Close*, 1447–54, 110. The property was described as late of John Cave. Extent as in n. 1.

[5] Until Richard came into residence the manor house and demesne had been farmed since the time of John Cave the father by members of the Hewet family (p. 146).

[6] *Cal. Inq*. Hen. VII (1), 302.

[7] CP 43/870/412.

[8] D/Ch/89/2. Exemplification of a recovery, Trinity Term 1 Hen. VII (1486).

[9] *Cal. Close*, 1447–54, 234.

[10] CP 40/821/338. Richard sued John's executors in 1466 for £6 14*s*. 10*d*. arrears. He was awarded £5 6*s*. 8*d*. and 40*s*. damages. He is described as of Sherington 'gentilman' in 1456 (*Cal. Close*, 1454–61, 146).

[11] PCC 11 Dogett, m. 87.

[12] *Cal. Inq*. Hen. VII (1), 302.

[13] Lipscomb, *History of the County of Buckingham*, IV, 337.

[14] See p. 9.

Hewet of Sherington

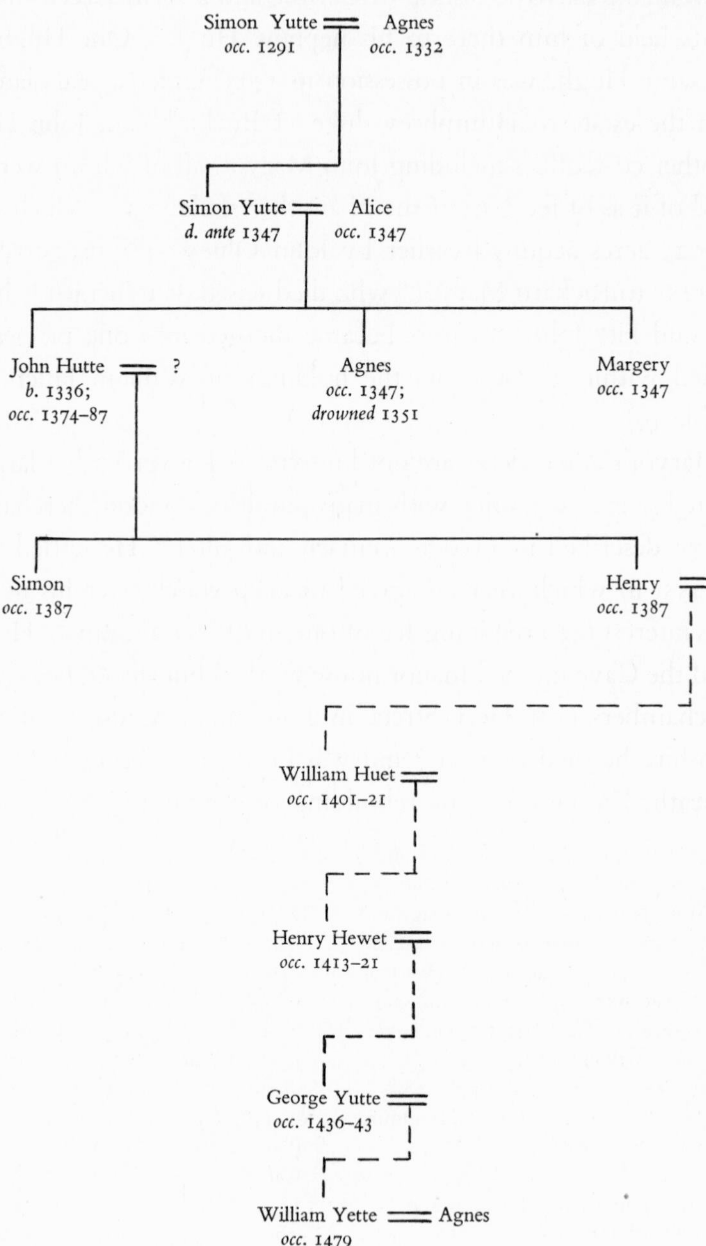

his executors to give to every poor householder in Sherington a cow or a heifer on conditions that these and any calves they produced should not be sold until the lapse of six years under pain of forfeiture. His daughter and heiress Jane was already married to Humphrey Catesby, the son of his old colleague Sir John Catesby, sergeant-at-law of Whiston, Northamptonshire. His widow Katherine, who came of a wealthy London merchant family of the name of Tate,[1] lived in the manor house at Sherington until her death in 1530.

The descent of the Grey of Wilton manor presents no unusual features and John, the eighth lord, settled it on his third son Edward Grey of Water Eton manor in Bletchley, who died seised in 1504.[2] The small Tyringham estate likewise underwent no change. The evidence for this is taken in part from inquisitions *post mortem* and is a good illustration of the point made by Crump that a draft of the jury's finding was often prepared beforehand in the escheator's office from a previous return and then read to the jury at the inquest.[3] In the present case the same (faulty) extent was repeated verbatim in seven consecutive inquisitions on Tyringham lands in Buckinghamshire between 1464 and 1615.[4]

In the previous chapter it was shown that the major part of the land held by peasants and smallholders in the early part of the fourteenth century had been absorbed into the larger estates—including those of Chibnall and Grendon—before 1400, and that the few remaining freeholds owing quit-rents to either the principal or Grey of Wilton manors did not represent more than about 14 and 38 acres respectively (Table 17). These small freeholds seem to have come through the next century without losing their individuality, for the appropriate quit-rents were still being duly recorded in manorial rentals of a later date. Very little land in Sherington

[1] She and her husband received a very substantial legacy from her mother Elizabeth Tate in 1480 (*Cal. Close*, 1470–85, 200).

[2] *Cal. Inq.* Hen. VII (1), 302.

[3] *Bull. John Rylands Lib.* VIII (1924), 140.

[4] The extent given was 4 messuages and 100 acres land, 20 acres meadow, 10 acres pasture, 6 acres wood called le Hoo with hedges and ditches to the same wood adjoining and 15*s.* rent of assize. In the first three inquisitions the estate was stated (incorrectly) to be held of Thomas Ardes instead of John, Michael and Anthony Ardes respectively. The true extent was 4 messuages and 1 carucate land (equivalent to about 100 acres land and 2–3 acres meadow) and 8 acres wood, as claimed in dower by Alice, widow of John Tyringham and sister of Robert Olney in 1405 (CP40/578, m. 362d), which tallies with the property held by the Tyringhams during the reign of Elizabeth, when detailed record again becomes available. The assize rents were apparently created when John Linford disposed of most of his open-field land to Thomas Grendon in 1383–8 (see p. 136), for in 1571 Edward Ardes owned 4 messuages, late of Thomas and Richard Grendon, which were held of Tho. Tyringham in free socage and were said to be worth 19*s.* per annum.

other than that acquired by Richard Maryot was, indeed, changing hands during the fifteenth century, an observation that helps to explain why so few land charters for that period have survived.

TABLE 20

Working population in Sherington during the later middle ages

(for summary see Table 21)

L signifies a labourer or peasant and S a smallholder, tenant farmer or tradesman

Date		
c. 1345	L	Adam, Bouchmaler, Bozard, Chandler, Copshot, Dayrel, Gille, Key (Gegh), Shore
	S	Brittain, Brut, Carpenter, Carter, Clerk, Courage, Course, Coyte, Elliot, Fisher, Frere, Gerveys, Gunnild, Herman, Heyne, Huet, Jones, Jory, Kenet, Kynbell, Long, Mason, Mathew, Palmer, Rafenyld, Richer, Savage, Shepeherde, Smith, Stachedone, Stouton, Taylor, Troup
c. 1400	L	Bozard, Chandler, Gille, Key, Shore, Smart
	S	Barker, Brittain, Britte, Carter, Clerk, Colyns, Clyfford, Course, Coyte, Elliot, Fisher, Frere, Herman, Heries, Heyne, Huet, Kynbell, Mason, Mathew, Mulsoe, Prykke, Savage, Shepeherde, Smith, Stachedone, Stouton, Taylor
c. 1460	L	Chandler, Clerk, Key, Millward, Shore
	S	Banister, Barker, Brittain, Britte, Carter, Colyns, Course, Coyte, Dedipas, Elliot, Everard, Fisher, Frere, Grenewich, Heries, Herman, Hooton, Huet, Mathew, Mulsoe, Sampson, Shepeherde, Smith, Taylor, Underwood
c. 1520	L	Beamond, Bocher, Elyott, Glaunder, Grenewich, Hed, Henley, Key, Millward (Millard), Overend, Smith, Williamson
	S	Adyngton, Bocher, Brittain, Chibnall, Course (2), Elyott (2), Field, Fisher (2), Grendon (2), Overend, Paynter, Pell, Sampson, Sheriff, Shortred, Smith (2), Taylor

Conditions in the village, however, did not remain as static as these observations might suggest, for there was a slow but continuous turnover of the population (Tables 20 and 21). The records available for the first two and the last of the dates mentioned in the tables are comprehensive and it can be claimed with confidence that the estimates given for these in Table 21 are not significantly in error. For the third date, *c.* 1460, the situation is less clearly defined. The relatively small number of charters and other evidences that have survived were the concern of the estate owners and some of the smallholders: they seldom mention the peasants and labourers. Information about these latter groups can, nevertheless, be deduced indirectly from other sources, for when a family known to have been living in Sherington *c.* 1400 was still there in the early part of the sixteenth century we may assume that it remained *in situ* during the intervening years. Tentatively, therefore, it is suggested that the estimates for the smallholders and tenant farmers *c.* 1460 given in Table 21 are realistic, but that those for the peasants and labourers may be somewhat low.

TABLE 21

Estimates of the number of working families in Sherington during the later middle ages

Sources. *c.* 1345: Table 18 and Throckmorton charters.
c. 1400: Throckmorton charters, Close Rolls, various inquisitions and a list of tenants of the Grey de Wilton manor.
c. 1460: Land deeds, Close Rolls, various inquisitions and a list of tenants of Fitz John's manor.
c. 1520: Muster Survey 1522, subsidy of 1524–5 and Court Rolls of the Mercers' Company.

The columns headed Old and New under a given date contain the numbers of those whose family was established in Sherington at the time of or after the preceding date respectively.

Time ...	*c.* 1345	*c.* 1400			*c.* 1460			*c.* 1520[a]		
	Total	Old	New	Total	Old	New	Total	Old	New	Total
Cottagers and labourers	9	5	1	6	3	2	5	5	7	12
Smallholders, tenant farmers and tradesmen	34	20	6	26	15	9	25	13	8	22
	43	25	7	32	18	11	30	18	15	34

[a] The 1524–5 subsidy shows that in some cases a family name was borne by more than one family and the estimates allow for this. There is no comparable information for the earlier years.

The Black Death reduced the working population by at least twelve members—four peasants and eight smallholders—but the further slight loss during the rest of the century due to migration or recurrent pestilence was balanced by immigration from outside. Meanwhile the average amount of land per head available to the tenant farmers was not substantially increased, for about two hundred acres of the open common fields had gone to form the new small estates of Chibnall and Grendon.

The next half century or so (1400–50) included the unsettled period of Henry IV and the Wars of the Roses. During the early years at least six families with roots back in thirteenth-century Sherington either migrated elsewhere or died out from pestilence: John Stouton, for instance, following in the footsteps of John Cave, became a citizen and draper of London. Newcomers before 1460 included Thomas Underwoode, who farmed the Fitz John demesne and two emigrants from Tyringham, Richard Dedipas and Thomas Hooton. In light of the discussion given above the small fall in the total number of smallholders in *c.* 1460 shown in Table 21 may not be significant, yet it is in keeping with evidence from independant sources showing that all was not well with the village in the middle period of the fifteenth century.

The situation in Sherington since the time of the Black Death had, in fact, been typical of that in many other parts of the country. In varying degree there was impoverishment and a sufficient drop in the population level to assuage the land hunger that had prevailed from the twelfth until the early part of the fourteenth century. As a consequence land had in some cases gone out of cultivation, and at the Parliament of 1432 during the troubled minority of Henry VI a measure of relief from taxation was granted to such places as were in need of help. Buckinghamshire may have benefited at once from this concession but we have no record of what happened before 1446, following two very bad devastations of the plague. In April of that year Parliament granted a whole and a half fifteenth and tenth, to be paid in three yearly instalments of one half. Relief was to be granted to such villages, cities and boroughs as were desolated, wasted, depopulated or overburdened with taxation, and the instructions to the commissioners appointed to make the deductions[1] laid down that a flat rate was not to be imposed, but account was to be taken of local needs. Their award to Sherington and other villages in the neighbourhood, as set out in Table 22, shows that they found conditions in the northern sector of the Newport Hundreds far from uniform.[2] The towns engaged in trade—Newport

[1] Edmund Grey of Ruthyn, knight, John Cheyne, knight and John Hampden of Hampden esquire. Schedule to E179/77/65.

[2] The village quotas fixed in 1334 are given in Table 22. The total assessments to the fifteenth for the county was £636 18*s.* 8*d.* and to the tenth for the boroughs and ancient demesnes £49 6*s.* 8*d.* For the whole county the deduction on the fifteenth was £108 5*s.* 8*d.*; by circumstance or more probably by design the relief was fairly evenly distributed among the different parts of the county, the percentage rates for the various Three Hundreds varying between 15·1 and 19·0. The reliefs became conventionalized and were applied in 1488–9 and 1513–14 in spite of the more flourishing conditions then prevailing.

Pagnell, Olney and to a minor extent North Crawley seem to have been holding their own, but we have insufficient information to say why Chicheley with Little Crawley for instance received practically no relief at all, while Stanton with Bradwell were given a rebate of nearly one half; in both of these cases the land was largely in the hands of monastic foundations.

TABLE 22

Taxation relief in 1446–7

	Normal assessment to the fifteenth and tenth[a] £ s. d.	Relief (%)
Stanton and Bradwell	2 6 8	44·6
Great Linford	2 10 0	31·3
Willen and Caldecote	2 3 4	31
Lathbury	5 4 0	27·7
Astwood	2 6 8	23·8
Gayhurst	3 10 0	22·4
Moulsoe	4 0 0	20·8
Sherington	3 6 8	20·0
Clifton with Newton Blossomville	3 13 0	18·2
Emberton[b]	3 6 8	17·0
Hardmead	2 10 0	15·0
Lavendon	5 0 0	13·3
Weston Underwood	3 10 0	11·8
Tyringham with Filgrave	3 6 8	10·0
Olney	9 0 0	3·7
Newport Pagnell and Tickford with le Mersh	12 0 0	3·5
Chicheley with Little Crawley	3 13 4	3·0
North Crawley	5 0 0	2·3

[a] E 179/77/4; assessment for 1336–7.
[b] This would include Petsoe and Ekeney.

The generous allowance for decay allowed to Sherington shows that it must have been subject in some degree to one or more of the calamities envisaged by Parliament and the point is of such importance that it needs probing. In the first place there is good evidence that the smallholders and tenants were not so impoverished that the land in the open common fields was lying untilled and reverting to waste. They were, on the contrary, prepared to pay rents very little if any less than those that had been current in the preceding century and were to hold in early Tudor times. In 1433, for instance, John Tyringham leased half a virgate of land, 7 acres of pasture and ½ acre of meadow to a substantial smallholder, George Huet, for twenty years at a rent of 23*s.* per annum.[1] This was little more in proportion than that paid for a lease of open-field land in 1312[2] and near to the average rent of Buckinghamshire arable land and pasture that had been considered worthy of enclosure before the Parliamentary inquiry of 1517.[3]

Ten years later, in 1443, Margaret, the widow of Richard Grey of Wilton, was given one-third of the profits of the Sherington manor as part of her dower. The land and rents concerned are described in the escheator's award[4] and besides one-third of the freehold rents she was allotted a rent of £1 12*s.* 2*d.* from about 2 virgates of customary land. This last sum represents about 10 per cent less than the rent (17*s.* 6*d.*) paid for a virgate of this manor in 1302[5] and also much later, in 1577.[6] As the land concerned was all in the open common fields there is again no evidence that the tenants were in any real difficulty.

It is when we come to consider the outlying portions of the demesne sector that we are given our first insight into a possible shortage—not of land but of labour. Le Hoo Park, the cause of so many legal squabbles in the past, is a case in point. It lay on high ground to the south-east of the demesne sector and in the thirteenth century it had been either part of the Carun demesne or in the ownership of someone of the same class. If tilled at all in those days it must have been by hired labour. In the century under review, with demesne farming giving place to leasing, it would

[1] NRO *Brudenell Coll.* A. XI. 10. Indenture between John Tyringham, lord of Tyringham, and George Yutte of Sherington. John married Elizabeth Brudenell, which accounts for the presence of this deed among the Brudenell muniments.

[2] NRO *Ecton*, 1190. m. 1d. Court roll of Carun manor dated 4 Oct. 1312; 4½ acres in the open fields leased for six years at 3*s.* 6*d.* per annum.

[3] Leadam, *Domesday of Enclosures*, II, 635. The average annual rental per acre of the arable land was 10¼*d.* and of the pasture 1*s.* 3*d.*

[4] C139/146/12. She was awarded freehold rents totalling 16*s.* 5*d.*, 8½ acres wood, and rents totalling £1 12*s.* 2*d.* issuing from 53½ acres land, 4 acres pasture and 2⅓ acres meadow. The free tenants were Hugh Horsington, Henry Coyte, Richard Chubbenhale, Henry Course, William Frere, William Smart, George Yutte and Richard Clerk; the customary tenants George Mathew, Henry Grendon, Richard Herrys and John Millward. The award was equivalent to a gross rental of £7 6*s.* 9*d.* (cf. n. 2, 3). At the inquisition *post mortem* of her husband in 1442 the value of the manor was returned for fiscal purposes at £7, or about 6*d.* per acre on the copyhold land.

[5] See p. 75, n. 4.

[6] See p. 183.

not have proved attractive as arable land to a local tenant during a period of labour shortage, for it was far removed from the open common fields wherein the tenant would have kept his implements. Under such conditions the land would probably revert to rough grazing and there is evidence that this must have occurred. The western half of the old park, the tillage of 50 acres referred to in the fourteenth century as 'le Stoking', came into possession of the Basset family of Drayton in 1323, when it was valued for fiscal purposes at *6d.* per acre.[1] The last Basset died in 1390 and in that year,[2] as well as in 1398[3] and 1403[4] it was still valued at the old rate. In 1423, however, an abrupt fall to *2d.* per acre was recorded.[5]

That this slump in the value of outlying land was the result of a labour shortage, due to migration or more probably to death from pestilence finds strong support in the contemporary fate of the hamlets Petsoe and Ekeney, which lay to the north of Chicheley and less than a mile—almost within a stone's throw—of le Hoo Park. Lying side by side and jointly extending to no more than 400 acres including woods, these lonely settlements were so far removed from the nearest main road or village that each soon acquired a tiny independent chapel of its own. In 1252[6] the yearly value of that in Petsoe was only 2 marks and in Ekeney but ½ mark. During any real shortage of labour one would have expected the workers in these vills to migrate to areas where conditions were more favourable, and this is what happened in the latter half of the fourteenth and during the fifteenth century. Between 1408 and 1439 the annual value of the enclosed demesne land, let with the capital messuage to a family called Markaunt, had risen from 8½*d.* to 9½*d.* per acre, whereas that of the open-field customary land had slumped from *5d.* to 2½*d.* per acre.[7] The small population reflects these lean times. A very complete survey made in 1473 shows that the combined hamlets comprised no more than the capital messuage and four cottages, two of which were owned by widows. There is a clear indication, nevertheless, that many other tenements, probably cottages, had recently become derelict because the survey records ten pightles butting on the byways, some of which were still bearing local family names. It is probable that the peasants concerned were

[1] Cal. Inq. Misc. II, 147.
[2] E149/56/2.
[3] C136/107/46.
[4] C137/38/41.
[5] C139/10/20.
[6] *Valuation of Norwich*, Ed. W. E. Lunt.
[7] C139/92/1. It was rated at *5s.* per virgate. For comparative purposes it may be mentioned that in Sherington the fiscal valuation of the Grey of Wilton open field land in 1442 was about *17s. 6d.* per virgate (E149/173/10).

either dead or they had migrated to the neighbouring villages.[1] This creeping decay, due to pestilence, was bound to effect the far east sector of Sherington as well, and it must have been because of the hardship thereby inflicted on the *landowners* that the commissioners were prevailed upon to grant the village some relief from taxation in 1446–7.

During the last 30 years of the century the village became progressively more prosperous, probably reflecting the business acumen of Richard Maryot who by 1480 was virtually in control of more than half the land in the open common fields.[2] Until he came into residence at Cave's manor house the only resident squire for very many years had been John Ardes, a newcomer with no roots in the village whose attenuated estate was almost wholly dispersed in the demesne sector so that he was not necessarily brought into very close working contact with the cropping programme that was then being applied to the open common fields.

The closing years of the fifteenth century were indeed heralding in a new era; more tenant farmers were coming in and the larger farmers like Thomas Chibnall and Henry Grendon were already extending their operations to neighbouring villages where proportionately more land was available as pasture. One scion of an old thirteenth century peasant family, John Mathew, who became a citizen and mercer of London was to provide Sherington with its proverbial 'Lord Mayor of London', for he was mayor there in 1490. He retained, nevertheless, his old family property, mostly copyhold, in Sherington, and on his death in 1498 he bequeathed 5 marks for the repair of the church there, a barrel of white herrings to the friars of Dunstable and 1 mark a year 'until ten marks be content' both to John Field and to young Barry.[3] The descendants of this John Field, a newcomer to the village at the time, still flourish there after the lapse of nearly half a millennium.

The fabric of the church has not so far been discussed in the present work because no new data for the various periods under review have come to light which could usefully add anything to the excellent account published by the Royal Commission on Historical Monuments (England).[4] It is pertinent to inquire, nevertheless, whether

[1] This account of Ekeney cum Petsoe is based on deeds in possession of Lincoln College, Oxford. The writer hopes to publish a detailed history of these interesting hamlets in the near future.

[2] He was also the farmer of the enclosed demesne land of Ekeney cum Petsoe in 1473 at a rent of about 10½*d.* per acre. The open-field land was then being rented by husbandmen from Emberton and Hardmead for 8¾*d.* per acre.

[3] PCC 29 Howe.

[4] *Buckinghamshire* (*North*), p. 259.

the Commission's observer was correct in ascribing the re-roofing of the church to the sixteenth century. The relevant statement is as follows 'The sixteenth century roof of the nave is supported by moulded principal and secondary beams and at the foot of these principals are shields charged, 1st a cross, 2nd a saltire and 3rd apparently a chevron between 3 roses'. The first shield, at the top of the nave on the south side is inaccurately described. It is a shield per cross (with no charge) for Fitz John

TABLE 23

Armory of Sherington

The list contains the coats of arms borne in the days of feudal military service: it excludes those assumed after Edward III instituted the Garter and heraldry became the playboy of pomp and circumstance.

Carun of Sherington[a]	Argent a lion rampant vert holding a cross formy fitchy gules
Linford of Sherington[b]	Argent a chevron between three roses gules
Ardres of Turvey[c]	Argent a bend between six molets sable
Fitz John of Hanslope[d]	Per cross (tinctures not known)
Cave of Sherington[e]	Not observed
Tyringham of Tyringham	Azure a saltire engrailed argent
Mountgomery of Ecton	Or an eagle azure

[a] T 41 carries the armorial seal of Roger de Carun.

[b] It was quartered with Carun on the Ardes monument in Sherington church.

[c] The earliest Ardres armorial seal among the Stopford-Sackville muniments is attached to a charter of John Dardres of Turvey dated 6 March 1351.

[d] Seal of John Fitz John of Hanslape on deed dated 27 July 1271 (Newton Longeville charters, New College Oxford: *ORS*, III, 17).

[e] See p. 127, n. 10.

of Hanslope (Table 23). The second and third shields, at the bottom of the nave on opposite sides of the large west window, are for Tyringham and Linford respectively. These three shields were borne by the squires resident in the early part of the fifteenth century and the very fact that the fourth shield—opposite the first—is blank, and does not display the coat of Ardes, is good evidence that the repair of the roof or at least the setting in place of the principal beams was undertaken before the heiress of the last John Linford married John Ardes about 1438.

There is a tradition that Dr William Barrow,[1] who was rector from 1407 to 1423

[1] The sequence of rectors during the century was as follows: William atte Crosse (p. 136, n. 3) exchanged with William Ryal in 1401 and he with John Disworth on 10 Aug. 1405 (Linc. Reg. 13, 297; 14, 426). In his turn he exchanged with William Barrow, LL.D., who retained the rectory while he

and during the last five of those years bishop of Bangor as well, built the south porch, for a shield which is now used as the arms of that see occurs as the dexter of two on the ringed handle of the south door.[1] It may well have been that the bishop—who retained an interest in Sherington until his death in 1429[2]—prevailed upon the three local squires of his day to help improve the church fabric and the oak shields of their arms were affixed to the roof beams in recognition of their generosity. When Brown Willis visited the church in *c.* 1735 he observed that one of the north windows contained a shield of four quarters with Tyringham in the first.[3] Cole, when he edited Willis's notes, wrote in 1761 'by the arms of Tyringham being put in the windows and carved on the beams of the church I presume they were in Henry 4th time great benifactors to the building of the present fabric, which I conceive it was then erected'.[4] His dating is in agreement with the suggestion made above.

The heraldic window mentioned by Willis, like the late medieval monument and two mural brasses that he described, disappeared during the restoration of the church in 1870. The brick altar monument, which stood against the wall of the north aisle, was covered at the top with a white marble whereon was cut the portraits, much worn in his day, of a man and a woman with a shield of arms at their feet showing: quarterly 1st and 4th Ardes; 2nd and 3rd Butler of Hardmead (three covered cups); impaling 1st and 4th Carun, 2nd and 3rd Linford. These achievements, and the dates of death given in the partly obliterated inscription around the edge of the marble, show that the monument was to John Ardes and Isobel his wife. One of the

was bishop of Bangor (1418–23) but resigned on appointment as bishop of Carlisle. He was followed in succession by Peter Horton, STP, on 20 July 1424, Robert Mouter on 13 June 1426, William Derby, archdeacon of Bedfordshire, on 26 July 1433 (Cant. and York Society, 45, 322, 348; 15, 48); Thomas Dawson on 5 Oct. 1437 (*Cal. Pat.* 1436–41, 93); Robert Kirkham before 1445, Gilbert Altoft on 13 Feb. 1445, William Grayburn, STD, sometime Fellow of Clare College on 10 Nov. 1474 and John Proctor on 20 Sept. 1486 (Linc. Reg. 18, 193; 21, 97; 23, 346).

1 Lysons gives an interesting sketch of this door handle as it was in the early nineteenth century. The original back-plate he depicts has long vanished and had been replaced by a new one of quite different design. The wyvern on the left of the handle, a merely traditional ornament of such rings, is nearly worn away and the arms are also considerably worn. The dexter shield is that which Barrow bore either in his own right or in that of the see—but I imagine in his own right; his arms, like those of St Thomas of Cantelo at Hereford, being adopted later for the see. The sinister shield is charged with a crudely distorted cross: Lysons depicts it as a cross patée, but it may well be a worn relic of a cross counter-componé borne by Cockfield of Nuthall, Nottinghamshire, a name which would still have been a commonplace one in Sherington at that time (cf. Table 12).

2 See p. 145.

3 Bodleian Library, MS Willis 24, 93.

4 Add. 5839, 175d.

two mural brasses was in memory of Richard Maryot, who has already been mentioned, and the other of Robert Yonge, who died in 1517, depicting him with his wife and four children.[1] Both brasses have been fully described by local historians.[2]

[1] He succeeded Richard Maryot as the lessee of the Ekeney cum Petsoe demesne lands and retained them until his death.

[2] Lipscomb, *History of the County of Buckingham*, IV, 337. Radcliffe, *History and Antiques of the Newport Hundreds*, pp. 204–5.

21

ECONOMIC CONDITIONS IN SHERINGTON UNDER HENRY VIII

THE progressive improvement in the economy of the village that became apparent during the reign of Henry VII was maintained during the first four decades of the new century and the dominant theme, as one would have expected in such a community, was sheep farming. Changes in ownership during the period, either as freeholder or tenant farmer were few, and the only noteworthy occurrence was the acquisition by the Mercers' Company of Cockfield manor. This property was henceforth to be managed from London by the Company's Court of Assistants, a shrewd group of men who would have little if any contact with their tenants in Buckinghamshire. The records of this court, nevertheless, are unusually complete for the whole of the 400 years that the Mercers retained the estate and it is from these that many of the interesting incidences woven into the narrative of this and later chapters have been culled.

Sir Henry Colet, of a family settled for some generations in Wendover, Buckinghamshire, was a leading citizen of London during the reign of Henry VII, being an alderman for the first time in 1476 and mayor in 1486. By trade a mercer, he served for many years on the Court of Assistants of the Mercers' Company and like most of the liverymen of his period he was also a Merchant Adventurer, exporting cloth to pay for the mercery he imported. Much of the wealth thus acquired was invested in Buckinghamshire land, and only a few months before his death in 1505 he had purchased Cockfield manor from Edmond, Lord Grey de Wilton.[1]

This rather scattered holding of Sir Henry's in Buckinghamshire, worth about £61 per annum, passed with the rest of his real estate to his only son John Colet, dean of St Paul's cathedral, London, who decided some four years later to devote

[1] In 1472 Reginald, Lord Grey de Wilton, settled the manor, with that of Vache in Aston Clinton, on his third son Edward Grey of Bletchley, after whose death without issue in 1504 the manors reverted to his nephew Edmond, then Lord Grey de Wilton (*Cal. Inq.* Hen. VII, III, 461). Edmond sold them, with Barton manor in Cambridge, to Sir Henry Colet on 5 May 1505 for £240 (ECL, 40d, 42, 43).

part of his patrimony to the foundation of a new school in St Paul's churchyard. As the endowment for this would have to be vested in trustees he persuaded his father's old company, the Mercers', to assume this obligation. Royal licence for the holding in mortmain of lands in Buckinghamshire worth £53 per annum—including Cockfield manor—was granted on 6 June 1510 and on 12 July 1511 the dean conveyed them to the wardens and commonalty of the 'Mistery of Mercery' as the company was called in those days. Formal seisin of the Sherington property was taken on the following 1 August by two members of the Court of Assistants in the presence of most of the tenants and a number of other inhabitants of the village.[1]

A landlord domiciled at a distance and hence in no position to vex with petty interference may have been welcomed by the Mercers' tenants, but in the early days there was undoubtedly a lack of contact and even of control. The Ouse fishery was a case in point. The tenants presented at the manorial court in 1523 that time out of mind they had enjoyed the right to fish in the river, but recently Anthony Ardes had claimed two-thirds and Katherine Maryot the other third as their respective exclusive rights. The Mercers were asked for their conciliation and it took them seven years to reach an agreement satisfactory to the tenants.[2] Enclosure problems were also subject to very considerable delay, as we shall see in the next chapter.

The two resident manorial families have left little record of their activities during this period. Anthony Ardes, who had succeeded his father Michael in 1503[3] was among those who received a general pardon from the new king in 1509[4] and acted as foreman of the juries empanelled in 1525 to inquire into the lands of the suppressed priories of Tickford and Ravenstone, the revenues of which were to form part of the endowment of Wolsey's new Cardinal College in Oxford.[5]

[1] Tenants: Henry Ipswell, Richard Sampson, William Beirey, Thomas Chibnall, John Whedon (recte Hooton) de Filgrave, Thomas Course of the same, Richard Frere, John Smythe husbandman, John Bocher, Cristofer Clerk, Robert Cooper, John Fylde, William Dosyndon. The public: Henry Eliet, John Awbell, John Dosyndon, Thomas Alyn, William Smyth and John Cheyne, esq., the last probably representing Lord Grey de Wilton.

[2] MCR, 1523, 1530. 'The tenants of this manor are informed that in the future they may use the fishery in the stream called the River annually for 3 days in any week at any time at their pleasure as in times past the tenants of the lord here were accustomed.' Any right of Cockfield manor to the fishery must have been acquired during the late fourteenth or the fifteenth centuries; before then two-thirds of it belonged to Linford manor and the other third to Fitz John manor.

[3] See p. 143.

[4] L and P, Henry VIII, I, 210. He is described as of Sherington, Buckinghamshire, of London, and of Manton, Rutland, where he had a small manor inherited from his Linford ancestor (see p. 125, n. 3).

[5] C142/76/Bucks, nos. 2, 3. Both inquisitions are signed by Anthony.

The joint Cave–Fitz John manor had been settled by Richard Maryot on his wife Katherine for life and the moated manor house was her home until she died in 1530. Meanwhile the management of the estate was in the hands of Sir Humphrey Catesby of Whiston, Northamptonshire, the husband of her daughter Joan and on his death in 1503 it passed to the grandson and heir Anthony Catesby.

Anthony took up sheep farming on a large scale and as his main estate was grouped around his Northamptonshire home at Whiston he delegated the running of his Buckinghamshire property—which included a small manor in Hardmead—to Thomas Chibnall until his own son Thomas was old enough to assume control about 1530. To increase the stock-carrying capacity of the land, especially in the demesne, both landlord and agent would have been alive to the advantage of substituting a three-field for a two-field system of tillage, whereby a smaller proportion of land would be lying fallow each year and there would be more stubble. Under good management, moreover, the demand for labour in the open fields would increase. The old system was still being followed in 1514,[1] but the change had been made some time before the Mercers' survey was ordered in 1561 and probably at the instigation of Thomas Chibnall at the end of the period 1515–35, which was one of rising prosperity in the village. Throughout these latter years the wool market continued on the upgrade and Thomas made money for himself as well as for his employer.

Shortage of meadow and pasture in the open-field section of Sherington, however, was still a drawback to the progressive farmer and when Thomas wanted to expand his programme he was forced to look to neighbouring villages such as Astwood, where only about one-quarter of the land was lying in open common fields. By 1521 he had acquired a small manor in Chicheley,[2] some parcels of land in Emberton under the manors of Ekeney and Patsoe[3] as well as an estate of about 200 acres grouped around Astwood.[4] Meanwhile some time before 1514 he had become tenant of one of the manors in Astwood[5] and from then onwards the Sherington

[1] See p. 221.

[2] 1 messuage and 60 acres land, 4 acres meadow, 10 acres pasture and 12*d.* rent (CP25(2)3/13).

[3] Extent not known (Lincoln College, Oxford: court rolls of Ekeney and Petsoe manors, 1502–20).

[4] 3 messuages and 133 acres land, 7 acres meadow and 63 acres pasture in Astwood, Hardmead, the Crawleys, Chicheley and Stagsden (CP25(1) 22/128, 129; CP25(2) 3/11/13; SS, 1435, 1456).

[5] There are numerous references to him as such, e.g. Tho. Chibnale gent. *versus* Richard Walis of Astwood, who overturned his ploughs and did great damage to property (CP40/1045/90).

farm was left in charge of his nephew Thomas Chibnall junior, who acquired by 1525 a farm in Astwood and a little later another in Hardmead, in which half the land was pasture.[1] On the death of Thomas senior in 1534[2] the old Sherington holding with his other property passed to his only son John, who had followed the custom of the day and spent his early years at one of the Inns of Court and in land management.[3] In 1544 John exchanged the Sherington holding with his cousin Thomas junior,[4] who gave in return the farm in Astwood.[5] John's descendants became in due course squires of Astwood, while those of Thomas junior remained on in Sherington for another 250 years.

Richard Grendon, of another old Sherington stock, was also able to take advantage of the new conditions and acquired much pasture ground in neighbouring villages, all of which his own Thomas[6] disposed of when he purchased Grymsberry manor in Bolnhurst, Bedfordshire.[7] The Course family, of a long line of Sherington small-holders (Table 3) flourished as tenant farmers in Tyringham and Filgrave, but its prosperity there was to be short lived.[8] These changes in the Sherington hierarchy are reflected in the survey of the national wealth made in 1522.

Early in the 1520's Wolsey was finding it increasingly difficult to finance the king's wars in Scotland and France. The normal medium of taxation, the fifteenth and tenth, had long since ceased to bear any relation to the wealth of the individual taxpayer, and an attempt in the immediate past to substitute for this the equivalent of a modern income tax had caused much resentment and led to widespread evasion. Wolsey was alive to the weakness of his position and recognized that he would be unable to raise the large sum he needed unless he could procure some up-to-date information about the taxable capacity of the country. Crafty man that he was, he knew that he could only obtain this by subterfuge and so, without disclosing his hand, he called upon the commissioners for musters in each county to make a survey —ostensibly for the furnishing of harness—of all rents, revenues, goods, etc., both

[1] 1 messuage and 40 acres land and 40 acres pasture (CP25(2) 55/395).

[2] Mural brass in Astwood Church (O. Ratcliffe, *History and Antiquities of the Newport Hundreds*, p. 179).

[3] Register of Admissions, Middle Temple, 4 July 1519.

[4] 1 messuage and 100 acres land, 6 acres meadow and 10 acres pasture (CP25(2) 3/17/52).

[5] 1 messuage and 40 acres land, 6 acres meadow and 10 acres pasture (CP25(2) 3/17/53).

[6] CP25(2) 55/395. The old farm in Sherington (Table 19, no. 177) was sold to Edward Ardes, another farm in Hardmead to Thomas Chibnall and some outlying parcels of land in Sherington to Ralph Smith.

[7] *Cal. Pat.* Ed. VI, 3, 32. *VCH Beds*, III, 126.

[8] See p. 174.

Chibnall of Sherington

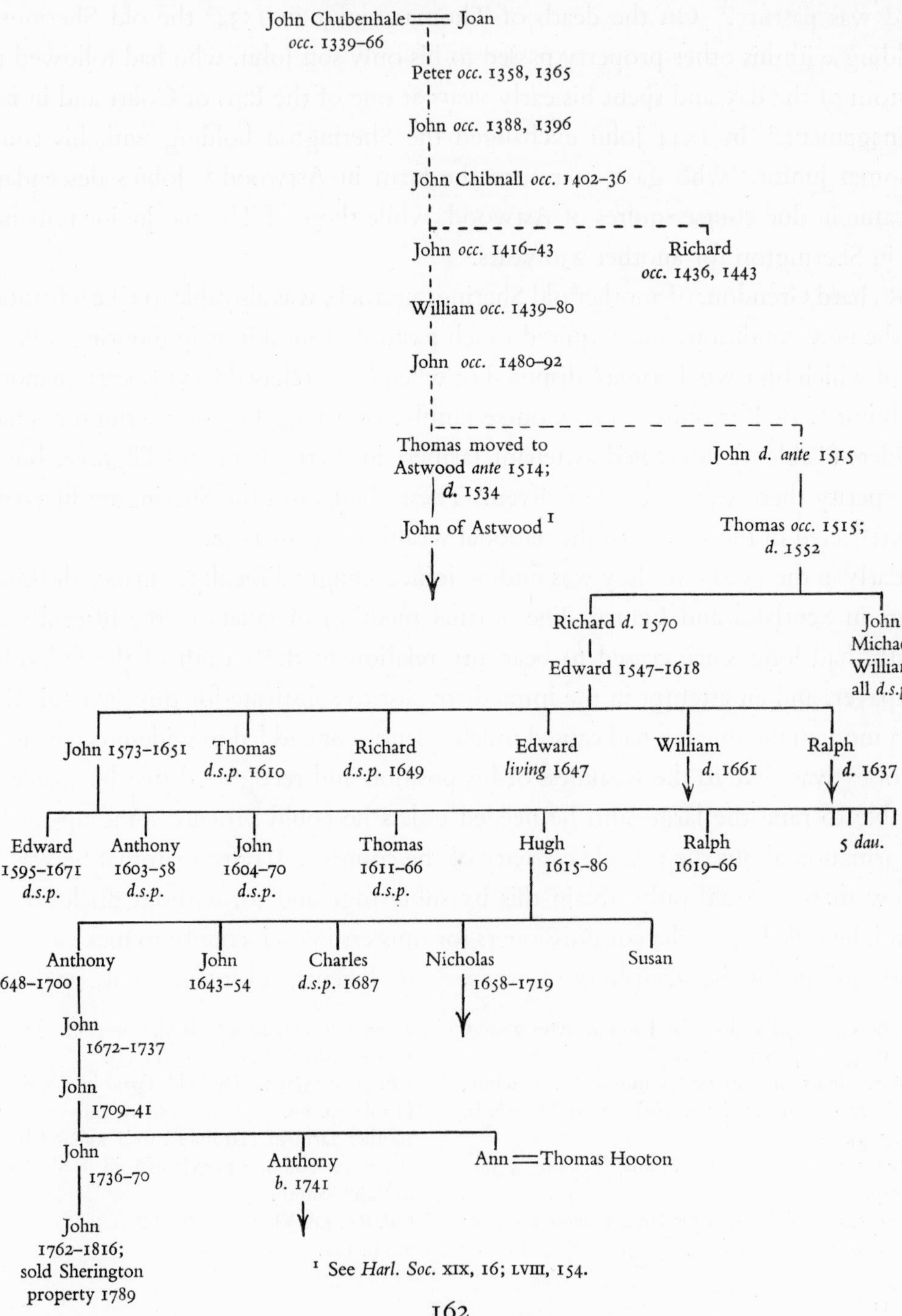

[1] See *Harl. Soc.* XIX, 16; LVIII, 154.

spiritual and temporal. It was impressed on them that they were to search out full values and to take all evidence on oath; at the same time they were to take care that no rumour was noised abroad as to the true intent of the inquiry. The results were to be incorporated in a 'book', which was to be sent to the exchequer without delay. By the spring of 1522 Wolsey had the information he needed and was thus able to deal effectively with the wealthier members of the community from whom he wanted an immediate loan, and to arrange the forthcoming subsidy of 1524, a graded tax on land, goods and wages.[1]

TABLE 24

Value of lands belonging to Sherington freeholders in the Muster Survey of 1522

Values quoted in italics are for goods of those domiciled elsewhere

	Anthony Ardes £ s. d.	K. Maryot and Anthony Catesby £ s. d.	Thomas Tyringham £ s. d.	Thomas Chibnall Senior £ s. d.	Thomas Chibnall Junior £ s. d.
Sherington	10 0 0	25 0 0	5 0 0	2 0 0	2 0 0
Chicheley	1 6 8	—	4 0 0	2 0 0	—
Hardmead	4 0	6 0 0	—	—	—
				20 0 0	
Astwood	—	—	—	8 0 0	1 6 8
			80 0 0		
Tyringham	—	—	20 0 0	—	—
Emberton	—	—	4 0 0	1 6 8	—
North Crawley	—	—	—	2 0 0	—
Great Linford	—	—	3 6 8	—	—
Lathbury	—	—	2 4	—	—
Total value of lands	11 10 8	31 0 0	36 9 0	15 6 8	3 6 8

The surviving records of this survey are in most instances fragmentary,[2] but the 'book' for Buckinghamshire, delivered to the Star Chamber at Westminster on 18 March 1522, fortunately survives complete in an early seventeenth century copy.[3] A valuable feature is the treatment of freehold land. When a taxpayer owned this in more than one village it was valued piecemeal under the various villages concerned (Table 24) whereas in the subsidy return of 1524 a summation was entered under the

[1] Cf. *BRS*, VIII, xii.

[2] Cf. Julian Cornwall, *RB*, XVI, 258.

[3] Bodleian Library, MS Eng. Hist. e, 187.

TABLE 25

Muster Survey in 1522: Sherington

	Value of goods	Value of land and tenements	Computed value of land: Mercers' rating[a]	Computed value of land: Maryot's rating[a]
	£ s. d.	£ s. d.	£ s. d.	£ s. d.
The king, lord in chief	—	1 13 0	—	—
Robert Kingscott, rector	25 0 0	20 0 0	—	—
Edward Skinner, clerk	4 6 8	—	—	—
Anthony Ardes, gent	13 6 8	10 0 0	11 5 7	15 15 4
Katherine Maryot	13 6 8	20 0 0 }	18 1 6 (Katherine Maryot and Anthony Catesby)	25 15 4 (Katherine Maryot and Anthony Catesby)
Anthony Catesby	—	5 0 0 }		
Thomas Catesby	13 6 8	—	—	—
Mercers' Company	—	6 6 8	7 17 6	—
Thomas Tyringham	—	5 0 0	4 3 2	5 15 0
Earl of Wiltshire	—	1 0 0	18 0	1 0 0
Prior of Tickford	—	6 8	—	—
Abbess of Delapre	—	1 0 0	—	—
Robert Mathew	—	1 6 8	1 2 6	1 6 8
Elizabeth Ardes	—	4 0	—	—
Thomas Chibnall, senior	—	2 0 0 }	4 1 0 (Thomas Chibnall, senior and junior)	5 16 0 (Thomas Chibnall, senior and junior)
Thomas Chibnall, junior	10 0 0	2 0 0 }		
Richard Grendon	4 0 0	2 0 0 }	2 10 9 (Richard and Thomas Grendon)	3 12 9 (Richard and Thomas Grendon)
Thomas Grendon	8 0 0	1 8 }		
John Smith	2 0 0	3 4	—	—
Henry Affeilde	1 6 8	5 0	—	—
Heirs of Henry Course	—	8 0	5 0	7 3
William Fisher	—	6 8	—	—
Thomas Course	—	6 8	6 6	7 6
John Walker	—	3 4	—	—
Thomas Butavont	—	2 0	—	—
John Addington	6 13 4	—	—	—
William Overend	5 6 8	—	—	—
Robert Grendon	2 0 0	—	—	—
William Fisher (a bill)	2 0 0	—	—	—
Richard Chibnall	1 0 0	—	—	—
Thomas Fisher	4 0 0	—	—	—
John Course	2 0 0	—	—	—
John Bocher	2 0 0	—	—	—
John Sampson	1 14 4	—	—	—
Richard Paynter	2 0 0	—	—	—
Richard Brittain	1 0 0	—	—	—
George Shortared	1 0 0	—	—	—
Thomas Eliot	2 0 0	—	—	—
Richard Eliot	1 0 0	—	—	—
Thomas Pell	2 0 0	—	—	—
Michael Smith	1 6 8	—	—	—
John Smith (a bill)	—	—	—	—
	Noe Harnesse			

[a] See text.

TABLE 26

Taxpayers in Sherington and neighbouring villages c. 1522

Compiled from the Muster Survey of 1522 and the Subsidy Roll of 1524

	Sherington	Lathbury	Hardmead	Tyringham cum Filgrave	Astwood	Chicheley	Emberton	Gayhurst
Religious[a] and civic[b] institutions	4	3	4	4	3	2	2	3
Non-resident freeholders								
With land worth £2 or more	3	3	2	—	3	2	6	—
With land worth £1 to £2	2	—	1	2	3	4	4	—
With land worth 10*s.* to £1	—	2	3	2	—	—	1	—
With land worth less than 10*s.*	5	4	4	4	—	9	7	4
Resident manorial families	2	—	—	1	—	—	—	1
Resident freeholders								
With land worth £2 or more	2	1	1	1	1	1	1	—
With land worth £1 to £2	—	—	—	—	2	5	—	—
With land worth 10*s.* to £1	—	1	1	1	2	3	5	—
With land worth under 10*s.*	3	2	2	—	1	6	8	2
Resident tenants								
With goods worth £2 or more	12	5	6	13	3	2	8	—
With goods worth £1 to £2	2	1	1	3	3	7	4	3
With goods worth £1	4	3	3	4	—	7	6	4
Labourers taxed at £1 on wages	12	19	10	5	8	5	4	5
Total number of resident lay taxpayers	37	32	24	28	20	36	36	15
Number of taxpayers, Subsidy 1524	33	39	22	29	20	32	31	16
Number of households, Lincoln Survey 1563	41	33	15	14	19	33	39	—

[a] Priories of Tickford, Ravenstone, Lavendon and Delapre.

[b] Mercers' Company.

one where he lived.[1] Goods were valued at home, so that when a village list includes a freehold rating unaccompanied by a value for goods an absentee ownership may be inferred. The survey of Sherington (Table 25) illustrates these points. Anthony Ardes and Katherine Maryot were resident but neither Anthony Catesby nor Thomas Tyringham. Four of those paying tax on land with less than 10*s*. per annum were smallholders and it is possible to tell from the place where their goods were listed that Fisher and Butavont lived in Chicheley, while Thomas Course and John Walker lived in Tyringham cum Filgrave. The rating of Elizabeth Ardes shows how effectively the commissioners had done their job: she was the heiress of her father Humphrey Ardes of Tansworth, Northamptonshire (p. 185), who had died on 3 August 1520 seised of a messuage, garden and orchard in the 'churche ende' of Sherington.[2] The subsidy roll of 1524 mentions many people assessed at one pound who were not recorded in the survey; these must be labourers taxed on their wages and accordingly they have been entered as such in Table 26. The number of resident taxpayers in Sherington was 37.

The question has often been raised by those interested in population studies whether the 1524 subsidy accurately reflects the number of households in the village.[3] For Sherington the answer is a qualified yes. The array of names given under the various headings in Table 20 shows what a sweeping change had occurred in the village population since the advent of the Tudors. That there was probably a slow but continuous shift of people from one village to another is suggested by the data assembled in Table 26, where the surprising feature is the large number of non-resident smallholders recorded under all but two of the villages concerned. These holdings were probably acquired by inheritance or marriage and so tenure may have been short. Fleeting ownership is the bugbear of population studies and the absentee landlord can fog the issue.[4] My estimate that in 1522 the number of householders in Sherington was about 38, including the rector, the resident squires and large freeholders like Thomas Chibnall, junior, and Richard Grendon is based

[1] Cf. *BRS*, VIII, xii.

[2] E150/25/10. The property no. 139 was valued at 6*s*. 8*d*. and owed a quit-rent of 1*s*. 3*d*. to Anthony Ardes. It also owed a quit-rent of 1*d*. to the Mercers' manor (Table 6).

[3] Cf. Julian Cornwall, *RB*, XVI, 258.

[4] E.g. Thomas Hooton owned 7½ acres land in Sherington, an amount too small for separate taxation, at a quit-rent of 2½*d*. to the Mercers. Between 1523 and 1537 he served repeatedly as a juror in manorial courts or as a witness to local deeds, but the survey shows that he lived in Tyringham cum Filgrave.

on a wider reading than I can claim for the other villages listed in Table 26: all the estimates, nevertheless, are in fair agreement with those given in the subsidy roll and compare favourably with the number of households recorded in the survey of Lincoln diocese made in 1563,[1] although in this latter case there are certain characteristic differences reflecting the progress, meanwhile, of the enclosure movement, to which reference is made in the next chapter.

More important perhaps than the number of householders shown in the survey is the intrinsic value of the assessments. At this distance of time we have no means of gauging the quality or quantity of a man's goods, but there are contemporary local records which make it possible to compute the value of his freehold land and thus enable us to throw some light on the question of whether Wolsey's subsidy of 1524 was extortionate, as proclaimed at the time, or just realistic.

When John de Grey reconstituted Cockfield manor *c.* 1300 the customary land, including the meadow, was worth about £5 18*s.* 6*d.* (Table 10). The value had slumped to £5 8*s.* 6*d.* in 1443[2] and was still at this figure when Colet handed over the manor to the Mercers in 1511. Under them the customary rents remained unchanged until well into the seventeenth century, and an analysis of the various tenancies set out in their survey of 1577[3] shows that the customary rent of arable land was about 6*d.*, of pasture 1*s.* and of meadow 1*s.* 8*d.* per acre respectively.[4]

Those rates must have been current during the lean years 1420–50 and showed no improvement later in the century. A survey of the nearby Ekeney cum Petsoe manor made in 1473, to which attention has already been drawn,[5] shows that under Richard Maryot the rents there had improved to 10½*d.* per acre for enclosed demesne and 8½*d.* for open-field arable land, values that are reasonably close to those Leadam computed for land in Buckinghamshire that had been enclosed before 1519, i.e. 1*s.* 3*d.* for an acre of pasture and 10½*d.* for that of arable land.[6]

The land distribution in 1522 differed from that of 1460 (Table 19) in certain minor respects; the Maryot estate included Fitz John manor as well as the holdings of Colyns and Huet, while Thomas Chibnall, junior, owned the holding of Alice Barker. The small freeholders mentioned in 1460 were those paying a quit-rent to

[1] Cf. Julian Cornwall, *RB*, XVI, 258.

[2] Cf. p. 152, n. 4.

[3] ECL, f. 143.

[4] Cf. Table 30. The rents of the tenants holdings were as follows: Fisher, £2 10*s.* 2*d.*; Chibnall, 19*s.* 8*d.*; Pierson, 8*s.* 9*d.*; Grome, £1 1*s.* 8*d.*; Disher, 8*s.* 3*d.*

[5] Cf. p. 154, n. 2.

[6] Cf. p. 152, n. 3.

Cockfield manor. No such records exist for the other three manors, but from earlier and later rolls the acreages concerned are known to have been small. With these observations in mind the value of every holding given in Table 19 has been computed both on the Mercers' and Maryot's rating and the results—for comparison with those of the muster survey of 1522—are shown in the last two columns of Table 25. It is to be remembered that the three manorial estates and that of Tyringham included freehold rents.[1]

The Mercers were absentee landlords and the school lands were in the hands of a bailiff responsible to the Company's surveyors.[2] Management and upkeep cost £1 2*s.* 0*d.* per annum and 8*d.* went in feudal dues,[3] so that the net annual income available to the school was £6 7*s.* 0*d.* in close agreement with the Survey. The spiritualities were undoubtedly taken from contemporary records in possession of the exchequer and call for no comment,[4] but the money due to the king for the fee held *in capite* (certainty money) is an interesting survival that has come to the writer's notice but once before—in the hundred rolls.[5] In most of the other cases the survey values are in general agreement with the Mercers' ratings. Anthony Ardes as a prominent man in local affairs would have been associated with the muster commissioners and his assessment in the survey was low: in the subsidy itself, however, he paid at the Maryot rating, as did his fellow landlords Katherine Maryot and Anthony Catesby. The present study, limited though it be to one village, would suggest that land was assessed by the survey commissioners at a realistic contemporary value and that its taxation in the subsidy of 1524 was in no sense extortionate.

[1] Linford manor, £1 15*s.* 0*d.*; Cave and Fitz John manors, £1 4*s.* 8*d.*; Mercers' manor, £2 8*s.* 11½*d.*; Tyringham 15*s.*

[2] The accounts of the 'Surveyors of School lands' from 1511 to 1620 are no longer available, but an old Mercers' Report mentions the account for 1524, which included 8*s.* 9*d.* for repairs at Sherington.

[3] Annual payments were £1 to the bailiff, 2*s.* to the local keeper of the woods and 4*d.* each to the Hundred Court of Bunsty and to Mrs Maryot's Court.

[4] The Delapre holding was leased for 22*s.* per annum (E318/755), the Tickford holding for 7*s.* 6*d.* per annum (E36/165/98) and the rectory during the reign of Henry VIII was worth £20 0*s.* 1*d.* clear (*Val. Eccls.* IV, 243).

[5] Cf. p. 60, n. 4.

22

THE BATTLE AGAINST ENCLOSURE

THE increase in wealth of the more opulent members of the community had its repercussions in the village where the poorer husbandman, with his few sheep and lambs, complained of overstocking to his detriment. The first rumblings came in 1525, when the jury at a Mercers' manorial court presented Lord Grey de Wilton for keeping sheep on the common fields.[1] As the Grey family had ceased to have any rights in Sherington after the sale to Sir Henry Colet just twenty years earlier we may see in this small incident the fantastic lengths to which the gentry in those days were prepared to go in order to maintain their inflated flocks. It was three years later, at the court of the same manor, that Anthony Catesby was presented for overstocking the common with sheep and his son Thomas, presumably living in the moated manor house, for overstocking with draught cattle.[2] As yet, however, there was no complaint about enclosing, although this had already occurred to a limited extent in Tyringham, Lathbury and Gayhurst during the early years of the century.[3]

The enclosure movement did not become widespread in north Buckinghamshire until about 1560 and then it was very largely due—as in other parts of the champion country—to the fall in the value of money. Landlords found themselves with incomes from land worth effectively only about one half of what they had become accustomed to in the past, and rents could not be increased overnight to counter it. A more immediate remedy lay in the fattening of cattle and sheep for the market or an increased production of wool, the choice being to some extent dictated by the nature of the land and outlets for the sale of agricultural produce. The outcry against enclosure, which was a feature of the period, was not always justified. There was a

[1] MCR, 23 Oct. 1525: 'the Lord John (recte William) Grey knight to remove his sheep from the fields of this manor, in which place he has no commons, before the feast of St Michael next under penalty of 3*s.* 4*d.*'.

[2] MCR, 28 Sept. 1528: 'They present that Anthony Catesby esq. has overstocked the commons of the lord there with his sheep. He is instructed to remove most of these sheep before the next court under penalty of 6*s.* 8*d.*'. 'They present that Thomas Catesby gent. has overstocked the commons with his draught beasts. He is instructed to remove them before the next court under a penalty of 3*s.* 4*d.*'

[3] Leadam, *The Domesday of Inclosures*, II, 574.

difference between 'enclosing to keep land for one's own intention, and forcibly turning tenants out of holdings', as Tawney so tersely put it, but not every complaint voiced in those days can be dealt with in such simple terms as this.

When Edward Ardes, for instance, fenced a piece of his own demesne land over which his villagers claimed right of common he denied them this right but did no other wrong. Sherington, however, had no open waste and grazing of all sorts was in short supply, so that every acre over which the villagers could claim right of common was precious.

To appreciate the attitude of these people to even minor enclosures in Sherington one must recall briefly the changes in the ownership of demesne pasture rights that took place during the thirteenth and fourteenth centuries. Originally these had belonged exclusively to those owning land in the demesne, but successive members of the Carun and Linford families had, on payment, allowed them to various freeholders and tenants of the open fields,[1] with the result that in 1374 a local inquisition jury could declare that the Linford demesne lands were worth nothing when fallow,[2] a sure indication that they had become subject to common of pasture. The situation presumably remained unchanged down to 1560, the only holdings in the village that were free from customary rights in one form or another being the home closes, as was traditional.

The first complaint was voiced at a manorial court of the Mercers in 1562. Edward Ardes was presented for enclosing Gowles Close (12 acres) and Stocking Close (8 acres) wherein from time immemorial the tenants had rights of common and also for overloading the commons with his sheep. He was amerced £3 *6s.* *8d.* and asked to take council with the lord, the jury asserting that he was entitled to a share of 250 sheep and no more without risk of encroaching.[3] In the same year the government sent a commission of inquiry to Buckinghamshire and both Edward Ardes and Thomas Catesby were presented for enclosing.[4] Six years later the appeal to the Mercers was a little more insistent: Edward and Thomas had fenced 60 acres to make one large close of pasture and in so doing the former had obstructed a common way

[1] Cf. pp. 108–110.

[2] C143/384/19.

[3] MCR, 29 June 1562. In the court orders of 1682 the stint for sheep was two for every acre in the fallow field and three for every acre of ley or glade. Assuming that all Edward's arable land (194 acres) was commenable—as the jury claimed—and allowing for 56 acres of ley and glade (Table 47) the number of sheep would be 260, suggesting that the same stint held in Elizabethan times.

[4] E178/424/5. Catesby was presented for 22 acres; the paragraph about Edward Ardes cannot be deciphered.

called Mill lane leading to the Sherington woods.[1] Both were also presented for overloading the common pasture to the extreme rating and stint.

The Mercers apparently took no notice of these complaints until the manorial court held in 1575, when presentments were made against Edward Ardes's widow Catherine (73 acres), William Mountgomery (18 acres) and three tenant farmers Richard Pierson ($1\frac{1}{2}$ acres), Robert Wallis ($1\frac{1}{2}$ acres) and Thomas Boswith ($1\frac{1}{2}$ acres) for enclosing.[2] A draft record of the proceedings, jotted down by the foreman of the jury while the court was in session, is preserved at Mercers' Hall and a selection of the presentments, in the day-to-day language of the period, is given in Appendix 2. The very fact that the lords of the other manors in Sherington were implicated in these complaints meant that the Mercers' Court was the only one in which such grievances could be vented, so that the presentments of their own tenants had wider implications than usual. The Mercers could not ignore the matter any longer and accordingly instructed their bailiff Thomas Fisher to institute proceedings against Catherine Ardes in the court of Star Chamber.[3]

Meanwhile there were discussions in London. John Isham, who had retired from a successful career as Mercer and Merchant Adventurer in 1572 to found a county family at Lamport in Northamptonshire, was now back in London for a year as Master Warden. It was fortunate for his colleagues that the affair had been left until his period of office, for he was well versed in the delicate negotiations that must precede enclosure by agreement, having effected this successfully at Lamport in 1570.

The next recorded step was taken at the Court of Assistants held on 31 January 1577 'At this court Mr John Isham and Mr Cokeram are appointed to ride down to Sherington between Easter and the beginning of next term and to take some good order with Mr Ards for the wrongfull inclosing of the Comens there as they shall think best either by way of exchange or stint as they shall find most comodious for the Company'. As good business men they added the rider 'and also to make sale of the old asshes there to such as will give most for them'.[4] Isham's journey into

[1] MCR, 11 Sept. 1568. The enclosure was approximately the medieval le Hoo Park: Upper Berrie Piece (24 acres), Stocking Piece (20 acres), Gowles Close (12 acres) and Dawes Gap Piece (8 acres). Thomas Tyringham was presented for overstocking.

[2] MCR, 16 Sept. 1575.

[3] St. Ch. 5, A1/23 (1576). Edward Chybnall, Anthonie Smith, Rauf Wotton and Thomas Wotton against Katherine Ardys for denying them their common of pasture in a place called the Deane (8 acres). The bill is lost, but the answer—claiming that the Deane had always been private—is preserved.

[4] MAC, 1512–1622, f. 184.

the country,[1] probably on his way home at the end of his period of office, did not immediately achieve its object, for at the court on 26 November 1578

It is agreed that Mr John Isham be written to by Mr Warden that he procede in the takinge some order with Mr Ardes for the Comens at Sherrington as he hath begonne, and to certifie him that Mr Cockeram is appointed to ride down before Easter term next, and to joyne with him therein if they shall think good and in the meanetyme the sute of Mr Fisher against Mr Ardes to stay. And further they to take order for the loppinge or felling of such old trees there as they shall thinck mete. And the charge of 20*s.* that Mr Isham disbursed in his travel the last lent is agreed to be allowed him.[2]

Fisher was also allowed the cost of his suite.[3]

As a mediator John Isham seems to have acted with courage and considerable acumen. There is no contemporary record of his discussions with Richard Ardes, but a later agreement on stinting shows that the villagers were willing to allow him to hold various parcels of land in the demesne totalling 47 acres in severalty, with the proviso that his tenant should make no claim to common in the open fields. He was also allowed a stint of three sheep per acre in demesne arable closes totalling 32 acres.[4] Richard was thus allowed exclusive rights over about 9 per cent of the demesne lands, or no more than 3½ per cent of the land over which the villagers claimed right of common. The outcome was really a significant victory for the villagers, seeing that Richard and his fellow landowner William Mountgomery would eventually have followed the lead of most of their neighbouring squires and enclosed the whole of the demesne land if a powerful outside body had not put a curb on their activities. As he gazed towards the west from the upper windows of his manor house alongside the church, and observed that all the fields spread over Tyringham hill had been enclosed, Richard must have felt that John Isham had given him a raw deal!

Thomas Tyringham, who had enclosed these fields in 1562, has been pilloried as a typical depopulator who turned people out of their tenements and the prime cause

[1] He was in Sherington with Cockeram on 19 Sept. 1577 and as surveyor of the school lands he drew up a complete rental and survey of the estate on the testimony of Edward Chibnall and three other tenants. The original document is preserved at Mercers' Hall and a copy is in RCL, 143–164 (cf. Tables 6, 47–51).

[2] MAC, 1561–1595, f. 324.

[3] MAC, 1512–1622, f. 187.

[4] Cf. p. 262, Table 48: Wood Close (8 acres), Spinney bushes or Dry Bank (7 acres), Gore Leys (20 acres) and Little Hill piece or Cowley's fields (12 acres) were to be held in severalty; part of Nether Berry Piece (8 acres) and Upper Berry Piece (24 acres) were to be stinted.

of much local discontent. Superficially this view could be correct, for he admitted to the destruction of seven homes of husbandry, but a closer look at the situation suggests that his move was part of a planned economy and that those most nearly concerned suffered little if any hardship. The urge to enclose would have been in the blood of the family ever since the creation of new sheep-walks became profitable, for the various members must have been fully aware of the value of their land, as put so appositely by a later authority on Buckinghamshire agriculture 'It is not a question with me, nor does a doubt exist in my mind that the grazing lands in the extreme parts of the county . . . and along the Ouse at Tyringham are equally as rich and fertile as any in the vale of Aylesbury'.[1] The first attempt to improve his land was made by Thomas Tyringham in 1509 when he pulled down two houses and enclosed 77 acres of arable land. He admitted this at an inquest held in 1517, but when summoned before Wolsey three years later he declared that one of the houses had been rebuilt and that all the land had gone back to tillage.[2] The muster survey of 1522 for Tyringham cum Filgrave is fully in keeping with such situation. There were then ten small freeholders—about the same as in the Hundred Rolls of 1279[3] and of these, eight were non-resident (Table 26). But the most interesting feature was the presence of nine tolerably wealthy tenant farmers (Table 27), about double the number at that time in Sherington, with approximately the same total acreage. The general picture is that of a prosperous community with the lord of the manor farming his own demesne of 400 acres,[4] including 50 acres of meadow.[4]

A short while before his death in 1526 Thomas was frustrated by the abbot of Lavendon[5] in his attempt to enclose 30 acres in Filgrave. His son, another Thomas, was more successful in 1562; he destroyed seven farm houses and enclosed the 480 acres of land that went with them. This was reported at a government inquiry held three years later,[6] but no remedial action was taken and he received pardon for the enclosure in 1578.[7] What had happened in the meanwhile to the prosperous tenant farmers of 1522? Had their sons and grandsons been turned out as popular tradition assumes? Thomas Course junior, the son of Thomas senior (d. 1557) and grandson

[1] Rev. John Priest, *General View of the Agriculture of Buckinghamshire* (1810).

[2] Leadam, *The Domesday of Inclosures*, I, 195.

[3] *Hundred Rolls* (Rec. Com.), II, 348. The Tyringham estate embraced a large part of Filgrave and was generally referred to in later deeds indifferently as such or as Tyringham cum Filgrave.

[4] C133/7/6.

[5] C1/536/15.

[6] E178/424.

[7] C66/1174/45, 46.

TABLE 27

Thomas Tyringham and his tenant farmers in Tyringham cum Filgrave

From the Muster Survey of 1522

	Annual value					
	Land			Goods		
	£	s.	d.	£	s.	d.
Thomas Tyringham	20	0	0	80	0	0
Ralph Course	—			8	0	0
Thomas Course, senior	—			16	13	4
Thomas Course, junior	—			1	3	4
William Course	—			6	13	4
John Malyns	—			10	0	0
Richard Malyns	—			5	0	0
Thomas Walker	10	0		8	0	0
Thomas Darling	—			6	0	0
John Marshall	—			6	0	0

of Ralph (d. 1547) died in 1557 leaving an only child Elizabeth, then under age.[1] John Malyns was dead in 1525; his only son Richard (d. 1547) had an only son of the same name who died childless in 1560.[2] Thomas Walker died in 1539, also childless.[3] Thomas Tyringham exhibited a list of twenty tenants in Filgrave when challenged about enclosure there by Catherine Ardes of Sherington in 1571.[4] All the old family names mentioned in Table 27 had gone except that of Marshall, and in the intervening years at least six, if not seven, farms would have reverted to him as landlord by death without direct heirs. Those which were on Tyringham hill, to the south of Filgrave and bounded on the south and west by the Ouse he kept in hand as demesne so as to be able to enclose when he thought fit. This can be inferred from his statement in reply to Catherine Ardes. It was the land grouped around his manor house, stretching right across the hill and down to the river—extending to about 800 acres, including his old demesne, that he enclosed in 1562. He would, of course, have denied some of the smaller villagers their right of common, and presumably he transferred these rights to Filgrave, where, he stated, there were still 600 acres under tillage. The hardship that he inflicted may thus have been no more severe than that

[1] MCR, 29 Jan. 1562. D/A/We/4, f. 159. D/A/We/10, f. 52. D/A/We/11, f. 169.

[2] D/A/We/6, f. 271; 11 f. 68.

[3] D/A/We/3, f. 227.

[4] St. Ch. 5, A37/20.

experienced by the smaller villagers during the many enclosures by agreement referred to in later chapters. The case illustrates from a different angle than usual the phenomenon that is apparent throughout all these studies on Sherington: a shifting population with families dying out or migrating at a rate that is surprisingly fast. Thomas Tyringham 'depopulated' Tyringham in the parlance of the day, but it is the writer's firm conviction that he did not turn many people out—he merely refrained from filling up vacancies when nature conveniently provided them for him.

23

THE LEASING OF SHERINGTON RECTORY

DURING the late fifteenth and early sixteenth centuries heretical views based on the exercise of 'private judgement' were widely held in Buckinghamshire, especially in the south, and as Sister Elspeth has suggested, these may have contributed to the deplorable state in which Bishop Atwater found the churches when he made a visitation of the archdeaconry in 1519.[1] The majority of the churches were ill-kept and forlorn, and only 22 were returned as *omnia bene*. The church at Sherington was so described,[2] perhaps because the parishioners had had with them for very many years past a stipendiary curate as well as a resident rector to keep them in tune with the old faith.[3] This happy situation, nevertheless, was not likely to continue indefinitely, for a benefice that provided for a curate in this way was a tempting bait for those who had to cater either directly or indirectly for the public service.

Robert Kencot, appointed rector in 1520, died early in 1535[4] and within a few weeks the bishop of Lincoln collated his own chaplain, Thomas Robertson.[5] This brought him into conflict with Henry VIII's minister Cromwell, who wanted the benefice for his own nominee Christopher Rookes, sometime chaplain to the old duchess of Norfolk. Assuming that the right of presentation was with the Crown Cromwell gave Rookes the king's mandate to the bishop, who demured. In a letter to Cromwell he pointed out that the bishops of Lincoln had been patrons for 242 years, and if now he were to obey the king's mandate he or his successors would find it difficult to sustain their title in the future. Robertson had already been instituted and had paid £10 for his first-fruits 'there were few men so learned in divinity,

[1] *VCH Bucks*, I, 297.

[2] *LRS*, XXXIII, 54.

[3] Richard Hawardyn, who succeeded John Proctor in 1510, died in 1518. The next rector Richard Mawdley was a pluralist and absentee, but he resigned a few months later and the bishop collated Robert Kencot in 1520. When a clerical subsidy was collected in 1526 Robert was taxed on £20 per annum and his curate Edward Skinner on £5 6*s*. 8*d*. (*OHS*, LXIII, 232).

[4] He was a man of some wealth (Table 25) and in his will left generous sums of money to his church and many local people (D/A/We/3, f. 74).

[5] Lincoln Reg. 27, f. 220.

latin and greek, or so meet to serve your Highness as touching good letters. He lately preached a sermon against the usurped power of the bishop of Rome, such as few in the realm have done.' Rookes, on the other hand, was 'but a bare clerke and of slendre lerenyng'. He begged to be allowed to exhibit his title. Cromwell agreed, and no more was heard of the matter.[1]

Thomas Robertson was a worthy scholar and one of the compilers of the Liturgy; as such he needed financial support and this was provided on a generous scale by his many preferments. Sherington to him was no more than one of his sources of income: he was an absentee and during his incumbancy the spiritual welfare of the village was delegated to the curate John Robertson.[2] He resigned in 1544, having sometime before then leased the rectory to William Hatton, a king's servant who, dying in that year, bequeathed the remainder of the term to his wife Elizabeth.[3] Yet in spite of this diversion of the rectorial dues Thomas, with the bishop's approval, was assigned for the rest of his life a pension of £5 per annum. He was to become dean of Durham in 1557, but two years later was ejected as a papist, when presumably all his clerical emoluments lapsed.

His successor in Sherington, William Rolston,[4] who took over a sadly denuded benefice in 1544, kept in close contact with his people[5] and guided them successfully through the Marian religious upheavals. He died soon after that queen in 1558, and was succeeded by John Man,[6] a pluralist who within a year exchanged for Adstock, Buckinghamshire, with Francis Babington the rector of Lincoln College, Oxford, a corporation owning the neighbouring hamlet of Ekeney cum Petsoe. Francis, likewise a pluralist, found the rectory free from outside commitments in 1559 and thereupon leased it for nine years to William Capon, a fortunate move on his part because he remained a papist during the early years of Elizabeth and by 1562 was forced to resign all his benefices.

The leasing of a rectory, even for a very long period, was not illegal in those days and Francis was but following the lead of others—many of them in the episcopate—when he mortgaged the future of his benefice and jeopardized the livelihood of his successors in return for ready cash. Many shrewd financiers, especially in the city of London, were alive to the trend of economic change through which England, like

[1] L and P, Henry VIII, IX, 117, 349, 453, 471, 569.

[2] Lincoln Archives: Epis. visitation, 154d, f. 60d.

[3] D/A/Wf/1/301. The conditions of the lease are not known.

[4] Lincoln Reg. 27, f. 227.

[5] He witnessed many local wills.

[6] Lincoln Reg. 28, f. 147.

the rest of Europe, was then passing and they were only too willing to put out their money in such a way. Details of Francis's lease are lacking, but within a fortnight of its sealing William Capon sold it for £20 to Gregory Coulton.[1] Francis was succeeded in 1562 by Giles Snell[2] who seems to have died six years later.

The next rector Henry Barlow was a dissolute fellow whose ill-treatment of the benefice had a far more lasting effect. His life in Sherington as a priest was so irregular that two of the leading inhabitants, Edward Ardes and Christopher Hollyman, on behalf of the general community, waited on the bishop in 1575 at his palace at Buckden to lodge a complaint against him.[3] The archdeacon also was repeatedly citing him for neglect in allowing the parsonage house to fall into ruins.[4] The Babington lease having expired in 1568 Henry, only a few weeks after he had been admitted to office, himself leased the rectory on 24 December for 80 years to William Collinson, reserving a stipend of £28 per annum for the rector.[5] Long leases such as this were keenly sought after by the financiers: John Isham, for instance, who was concerned a little later with the Mercers' manor,[6] had in the same year negotiated a 99-year lease of the rectory of Lamport, Northamptonshire, a village in which he had lately acquired much land.[7] Many of the rectors in the decades following the reformation were men of mean intellect who could be easily tempted by what seemed a generous offer of ready cash and by 1571 the abuse was becoming so widespread that parliament was forced to set a limit to the provisions of such leases.[8]

Sherington rectory had been taxed at £20 10*s*. 8*d*. per annum in 1535[9] and so at first sight a stipend of £28 per annum in 1568 may not appear ungenerous. Since 1530, however, there had been a sharp fall in the value of money, due to the influx of silver, and a corresponding rise in the value of tithe and agricultural produce. To use a modern expression, the financiers of the period knew that they were operating in a rising market. Less than a fortnight after the attesting of Barlow's lease—which had been approved without delay (for a substantial fee?) by the bishop of Lincoln and the dean and chapter of Lincoln cathedral—Collinson sold it to Francis and

1 C3/33/69. The two financiers quarrelled over payment.

2 Lincoln Reg. 28, ff. 69, 214.

3 *LRS*, II, 136.

4 D/A/V/1, ff. 32, 43.

5 *BAS*, 915/43. Lincoln Patent Book, Bij. 3.17, f.2. The rector at his own cost was to maintain the various buildings and the chancel of the church, as well as pay all taxes.

6 Cf. p. 171–2.

7 Mary E. Finch, *The Wealth of Five Northamptonshire Families*, *NRS*, XIX, 20–2.

8 Cf. Mary E. Finch, *loc. cit.* p. 21, n. 6.

9 *Val. Eccl.* (Rec. Com.), IV, 243.

Nicholas Bullingham, who disposed of it six years later to Dr John Belley.[1] In his turn Belley sub-let it on a yearly basis for £50 per annum to Christopher Hollyman of Sherington, who was then serving in Queen Elizabeth's guard. Clearly the rectory must have been already worth more than £78 per annum.[2] John Isham, who has been mentioned above, boasted that within a very few years of its purchase, Lamport rectory was showing a clear profit of £100 per annum. On John Belley's death in 1600 the lease was inherited by Sir Thomas Belley, who sold it in 1615 to Sir William Andrews of Lathbury. The latter disposed of the last 21 years of the lease in 1627 to Roger Nichols of Clifton Reynes for the large sum of £1000, showing that the rectory by then must have been worth more than £100 per annum.[3]

It is not until we turn back to the benefice itself that we see this long drawn out and disgraceful financial episode in true and melancholy perspective. Barlow had died in 1581 and his successor John Martin, who came of good family, was forced to reside elsewhere because Sherington could offer no habitable parsonage house.[4] In 1600 he took to wife 'a woman of good lyffe and honest conversation', in keeping with Queen Elizabeth's injunction,[5] and seven years later he built at his own expense a new parsonage house[6] which, with a few eighteenth-century additions, survived more or less unaltered until recent times. There he lived until his death in 1626, drawing throughout the whole of his incumbancy the stipend of £28 per annum that had been clamped upon him and his successors by Henry Barlow. When Sir William Andrews sold the lease in the following year his conscience must have been giving him just a little twinge, for the conveyance contains a clause to the effect that Roger Nichols should pay to the rector of Sherington 40*s*. per annum 'if the said parson will receive the same'.[7] One feels that John Martin would have spurned the miserable peace-offering, but his successor Thomas Gilder may have been forced by circumstances to be more humble and conciliatory.

[1] *BAS*, 915/43.

[2] Req. 2/131/10.

[3] *BAS*, 915/43.

[4] *LRS*, 23, *Liber clerici* (1585).

[5] Lincoln: certificates for ministers wives, 7, f. 11. His wife was Marie Copley.

[6] Lincoln archives: VIII, Terriers, 1625, p. 2, vol. 6. 'A parsonage house newly built by the incumbant now lifyng contaynynge five bays, all of stone, a hall, a parlor, a kytchyn, a buttery and a bouldynge house, with chambers over every one well and sufficiently bourded. An above house annexe thereunto of one baye and there is also a parsonage barne of seaven bayes, repaired also by the saed incumbant. A hay barne and a stable of 3 bays.'

[7] *BAS*, 915/43.

24

THE IMPOVERISHMENT OF THE MANORIAL FAMILIES

WITH its four little manors now merged into three Sherington during the reigns of Elizabeth and James I reflects the economic forces that were inexorably changing the social structure of England. The owners of two of the manors, representatives of very old but lesser gentry, were unable to adapt themselves to the new world into which they were moving; the one because of personal extravagance and malpractice, the other—so it would seem—from sheer inertia. Even the Mercers, those astute businessmen who recognized the need to counter inflation, were forced by reasons that will be made clear later to accept a slow rate of growth in income from Sherington. Only the freeholders and the larger tenant farmers were on the upgrade. As the Mercers' holding provides a stable background against which those of Ardes and Mountgomery can be assessed it will be convenient to discuss its economy first.

The Mercers' tenants in Sherington were able to weather the inflation storm in the last half of the sixteenth century without embarrassment because land there was held by custom of the manor and this was not readily susceptible to change. Such conditions did not hold in many of the other properties in the Colet Trust and there had been an overall increase of income more than sufficient to meet the rising cost of running the school. The Mercers could thus afford to treat their tenants in Sherington with a benevolence that would have been quite unrealistic on the part of the other two manorial owners there, neither of whom had outside support to help counter the ever-increasing cost of living.

Freehold tenants of Mercers' manor owed a relief of a year's rent on death or exchange: copyhold tenure, at rents fixed when the manor was created *c.* 1300, were for life, a heriot of one year's rent being due on death or exchange of tenant. A copyholder paid a fine on admission or for permission to bring in a second life, and the sum of money demanded was the only item in the manorial economy that could be varied by the lord. The profits of court for successive decades until 1620

TABLE 28

Profits of court, 1511–1520

(Mercers' manor)

	Freehold reliefs £ s. d.	Customary heriots £ s. d.	Customary fines for entry £ s. d.	Total for decade £ s. d.	Decade average per annum £ s. d.
1511–20	—	—	3 0	3 0	3½
1521–30	3 9½	—	2 0	5 9½	7
1531–40	1 13 2½	—	5 4	1 18 6½	3 10¼
1541–50	1 19 7½	1 6 8	3 4	2 19 9¼	5 11¾
1551–60	1 11 1	19 8	4 0 0	5 11 1	13 4
1561–70	2 4 5½	3 9 10	3 0 0	8 14 3½	17 5
1571–80	6 11½	—	2 0 0	2 6 11½	4 8½
1581–90	—	8 9	20 0 0	20 8 9	2 0 10½
1591–1600	—	—	30 0 0	30 0 0	3 0 0
1601–10	4 2½	—	20 0 0	20 4 2½	2 0 5
1611–20	2 0 4½	1 19 2	52 10 0	56 9 6½	5 13 0

are set out in Table 28.[1] The fines for entry remained nominal until about 1550, but by the turn of the century they had risen to ten times the annual rent for one life and double that amount for two. As rents remained fixed these increases were modest.

The copyhold of the Chibnalls (Table 30, n. 158), which ran for an extraordinary long period without interruption, illustrates many of these points. Thomas was granted the cottage, pasture and meadow for life in 1512 at a rent of 10*s.* 8*d.* per annum and a fine of 2*s.* The arable land was added in 1537 at a rent of 9*s.* and a fine of 3*s.* 6*d.* The inclusive rent of 19*s.* 8*d.* was being paid by his grandson Edward in 1593 when he gave the Mercers a fine of £20 to bring into the copy his sons John and Edward. At the Court of Assistants held on 12 March 1613 Edward junior surrendered his interest in favour of John's son John, a boy of 8. When granting this privilege the members of the court showed that they could, at times, put pleasure before business. The election feast of the new master warden would be held in a few weeks time, and the entry in the court book ends with 'John gave the lord a fine for one of his status and there was to be had for it two fat bucks'.[2] John the grandson

[1] Compiled from court rolls. There are gaps in the series of rolls before 1560, but the missing items would add but a few shillings to the totals given.

[2] MAC, 1513–1622, ff. 311–12, March 1613. MCR, 24 July 1623.

survived until 1670, so that the fine of 1593 was equivalent to an increase of 5*s.* 2*d.* per annum rent for the next 77 years.

Another source of revenue from Sherington was the sale of wood. The hedgerows of the home closes abounded with oak, ash and elm, so that village needs could be readily satisfied without cutting timber from the main wood.[1] It must be remembered, nevertheless, that a copyholder could not cut timber growing on his holding without the lord's permission, but the Mercers granted this at frequent intervals, the allowance being reasonably generous.[2]

There is no information about the exploitation of Mercers' Wood before 1544. The trees would have been felled on occasion when the local market for timber was good,[3] but replacement was probably left to chance or even to nature. As the century unfolded, however, the national demand for timber increased decade by decade and the government rightly took steps to encourage the more enlightened system of 'coppice with standards', which was given statutory sanction in 1544, the number of standards being fixed at twelve per acre.[4] The Mercers were alive to the change and a few months previously had ordered their surveyor of lands to clear out all old timber to the best advantage.[5] Anthony Cave, who was then negotiating with the king for the purchase of some of the Tickford priory property in Chicheley, mentions that the wood sales at Sherington in May of that year were not going well.[6] The Mercers applied the coppice system to Mercers' Wood in 1545 and at the end of fifteen years the new growth was sold to John Marshe of the city of London for £30 (30*s.* per acre) on condition that he removed the timber within two years, that he left a sufficient number of standrels, and that he kept the wood fenced during the ensuing eight years to protect the spring (young growth) according to the statute of Parliament. He was moreover to discharge the Company of all tithe that might acrue to the parson of Sherington. Similar leases for terms of ten or fifteen years were subsequently granted in succession to the surveyor Thomas Coleshill, to Henry Isham, Gregory Isham and Alderman Sir Thomas Bennett, all of whom were, in turn, master warden of the Company.[7] As the current rate for timber during the

[1] The Mercers' survey of 1577 shows 586 trees growing in the home closes of the manor (RCL, ff. 143 *et seq.*).

[2] Cf. p. 278.

[3] In 1526 the local bailiff was instructed not to sell wood or underwood without the consent of the surveyor (MAC, 1513–1622, f. 26).

[4] S. T. Bindoff, *Tudor England*, p. 11.

[5] MAC, 1573–1620, f. 40 (12 Dec. 1543).

[6] L and P, Hen. VIII, XIX, part 2, 482.

[7] MAC, 1513–1622, f. 70 (12 Dec. 1560); f. 160 (18 Jan. 1571); f. 175 (16 Feb. 1575); f. 222 (16 July 1586); f. 255 (28 Aug. 1594); f. 279 (22 April 1601).

period in question was 5*s*. 6*d*. to 6*s*. 6*d*. per acre the trusteeship was being judiciously blended with a modicum of private gain.[1]

The net income of the Mercers' manor decade by decade until 1620 is given in Table 29.[2] At the end of the century the increase was of the order of 50 per cent, very much less than would be shown by many an estate in private hands and, as already mentioned, by the Colet foundation as a whole. The contrast with the other two manorial estates in Sherington, however, is a rather sorry one, for both were in low water and outlying farms had either been sold off or were to become so within a few years.

TABLE 29

Annual income of the Mercers' estate, 1511–1620

Period	Freehold and customary rents £ *s*. *d*.	Rent from Woods £ *s*. *d*.	Profits of court £ *s*. *d*.	Total receipts £ *s*. *d*.	Outgoings[a] £ *s*. *d*.	Net income £ *s*. *d*.
1511–20	7 17 6	—	3½	7 17 9¾	1 1 8	6 16 1¾
1521–30	7 17 6	—	7	7 18 1	1 1 8	6 16 5
1531–40	7 17 6	—	3 10¼	8 1 4½	1 2 8	6 18 8½
1541–50	7 17 6	—	5 11¾	8 3 5¾	1 2 8	7 0 9¾
1551–60	7 17 6	—	13 4	8 10 10	1 2 8	7 8 2
1561–70	7 17 6	3 0 0	17 5	11 14 11	1 2 8	10 12 3
1571–80	7 17 6	2 0 0	4 8½	10 2 2	1 4 0	8 18 2
1581–90	7 17 6	2 0 0	2 0 10½	11 18 4½	1 4 0	10 14 4½
1591–1600	7 17 6	2 0 0	3 0 0	12 17 6	1 4 0	11 13 6
1601–10	7 17 6	2 0 0	2 0 5	11 17 11	1 4 0	10 13 11
1611–20	7 17 6	2 0 0	5 13 0	15 10 6	1 4 0	14 6 6

[a] Cf. p. 168, n. 3. Payment for the care of the wood was 1*s*. per annum until 1530, 2*s*. per annum from 1531 to 1570 and thereafter 3*s*. 4*d*. per annum.

Linford manor had been settled by Anthony Ardes *c*. 1540 on his son Edward, who was then acting as bailiff and collector of the lands surrendered by Lavendon abbey at its dissolution in 1536.[3] As such he would appear to have taken no direct part in the scramble for monastic land that was a feature of the period, but within a few weeks of relinquishing the appointment on 25 February 1545 he acquired

[1] NRS, XIX, 118, n. 6; 163, n. 4.

[2] John Harrison, highmaster of the school in 1595, sued the Mercers as trustees in that year before the Court of Arches: *inter alia* an account was given of the school income and expenditure for the ten years to 1595. The rents at Sherington were returned as £7 17*s*. 6*d*. per annum and of the wood as £2 per annum. Profits of court were not itemized. (E 101/522/8 A.)

[3] L and P, Hen. VIII, XX, part 1, 676.

from Nicholas Wallis of Sherington a small farm there (Table 19, no. 138, late Delapre abbey)[1] and from Thomas Lawe of Olney a small estate in Lathbury worth £6 5*s*. 4*d*. per annum (late of Lavendon abbey) as well as the advowson of Hardmead (late of Merton priory)[2] suggesting that in the meanwhile his friends have been active on his behalf. He continued to serve the government as one of the feodaries of the Court of Wards and in 1563–5 was the escheator for Buckinghamshire. It was during this latter period, towards the end of his life, that he seems to have become worried about the spendthrift propensities of his eldest son Richard, for within a few weeks of his death on 3 November 1570[3] he entailed the Sherington estate in a way that showed his distrust. With royal permission[4] he enfeoffed trustees, including his cousin Thomas Snagg, to hold to the use of his wife Catherine for life and ten years after, then to the use of Richard in tail male, with contingent remainders to his eight other sons in succession.[5] Richard was thus barred from his inheritance until ten years after his mother's decease. The breach between father and son seems to have been complete, for in his will Edward left all his outlying property in Hardmead and several other nearby places to his second son Thomas, who was made joint executor with his mother. Richard was not mentioned.[6]

Educated at Cambridge,[7] Richard was already in debt by 1570,[8] even though his first wife Margaret, who died at Turvey, Bedfordshire, some four years later, had a life interest in an estate at Graveney, Kent.[9] Unlike his brothers Thomas and Edward, who had come into immediate possession of their patrimony,[10] Richard was dependent on the goodwill of his mother and her trustees for financial support.

1 E368/385.

2 L and P, Hen. VIII, xviii, part 1 g, 981(41); R. E. C. Waters, *Chester of Chicheley*, I, 85.

3 C142/217/114.

4 C66/1069.

5 The abstract of title to Linford manor states that the grant to trustees was made by deed pole, to hold to the use of a pair of indentures dated 11 September 1570 (D/Ch/188/1). The originals are lost, but the provisions were recited by Catherine the widow when distrained to show her title to the manor in Trinity Term 1571 (E368/385).

6 PCC 31 Martyn.

7 With his brother Thomas he matriculated from St John's College in Michaelmas Term 1554.

8 C54/817, recognizance for £80, to be void if £40 be paid to Thomas Chibnall at his mansion house in Husbands Crawley, Bedfordshire, before a certain date. Req. 2/167/37, mentions debt of £60.

9 C142/172/146. The estate passed at her death to a son by a previous marriage. Richard was sued for £33 6*s*. 8*d*. in connexion with the son's marriage (Req. 2/202/7).

10 Thomas inherited the Linford property in Manton, Rutland, which he sold in 1571 and a manor in Hardmead, with lands in Chicheley and Astwood, all of which were sold in 1581 (*VCH Rutland*, 80; CP40/1404/160). He acquired Flavell's farm in Renhold, Bedfordshire (*VCH Beds*, III, 216). Edward inherited a 21-year lease of John Newman's farm in Emberton.

Ardes (Ardres) of Turvey (T), Hardmead (H) and Sherington (S)

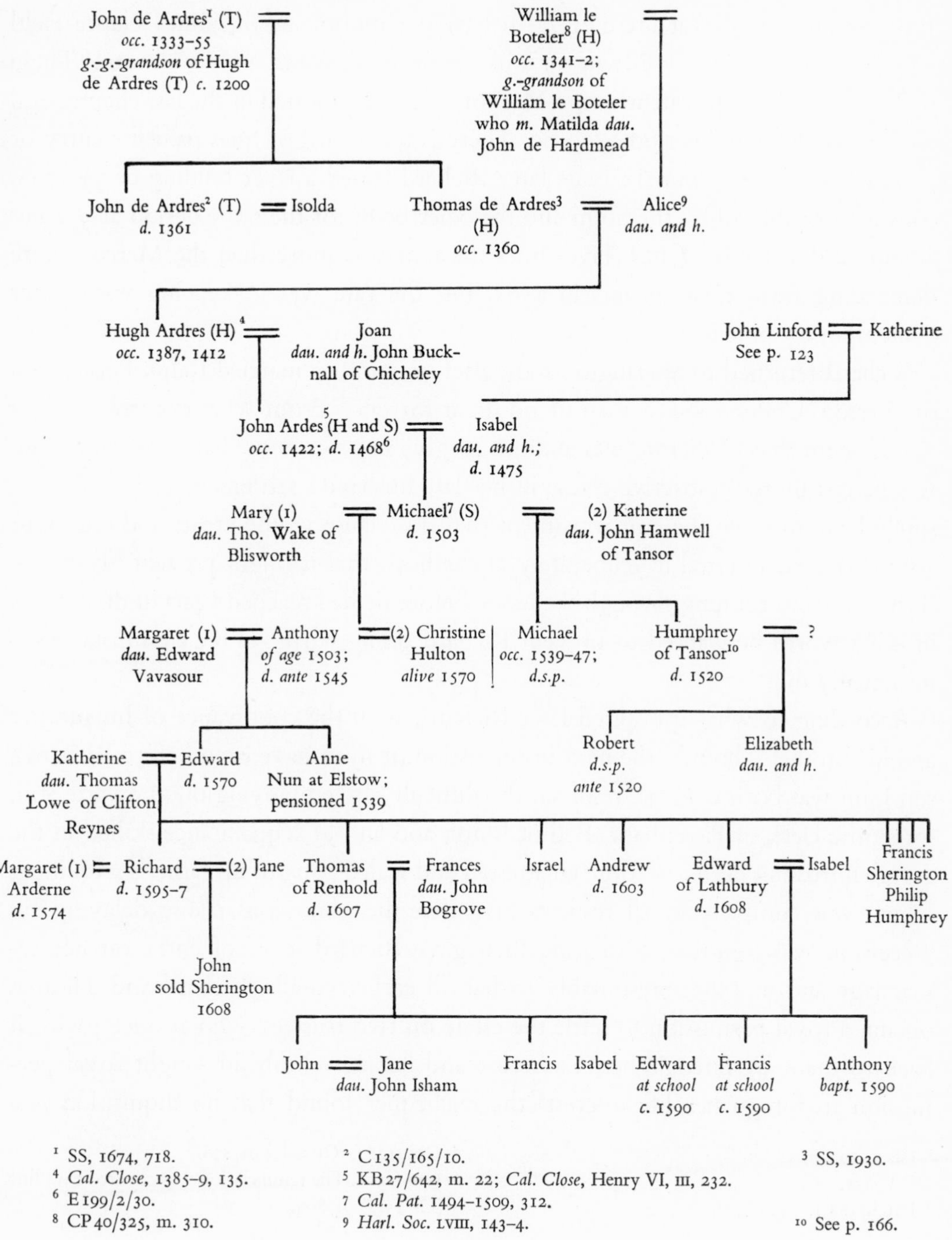

1 SS, 1674, 718.
2 C135/165/10.
3 SS, 1930.
4 *Cal. Close*, 1385–9, 135.
5 KB27/642, m. 22; *Cal. Close*, Henry VI, III, 232.
6 E199/2/30.
7 *Cal. Pat.* 1494–1509, 312.
8 CP40/325, m. 310.
9 *Harl. Soc.* LVIII, 143–4.
10 See p. 166.

Catherine was running the estate in 1576, when she leased the farm that her husband had acquired from Richard and Thomas Grendon (Table 30, no. 177) to Robert Bosworth for 21 years at a rent of £4 10*s.* 0*d.* per annum and the joint Delapre-Field farm (no. 138)[1] to Henry Edwin for a like period at £2 13*s.* 4*d.* per annum.[2] These rents are roughly equivalent to the Maryot rating mentioned in the last chapter and were modest for the period 1570–80. There is no record of fines paid for entry or perhaps for renewal, but six years later Richard leased a river holding of 3½ acres, consisting of the cobbs, the holm and the ozier beds, for the same period at £2 per annum and a fine of £10.[3] Five times the rent was more than the Mercers were demanding from their tenants in 1565, but the rate was in keeping with other contemporary practice.

Richard returned to Sherington soon after his mother married Ralph Pemberton of Weston Underwood, a man of no great fortune. From what occurred later it would seem that Catherine was anxious to give her son immediate possession, but was barred by the restrictive clause in her late husband's settlement. Edward must surely have foreseen the embarrassment that this clause would create and one must assume that he inserted it deliberately in the hope that it might prevent his spendthrift son from running through the estate before he had reached years of discretion: in other words he wanted to prevent Richard doing what—in the circumstances—he actually did.

According to what transpired later Richard, with the connivance of his mother and his brother Thomas, the next in succession (it must have been before Richard's son John was born *c.* 1574), resolved the difficulty by employing one Edward Still, sometime clerk of Pavenham, Bedfordshire, and an old acquaintance skilled in the art of engrossing deeds, to forge an attested and sealed copy of his father's settlement which was complete in all respects save that the obnoxious clause delaying his succession was omitted. Catherine then gave Richard leave of entry on her remarriage and in 1585, presumably to bar all earlier entails, Richard and Thomas obtained royal permission to settle the estate on two trustees, who at once passed it back to them by fine.[4] When Catherine and her new husband sought royal permission to forego her life interest[5] the exchequer found that no inquisition *post*

[1] Cf. p. 192, n. 1.

[2] D/C/1/1.

[3] D/Ch/188/1. D/C/1/2.

[4] C66/1267. CP25(2) 91/806.

[5] C66/1311. The renunciation was covered by a fine (CP25(2) 91/809).

TABLE 30

Holders of land in Sherington in 1580

Numbers shown thus, 63*, are not included in the area shown on Map 8; the direction in which they lie is indicated on the map.

No. on Map 8	Owner	Tenant or description	Messuages	Cottages	Demesne Pasture (a.)	Demesne Arable (a.)	Open fields Pasture (a.)	Open fields Arable (a.)	Meadow (a.)	Wood (a.)
188	Richard Ardes	Manor and demesne	1	4	77	194	—	—	8	20
	Richard Ardes	Tile house, Robert Bosworth	1	—	$5\frac{1}{4}$	—	—	70	$3\frac{1}{4}$	—
177	Richard Ardes	Ralph White	—	1	—	—	—	11	—	—
138	Richard Ardes	Henry Edwin	1	—	6	—	$2\frac{1}{2}$	$65\frac{1}{2}$	$2\frac{1}{2}$	—
19		Ralph Hooton								
52	Thomas Tyringham	Thomas Bauswell	1	3	26	—	—	76	4	6
54		John Barnes								
120*	Lord Mordaunt	Edward Fisher	1	—	27	—	—	—	—	—
89	Wm. Mountgomery	Manor and demesne	1	—	44	140	—	—	4	36
15	Wm. Mountgomery	John Knight								
18	Wm. Mountgomery	Thomas Orpen								
33	Wm. Mountgomery	Bartholomew Course								
46	Wm. Mountgomery	John Hall	5	7	11	—	8	346	13	—
53a	Wm. Mountgomery	William Field								
106*	Wm. Mountgomery	Richard Ford								
182	Wm. Mountgomery	Edward Wallis								
153, 159	Mercers' Company	Manor farm, Thomas Fisher	1	1	15	11	—	50	3	20
158	Mercers' Company	Edward Chibnall	—	1	—	2	$2\frac{3}{4}$	$12\frac{3}{4}$	4	—
162	Mercers' Company	John Pierson	—	1	$1\frac{1}{2}$	—	—	$13\frac{1}{2}$	$\frac{1}{2}$	—
178	Mercers' Company	Agnes Grome	1	—	$3\frac{3}{4}$	$6\frac{1}{2}$	—	$35\frac{1}{2}$	—	—
		Thomas Disher	—	—	—	—	$2\frac{1}{2}$	—	4	—
157, 41	Edward Chibnall	—	1	2	—	—	10	$129\frac{1}{2}$	6	—
198	Anthony Smith	—	1	—	—	—	—	8	—	—
53	Thomas Orpen	—	1	—	—	—	—	10	—	—
63*	John Springnell	—	1	—	—	—	—	7	—	—
40	Ralph Hooton	—	1	—	—	—	—	20	—	—
179	Rector	—	1	—	$4\frac{1}{2}$	—	—	15	$1\frac{3}{4}$	—
			21	20	225	$353\frac{1}{2}$	$25\frac{3}{4}$	$870\frac{3}{4}$	54	82

mortem had been called for after the death of Edward, a tenant in chief. Somewhat belatedly this was held on 8 February 1588 and among the various documents of title exhibited to the jury was the forged indenture giving Richard the reversion on his mother's death.[1]

When Richard first gained possession the open-field farms were on lease to the sitting tenants until 1597. To raise money he granted a reversionary lease of these farms, together with 8½ acres of demesne pasture, to his friend Christopher Hollyman, for 21 years from Michaelmas 1598 at a rent of £47 per annum.[2] Such a sum was equivalent to about 5*s.* 3*d.* per acre per annum for arable land and 10*s.* per acre for meadow and pasture, values in reasonable accord with those current in neighbouring counties at the turn of the century.[3] Christopher paid a fine for entry of £20,[4] or at the rate of 2*s.* 3*d.* per acre, a sum that seems very small in light of Richard's needs, but again it was in keeping with current practice.[5]

Having thus obtained some ready cash and assured himself of what seemed a reasonable income from the farms until 1619, Richard decided to sell the various freeholds concerned. He approached his powerful neighbour at Tyringham. In Thomas Tyringham's own words 'Richard, by his loose dealings drawne into distresse and myserye did labor (him) many times to purchase parcels of the manor lands'. Whereupon Thomas 'altogethere ignorant of the forgerye and synister practices beforehand by Richard and his friends, and pitying his distress and favouring him as a neighbour and friend, and reposing great trust in him, did purchase several parcels of land'. The sale by Richard and his brother Thomas, with royal licence, of the two farms and various small parcels of land to Thomas Tyringham and his son Anthony for £370 was made on 7 March 1588, the purchasers to recive the rents under the existing leases, but only £10 16*s.* 0*d.* per annum from the enhanced rent to be paid by Hollyman after 1598.[6] The next year there was a further agreement between the same parties for the sale of the manorial rights for £165,

[1] C142/217/114.

[2] D/C/1/1.

[3] In 1609 the extensive lands of the Queen's manor of Newport Pagnell were valued per acre per annum at 5*s.* for arable land, 10*s.* for meadow and 13*s.* 4*d.* for pasture respectively (F. W. Bull, *A History of Newport Pagnell*, p. 52; cf. also M. E. Finch, *NRS*, XIX, 73, 149).

[4] Richard entered into a recognizance for £40 to observe performance of the lease: I presume that, as was customary, the sum was double that which he received (C54/1221).

[5] Cf. M. E. Finch, *NRS*, XIX, 150.

[6] D/C/1/1. C66/1314. CP25(2) 91/809. Hollyman died in 1589 (D/A/Wf/11, proved 8 Oct. 1589) so it is doubtful if his lease was operative.

leaving Richard in undisturbed possession of his demesne lands.[1] It will be seen that to date Richard had provided for his present and his future very comfortably at the expense of his heirs.

The direct heir John, his own son, however, was not complaisant. Although still under age he must have heard talk at home of the original indenture and in 1590 he informed Thomas Tyringham that he intended to recover possession of the land and tenements his father had sold. Thomas promptly appealed to the Star Chamber and insisted on subpoening all the actors concerned, including Still.[2] In his bill of complaint, relevant abstracts from which have already been quoted, he pointed out the great expense to which he had already been put for licences, fines, etc.[3] The dependants all denied any illegal action and the case dragged on for ten years before judgement in favour of Anthony Tyringham was given in the court of common pleas.[4] By order of the court John Ardes was compelled to suffer a recovery of the property in 1601.[5]

The principal manorial rights in Sherington, the embodiment of the original Carun fee, had thus been sold for the first time after an unbroken tenure of nearly 500 years, and John, the heir of this long tradition, was left with no more than an attenuated portion of the demesne lands. For a minor gentleman or a prosperous yeoman such an estate would have been a fine holding, but to a young squire of Norman descent who could quarter the arms of Carun and Linford it must have seemed woefully inadequate. It is unfortunate that no personal information about the family has survived: we know so little about this John and his father, even of his grandmother Catherine, the daughter of the Thomas Lowe of Clifton Reynes who had been an esquire of the body and captain under Henry VIII. Married young, *c.* 1540, she had as a middle-aged widow to provide for a string of younger sons as well as a daughter separated from her husband. With the economic outlook changing almost year by year her life cannot have been an easy one and this seems to have made her a rather querulous neighbour. In 1571, for instance, she accused Thomas

[1] D/C/1/2; another copy D/Ch/188/3. The schedule attached is a detailed terrier of all the demesne lands retained by Richard and was of great use in the reconstruction of the strip map for 1580 (pp. 259–76).

[2] St. Ch. 7/Add. 6/9, 10. St. Ch. 5/T 10/11; T 12/11.

[3] By the time that Thomas secured undisputed possession in 1601 I estimate that he would have put out between £25 and £30 in legal fees and expenses (Copies of Bills of Costs and Law Charges from 1557 to 1665: MS volume, Law Society Library, London).

[4] D/Ch/188, 1, 2; the latter is an enrolled fine reciting the full proceedings of the fine levied in Easter Term 1588.

[5] CP 43/73/87.

Tyringham of defrauding her of a quit-rent of *2s. 4d.* in Sherington and her bill of complaint was a long rambling document full of irrelevancies—declaring that he had forcibly enclosed the whole of Tyringham and Filgrave to the grave damage of the inhabitants and insinuating that he was preparing to do the same in Emberton.[1] She was evidently a masterful as well as excitable woman, but her eldest son Richard seems to have been able to bend her to his will. She outlived him and in her old age became garrulous.[2]

John Ardes did not retain his lean patrimony for long. We do not know whether his debts were inherited or of his own making, but on 22 May 1609 he conveyed the estate for £1800 (about £7 per acre) to his grandmother's nephew Reynes Lowe of Clifton Reynes,[3] who settled it two years later on his younger brother Thomas.[4] John's fate is not known, but he may be the person of the same name who was underkeeper of Wychwood Forest, Oxfordshire, in 1612, and died at Shipton under Wychwood in August 1621.[5] His cousin John, son of his uncle Thomas Ardes of Renhold, who had married a daughter of Thomas Isham of Lamport, also fell on evil days and had to leave Bedfordshire.[6] The later history of this old family is thus rather pathetic[7] and we may perhaps end our account of it with an enigma from the parish register of Irthlingborough, Northamptonshire, 'buried on 13 August 1617 Lawrence Ardes, an ancient gentlewoman'.[8]

When Thomas Catisby died in 1571 his son, another Thomas, exchanged the Cave–Fitz John manor in Sherington for that of Ecton, Northamptonshire, owned by William Mountgomery, which lay adjacent to his main estate at Whiston.[9] The Mountgomerys had held Ecton since the early twelfth century[10] and for the last 100

[1] St. Ch. 5/A41/18.

[2] Lincoln Record Office: episcopal visitation 1607, f. 16: 'Sherington, Katherine Eards and Emme Simmonds for callinge one another whore in the churchyard the 19 of July 1607 and using other words'. She continued to use the name Ardes after her second marriage.

[3] D/Ch/188/4.

[4] D/C/1/3, 4. CP25(2) 275, Mich 9 James I.

[5] SP Dom. James I, 1611–18, p. 122: Arch. Court Oxon, Act Book A, p. 126.

[6] Lamport Hall, Isham Collection 1 L2113; Isham correspondence, no. 164.

[7] When William Cole the antiquary was staying with his friend Philip Barton, the rector, on 15 May 1761 he visited the old Linford–Ardes manor house, then part of the Chester estate and let off as two tenements. Painted on the walls of the great parlour, which had been partitioned into three, were the following achievements of arms: (1) Ardes, quartering Bucknall, Linford and Carun; impaling Vavasour and de la Hay, (2) Ardes impaling Reynes, (3) Ardes quartering Butler, (4) Ardes impaling Wake. Linford was displayed over the chimney (Ad. MSS 5839, p. 175d).

[8] Northants Record Office: Isham–Longdon MSS, xxx; extract from parish register of Irthlingborough.

[9] D/Ch/89/3, 4.

[10] *VCH Northants*, IV, 123.

years a junior branch of the family had been in possession so that the exchange brought to Sherington another feudal family of ancient lineage like the Ardes.

No records of the Catisby–Mountgomery régime during the last two-thirds of the sixteenth century have survived and we can only conjecture the way the estate was run from the turn of events in the early seventeenth century. It would seem that the various farms, as in Richard Maryot's day, were let out on lease and that the increase in rents as time went on did not keep pace with the rise in the cost of living or in the profits of farming, so that at the end of the century William Mountgomery was in straightened circumstances, whereas his tenants had accumulated savings sufficient to allow them to purchase their holdings. The situation was similar to that of Richard and John Ardes, except that William dealt with his tenants directly and not through an intermediary like Christopher Hollyman, whose prime object must have been the forcing up of tenants' rents.

As a preliminary to the marriage of his heir Sherington Mountgomery in 1601 William settled on him the whole estate, reserving to his wife Margaret and himself no more than an annuity of £13 6*s*. 8*d*., together with a life interest in a corner of the old moated mansion house and 15 acres of the demesne lands.[1] He died in 1610[2] and within two years Sherington—presumably to pay off his own and his father's debts —had sold off all the outlying farms and much of the demesne, retaining no more than a 'gentleman's farm' of even smaller acreage than the one which Thomas Lowe had obtained from John Ardes.[3]

The contrast between the affluence of the tenant farmers and the poverty of the old manorial families shows up in the subsidy return for 1599 (Table 31). The annual value of the taxpayer's land or goods was assessed on an outdated formula and is no real guide to his wealth, but the sums recorded are comparable one with another and so serve their purpose. It is interesting to note that few of the tenants listed represent families that go back even as far as the muster roll of 1522 (Table 25)

[1] Indenture 8 March 1601: the Cave–Fitz John manor was settled on Sherington Mountgomery; William and his wife to retain for life the use of their bedchamber, the chamber over it, the adjoining privy and the little chapel chamber—parcel of the moated manor house; the dove house, the little stable, an orchard, Park Close (2 acres), Grove Close (6½ acres), the right to fish in the river and 15 acres of demesne land which Sherington was to cultivate for them (D/Ch/89/5, 6) The marriage settlement was dated 10 Dec. 1602 and the bride was Anne, sister of Humphrey Smith, citizen and grocer of London (D/Ch/89/9–10).

[2] Lincoln Consistory Court, 1627, F, 63. It exhibits gentile poverty: three younger sons, Ferdinand, Michael and Theodore receive £14 13*s*. 4*d*. each also two daughters £8 each.

[3] Cf. Table 32, n. 89, 188.

and this applies also to the tenants who held in 1580 (Table 30). During the intervening years there had been considerable change in the make-up of the agricultural community and in general the tenants sprung from the older stocks had fared worse than those from outside who had, in fact, just about held their own. The Fields were a case in point. Henry the grandfather had had to sell his small freehold farm to

TABLE 31

Sherington Subsidy Roll 1599[a]

In terris (t), in bonis (b)

		Value of land or goods £	Tax s.	d.
William Mountgomery, gent.	t	8	32	0
John Ardis	t	4	16	0
Edward Wallis	b	5	13	4
John Chubnall	b	3	8	0
Thomas Orpin	t	1	4	0
Edward Chubnall	t	5	20	0
Raphe Houghton	b	4	10	8
Thomas Bauswell	b	4	10	8
John Hall	b	3	8	0
John Knight	b	3	8	0
Bartholomew Coursse	b	3	8	0
Maurise Affeeld	b	3	8	0

[a] E179/79/234.

Edward Ardes in 1551[1] and became a tenant of the Catisby–Mountgomery estate; his son William[2] and grandson Maurice carried on after him, but when the outlying portions of the estate were sold the latter had insufficient wealth to buy the freehold of the farm. The same applies to Bartholomew Course, of old Sherington stock. When the various Mountgomery farms were disposed of between 1608 and 1612 the major part of the land was divided between Edward Wallis, whose father Nicholas

[1] D/Ch/188/1. Indenture 2 Jan. 1551: a messuage (probably no. 193), a close adjoining, 22 acres arable land and 2 roods meadow—sold for 40 marks. The holding would appear to be an old virgate; Henry Field, like his ancestors, had paid a quit-rent of 2*s.* 4*d.* to the Tyringhams (St. Ch. 5, A37/20).

[2] He died in 1588 and an inventory of his goods, valued at £53 8*s.* 4*d.* is preserved at Lincoln (Inv. 76/187).

had come in from Astwood about 1540, and John Knight, who had only recently migrated from Lathbury.[1]

In Sherington, as elsewhere, it was the freeholders like Edward Chibnall, whose branch of the family had only recently climbed into the ranks of the minor gentry and was still in close contact with the land, who were able to take full advantage ot the inflation in the latter half of the sixteenth century. Edward had farms in Hardmead and Milton Keynes as well as in Sherington, and these were run for him as soon as they were old enough by his sons John and Richard. This gave him the leisure in later life to play a part in local government; he was, for instance, one of the feodaries for Buckinghamshire and in 1600 was high constable for the Three Hundreds of Newport.[2]

Inflation, however, was not the only factor that was working to improve the lot of the tenant farmer: education had been made available to him and he was taking advantage of it. In 1545 Anthony Cave, a wealthy merchant of the Staple from Calais, had acquired certain lands in Lathbury that were formerly in the possession of Lavendon abbey as well as the rectory and the two Tickford priory manors in Chicheley. His conscience may have been troubling him, or more likely his business experience had impressed on him the need for more general education, for a few years later he decided to build a grammar school in Lathbury. In 1553 he arranged for this to come under the supervision of Christ Church, Oxford, and set up a family trust under a 99 year lease of the impropriate rectory of Chicheley to provide a stipend of £12 a year for the schoolmaster. The children of poor parents were to be taught free by the undermaster, but he could receive 3*d.* per quarter for each child whose parents had reasonable means and double this amount if they were worth £20 or more per annum.[3] A unique but decayed list of scholars *c.* 1595 was in the possession of a local Lathbury squire early in the nineteenth century, who made a copy which is available today.[4] He was able to transcribe 50 out of a total of 80 names on the list and these represent families of all degrees within a radius

[1] Of the farms cited in Table 30, no. 106 went to Hugh Windmill and Anthony Newall (CP25(2) 274; CP43/103/46); no. 46 was bought in by John Hall (CP25(2) 275); no. 182, Fitz John manor farm, where the mansion was in ruins (CP25(2) 92/826) and no 18 went to Edward Wallis; no. 15 and no. 33 to John Knight; and no. 53a to Phillip Kirtland (CP25(2) 275; CP43/119/72).

[2] Bodleian Library, Oxford, MS Willis 30.

[3] E. G. W. Bill, *Calendar of Estate Papers at Christ Church, Oxford*, I, f. 4.

[4] Gough MSS Buckinghamshire Record Office: the list was copied out by Mansel Dawkins Mansel at Lathbury some time before 1823.

of 6 or 7 miles of the school. The farming community, including the modest smallholder, was well to the fore.[1]

There is no doubt that this school had a pronounced cultural effect on the district. The writer has had occasion to examine many score of late sixteenth and early seventeenth century deeds for the area and can vouch for the excellent penmanship, as portrayed by signatures and drafts of deeds, of the people concerned. The writing of ordinary people in Elizabethan times was usually vile. Anthony's trust deed expressed the hope that his successors at Chicheley would continue to support the school after his lease expired in 1652. In the event this was not possible; Chicheley hall had been sacked and plundered by the parliamentary forces and Sir Anthony Chester was a refugee in Holland. The school in due course was closed, and with the permission of Christ Church the materials were used for the repair of the parsonage house in 1698. The effect on the local farming community was all too plain: in so many cases the neatly written signature had given place to a large and sprawling script—a sure sign of illiteracy.

[1] The fourteen boys from Sherington were Edward and Francis Ardes; Edward, William and Richard Chibnall; Thomas, Arthur and William Barnes; Thomas Hollyman, John Hooton, Thomas Pierson, William Hall, Richard Cole and John Orpin.

25

THE RISE AND FALL OF THE YEOMANRY, 1600–1750

THE sale by Sherington Mountgomery of his outlying farms at the end of the first decade of the new century meant that Anthony Tyringham, who owned about 300 acres,[1] was now the largest landowner in the village. The family did not hold the position for long, however, as the eldest son Thomas, who succeeded in 1615, mortgaged the Tyringham estate so heavily that on his death in 1636 his brother and heir John was forced to raise money by selling the five Sherington farms, retaining there no more than the manorial rights and Linford Wood. Three of the farms, which had been purchased from Richard Ardes in 1588–9 for £2 per acre were sold for £1992 10*s.* 0*d.* or about £7 per acre,[2] and so showed a profit commensurate with the increased value of land; the other two, which were sold to Joseph Lake of Sherington, were the original Tyringham holding in the village.[3] These changes, as well as the sale by Edward Wallis and his son Robert of the two farms acquired from Mountgomery[4] meant that the distribution of land in 1650 (Table 32) was very different from what it had been in 1580 (Table 30).

The two old manor houses were still inhabited by minor armigerous families. Thomas Lowe, who had inherited from his father Thomas in 1642 about 230 acres of the Ardes demesne and had no property elsewhere, would have enjoyed an income of not more than £200 a year unless he had farmed most of the land himself. He was already in financial difficulties and his estate was to be broken up within the next ten years, the house and about 90 acres passing to John Adams, a yeoman of Little Horwood.[5]

[1] He had purchased a third small farm (no. 177) from Richard Ardes about the year 1590.

[2] C54/3125, m. 2; CP43/221, m. 28: John Chibnall took farm no. 138, John Newman of Bradwell no. 54 and Hugh Smith of Broughton no. 177.

[3] MCR, 1642, 1648, 1658: Joseph Lake sold farm no. 52 in 1649 (D/Ch/52/1) to John Cunningham for £270 or about £10 per acre, and farm no. 19 to Christopher Rookes of Calverton (CP25(2) 537, Hil. 1656).

[4] Fitz John manor farm no. 182 was sold to Richard Babington (CP26(2) 536, Trin. 1649), and the smallholding no. 18 to John Chibnall in 1626 (D/Ch/138/1).

[5] D/C/1/5.

TABLE 32

Holders of land in Sherington in 1650

Numbers shown thus, 63*, are not included in the area shown on Map 8; the direction in which they lie is indicated on the map.

No. on Map 8	Owner	Tenant or description	Messuages	Cottages	Arable land (a.)	Pasture (a.)	Meadow (a.)	Wood (a.)	Number of single cow-commons	Number of hearths[a]
188	Tho. Lowe	Linford manor house or The Hall	1	4	130	13	8	—	16	—
16	Tho. Lowe	Ambrose Cowley	1	—	30	46	—	—	9	—
138	John Chibnall	John Foulsham	1	—	67¾	14	5¾	—	8	3
54	Tho. Newman	Tile house, Michael Baker	1	—	81	5¼	—	—	—	—
177	Tho. Chibnall	Tho. Marshall	1	—	58	6	4	—	7½	4
—	Sir William Tyringham	Daniel Boughton	1	—	6	8	—	18	—	1
19	Joseph Lake	Catherine Wheel, Richard Cole	1	—	67¾	2	4½	—	4	6
52	John Cunningham	Buswell's farm	1	—	36½	11	3¾	—	5	2
89	Brett Norton	Cave manor house	1	—	107	34	4	40	4	11
182	Richard Babington	Fitz John manor farm	1	2	77½	4½	4	—	8	5
15	Margaret Knight	—	1	2	83	7	3	—	8	3
33	Robert Knight	—	—	1	50	1	3	—	14	4

46	Richard Lord	—	—	1	12	2	—	—	4	—
159	Mercers' Company	Manor farm, John Wells (Thomas Clifton, under-tenant)	1	—	35	$6\frac{1}{2}$	$1\frac{1}{2}$	—	3	2
158	Mercers' Company	John Chibnall (Edward Henley, undertenant)	—	1	$14\frac{3}{4}$	$9\frac{1}{4}$	4	—	3	—
162	Mercers' Company	John Pierson (Richard Brittain, undertenant)	—	1	$15\frac{1}{2}$	3	1	—	3	1
178, 153	Mercers' Company	Annis and Thomas Course	1	1	$42\frac{1}{2}$	$3\frac{3}{4}$	$\frac{1}{4}$	—	4	—
152, 224	Mercers' Company	Tho. Norman	—	2	14	$1\frac{1}{4}$	1	—	4	—
—	Mercers' Company	Ralph White	—	—	—	$3\frac{3}{4}$	4	—	—	—
—	Mercers' Company	John Peters	—	—	—	—	—	21	—	—
18	John Chibnall	Richard Hunt	1	—	10	3	$\frac{3}{4}$	—	4	—
41	John Chibnall	Edward Laughton	1	—	20	1	2	—	4	2
63*	Richard Field	Stonepit house	1	—	7	—	—	—	4	1
106*	Anthony Goodred	Park Cottage, Elizabeth Goodred	—	1	22	4	5	—	6	—
120*	John Cowley	Gowles farm (Dukes Pieces)	1	2	48	—	—	—		
20	Tho. Richards	—	—	1	12	$\frac{3}{4}$	—	—	3	—
157	John Chibnall	—	1	5	130	10	8	—	10	5
198	Tho. Harman	Edward Boddington	1	1	$22\frac{1}{2}$	—	$2\frac{1}{2}$	—	4	3
53a, 53	Rich. Hooton	—	1	1	33	6	4	—	10	—
179	Rector	Rectory and Glebe	1	—	15	$4\frac{1}{2}$	$1\frac{3}{4}$	—	11	4
			21	26	$1247\frac{3}{4}$	$210\frac{1}{2}$	$75\frac{3}{4}$	79	$160\frac{1}{2}$	—

[a] E 179/80/349—hearth tax roll for 1662 (?)—partly perished.

Sherington Mountgomery died in 1627 and his heiress Ann, the wife of Richard Halford of Edith Weston, Rutland, sold the Cave–Fitz John manor to William Norton of Hinxton, Cambridgeshire.[1] Under the terms of Sherington's will a quit rent of 8*s*. 4*d*. issuing from a tenement in the occupation of Edward Lord, now called Water lane farm no. 46, was vested in trustees for the benefit of the poor people in the village.[2] The charity was duly reported to the Commonwealth Commission of Inquiry in 1653[3] and is mentioned in the Cave–Fitz John court roll of 1708,[4] but no later reference has been found and it must have lapsed through the inability of the trustees to carry on or exact payment. Brett Norton succeeded his father in 1641. The moated manor house of those days was a large building taxed on eleven hearths, and to support this he had only 180 acres of demesne and woodland worth at the most about £200 a year, a small competence for one who was on the fringe of the squirearchy and jealous of its privileges. He was a justice of the peace and much of the detail of local government in this rather remote corner of Buckinghamshire was in his hands. How he was able to keep solvent during the restoration period is a mystery,[5] for his son Owen Norton was in financial difficulties soon after inheriting around 1680 and from 1688 onwards the estate became so heavily mortgaged that twelve years later the mortgagees foreclosed and sold it to Thomas Pargiter of Passenham, Northamptonshire.[6]

John Chibnall, whose Elizabethan house (Pl. IV) is now called the Old House, had become one of the minor gentry[7] and accepted his full share of local leadership. His estate, including the small farm he rented from the Mercers, extended to more than 300 acres and he had half as much again in the neighbouring villages of Hardmead, North Crawley and Milton Keynes. The years leading up to the civil war and the period of the restoration were the heyday of the yeomanry and of all those listed in Table 32 only Thomas Newman of Bradwell was domiciled elsewhere. Such a

1 D/Ch/89/23–26.

2 Lincoln District Probate Registry, Misc. Wills Book F, no. 63. The trustees were his well-beloved friends Francis Say, Francis Muscote, John Chibnall and Edward Wallis.

3 C93/23/3. Payment by Richard Lord, Edward's son, was then six years in arrear.

4 A quit-rent of 9*s*. was payable on the cottage and garden, of which 8*s*. 4*d*. went to the poor and 8*d*. to the lord of the manor. The succession was Richard Lord, William Field, Robert his son, James Brittain, William and James his sons (D/Ch/46/1–3).

5 William Norton had held a lease of Hinxton rectory, but it is not known when this expired (D/Ch/89/27).

6 D/Ch/89/47–52. The sale price was £1300.

7 When the heralds visited Buckinghamshire in 1566 his father Edward had not attained manorial status and so was not recognized as armigerous like his cousins of Astwood, who had later migrated to Orlingbury, Northamptonshire.

happy situation, however, was not to last, for it contained within itself elements that were unstable. Sherington in those days had a large preponderance of open-field land and inadequate facilities for grazing, conditions that tended to maintain a low standard of farming and called for the conversion of some of the tillage to pasture.

Any move in this direction, however, would have been unpopular with the numerous freeholders and tenant farmers who then held sway in the village, for we saw in the last chapter how the Ardes–Mountgomery attempt to enclose only a small portion of their own demesne had been frustrated by the Mercers' tenants. In the neighbouring villages, however, where the whole or a large part of the land belonged to one owner the conversion of pasture to tillage went on steadily during the early years of the seventeenth century and the attitude of the government was, on the whole, tolerant. When corn prices were low, as in 1619, a commission was appointed to grant pardons to offenders, who thereby acquired the right to retain their pastures; yet in 1629–31, when there was a scarcity of corn, the Privy Council got flurried and ordered the removal of all enclosures during the preceding two years. Anthony Chester, however, who had made extensive enclosures at Chicheley, mostly by agreement with his tenants, had paid a fine of £100 in 1619.[1] Other villages enclosed by agreement just then were Weston Underwood in 1617,[2] Hardmead[3] and Ekeney cum Petsoe.[4] Filgrave had been partly enclosed before 1607,[5] while the Clifton pastures lying alongside the Ouse, and the most fertile part of Clifton Reynes, had been forcibly depopulated by Francis Lowe as far back as 1565.[6] The situation in Lathbury was interesting. Before and during the time of Anthony Cave the land there had been tilled on the three-field system but on division of the estate after his death in 1555 one of the heirs enclosed a whole field for pasture, while the other kept the remaining two fields as arable, the tenants being forced back to a two-field system of husbandry.[7]

[1] In 1616 Anthony owned 1464 acres of the 2070 acres in Chicheley: of this only 303 acres was in the open common fields (Bedfordshire Record Office, DDBC, 479, f. 9). The Chester muniments include several agreements with tenants, dated between 1615 and 1620, to extinguish pasture rights. There was still a small amount of open common field in the early eighteenth century (D/C/1/163).

[2] T Deeds: agreement 3 Nov. 1617.

[3] Map of 1638 in possession of Group-Captain G. Powell-Shedden.

[4] Map of 1641 in possession of Lincoln College, Oxford.

[5] St. Ch. 8/15/12; it was fully enclosed in 1707 agreement about glebe (D/Ch/Tyr/1–3).

[6] E 178/424, m. 5.

[7] C2/Eliz./Pp. 6/34.

Sherington, with its neighbours Emberton and Lathbury, was thus encompassed by a ring of villages in each of which the old traditional system of tillage was being wholly or in part discarded in favour of sheep farming. While it is by no means certain that all the new enclosing in this outer periphery was for the purpose of transforming arable land to pasture it is clear that in the neighbourhood taken as a whole the amount of land under tillage was being reduced, with the corollary that there would be some displacement of the working population. The Leicestershire minister John Moore, a contemporary moralist bitterly opposed to enclosing, declared that 'the cottiers, who earn their living in work connected with the plough, are now cast adrift and wander towards the nearest open-field village—thus it comes about that the open-field towns have about double the number of cottiers they used to have, and are hard put to it to provide for the poor which the enclosures have made'.[1] The situation in Sherington was, indeed, far more serious than this, for there had been a threefold increase in the number of cottagers since the days of Elizabeth.

On the plausible assumption that in 1522–4 the resident freeholders and such of the tenants as were rated at £2 or more per annum on their goods lived in farm-houses, the labourers and rest of the tenants would have required between them about eighteen cottages (Table 26). Other habitations in the village at that time were the rectory, the two manor houses of the resident squires, and the house of Elizabeth Ardes,[2] so that the total number of households was about thirty-nine (Table 33). In 1580 (Table 30) the number of farms had increased to 23 and of households to 45, in line with the lesser increase recorded in the Lincoln survey of 1563.

In 1681 Sir William Tyringham sold the Linford manorial rights acquired from Richard Ardes in 1589, to Roger Chapman, an attorney of Newport Pagnell. The manor was the principal one in the village and the lord had view of frankpledge. Roger held a view the following year and *inter alia* the jury presented that 34 cottages, listed under their owners names, were being held contrary to the statute of 31 Elizabeth, c. 7, which laid down that each one must be provided with a quota of 4 acres of land. He held another view in 1708, in which year also Thomas Pargiter, the new owner of the Cave–Fitz John manor, held a court baron, and the respective

[1] Quoted by Margaret James, *Social Problems and Policy during the Puritan Revolution 1640–1660*, p. 107.

[2] Cf. p. 166, n. 2. The house no. 139 reverted at her death to Edward Ardes: a quit-rent of 1*d.* per annum was payable to the Mercers' Company (Table 6) and the subsequent history of the house can be traced through their court rolls.

rolls show that there were then 33 old-established cottages on which a small quit-rent was payable to one or other lord (Tables 34, 54). These cottages, together with one held freely of the Mercers and another that was their copyhold (Table 32, no. 152) comprised the 34 cited in 1682 as being contrary to the statute.[1]

TABLE 33

Number of households in Sherington

	1522–4	1580	1708[b]	1796
Rectory	1	1	1	1
Manor houses	2	2	1	1
Other houses	1[a]	1	1	11
Farms	17	23	26	16
Cottages	18	18	63	64
	39	45	92	93

[a] No. 139.

[b] A return by the rector *c.* 1705 gives 120 families (Lincoln Rec. Office, Speculum). Contemporary deeds show that many of the cottages and small tenant farms were then divided into two tenements.

From the facile way that the sites of some of these cottages 'pair-off' (Map 8) it is a fair surmise that they derive from an earlier holding that embraced both of them, the original quit-rent having been apportioned at the manorial court. Such a hiving off from a mother-site, which could have been in the home close of a farm, might have occurred more than once. As mentioned later,[2] the Mercers' court roll for 1648 records the emergence of cottage no. 197 from the old small-holding no. 198 and the apportioning of the quit-rent between them. Court rolls of the other two manors for the early seventeenth century have not survived, nevertheless the data assembled in Table 34 show with reasonable certainty that the 34 cottages of 1680–1700 derive from eighteen of an earlier period, in good agreement with the number postulated for 1522–4.

At Roger Chapman's first view in 1682 the jury had returned that fourteen cottages were standing on the manorial waste and at Thomas Pargiter's court of 1708 another fifteen were assigned to the waste of Fitz John's manor (Appendix 3

[1] There were presentments at the Buckinghamshire assizes in 1690–1 for building cottages in Sherington without assigning 4 acres of land (*BSR*, I, 363).

[2] P. 279.

and Table 55). These 29 cottages will have been erected with the respective lord's permission by the parish overseers under the Elizabethan statute of 1601 for the relief of the poor; there being no obligation in such cases to provide the 4 acres of land. It would seem therefore that although there had been no more than eighteen cottages in Sherington during the early part of the sixteenth century the number had gone up to 63 by 1708, 29 being inhabited by paupers and the remainder by villagers with less than 4 acres of land apiece. There had meanwhile been a corresponding increase to 92 in the number of households (Table 33).

This expansion in the ranks of the poorer people was greater than could be attributed to normal population growth and must have been due to an influx of strangers from the vicinity. The expression 'enclosure by agreement' was a convenient euphemism of the day for an operation that provided compensation for the farmer and smallholder, but left in the lurch the employees who laboured in one or other aspect of open-field tillage. As John Moore complained, these men and their families were forced by circumstances to migrate, and many of them drifted into Sherington to find shelter in the cottages or hovels on the manorial waste.

An equally illuminating picture of the housing position during the restoration period emerges from a study of the Hearth Tax returns. The tax roll of 1662, the only one preserved for the Three Hundreds of Newport,[1] shows that 42 houses were rated for tax in that year (Table 35). Of more immediate interest, however, are the returns from the various villages of those who, in the tax of 1671, were remitted through poverty.[2] The effect of enclosure stands out very vividly, for while no claim for exemption came from Tyringham cum Filgrave, Hardmead, Weston Underwood and Clifton Reynes, the returns for Chicheley, Emberton and Sherington certify exemption for 11, 31 and 51 paupers respectively, figures that tell their own story. The total number of buildings in Sherington—including the rectory—on which tax was either paid or remitted in 1662–71 was 93, in agreement with the number of households already postulated from evidence of different origin. While the data collected in Table 33 suggest that the number of dwellings remained fairly constant between about 1660 and the Enclosure Act of 1796 there was a definite

[1] E179/80/349. The roll is partly decayed and about a third of the householders names in Sherington is illegible.

[2] E179/80/362. The owner was exempt provided that his dwelling was not worth more than £1 per annum, that he neither owned nor rented land worth £1 per annum and that his dwelling had not above two chimneys, two firehearths or two stoves.

TABLE 34

Cottages and quit-rents in Sherington

Cottages, and farmhouses (F) are referred to by the number assigned to them in Map 8.

Manor	Period 1520–1600 Cottage or farmhouse	Quit-rent (*d.*)	*c.* 1700 (cf. Tables 35 and 55) Cottage or farmhouse	Apportioned quit-rent (*d.*)	No of single cow-commons
Linford	26	3¼	25	1¾	2
			26	1½	
	28	6½	28	6½	—
	32	1	32	1	—
	42	6	42	8¼	2
			47	1¼	—
	48	3¼	48	½	—
			49	1½	—
	54(F)	16½	54(F)	16	—
			55	½	—
			92	3	—
	93	6½	93	2½	—
			94	1	—
	96	1	96	1	—
			141	2	—
	143(F)	19½	142	8¼	—
			143(F)	9¼	2
			144	1	—
	145	3½	145	1½	—
			146	1	—
			160	1¾	—
	161	10¾	161	9	2
	165	7	165	7	3
	166	2¾	166	2¾	—
			183	½	—
	184	9½	184	4	—
			185	5½	—
Cave	16	6	16(F)	6	—
			20(F)	1	—
	20	1	20*a*	—	—
	40	3	40	3	2
			50	½	—
	51	1¾	51	1¼	—
			199	12	2
	201	28	200	14	2
			201	2	4
Mercers	198(F)	3*s.* 10*d.*	198(F)	2*s.* 1*d.*	—
			197	1*s.* 9*d.*	2
			152[a]	—	—
	153[a]	—	153[a]	—	—
Number of cottages	18		35		

[a] Mercers' copyhold, not freehold.

movement among the inhabitants. The lists of owners of cottages or their tenants in 1682, 1708 and 1796 respectively exhibit a continuous coming and going.

This influx of newcomers in the first half of the seventeenth century as the aftermath of enclosure elsewhere provided Sherington with a plethora of skilled workers —potential tenant farmers as well as labourers—all of whom were eager for employment. Freeholders accordingly found it easy and profitable to let their land or to take on extra hands so as to give themselves time for a second occupation. John Chibnall, with an estate worth £300 a year, remained active until his death in 1652, as also did his third son John who followed him. John Knight's two farms, worth about £70 a year, were run by his widow Margaret and son Robert. Six of the smaller freeholders and three of the tenant farmers listed in Table 32, however, coupled their farming with a trade or craft;[1] there may have been others, for some of the larger tenants especially are known to have sublet their holdings.

These favourable conditions held for a decade or so after 1650, but as the century drew to its close there was a subtle change which did not become marked until the new one was well advanced. One by one the farms were passing out of the hands of those who by tradition owed allegiance to the village community and were acquired by strangers with no local roots. Slowly but surely the influence of the old leading families was fading.

When John Chibnall the son died in 1670 the estate came to his only surviving brother Hugh,[2] rector of Walton, a village 5 miles south of Newport Pagnell, who settled it the next year on his eldest son Anthony.[3] Hugh, like his younger brother Ralph, had been at Oxford, and an elder brother Anthony had spent his working life as a fellow of Magdalen College there. Anthony the son had been reared in a rectory and at the youthful age of 23 was fortunate enough to find himself a man of property. He would have been acquainted already with the manners and customs of London under Charles II and a life of local activity in puritan surroundings such as had contented his grandfather and uncle John made no appeal. The lure of

[1] Butchers: Thomas Richards (no. 20), John Cunningham (no. 52) and Richard Brittain (no. 46). Grocers: Thomas Marshall (no. 177). Malster: Anthony Goodred (no. 106). Tailors: Richard Field (no. 63) and Richard Hooton (53 and 53a). Wheelwright, Richard Hunt (no. 18).

[2] D/Ch/157/1. Indenture dated 27 Aug. 1644: John Chibnall, senior, made provision for his wife Agnes and then settled the estate to pass successively to his sons Anthony, John, Thomas, Hugh and Ralph in tail male. The eldest son, Edward, a simpleton, was barred: he was looked after by Hugh at Walton and died *s.p.* in 1671.

[3] D/Ch/157/2, 3 lease and release dated 17 and 18 Oct. 1671 (CP 43/235/–).

London was his undoing and to appreciate how a young man of his small independent means could have got caught up in one of the financial scrambles of the day, it is necessary first to lay bare the position of his powerful neighbour Sir William Tyringham. When the latter succeeded his brother Sir John in 1644 the Tyringham estate—despite the sale of the outlying Sherington farms in 1637—was already mortgaged for over £5000. A heavy fine for delinquency during the civil war and personal extravagance in the early years of the restoration increased his indebtedness to more than £14,500 and by 1669 he was forced to sell the estate for £20,000 to Edward Backwell, goldsmith and alderman of London.[1] Edward, whose son John was to marry Sir William's daughter and heiress Elizabeth in 1678 (see p. 206), already owned the manor of Buckworth, Huntingdonshire, an estate extending to 1000 acres. As a prominent banker of the period his widespread activities were prone to political influence and when Charles's government stopped the exchequer in 1672—that is, withheld payment of part of its interest to the bankers so as to be able to use the money for other purposes, he was badly hit. Various creditors obtained judgement against him within a few months and to raise cash he settled Buckworth in 1673 on Edward Brewer, one of the collectors of the great customs in the port of London, and Anthony Chibnall for £11,400.[2] Anthony, whose stake in this large sum must have been relatively small, took over the manor house at Buckworth and his Sherington home was let. Brewer died in 1676[3] and as the exchequer started to pay some of its bankers' arrears of interest the following year, Edward Backwell was able to recover the Buckworth property by 1681.[4] The full details of this last transaction have not come to light and so it is impossible to say how much money this incursion into high finance cost Anthony, but he burnt his fingers and on his return to Sherington in 1682 he was so deeply in debt that he had to sell his farm in Hardmead and some cottages in Sherington as well as place a heavy mortgage on Marshall's farm (no. 138) with a Dr Waller of Newport Pagnell. When he died in 1701 his son John found the estate so encumbered that within a few years he was forced to sell Marshall's farm and two other small properties to his uncle Nicholas Chibnall of Newport Pagnell to settle outstanding debts.[5]

The history of the Knight family followed the same uneasy course. John, the son

[1] D/Ch/Tyr/4, 5.

[2] C 54/4394, m. 15 (23 Jan. 1673–4). BAS, 660/38.

[3] *Cal. Treas. Books V*, II, 1349.

[4] He presented to the church in that year (*VCH Hunts*, III, 24).

[5] D/Ch/138/1–3: the sale price was £760 or about £6 5*s*. 0*d*. per acre.

Tyringham of Tyringham, with Backwell and Praed

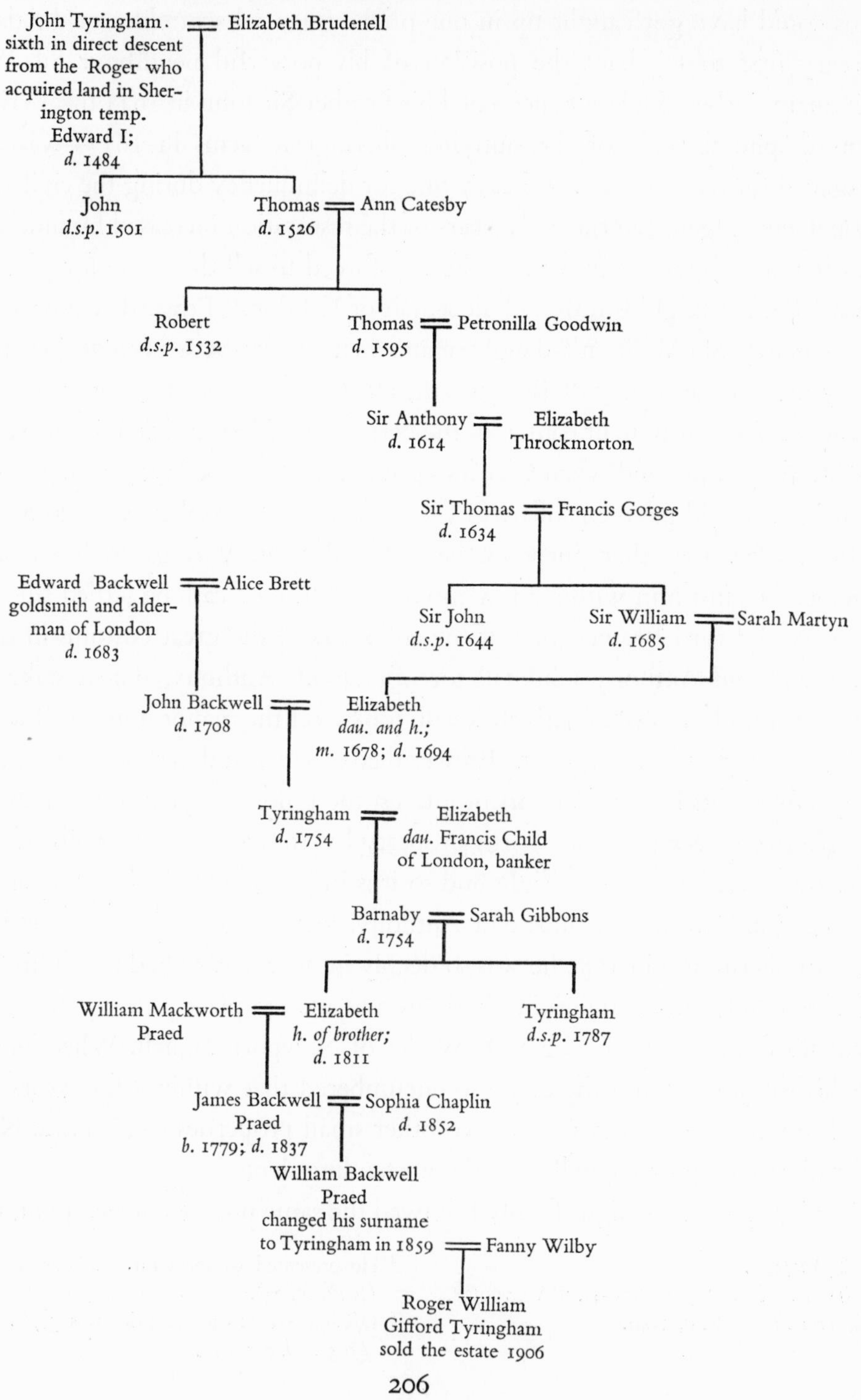

of Robert, lived on his rents, as also did his grandsons Thomas and Henry.[1] By the end of the century their debts forced them to seek employment and they became soapmakers in Southwark, Surrey. The effort was unrewarding and soon after Henry's death in 1713 Thomas was adjudged bankrupt for debts amounting to £600 on the petition of William Astell, a director of the South Sea Company. Because of the confusion over the 'South Sea Bubble' the court did not give Astell possession of the farms until twenty years later.[2]

There had been other changes of ownership before 1700, due to the foreclosing of mortgages,[3] inheritance[4] or sale,[5] as shown in Table 35 and the number of farmers who tilled their own land was only half what it had been 50 years before. The influence of the outside capitalist was on the increase.

Agricultural conditions deteriorated during the first half of the eighteenth century and the drift towards tenant farming went on unabated. By 1750 (Table 41) John Babington, of Fitz John manor farm no. 182[6] was the only resident freeholder, for Robert Rogers, who owned the small Water lane farm no. 46 was by trade a carrier on the London–Newport road. The old yeomanry were all but down and out.

[1] Farm no. 33 had been sold by Robert in 1665 to Roger Chapman (CP25(2) 628). His son John had purchased farm no. 177 from Thomas Chibnall (4th son of John) in 1658 (D/Ch/177/1).

[2] On his death they devolved on his daughter Margaret, who married John Thornton (D/Ch/15/1–10).

[3] No. 16, part of the estate of Thomas Lowe; no. 33, one of the Knight farms; no. 106, part of the Goodred estate (D/C/1/21); no. 53, part of the Hooton estate (D/Ch/53, Chubb. Abs. of title).

[4] No. 19 sold by Joseph Lake in 1656 to Christopher Rookes of Calverton, Buckinghamshire, whose daughter married Rev. William Carpenter, the rector there (CP25(2) 537; D/Ch/19/1).

[5] No. 198, part of the Goodred estate sold to John Ruddy (Chubb. Abs. of title); Sir William Tyringham sold the manorial rights, the wood and various pieces to Roger Chapman for £400 in 1681 (D/Ch/129/5–8).

[6] D/Ch/182/1–3.

TABLE 35

Holders of land in Sherington in 1700

Numbers shown thus, 63*, are not included in the area shown on Map 8; the direction in which they lie is indicated on the map.

No. on Map 8	Owner	Tenant or description	Messuages	Cottages	Arable land (a.)	Pasture (a.)	Meadow (a.)	Wood (a.)	Quit-rent payable to Linford (L), Cave cum Fitz John (C) or Mercers' (M) manor: Manor	£	s.	d.
188	Robert Adams	The Hall manor farm	1	—	61½	27	3	—	—		—	
138	Anthony Chibnall	Thomas Marshall	1	1	67¾	14	5¾	—	—		—	
54	George Newman	Richard Knight	1	—	81	5¼	—	—	L		1	4
177	Thomas and Henry Knight	Samuel Cunningham	1	1	58	6	4	—	L			4
16	Aldren Fuller	Tho. Loughton	1	—	30	46	—	—	—		—	
—	Roger Chapman	Daniel Boughton	1	—	6	8	—	18	—		—	
19	Wm. Carpenter	Catherine Wheel, Widow Fountaine	1	—	67½	2	4½	—	L		1	9½
52	Samuel Cunningham	—	1	—	27½	4	1¾	—	C			2
89	Tho. Pargiter	Cave manor house	1	1	108	34	4	40	M		3	1½
									L			2
182	Richard Babington	Fitz John manor farm, John Babington	1	2	62½	4	4½	—	L			6¾
15	Thomas and Henry Knight	Tho. Richardson	1	2	106	7	3	—	C		1	6

33	Roger Chapman	Anthony Lightwin	—	1	27	3	1	—	C	¾
46	William and James Brittain	Robert Rogers	1	—	18	2	—	—	L	4
									C	8
									M	1½
159	Mercers' Company	Manor farm, Edward Fuller (Tho. Clifton, undertenant)	1	—	35	6½	1¼	—	—	—
158	Mercers' Company	Anthony Chibnall	—	1	14¾	9¾	4	—	—	—
162	Mercers' Company	Edward Fuller (Tho. Clifton, undertenant)	—	1	14½	1½	½	—	—	—
178	Mercers' Company	Tho. Course	1	—	30½	3¾	¼	—	—	—
153	Mercers' Company	Edward Fuller	—	1	5½	—	½	—	—	—
152	Mercers' Company	Tho. Umney	—	2	17¼	3¾	5	—	—	—
224	Mercers' Company	Roger Chapman	—	—	—	—	—	21	—	—
18	Anthony Chibnall	Luke Watts, Robert Laughton	1	—	35½	3	3½	—	—	—
63*	Edward Hooton	—	—	1	5½	—	—	—	L	8
									M	1½
143	Edward Hooton	—	1	3	7½	22	¼	—	L	9¼
106*, 120*	Sir John Chester	Edward Richards, Edward Tickhill	—	1	70	4	5	—	—	—
20, 142	Tho. Richards	—	1	3	16½	2	4½	—	L	9¼
									C	6
157	Anthony Chibnall	Robert Adams, John Marshall	1	4	130	10	8	—	L	½
									C	1 0¼
									M	1 9 6
53, 198	John Ruddy	—	2	3	91	6½	4	—	L	2
									M	3 6
179	Rector	Rectory and Glebe	1	—	15	4½	1¾	—	—	—
			21	28	1237¾	239½	69¾	79		

26

THE EMERGENCE OF NON-CONFORMITY

THE Jacobean period was one in which various aspects of puritanism were stirring the imagination of many folk, especially of the more humble sort, in north Buckinghamshire. The movement appears to have taken root initially in Newport Pagnell and Olney, but by the end of the reign there was a strong nucleus in Sherington and the number of adherents was increasing as a result of enclosure in the neighbourhood. Many of the unfortunate families thereby turned adrift came knocking at the door of Sherington and to the lasting credit of the village they did not all knock in vain. One has a suspicion that those allowed entry were chosen because they already had puritan leanings, but be that as it may there is no gainsaying the fact that their descendants in the next generation provided the strong local support given to the new Society of Friends. The puritan was a harsh judge of himself as well as of those who did not measure up to his self-imposed standards and it was characteristic of him that kindliness often went hand in hand with intolerance.

At this Courte a Petition was read contayning a Complaint from the Inhabitants of the towne of Sherington against William Fisher the Companies tenant and bailiffe there for keeping inmates and suspitious vagrant persons to the general offence and annoyance of the whole towne. It is agreed that a letter be forthwith written unto Fisher to give him notice of the complaint and admonish him to reforme and amend the said misorders and abuse that the Company be not troubled with any further complaint otherwise the Company intend to take their business from him and settle it on some other person which is of honest name and conversation.[1]

The Fishers were one of the oldest families in Sherington (cf. Table 20) and William had succeeded his father Thomas as Mercers' bailiff and tenant of the manor farm in 1597. The wording of both complaint and reply smacks of self-righteousness, but in those days the presence of lodgers was the concern of the whole community, for if they were allowed to remain too long they could become a legitimate charge on the parish rates. There were, indeed, good grounds for dissatisfaction, for William disclosed to the Mercers two years later that he was deeply in debt to several

[1] MAC, 1513–1622, f. 320, *Assembly at Paules Schole 5 Feb. 1617.*

local people and asked permission to sell his copyhold for £300 to Philip Kirtland so that he could pay his creditors. They agreed, but insisted on evidence that all debts had been paid before the new tenant was admitted:[1] Fisher then left the village.

The number of dissenters continued to increase and during the years 1633–6 twenty people, including eleven women, were presented at the ecclesiastical court for attending meetings of their fellows in Newport Pagnell and Olney on Sundays instead of going to their own parish church.[2] The archdeacon, probably under pressure from archbishop Laud, viewed the situation—which was far worse than in any other village within walking distance of those two centres—with some alarm and appointed a commission of prominent local people to deal with it.[3] The three leaders Anthony Newall, Richard Hooton and Robert White were duly excommunicated[4] and the others were allotted special seats in church for their use during service. The recalcitrant parishioners, however, took no notice, and in January 1634 Mary the wife of Thomas Newall, Alice the wife of Richard Hooton and Goodwife Field were presented for refusing to sit in their appointed seats.[5] Two years later Goodwife Field, a woman of firm conviction, retaliated by smashing the one allotted to her.[6] Far from becoming attenuated the drift away from church gathered pace and at Easter 1637 there was a conventicle at Sherington itself.[7]

Meanwhile Philip Kirtland, very much in debt, joined Anthony Newall and others drawn from Newport and Olney to emigrate to Lynn, New England.[8] The Mercers were sympathetic and not only allowed him to dispose of his copyhold to advantage[9] but gave him 25 marks for his relief.[10]

[1] MAC, 1513–1622, f. 331, 17 Nov. 1620. William's copy was for three lives, including those of his wife and step-son, at the customary rent of 50*s*. 2*d*. per annum. The new copy to Philip was also for three lives, his own, wife Rose and son John, at the old rent and a fine of £50.

[2] D/A/V/2, ff. 99, 220d, 221; D/A/V/4, f. 43.

[3] D/A/V/2, f. 106, 1 Aug. 1633: the rector, Thomas Gilder, with Anthony Tyringham, William Norton, Thomas Lowe, John Chibnall, Edward and Robert Wallis, Thomas Knight.

[4] *Ibid.* f. 109d.

[5] *Ibid.* f. 220d.

[6] D/A/V/4, f. 84: Anne Feild the wife of Richard Feild presented for breaking a seate in the Church wherein she was appointed to sit (4 Nov. 1636).

[7] D/A/V/4, f. 114—Sherington—'present that we have heard there was a repeticon of Mr Seatons sermon (which he preached in the parish aforesaid) in one Michael Baker's house (farm no. 54) but by whom the repeticon was made we know not nor who was present there'.

[8] V. C. Sanburn, *New England Hist. and General Reg.* XLVIII (1894), 66–7. Hotton, *Emigrants to America*, 1600–1700, I, 44. Philip, his wife and eldest son John must have sailed for New England in February 1637–8; his younger sons Philips and Nathaniel had left in 1635.

[9] MCR, 14 July 1635. MAC, 1637–41, f. 22–30, Jan. 1637–8.

[10] MAC, 1634–8, 28 Jan. 1635.

During the Commonwealth period Sherington experienced some of the inevitable consequences of a many-sided puritan revolution. The Committee for Plundered Ministers[1] had sequestered the rector Thomas Gilder during 1647, presumably because he had royalist sympathies, and in the following January had appointed as his successor Ignatius Fuller, a young man from Olney[2] who had recently taken his degree from Emmanuel College, Cambridge, a centre of moderate puritanism. In the same year John Chibnall's second son Anthony, a fellow of Magdalen College, Oxford, was expelled from the university by the Parliamentary Visitors. He had held college office from time to time as dean of divinity, bursar and vice-president; he was also reputed to have been a proselytizing puritan in a community predominantly royalist during the presidency of Dr Accepted Frewen (1626–43). Like many in the university he refused to acknowledge the authority of the visitors, most of whom were presbyterians of the violent type, when summoned to appear before them on 28 April 1648 and was ordered into the custody of the garrison marshal. Deprived of all his college offices a little later he was released early in October, after having spent nearly five months in the garrison gaol.[3]

The Sherington community during the 1650's must have been an interesting one. The leading squire, Brett Norton, was a justice of the peace and a staunch upholder of the law, both inside church and outside it. Thomas Lowe, the other squire and quite a number of the farmers were moving away from conformity. John Chibnall, the largest landowner, had recently died and by a family settlement the estate passed to his second son Rev. Anthony of the preceding paragraph, who was an independent puritan with a rooted objection to presbyterians.[4] The new rector conformed, but he had puritan leanings and had come under the influence of the 'Cambridge Platonists' at Emmanuel.[5] Lastly, a fair sprinkling of the tenant farmers, tradesmen and cottagers, very many of whom had been taught to read at Caves' Grammar School in Lathbury and so could put their own interpretation on the Bible, had gone all the way with George Fox and were to become willing adherents of

[1] Set up initially in 1642 to deal with hardship among those turned out of their livings by royalists it had since assumed authority to act as ecclesiastical commissioners for a completely disestablished church (cf. W. A. Shaw, *History of the English Church 1640–1660*, pp. 194–5, 274).

[2] His brother John went with Kirtland and Newall to Lynn, New England, in 1638.

[3] Camden Society, NS, XXIX, 510.

[4] He had entered Magdalen as a demy in 1619 at the age of 17, probably as a scholar from Cave's Grammar School, Lathbury. The statement in *Accepted Frewen* by Thomas Frewen, London, 1783, that Anthony was Frewen's tutor is false: he was a tutor under Frewen as president.

[5] *VCH Cambs*, III, 476.

the Society of Friends when this was organized during the first half of the decade to follow.

These conflicting views made life difficult for the young rector. During his first year, 1648, which was the last under the Barlow lease, he received the old miserable stipend of £28, but after that he became entitled to the full profit of the rectory which, glebe excluded, was worth on his own computation about £300 a year. Nevertheless, he did not find his dissenting parishioners at all accommodating on the question of tithe, which they objected to paying on religious grounds and not for any love of the sequestered rector, as was sometimes the case elsewhere. John Cunningham, farmer and butcher as well as a follower of George Fox, not only withheld his own payment for 1649 but was urging his fellows to do likewise, 'there is noe manner of tithe due to the rector or any other minister of religion or parson whatever'. The crisis came three years later and in Hilary Term 1653 Fuller opened proceedings in the court of exchequer against Thomas Lowe and eighteen farmers for withholding tithe to the total value of £144 issuing from more than half the arable and pasture land of the village.[1]

The era of toleration that seemed to be ushered in with the restoration soon gave place to oppression under the Clarendon Code and dissenters were once more being harried for not attending church. A study of the rector's tithe suits, and of presentments made at the archdeacon's courts in 1662–4[2] shows that the number of dissenters was already in excess of 50 and of unbaptized children at least fourteen: 34 families were concerned, or more than a third of the village total.

A large proportion of these people joined the Society of Friends when this was organized in 1662–6 and came in for some harsh treatment from the civil authorities. When the bishop of Lincoln asked incumbents for information about them the rector reported that there had been a conventicle of quakers at the house of Richard Hunt since 1662, that they had no minister but taught themselves and that their number—already 20–30—was on the increase.[3]

Richard Hunt, a ploughwright whose cottage and workshop in Water lane (Map 7, no. 32) became the meeting place of the quakers, was mercilessly treated by the local justices, including Brett Norton and Anthony Chester, for absenting himself

[1] E 112/289/19, 20, 31, 34, 35. The case is dealt with fully in Ch. 28.

[2] D/A/V/6, m. 9; 7, m. 13 d *et seq.*

[3] Lincoln Record Office—Return of conventicles in Buckinghamshire, 1669.

from church and seems to have been gaoled for several weeks each year from 1662 onwards. There was a particularly vicious attack made on him in 1670

for preaching Truth in a meeting of Friends in the open street called Water Lane, at Sherington (being kept out of their Meeting house) on the 6th day of the fourth month, 1670, was fined ten pounds by Brett Norton and Thomas Farrar of Cold Brayfield, for which fine, on the fourteenth day of the same month the said Richard Hunt, being a Wheelwright, had a new cart and as much timber as was, with the cart, worth £12 14*s.* taken from him by Thomas Clifton and John Philip, Constables and Thomas Marshall, John Babbington and John Field, Overseers of the Poor.[1]

Stephen Marshall, John Cunningham and Richard Marks were others sent to gaol at Aylesbury, while Mary Chapman, widow, a tenant of one of the Mercers little farms (no. 162) was cited twice for tithe and in 1659 her Bible, probably her most cherished possession, was taken away for non-payment of church dues. The Mercers, on the contrary, treated her at this period with kind consideration and reduced her rent from £5 to £3 per annum to show their appreciation of the way she had renovated the premises at her own expense.[2]

As mentioned in Ch. 1, Ignatius Fuller himself was presented by his own churchwardens at the archdeacons' court in 1672 for departing from orthodoxy in the conduct of his ministry. By then he had, indeed, modified some of his earlier views and when preaching at the funeral service of Mrs Anne Norton, William's widow, he expressed general agreement with the doctrine of Falkland, one of the leading rational theologians of the day.[3] He sought to minimize the essentials of religion and to extend toleration, so that, like Falkland, he was dubbed a socinian by some of those who opposed him.[4] Such latitudinarianism, however, was not allowed to interfere with his campaign for tithe.[5] Richard Marks, a leading quaker, was sued by him in the ecclesiastical court in 1683 and committed to Aylesbury gaol. He remained in prison for ten months, during which time a fourth part of his corn was seized. Finally 'his Neighbours, not knowing how to do well without (he being the chief Smith in the Town) satisfied the greedy Priest and fetched Thomas home from Prison'.[6] It was in this year also that the persecution of dissenters, which had abated

[1] See F. W. Bull, *History of Newport Pagnell* (Kettering, 1900), p. 136.

[2] MAC, 1657–1663, f. 35; 1663–9, f. 41.

[3] Ignatius Fuller, 'A sermon at the Funerals of Mrs Anne Norton 12 July 1671' (Cambridge University Library, 9/55/57).

[4] H. John McLachlan, *Socinianism in Seventeenth Century England* (Oxford University Press 1951).

[5] He sued in the exchequer court in 1656, 1670 and 1703 (E112/289/70; 356/144; 779/43).

[6] Quoted from *BASRB*, I, 136, n. 33.

somewhat after the Declaration of Indulgence, flared up again under Archbishop Sheldon. At the Easter sessions in Aylesbury there was an order that 'the Lawes against Dissenters from Church be recommended to all the Justices of the Peace within this County to be putt into execution'. During the next three years 44 people were presented at the assizes and some of those, with six others, at the archdeacon's court. The number of dissenters was thus at least as great as it had been twenty years before, and this time over 40 families were involved.[1] The quakers stubbornly held their own and supported each other in a wonderful way.[2] Their conventicle in 1683 brought them a heavy fine from Owen Norton,[3] who had followed his father Brett as a justice of the peace, but they had not long to wait for relief: the Toleration Act of 1686 enabled Richard Hunt's cottage and shop to be registered as the official Meeting Place in Water lane, and his home close (no. 31)—in which he had mowed the hay that was part cause of his troubles over tithe—was henceforth to be the quaker burial ground. In 1705 the rector told the bishop of Lincoln that there were seventeen quakers in the village as well as many independants and anabaptists.[4]

[1] William Salt Library MS 33. Bishop Compton's census of 1676 gives 200 conformists and 30 non-conformists. The latter figure is low unless families are implied, which would make nonsense of the figure for conformists (cf. Clark, *The later Stuarts, 1660–1714*, p. 26).

[2] *BASRB*, I, 51. At a meeting at Mr Elwood's on 30 March 1677 the sum of £19 16*s.* 11*d.* was brought in from ten other meetings in Buckinghamshire to help those who had lately suffered by fire at Sherington. The money was sent to Stephen Marshall.

[3] *BSR*, I, 169.

[4] Lincoln Record Office, Speculum (1705–23).

27

SHERINGTON AND THE CIVIL WAR

NEWPORT PAGNELL was of great strategic importance during the civil war, for a garrison stationed there could bar all intercourse between Bedford and the west as well as intercept supplies from the Midlands destined for the capital. Four roads roughly conforming to the points of the compass converge on the town, but of these the one from the east merges with that from the north in Sherington, so that it is a joint stream of traffic that passes south over Sherington bridge to enter Newport by the north bridge there.

As an important link in the Newport defence system Sherington bridge would have been kept in repair by the troops, but in times of peace its upkeep had always been a source of friction between the villagers and the justices responsible for the care of roads. Few details of the period before the civil war have survived, but one incident is of interest because it introduces John Hampden, the most famous of all Buckinghamshire men. As a justice of the peace attending assizes in Aylesbury he would at times have been entrusted with business concerning the northern part of the county and in 1633 he was drawn into the age-long controversy over Sherington bridge. The local inhabitants had always objected to their being held solely responsible for this because the road from the village to Newport, called in those days Sherington lane, was the connecting link between two converging main streams of traffic and catered for a public far wider than a purely local one. The bridge, consequently, was in a chronic state of disrepair and periodically the village would be indicted at the assizes. There is no record of the proceedings in 1633, but a similar presentment was made some 50 years later and the outcome at that time will illustrate what must have transpired at the earlier hearing. Justices were appointed to look into the matter and they reported that 'Sherington ought to repaire the same bridge only as a Horse Bridge, and that it is fitt to be made a Cart Bridge, being the greate road between Oxford and Cambridge and chiefly the way from greate parte of Northampton and Bedford sheires to Newport Pagnell in this county and so to London'.[1]

[1] *BSR*, I, 268.

Justices had been appointed for the same purpose in 1633 and John Hampden, in a letter to his friend Sir William Andrews of Lathbury—an interested party—stated that he had had conference with Sir William Tyringham, who was on the bench at the time, John Chibnall and the two high constables of Newport Hundreds. He had then seen the clerk of assize and learnt that no issue would go out against the village if the indictment were to be ignored.[1] And so, as usual, nothing was done.

Hampden comes to mind again when we read under date 18 April 1638 'It is now reported to this court that John Chibnall the Company's bailiffe at Sherington hath caused the Company's wood there to be deeply assessed for Ship Money'.[2] The dispute over Ship Money presaged the break between king and Parliament, whose last measure of agreement dealt with the revolt of the Irish catholics in October 1641. The people of Buckinghamshire—irrespective of religious opinion—were deeply moved by the plight of the unfortunate protestants who had been ejected from their homes and when a call for voluntary contributions towards their relief was made by parliament the following February the Newport Hundreds responded generously. Every household in Sherington seems to have contributed and even the poorest cottager gave his 2*d*.[3]

The rival armies assembled in the summer of 1642 and inevitably the local gentry showed divided allegiance: Sir John Tyringham, Sir Anthony Chester of Chicheley and Sir Kenelm Digby of Gayhurst were for the king, while Sir William Andrews of Lathbury supported Parliament, as did all the London gilds, including the Mercers'. The first major clash came at Edgehill on 23 October, when Prince Rupert's troops fell back and a few hours later made a vain thrust towards Aylesbury. South Buckinghamshire, where Hampden held sway, was solidly behind Parliament and the upkeep of the garrison at Aylesbury was a first charge on the 'Weekly Pay' tax imposed by Pym to support the parliamentary forces.[4] The inhabitants of Sherington

[1] Stowe, 142, f. 40: holograph letter from Aylesbury manor dated 21 March 1633–4.

[2] MAC, 1637–42, f. 39.

[3] SP 28/149: Richard Greenville's accounts. Sherington contributed £5 3*s*. 9*d*.; John Chibnall gave £1, 30 farmers from 1*s*. to 5*s*. each and 57 cottagers from 2*d*. to 6*d*. each. In a few instances father and son contributed and I estimate the number of households at about 75. The sums given by neighbouring villages were as follows (number of contributors in brackets): Lathbury, £19 2*s*. 0*d*. (Sir William Andrews, £13 6*s*. 8*d*.); Tyringham cum Filgrave (34), £11 6*s*. 4*d*. (John and Lady Francis Tyringham, £5 each); Chicheley (35), £2 1*s*. 4*d*.; Hardmead (24), 10*s*. 4*d*.; North Crawley (144), £19 11*s*. 7*d*.; Emberton (106), £12 1*s*. 7*d*.

[4] Buckinghamshire was assessed at £425 per month and of this £200 was for the garrison.

were called upon for a monthly contributon of £4 2*s.* 6*d.*,[1] a burden that must have given them their first inkling of the difficult times ahead, for it was at a rate per annum five times as great as they had paid under the two subsidies granted by Parliament to Charles in 1641, just before the break.[2]

The Newport area had no effective contact with the fighting until Prince Rupert, on a sally from Oxford, swept through it on his way to capture Bedford on 17 October 1643. Four days later he withdrew to Stony Stratford, but left Sir Lewis Dyve and his troop in Newport itself with instructions to fortify. The earl of Essex, the parliamentary commander, was in the vicinity, and when he advanced Dyve, under some misapprehension, withdrew before the end of the month without giving battle. Parliament, recognizing Newport's key position, ordered a garrison to be maintained there and appointed Major-general Phillip Skippon as governor.[3] Henceforth the course of events in the area was conditioned by the needs of a garrison town and as Skippon was kept short of money the nearby villages like Sherington were subject to close requisitioning. In some other respects, however, the area was a favoured one, for it had come under the domination of the king for but a fleeting period and so never found itself like so many other places in the unhappy position of paying taxes first to one side and then the other.

Dyve had started to encircle the town with a water ditch and high mound; Skippon continued the work, but it was not completed until well into the new year by his successor Sir Samuel Luke. It must have been during these operations, or perhaps later in 1648, when Parliament ordered the slighting of the fortifications, that Chicheley Cross (Pl. II) was destroyed.[4]

A detachment of the garrison was maintained at Olney and accordingly there would have been frequent comings and goings between this bridgehead into Northamptonshire and its base: it is interesting to note therefore that the road to the east of Sherington church, which runs north to connect with the Olney road near the top of Emberton hill, took on the name 'Gun lane' at this time, indicating that it was being used either for the transit of artillery or more probably for its

1 SP 28/127, ff. 284–8. The garrison treasurer's accounts were incomplete. Under date 2 April 1643 the payment from Sherington was entered as 'John Chibnold and his tenants £1 2*s.* 6*d.* and ye towne £3'.

2 E 179/80/307.

3 For the history of Newport Pagnell during the civil war see F. W. Bull, *A History of Newport Pagnell* (Kettering, 1900); H. Roundel, *RB*, II, 206 *et seq.*; *VCH Bucks*, IV, 409.

4 Cf. p. 9, n. 4.

deployment.[1] There is indeed a local tradition that the trench running east–west across the meadow to the rear of Mr Field's farm was dug during the civil war[2] and it may well have been used for gun emplacements. It was on 1 March 1643–4 that Luke ordered Captain Purbeck Temple to quarter with his troops at Sherington and to requisition from there the hay and oats for his horses. Captain Ennis and his troop took over on 3 December and while he was away scouting for Luke in the early months of the new year[3] Captain Holmes's troop seems to have taken their place.[4] General Fairfax's army camped in the village on Saturday 5 June and after holding a council of war there three days later—traditionally in Bancroft field to the south of the old rectory—he proceeded via Stony Stratford and Northampton to join Cromwell the day before the decisive battle of Naseby on 14 June 1645.

This royal disaster ended the fighting in or near north Buckinghamshire and the garrison troops, now under the command of Major D'Oyley, were recalled to Newport Pagnell. As a period of inaction lay ahead the horses needed protection and some of the nearby villages earned D'Oyley's gratitude by offering money for the building of stables.[5] Many of the soldiers were quartered outside the town,[6] principally in Hanslope, Castle Thorpe, Loughton and Great Linford, but Captain Ennis's company at Sherington was not a burden for long as it was withdrawn for service in Ireland early in 1646.

During this period of quasi-peace D'Oyley should have been in receipt of the £4000 a month that Parliament had voted in December 1643 for the support of the garrison, but payment was woefully in arrear and on 17 October 1645 he made a bitter complaint to Parliament, pointing out that the clothing of most of his men was in tatters and that they had had no pay for months.[7] His treasurer's accounts, however, show that the villages in the Newport area had continued to give loyal support[8] in spite of the burdensome local levies to which they had been subjected.[9]

[1] It is first mentioned in Chester D. Lowe to Adams, 4 April 1660.

[2] Information supplied by the late Mr F. J. Field in 1945.

[3] *BHRS*, XLII, 18, 106.

[4] *RB*, II, 240; 6th Report Hist. MS Comm. p. 181: Holmes complained to Parliament that while his troops at Sherington were receiving constant pay Sir John Norris drove off the poor people's cattle and sold them to his servants.

[5] SP28/127, f. 100: Sherington contributed £2 10*s*. 0*d*.

[6] *Ibid*. f. 13: early in 1646 Sherington received £3 as against Loughton's £73.

[7] SP Dom, 1645–7, 208.

[8] SP28/149: Sherington was assessed at £6 15*s*. 0*d*. per month.

[9] MAC, 1641–5, f. 89: Mercers' wood was assessed at 20*s*. in 1643 'for the getting of 40 horses out of the towne'. MAC, 1645–51, f. 20: 16 Feb. 1645,

The withdrawal of the garrison in June 1646 must nevertheless have come as a great relief to the neighbourhood after years of strain, even though heavy taxation for the support of the Commonwealth army was maintained until the restoration.[1] Troops were back in the village once more during the march on London in the second civil war of August 1648, but only for a short spell.[2]

'John Chibnall . . . to pay such reasonable taxes for the wood at Sherington as shall be got thereupon'.

[1] SP 28/148: Sherington was assessed at £13 8*s*. 8*d*. in 1657 and double this sum in 1659.

[2] MAC, 1645–51, f. 161: 16 Jan. 1649, 'John Chubnall's note for quartering of soldiers, which he presents to be in regard of the companies wood at Sherington, whereupon there is no house, was now denyed to be paid him'.

28

AGRARIAN ECONOMY UNDER THE THREE-FIELD SYSTEM OF TILLAGE

THE Mercers' survey of their open-field land in 1577[1] showed that the two-field system of husbandry practiced in Sherington during the thirteenth and early fourteenth centuries[2] had given place sometime before then to one based on three fields. There is abundant evidence to illustrate these two systems at work before 1330 and after 1577 respectively, but the intervening years are barren and over the whole two and a half centuries only one descriptive land deed has come to notice which throws light on the intriguing question of when the change from the one system to the other took place. This is an indenture dated 20 January 1514 which describes a meese situated on Water lane as abutting south on South Field,[3] thereby demonstrating from the lay-out of the fields given in Maps 3 and 4 that the older system of tillage was still operative.

This valuable information[4] narrows the issue and the change must have come about between 1514 and 1561, the year in which the Mercers ordered their survey

[1] RCL, ff. 144–163; cf. Tables 46–50.

[2] Cf. Ch. 17.

[3] SS, 1456: the interpolated numbers in brackets refer to Map 8. Ratification of an exchange between Thomas Chubnale of Astwood and Thomas the son of John Chubnale of Sherington, of a meese in Sherington for a close in Stagsdon '. . . the qweche muse (41) sothely is sett and lyeth in Sheryngton a for' seide be twene ye londe (42) sum tyme of John Ardis upon ye north and a place cald haymesplace (40) and ye kynges way upon ye west and a fyld calde ye sowth fyld upon ye sowth and ye londe (43) sum tyme of William Chubnale upon ye east for oone tofte with a croft . . . in Stachedon'. It is to be remembered that in Tudor times a line drawn from the church towards the junction of Cross Albans wood and Mercers' wood was often taken as a pointer to the north, so that the town end of Water lane might well have been considered to run in that direction (cf. p. 263, n. 1).

[4] The meese (41), on which would have stood in those days a cottage, became a small tenant farmhouse when John Chibnall purchased a parcel of land from Richard Hooton in 1628 (*BAS*, 413/44). His grandson Anthony sold the cottage in 1681 to John Gilman and the close—then called Farthing Close—to Hugh Cowley. The cottage was derelict in 1756 and was pulled down before the enclosure award of 1797 so that it is not recorded on Map 7. Close no. 43, known later as Richard's Close, was a copyhold of Cockfield manor. William Chibnall, who died 1478–80, held under Edward Grey and Robert Mathew under the Mercers in 1515.

to be made.[1] As Lennard has pointed out,[2] written record of any such agrarian change, except when intercommoning between different communities was concerned, is extremely rare, the reason probably being that it was achieved by tacit agreement with no more difficulty than could have been met by friendly interchange of a few selions here and there. The evidence for Sherington is in accord with this view, even though it covers no more than 35 per cent of the open-field land. The original division between West Field and South Field was a natural one—the town ditch. The fence, however, that was erected under the new system to partition old West Field into Marehill Field and a part of Middle Field was no more than an artificial barrier devised so that existing holdings could be parcelled out into three nearly equal lots instead of the two that had previously prevailed. Many terriers drawn up on the three-field basis of farms whose origin antidates the change are still available[3] and these demonstrate that the land attached to each farm would have been as well balanced under the old system as it was under the new one (Table 36). As no extensive give and take between owners of strips was called for the change-over would have involved no action that required written record.

The replacement of biennial by triennial fallowing in the open fields would have necessitated a like change in the demesne sector. There is, fortunately, indirect evidence from an unexpected source that Anthony Catesby and Anthony Ardes, who between them owned most of the land there, met to discuss the matter *c.* 1530. Among the Sotheby manuscripts on loan to the Northamptonshire Record Office are the muniments of the Catesby family of Ecton, Northamptonshire, and these include a bundle of court rolls dated between 1290 and 1365 of Roxhill manor in Marston Moretaine, Bedfordshire.[4] These rolls were stitched together a very long while ago and interleaved between two of them is a roll for Carun manor in Sherington dated 21 September 1312, which includes, *inter alia*, a terrier of the manorial demesne that has been superscribed at a later date, in bold early Tudor

Robert White was given a life tenancy in 1623 and ever since then it has been known as White's Close (Map 2). Meese (cottage and pightle) no. 40 was owned by Henry Newall in the mid-seventeenth century: its earlier history is not known, but it became the parish workhouse in 1813.

[1] MAC, 1512–1622, f. 21.

[2] *Bull. Inst. Hist. Res.* XX (1946), 136.

[3] Cf. Table 51, holdings a, d, k and m: the other terriers are of farms created under the new system when the manorial lands were dispersed early in the seventeenth century.

[4] This had been acquired by Richard Maryot, whose son-in-law Humphrey Catesby left it to his second son Thomas. On the latter's death without issue in 1530 it passed to his elder brother Anthony, who had already inherited Sherington (*VCH Beds*, III, 310).

TABLE 36

Open-field holdings under different systems of tillage

Owner	Tenants c. 1530	Farm no.	Two-field system: West Field (a.)	Two-field system: South Field (a.)	Three-field system: Marehill Field (a.)	Three-field system: Middle Field (a.)	Three-field system: Windmill Field (a.)
Mercers' Company	Thomas Chibnall	158	$5\frac{3}{4}$	7	$4\frac{1}{4}$	$4\frac{1}{4}$	$4\frac{1}{4}$
Mercers' Company	William Fisher	159	$24\frac{3}{4}$	$25\frac{1}{4}$	$18\frac{1}{4}$	$13\frac{1}{2}$	$18\frac{1}{4}$
Mercers' Company	John Bocher	162	$6\frac{1}{4}$	$7\frac{3}{4}$	$4\frac{3}{4}$	$4\frac{1}{2}$	$4\frac{3}{4}$
Mercers' Company	Richard Chibnall	178	$19\frac{1}{4}$	$16\frac{1}{4}$	$14\frac{1}{4}$	$9\frac{1}{2}$	$11\frac{3}{4}$
John Chibnall	Thomas Chibnall	157	$51\frac{5}{12}$	$53\frac{2}{3}$	$35\frac{11}{12}$	$36\frac{1}{2}$	$32\frac{2}{3}$
Tho. Catesby	—	15	$35\frac{5}{6}$	$35\frac{7}{8}$	$22\frac{1}{6}$	$21\frac{7}{24}$	$26\frac{1}{4}$
Rector's Glebe	—	179	6	$8\frac{1}{12}$	$4\frac{1}{4}$	5	$4\frac{5}{6}$
			$149\frac{1}{4}$	$151\frac{7}{8}$	$103\frac{5}{6}$	$94\frac{13}{24}$	$102\frac{3}{4}$

script, with the marginal references North Fild, Est Fild, Sowth Fild and West Fyld respectively.[1]

One may well ask how this old Sherington roll, representing Anthony Ardes's inheritance, came to be lost among the muniments of the Catesby family, who never had any direct connexion with the Carun estate. It seems to the writer that these Tudor additions were made at the time the two Anthonys met to discuss a re-arrangement of their cropping programme so as to bring it into line with the new one the villagers wished to adopt in the open fields, and that after agreement had been reached to partition the old North Field so as to provide for the new Middle Field the Carun roll—which Anthony Ardes had produced as evidence of his holding—had been inadvertently taken away with his other papers by Anthony Catesby. As the latter did not inherit Roxhill until 1530 it is unlikely that the discussion took place before that date.

Very little information about the husbandry in Sherington under the new three-field system is available until the middle of the following century, when Parson Fuller's lawsuits over tithe provide information that is in many respects unique. Partly because of the spread of non-conformity he found himself at loggerheads with farmers who between them were tilling some 550 acres or 65 per cent of the

[1] The terrier is given in Table 53 and reproduced in Pl. IV.

land in the open common fields. In his three bills of complaint[1] dealing with tithe that should have been paid in 1653 he was careful to point out that his allocation of the various crops from any one holding might not be precise, but even so the overall picture that emerges (Table 37) shows that the rotation being followed was one that was widely practised at the time on the strong loamy and clayey soils in Bedfordshire, north Buckinghamshire and Huntingdonshire. To quote Thomas Stone's description for Bedfordshire, written in 1794

The common fields of those descriptions of soils, are generally divided into three parts, seasons or fields, one of which is annually fallowed, a moiety of which fallow field (according to the best mode of management is annually folded with sheep and sowed with wheat, the other moiety of such fallowed land is dunged and sown with barley in the succeeding spring, and that part which produces wheat is in succession sown with oats, that which is next after fallow sown with barley, is in the succeeding year sowed with beans, peas or other pulses, and then such land being again to be fallowed, that part which in the previous course of husbandry was sown with wheat, comes into rotation to be sowed with barley, by which procedure the same kind or sort of grain is only produced every sixth year.

He complained, nevertheless, that many short-sighted farmers infringed the practice and grew too large a proportion of one grain—he instanced wheat and oats—so that on part of the land repetition of the crop occurred every third year and the soil in consequence became exhausted and foul.[2] His criticism is germane to the situation in Sherington, where the cropping during the seventeenth and eighteenth centuries appears to have followed the practice set out in Table 38, which is based on relevant data from Table 37 and the manor Court Orders of 1682.[3]

In 1653 the ratio of barley to wheat sown in the tilth field was about 2:1[4] and of pulses and oats in the pease field about 3:1.[5] Rye was not sown.[6] A portion of the barley land was thus under the same sort of crop every third year. This unbalance

[1] E122/289/31, 34, 35.

[2] *General View of the Agriculture of the County of Bedford* (London, 1794), p. 14: see also the companion *Views for Buckinghamshire*, by W. James and J. Malcolm, and for Huntingdonshire by G. Maxwell.

[3] Pp. 283–5.

[4] The ratio was the same in 1649, when a different common field must have been concerned.

[5] Thomas Lowe, another objector to tithe, had the exclusive use of plots in the demesne sector. In 1653 he sowed 8 acres wheat, 20 acres barley, 12 acres beans and peas and 10 acres oats. Wheat + barley was 56 per cent of the total crop, as in the open fields.

[6] Cf. Priest, *General View of the Agriculture of Buckinghamshire* (1813), p. 187. The ryeslade in Middle Field derives from earlier Rereslade, either OE *Hryre*, fall, here perhaps landslide or else OE *rēar*, reed, unrecorded but possible counterpart of German *Rohr*, Scand. *rör*, the same. Rye furlong in Windmill Field has probably the same origin, but an earlier form has not been met.

TABLE 37

Crops grown in Sherington, 1653

Numbers shown thus, 63★, are not included in the area shown in Map 8; the direction in which they lie is indicated on the map.

Owner or tenant (T)	Farm		Acres sown	Acres under				Percentage of total acres	
	No. on Map 8	Arable acreage		Wheat	Barley	Beans	Oats	Under wheat and barley	Under oats, peas and beans
Tho. Marshall (T)	177	58	40	6	13	21	—	47·5	52·5
John Cuningham	52	36½	30	6	10	12	2	53·3	46·7
John Babington	182	77½	50	10	20	15	5	60	40
Margaret Knight	15	83	50	10	18	20	2	56	44
Robert Knight	33	50	40	8	12	12	8	50	50
Richard Lord	46	12	24	4	8	8	4	50	50
Edward Henley (T)	158	17	10	2	3	5	—	50	50
Edward Laughton (T)	41	20	14	3	4	7	—	50	50
Richard Field	63★	7	4	1	1	2	—	50	50
Elizabeth Goodred[a]	—	—	18	3	9	6	—	66·7	33·3
Anthony Goodred	106★	22	12	2	5	5	—	58·3	41·7
Mary Chapman	224	5½	6	1	2	3	—	50	50
Richard Brittain (T)	162	15½	10	2	4	4	—	66·7	33·3
Richard Hooton	53	33	20	4	6	10	—	58·3	41·7
John Foulsham (T)	138	67½	30	10	15	5	—	50	50
Henry Travell[a]	—	—	20	4	6	7	3	50	50
Richard Hunt	18	10	6	—	2	4	—	33·3	66·7
William White[b]	—	10½	6	1	2	3	—	50	50
	—	526	390	77	140	149	24	55·4	44·6

[a] Tenant holding not identified.

[b] He owned 7 acres freehold and rented 3¾ acres under the Mercers.

did not mean that the furlong instead of the field had become the fundamental unit of cropping, as Hilton has shown so convincingly for Kirby Bellars in the later middle ages,[1] for such a flexible system would be possible only where one lord of the manor had full control, a condition that did not hold in Sherington. The position there was similar to that of Bluntisham-cum-Earith, Huntingdonshire, during the period 1800–13, where the barley and wheat were grown in separate sectors of the same field in the ratio of about 4:1.[2] The stinting Agreement of Sherington in 1722[3] mentions a wheat field and a barley field, implying that about a third of each common field could be readily partitioned off by moveable fences or by existing cart tracks when its turn came to be used as tilth or pease field respectively.

A study by Hoskins of crops grown in Leicestershire at various times between 1393 and 1531, in part based on inventories of deceased farmers estates, showed a barley to wheat ratio of about $2\frac{1}{2}$:1, with an even greater disproportion later in the sixteenth century.[4] He postulated a rotation similar in outline to that described by Stone, but Orwin made fun of it on the score that such a large differentiation between the winter-sown and spring-sown crops would play havoc with the field economy.[5] Orwin's views on agricultural practice command respect, but in this particular case he was relying too much on what he had seen with his own eyes at Laxton and too little on what he might have read of earlier authorities on open fields. It is not a question of just guessing what happened in these barley-pulse fields, for the situation there was well known to those who wrote the *General Views on Agriculture* of the various counties drawn up in 1794 for consideration of the Board of Agriculture and Internal Improvement, particularly to Stone, already mentioned, to Maxwell, who wrote about Huntingdonshire and to James and Malcolm who wrote about Buckinghamshire. It is perhaps unfortunate that Monk, who described himself as an ensign of dragoons, did not think fit to mention the common fields at all in his very sketchy *View of Leicestershire*, but Hoskin's studies[6] make it clear that the situation there was no different from what it was in the more southern parts of the champion country.

Table 38 shows that the field work at Sherington under normal conditions would

[1] R. H. Hilton, *The Economic Development of some Leicestershire Estates in the 14th and 15th Centuries*, pp. 52–3, 152.

[2] C. F. Tebbutt, *Bluntisham-cum-Earith*, pp. lix–lxiv.

[3] Pp. 286–9.

[4] *Trans. Leic. Arch. Soc.* 1941–2, p. 2. *Essays in Leicestershire History*, p. 123.

[5] *The Countryman*, xxxv (1947), 250.

[6] Summarized in *The Midland Peasant* (Macmillan, 1957), p. 155.

TABLE 38

Calendar of the fields in Sherington, c. 1682

	Fallow field	Tilth field	Pease field
October	Common of pasture	Sow wheat	—
November		No horse, beast or sheep after 1 November	No horse or cattle after 30 November
December		—	—
January		—	—
February		—	Plough after 2 February, sow beans and peas
March		—	—
April		Plough and sow barley	—
May	No horse, colt or cow after 10 May	Horses and beasts allowed in after 10 May	Horses and beasts allowed in after 10 May
June	Various ploughings	—	—
July		—	—
August		Harvest wheat and barley	Harvest beans and peas. Cattle allowed in 4 days later
September		Beasts and sheep on stubble	—

not have been too unevenly distributed throughout the season. The tilth field needed treatment from mid-October to early December, when part would be sown with wheat. The turn of the pease field came during February, to prepare for the sowing of beans and peas, while in April the residual portions of the two fields would have to be prepared for barley and oats respectively. The fallow field would require attention in early summer. The programme of work in late winter and early spring would have been heavy, but in the case of Sherington the number of independent farmers was large and so a sufficiency of plough-teams may have been available. This could have accounted in part for the persistent cry that there was not enough meadow and pasture for the beasts that should be kept—though such an explanation would not necessarily hold in other villages that followed a similar cropping programme. Inclement weather in winter or early spring, of course, could hold back the field work on the stiff Sherington loam to such an extent that—as Orwin realized—the farmer would be forced to sow his spring crops late and on soil that had not been adequately prepared. This must have happened time and again, ultimately with disastrous results, but custom dictated the farmers' programme and even if he felt there was room for improvement he could not reject it as unworkable.

In the first hundred years or so after the change-over to the three-field system his husbandry was, indeed, reasonably successful and the yeoman made money.[1]

Parson Fuller's valuation of the crops sown in 1653 (Table 39) throws light on the standard of husbandry at that time. On the assumption that the price of grain was lower in 1653–4 than at any other time in the century[2] it can be calculated from his data that the open-field land in Sherington had produced, in 1653, 2·5 quarters wheat and the same amount of beans, 3·5 quarters barley and 4·0 quarters oats per acre respectively.[3] These yields refer to but one year's cropping and so may be fortuitous, but for wheat and barley they are in line with those recorded for the period 1612–21 by Loder, who farmed successfully under the two-field system at Harwell, Berkshire.[4]

Fuller's estimates of total income amenable to tithe in 1653 suggest that the farmers were enjoying a modest degree of prosperity. The largest farm (nos. 15 and 33) run jointly by Robert Knight and his mother was comparable in size (133 acres) to that of Loder at Harwell (120–130 acres, arable). During the period 1612–19, when Loder was growing about three of barley to one of wheat in the tilth field, with a subordinate amount of pulse in the fallow field, the average price he realized for these three grains was 18 (10–23), 28 (20–34) and 18*s.* per quarter respectively.[5] His average gross income from grains was £242 (204–297) and of hay £60 (53–64), a total from these two sources of £302 (257–336). He had various oddments of income (chaff, straw, orchards, etc.) and after deducting all expenses his average net income was £239 per annum, a comfortable living from a farm of this size.

The Knights, who were of course sowing two-thirds of their land each year, had a gross income from grains of £204 in 1653, roughly equivalent to Loder's average if due allowance be made for difference in selling price. Their farm, like all open-field farms in Sherington, was short of meadow (only 6 acres) and pasture (only 8 acres) and they sold no hay, but the tithable income from the calves and milk of fifteen cows and from the wool and lambs of 200 ewes and wethers was £80. There are no details of additional revenue or of working expenses, but by analogy with Loder their net income may have been between £200 and £250 a year or slightly less

[1] Cf. Ch. 25.

[2] Thorold Rogers, *History of Agriculture and Prices*, v, 209.

[3] He rated wheat and beans at 50*s.* per acre, with barley and oats at 10*s.* less. In 1653–4 wheat and beans were worth about 21*s.*, barley 13*s.* and oats 11*s.* per quarter, respectively. Because of its remoteness from London prices in Sherington would be about 2*s.* per quarter less than these (cf. MAC, 1619–25, f. 175).

[4] Camden Society, 3rd series, LIII, xvii.

[5] Loder does not detail his sowing of pulses and the value quoted is from Thorold Rogers.

TABLE 39

Gross tithable income of farmers in 1653

Numbers shown thus, 63*, are not included in the area shown in Map 8; the direction in which they lie is indicated on the map.

No. on Map 8	Owner or tenant	Acreage	Gross value of grain (£)	Meadow hay (a.)	Pasture hay (a.)	No. of milking cows	No. of ewes and wethers	Gross tithable income (£)
177	Thomas Marshall	58	120	4	4	8	40	136
52	John Cunningham	36½	90	6	15	10	30	147
182	John Babington	77½	115	—	—	10	—	135
15	Margaret Knight	83	114	—	—	10	100	154
33	Robert Knight	50	90	—	—	8	100	130
46	Richard Lord	12	52	3	—	12	—	58
158	Edward Henley	17	30	2	—	6	—	40
41	Edward Leighton	20	32	—	—	8	—	48
63*	Richard Field	7	9	—	—	4	—	9
106*	Elizabeth Goodred	36	32	—	—	8	—	48
—	Anthony Goodred	22	27	—	—	8	—	43½
224	Mary Chapman	5½	13½	—	—	4	—	13½
162	Richard Brittain	15½	23	—	—	6	—	23
53	Richard Hooton	33	60	3	3	6	80	88
138	John Foulsham	67½	75	—	—	10	—	95
—	Henry Travell	—	45	—	—	9	—	65
18	Richard Hunt	10	13	3	—	4	—	20½
—	William White	10½	13½	—	—	4	—	13½
188	Thomas Lowe	67½	90	20	—	6	—	102

than £2 per acre. All the farmers listed in Table 39 were presumably making as good a living proportionately as the Knights, but the tithe data is too restricted for one to judge what advantage, if any, had accrued from the adoption many decades before of the three-field system of tillage. The open-field land was clearly still in good heart, but during the next 30 years or so there was to be a distinct change for the worse.

To understand the full import of what was happening at that time it is necessary to consider briefly the question of common rights. By ancient custom the ownership of 1 acre in the cowpasture conferred the right to tether two cows or horses from 11 May until the harvest be home, when it became common (open-tide). A clause in a conveyance of Richard Ardes to Thomas Tyringham in 1588[1] is a good illustration '12 a. and 3 r. lease and grasse grounds lying in the Beasts Pasture of Sherington for the which it shall be lawfull for the said Richard or his heires to kepe 25 Beast and a half before the hearde'. Each acre was thus equivalent to two cow-commons, as they were called,[2] and as the cowpasture extended to about 100 acres there must have been about 200 of them in all. One hundred and sixty of these are known to have been appurtenant to farms (Table 32) and another 23 to cottages (Table 34); the rest have not been traced, but it is probable that the eighteen cottage holdings of the Tudor period had two cow-commons apiece. But of course the owners of the 40 or more little cottages built in the middle decades of the seventeenth century would have had no such rights, and one must assume from the crisis of 1682 mentioned below that the farmers and smallholders had tacitly allowed these poor destitute folk to tether a cow or two per family, with the result that in the course of time the cowpasture became overstocked. The situation there, moreover, was being aggravated by the ploughing up of some of the old Lammas lands.

The river meadow had never provided more than the feed required for the plough-teams, and to augment the supply of green fodder and hay a number of patches of land in the open fields, more generously watered than the rest through proximity to the river or a well, had been set aside as permanent grass.[3] The owners

[1] D/Ch/188/3.

[2] A cow-common was a negotiable hereditament of about the same value as a half acre of enclosed pasture (MAC, 1791–7, under date 16 June 1796).

[3] In Windmill Field: Bullock's Leys furlong, the lower part of Standhill Marsh furlong, Holloway Slade and the ley below the furlong under the Ash: in Middle Field, Clott's Close, Bridge Leys and parts of Hareland furlong: in Dropwell Field, the few selions in Stony Clay and Walcot furlongs which butted against the rithy from Bredenwell, Hazlemead.

of these leys, glades, slades or swards as they were variously called had the right to tether beasts or horses on them from 11 May until Lammas day (1 August), after which date they became common. The 'Lammas lands' were rated as meadow,[1] but when more grain was needed for the expanding village population many of these were brought once again under tillage and the evicted animals were turned into the cowpasture.

Pressure of population also affected the quality of grazing in the open fields. As tenants or owners of the little cottages on the manorial waste the emigrants from outside would have had no right to common of shack, but, as with the cows, it must have been humanly impossible to deny each destitute family permission to keep a sheep or two—with a lamb in season—so that in time the fallow field, like the cowpasture, became overstocked. By 1680 all these various practices—which presumably had been allowed in the first instance out of pity—had made such inroads into the village economy that the community was obliged to seek a remedy at the local court leet.

A view of frankpledge was appurtenant to the principal manor and during the period with which we have been dealing this was in the hands of the Tyringham family, whose steward had been casual in the holding of courts and had not engrossed any court rolls. Late in 1681 Sir William Tyringham sold the manorial rights, with a few remnants of the old Ardes estate, including Linford Wood, to an ambitious local attorney Roger Chapman, who held a view of frankpledge and court baron the following May.

There the jury and other inhabitants made and agreed orders[2] which, *inter alia*, limited the number of cows that could be put into the cowpasture to one for every double cow-common; allowed only four horses or six cows on the stubble at opentide for every 60 acres of arable land and ley; allowed two sheep for every acre of arable land and three for every acre of ley in the fallow field; and directed that all land then in tillage which had once been counted as Lammas land was to be put back to sward before 1 November. It was hoped that these measures—which would hit the poorest section of the community harder than any other—would bring the livestock situation once more under control. The tragedy, of course, was that these

[1] The totals under 'meadow' in Tables 32, 35 and 36 exceed the 52 acres of river meadow because it was the attorney's custom to include the Lammas lands as such in their classification of the property under conveyance.

[2] See pp. 283–5.

folk had no appreciation of factors other than overstocking—such as faults in their own cropping programme—which could be undermining the fertility of their soil.

Lack of prosperity in the village for a long period following the civil war is reflected once again in the unchanging price of open-field land at a time when the value of money was slowly depreciating. John Tyringham had sold his outlying farms in 1637 for about £7 per acre[1] and John Chibnall got slightly less than this for Marshall's farm in 1714.[2] The corresponding information about rents is rather diffuse, but is consistent and tells the same story. Richard Ardes had let his open-field farms in 1588 for a few pence over 5*s*. per acre, and Anthony Chester of Chicheley in 1623 could write of John Forde, his tenant of 7 open-field acres in Sherington 'he must plough me as much or pay five shillings the acre'.[3] During the first half of the seventeenth century the Mercers' farms continued to be held as copyholds for life at the old customary rents[4] and it was not until after the civil war, when so many feudal customs were allowed to lapse, that they decided to grant leases for 21 years at increased rents. The old custom of exacting a fine for entry, however, was not entirely discarded, for it offered an immediate reward that they found hard to resist. When John Wells, a city merchant who had been tenant of the little manor farm no. 159 since 1637 at the old customary rent of 27*s*. per annum died in 1677 his local undertenant, Thomas Clifton—who had farmed it for 35 years—offered the Mercers a rent of £16 a year for a 21-year lease, but could not afford a fine. Edward Fuller, citizen and joiner of London,[5] countered with an offer of £6 a year and a fine of £100, which the Mercers accepted on condition that Clifton remained undertenant at his proferred rent. They were thus prepared to forego the extra £110 that would accrue over the course of years for a lump sum down.[6] In contrast, the old copyhold farm no. 158, which fell in during 1670[7] on the death of John Chibnall, was leased to his nephew Anthony Chibnall for 21 years at £11 a year without a fine.[8]

The Mercers were aware that conditions in Sherington had deteriorated since the civil war. The local bailiff Anthony Chibnall had been unable to collect many of the

[1] See p. 195.

[2] See p. 205: in the meanwhile three farms, nos. 33, 46 and 52 had been sold for about £8 per acre.

[3] Bedfordshire Record Office, DDBC, 479, f. 26.

[4] See pp. 180–2.

[5] A relative of Ignatius the rector and founder in 1705 of Fullers' charity. An annual rent charge of £5 was to provide £1 for the rector to preach a sermon on 27 March, 10*s*. for the rector and churchwardens on the same day, 2*s*. 6*d*. each to 26 poor people and 5*s*. to the parish clerk.

[6] MAC, 1675–81, ff. 45, 56, 60.

[7] See p. 181.

[8] MAC, 1669–75, ff. 96d, 98.

small quit-rents for some years before 1680 and his account was showing a deficit of about £40, nearly a year's total rents.[1] Farms, smallholdings and land were changing hands at a rate well above normal, and at a Court of Assistants held early in 1682 the clerk of the Company warned the members that if they did not hold a manorial court before long to register the freehold tenants they were in danger of losing their quit-rents. He also pointed out that a view of the property was urgently needed so that when an old copyhold lease ran out it could be replaced by one for 21 years at an equable rent.[2]

The master and wardens, with their surveyor, visited Sherington on 16 July 1682. They first examined the trees growing in the home closes. Most of these, from neglect, were 'touch't with Rottennesse in one parte or other of the tree' but the 252 that were thriving were sold for an average price of just under £1 apiece. The coppice wood, on lease to Roger Chapman the attorney, was valued at £8 per annum.

On the next day they held a court baron and in collaboration with Anthony Chibnall they valued the estate. Excluding timber they judged it to be worth £72 10*s.* 0*d.* per annum, the various holdings being rated at an annual rent of £1 for a cottage, 17*s.* for an acre of meadow or pasture, and only 4*s.* 6*d.* for an acre of open-field arable land.[3] These rates, which could not be applied until the old leases ran out (Table 40) were low even for this lonely corner of Buckinghamshire and were symptomatic of the depressed state of Sherington husbandry. There is a further illustration of this at the turn of the century, when one of the wardens visited Anthony Chibnall to discuss a new lease of his little farm no. 158. Anthony offered to renew at the old rent of £11 per annum but refused to pay a year's rent as fine; whereupon the warden reported at a Court of Assistants held on 26 June 1700 '. . . I find him very positive not to meddle with it on any other terms than he had it before and indeed I looke upon it to be as hard lett at that as anything you have in Bucks'.[4] The coppice was also a cause for concern at this period. When Roger Chapman's lease expired in 1711 nine and a half years rent remained unpaid and the trees had been so abused that the surveyor was unable to find a new tenant. It was finally stocked up in 1723 to make a paddock of enclosed pasture.[5]

[1] SAB, 1664–81.

[2] MAC, 1681–7, f. 10.

[3] Book at Mercers' Hall entitled 'St. Paul's School lands', P.S. No. 13[a], anno 1682, ff. 28–37.

[4] MAC, 1693–1700, f. 189.

[5] MAC, 1734–42, f. 171.

TABLE 40

Annual income from the Mercers' estate in Sherington

Period	Freehold and copyhold rents £ s. d.	Fines, heriots, etc. £ s. d.	Lease of wood £ s. d.	Estate leases £ s. d.	Gross income £ s. d.	Outgoings £ s. d.	Net income £ s. d.	Income actually received £ s. d.
1621–30	7 17 6	9 8 0	2 0 0	—	19 5 6	0 4 0	19 1 6	19 1 6
1631–40	7 17 6	4 3 0	2 0 0	—	14 0 6	0 4 0	12 8 6	12 10 3
1641–50	7 17 6	14 1 0	2 12 0	—	24 10 6	1 12 0	22 18 6	20 6 4
1651–60	7 17 3	2 12 4	9 10 0	1 4 0	21 3 7	1 0 0	20 3 7	21 4 6
1661–70	7 5 9	8 0 0	7 0 0	5 16 0	28 1 9	1 0 0	27 1 9	22 11 3
1671–80	5 8 6	10 0 0	7 0 0	18 15 9	41 4 3	0 18 0	40 6 3	39 2 0
1681–90	3 18 6	10 10 0	7 0 0	23 0 0	44 8 6	0 10 0	43 18 6	52 5 0
1691–1700	3 19 0	12 0 0	7 0 0	24 16 0	47 15 0	0 16 0	46 19 0	44 13 0
1701–10	3 11 0	—	7 0 0	38 0 0	48 11 0	1 0 0	47 11 0	33 13 3
1711–20	2 9 2	12 10 0	—	44 15 0	59 14 10	—	—	—
1721–30	2 9 2	—	—	58 16 0	61 5 2	—	—	—
1731–40	2 9 2	10 10 0	—	65 4 0	77 13 2	—	—	—
1741–50	2 9 2	—	—	80 0 0	82 9 2	—	—	—
1751–60	2 9 2	—	—	88 4 0	90 13 2	—	—	—
1761–70	2 9 2	—	—	94 0 0	96 9 2	—	—	—
1771–80	2 9 2	—	—	95 4 0	97 13 2	—	—	—
1781–97	—	—	—	105 0 0	105 0 0	—	—	—

The general agricultural situation did not improve as the new century got under way. The court orders of 1682 had apparently failed to have the desired effect and in 1722 all those concerned as freeholders or tenants drew up an Agreement on Commons which they bound themselves to observe for the next 21 years.[1] The preamble states that the arable lands in the common fields were not getting the necessary amount of dung because the pasturage available in those fields was insufficient for the number of sheep that ought to be kept and folded there for the purpose. The quantity of meadow and enclosed pasture, moreover, was too small to provide enough grass for the horses and cows the farms ought to maintain. The three main provisions of the agreement were intended to remedy these deficiencies. In the first place the field-tellers were required to set out strips of land 16½ feet wide between each furlong for use as a headway, drift-way or cart-way. Next, every selion of ½ acre was to have a strip 1 foot wide on each side of it kept as sward. Larger pieces of compacted selions were to be given suitably modified treatment in the proportion of 4 feet of sward to the acre. This 'ribbon development' connecting the headway of one furlong with that of the furlong immediately below it seems fantastic, for in effect it meant the setting aside of between 1500 and 2000 strips of sward. Lastly, all the farmers were to lay down for sward 5 out of every 30 acres they had in the open fields, and so on in proportion. As all the farm holdings except a very few in the demesne sector were in scattered selions this must have created a really tangled network of sward in the open fields.

There is no information about the success or failure of this interesting attempt to raise the standard of husbandry in Sherington, but the situation there must have been similar to that discussed by an unknown author of 1773 who maintained that land in balk was largely wasted

balks are of different widths, from two to sixteen feet; they are never ploughed, but are kept in grass under pretence of their being common field pasture. They are literally of no benefit to either the occupier or the Poor; for they are too narrow either to mow, or to graze without a boy to attend to each beast with a halter; and when the corn is off them, their grass is too old to feed; nor ought the common field to be kept open till it is consumed, for that must prevent putting in wheat in the proper season and is a total prohibition of turnips and cabbages.[2]

[1] See pp. 286–9.

[2] Quoted by E. C. K. Gonner, *Common Land and Inclosure*, p. 27, n. 1.

The provisions, nevertheless, would not have been too difficult to implement if a hypothetical application of it to the old Chibnall farm no. 157 can be taken as a guide. There, 105 acres in the open fields were made up of 289 selions grouped in 142 pieces of land. John Chibnall could have selected for sward nine of these pieces, each of 2 acres or more, a not unreasonable size for the purpose.[1] These new Lammas lands, for such they would to all intents and purposes have become, together with the ancient holding of 3½ acres in Clotts Close, would have more than provided John's quota of sward. Whether the arable land in question was suitable for conversion in this way is another matter: all one can suggest is that its withdrawal from the arable fields would not have unbalanced the cropping programme there. On the assumption—for which, may be, there is no justification—that all the other farmers concerned could have brought about a change with as little disturbance as this, the pasturage in the open fields would have been increased by some 500 acres. It was, presumably, in anticipation of such a benefit that the sheep stint was raised from two per acre of fallow to one per acre of arable land. The cow stint, nevertheless, was reduced from six to four per 60 acres of arable land and ley in the open fields. Sir John Chester retained the right of pasture for 100 sheep on a particular 32 acres in the demesne sector[2] and to enclose the 'Duke's pieces' that were part of Gowles farm no. 120.[3]

Indirect evidence discussed below suggests that the agreement lapsed after its 21-year course. The spirit of adventure among the local farmers was not lacking, but unhappily they do not seem to have understood that overcrowding of the cow-pasture and a shortage of pasture in the open fields were not the only factors slowly undermining the fertility of their soil; they had yet to learn and appreciate the inborn errors of their cropping programme. In any case the venture would have needed the willing co-operation of all concerned and with the lapse of years this might have become increasingly difficult to obtain because the drift towards capitalist farming went on unabated. As the new century unfolded the old freehold farmers dropped out one by one. Samuel Cuningham of no. 52 was in debt to Dr Waller of Newport

[1] D/Ch/157/8.

[2] See p. 172. This was under the Isham–Ardes agreement of 1578 on Enclosure: the arable lands concerned being Upper Berrie piece (24 acres) and part of Nether Berrie piece (8 acres). These lands came to Chester from Roger Chapman, who had purchased from Thomas Lowe in 1654.

[3] Recalling Humphrey, duke of Buckingham, who was killed at the battle of Northampton in 1460. The land remained with the Staffords until sold to Lord Mordaunt soon after 1570. See Tables 19, 30 and 32.

Pagnell, who foreclosed in 1711; Robert Adams was so deeply in debt when he died that his sons sold the remnant of the old Ardes estate—including the manor house no. 188, then used as two tenements—to Sir John Chester.[1] Robert Crichton, a lace dealer of Newport Pagnell, purchased farms nos. 18, 41 and 138 from the representatives of Nicholas Chibnall of Newport Pagnell in 1722.

John, the son of Anthony Chibnall, died in 1737 and when his only son, another John, who was a Cambridge graduate, had paid off the family debts his only asset was the ancestral holding no. 157, which he decided to farm himself. He died of smallpox, however, in 1741 before he had proved his mettle and as his heir, yet another John, was only 4 years old the estate had once more to be let. By 1750 (Table 41) John Babington of Fitz John manor farm no. 182 was the only resident freehold farmer,[2] for Robert Rogers, who owned the small Water Lane farm no. 46, was by trade a carrier on the London–Newport Pagnell road.

The data assembled in Table 42 illustrate the profound change that had taken place in the land ownership since the civil war. In 1650 only about 12 per cent of the land was owned by non-residents; the rest was divided more or less equally between the local gentry and the farmers. The profits of the land therefore were in large part spent locally—for current consumption or for the benefit of the farms. One hundred years later the tables had been turned: those living outside the village—widows, maiden ladies, and merchants in Newport Pagnell or London—owned two-thirds of the land and the farmers as a group divided the rest with the scant local gentry. Rents were low, but so also were farm profits and the tenants, most of whom operated on a small scale, may well have felt neglected.

At this particular juncture the Mercers handling of their estate was as inept as it could be. They had not visited it since 1707, and when a lease expired they continued the policy of demanding a substantial fine for re-entry. This militated against the small local farmer with no reserve of capital and by 1732 two lace dealers of Newport Pagnell, Robert Crichton and Mathew Hartwell, with William Chibnall a mercer there and the Rev. John Hooton, vicar of Astwood, held between them all the Mercers' leases (cf. Table 41). Such treatment gave the local farmers no encouragement. The Mercers remained complacent, however, until serious arrearages of rent were brought to their notice in 1741,[3] when they sought advice from a Luton estate

[1] D/C/1/19, 20.

[2] D/Ch/182/1–3.

[3] MAC, 1735–42, f. 245d.

TABLE 41

Holders of land in Sherington in 1750

Numbers shown thus, 63*, are not included in the area shown on Map 8; the direction in which they lie is indicated on the map.

No. on Map 8	Owner	Tenant or description	Messuages	Cottages	Arable land (a.)	Pasture (a.)	Meadow (a.)	Wood (a.)
188	Sir Anthony Chester	John Field	1	—	61½	33	4	—
138	Robert Crichton	—	1	1	67¾	14	5¾	—
54	Robert Webster	Sarah Adams, John Lane	1	—	81	5¼	—	—
177	Edward Paine	Thomas Caves	1	1	81	6	4	—
16	Susan Harris	—	1	—	30	46	—	—
	Barnaby Backwell	—	—	—	6	8	—	18
19	John Chubb	John Fountaine	1	—	67¾	2	4½	—
52	Richard Perrot	John Babington	1	—	27½	4	1¾	—
89	Thomas Smith	Cave manor house	1	1	108	34	4	20
182	John Babington	Fitz John manor farm	1	2	62½	2	4¾	—
15	Margaret Thornton	—	1	2	106	7	3	—
33	John Course	Richard Herbert	—	1	41	1	4½	—
46	Tho. Rogers	Benjamin Griggs	1	—	18	2	—	—
159	Mercers' Company	John Line, undertenant to Mathew Hartwell	1	—	35	10¾	1¼	—
158	Mercers' Company	Wm. Course, undertenant to Wm. Chibnall	—	1	14¾	9¾	4	—
162, 224	Mercers' Company	Richard Fisher and Benjamin Cole, undertenants to John Stubbs	—	2	22	1½	1	—
178	Mercers' Company	Thomas Platt, undertenant to Mathew Hartwell	1	—	30½	3¾	—	—
152, 153	Mercers' Company	Wm. King and James Tomkins, undertenants to Robt. Crichton	—	2	14	21¼	1	—
152, 153	Mercers' Company	Elizabeth Rogers	—	—	3¼	2½	4	—
18	Robert Crichton	Tho. Herbert	1	—	35¼	3	3½	—
142	Thomas Hooton	Ann Richards, Tho. Line	1	3	16½	2	4½	—
63*	John Battison	William Petts	—	1	5½	—	—	—
143, 139	Anne Glasbrook	Thomas Richards, John Stubbs	1	3	40	27½	3½	—
106*, 120*	Sir Anthony Chester	Richard Harrison, Thomas Tebbutt	1	—	70	4	5	—
157	John Chibnall	William King	1	4	130	10	8	—
198, 53	Ann Lucas	Edward Lane	1	2	63½	4	2½	—
179	Rector	Rectory and Glebe	1	—	15	4½	1¾	—
			20	26	1250¾	248¾	76¾	38

agent, John Nodes. He found that the vicar of Astwood, who owed $5\frac{1}{2}$ years' rent (£55) was insolvent[1] and instructed the undertenant John Stubbs to pay his rent direct to the Company in future, while Mathew Hartwell owed three years' rent (£88)[2] for his two little farms. Nodes was able to sell timber from the home closes for £100 and arranged with the tenants to send in terriers of their lands.[3]

TABLE 42

Distribution of land in Sherington among various classes of owners

	Acreage			Number of owners		
Date	Local gentry	Absentee owners	Freehold farmers	Local gentry	Absentee owners	Freehold farmers
1312	790	416	327	4	4	4
1460	880	385	317	4	5	9
1580	1083	299	190	3	2	5
1650	684	207	703	3	2	14
1700	642	601	340	4	7	6
1750	277	1076	270	3	14	3

It was not until 20 May 1748 that the Court of Assistants shook off its lethargy and appointed a committee of its own members to review the working of the Colet Trust. The inquiry was a searching one and the report recommended that in future leases should be granted at full economic rents without fines, that efforts should be made to collect arrears of freehold rents, amounting in the case of Sherington alone to £82, and that all the Buckinghamshire estates be visited in turn for the purpose of keeping manorial courts.[4] Two of the wardens, with the clerk and surveyor, accordingly visited Sherington on 19 September to hold the first manorial court there since 1686. They viewed the estate and saw with their own eyes the fruits of their Company's neglect during the past two or three decades.

The farm houses and outbuildings which the tenants, according to their leases, were expected to keep in repair were intended for their own use or that of their undertenant. The Mercers now found to their surprise that the three main tenants, Hartwell, Crichton and Stubbs had leased off the farm lands to be worked in

[1] MAC, 1742–7, f. 42d: 'he has a family of thirteen children and is in very low circumstances'.

[2] MAC, 1742–7, f. 83.

[3] The terriers are preserved at Mercers' Hall.

[4] MAC, 1747–51, ff. 77–101 *passim*.

connexion with other farms and that the buildings were being allowed to become more or less derelict. All of them were of stone and thatched, but only two could be regarded as in good condition, no. 224 sub-let to James Tomkins for 33*s*. per annum and no. 153, sub-let for 3*s*. less to Richard Robinson. Both of Hartwell's farm houses were in ruinous condition and no. 159, the little manor house, was sub-let to John Line, a matmaker, for 50*s*. per annum. The two cottages, nos. 152 and 162, sub-let to widow Smith and William Watts for 30*s*. a year each respectively, were fit only to be pulled down or turned into barns. The estate had thus become dispersed, with the land integrated with other farms and the buildings in use as working-men's tenements.[1]

The Mercers had learnt their lesson. Mathew Hartwell was some years in arrear with his rent and they foreclosed on both farms, which they offered at the old combined rent of £32 a year (only 4*s*. 6*d*. an acre for arable land) to Thomas Platt on condition that he spent £100 on renovating farm house no. 178, which was henceforth to be the manor house. For this purpose he was to be allowed the materials of the old manor house, no. 159, which could be rebuilt as a cottage.[2] Under conditions then prevailing in Sherington small isolated farms were not an economic proposition, and at the Court of Assistants on 8 March 1754 it was resolved

That it is the opinion of this Court that if the Farms at Sherrington in the possession of William Stubbs, James Buchanan [son-in-law and heir of Robert Crichton], William Chibnall and Elizabeth Rogers could be united into two farms, and the Farmhouses and Barns putt into good Repair by the Company, and lett afterwards to Tenants who will live in the Farmhouses and plow and till the Land themselves; and be obliged to spend all the Dung and Compost arising therefrom upon the said Farms and keep the Farm Houses and Out houses thereunto belonging in Tenentable Repair fit for tenants to live in, it would make an improvement of the Company's Estate at Sherrington, and be the means to have industrious Tenants of substance that understood Husbandry to occupy the same.[3]

As the farm terriers sent in by the tenants some ten years earlier were considered inaccurate they asked their surveyor, Richard Saunders, to prepare a new one for the whole estate.[4]

[1] MAC, 1747–51, f. 27–8. A survey made in 1753 describes the buildings in detail. No. 159, the manor house, had three rooms on the ground floor and two upstairs: there was a barn of three bays; no. 178—built by Thomas Course *c*. 1645, had a kitchen, parlour, dairy, drink room on the ground floor with four rooms upstairs: there was a stable of two bays and a barn of three bays. The smaller farmhouses 16, 153 and 224 had three rooms on the ground floor and two above; the cottages 152 and 158 had one room on the ground floor and one upstairs.

[2] MAC, 1751–6, 1 March 1754.

[3] *Ibid*. 8 March 1754.

[4] This is preserved at Mercers' Hall. It is referred to on pp. 271–2.

Sir John Chester, by now the largest landowner in the village, also realized the uneconomic nature of small units and grouped his property into two farms, one based on the old Ardes–Adams holding no. 188 with its newly built farm house on lease to John Field and the other based on Park farm no. 106 on lease to Thomas Tebbutt. There were still too many small farms belonging to absentee owners, however, and judging by the rents still current in the period 1750–60[1] the Stinting Agreement of 1722 had had no appreciable effect on the standard of husbandry.

The dearth of resident freeholders of any standing deprived the village community of the local leadership that it needed. The various manors were all held by those who resided at a distance—the principal one by Barnaby Backwell, the owner of Tyringham,[2] who lived in London and Cave's manor by Dryden Smith, who was a shipbuilder in Wapping. John Chibnall, who came of age in 1758 might have taken the lead in due course had he not been stricken with smallpox, like his father, before there had been time to establish himself. He and his wife Velebet died in 1770 and farm no. 159 had once more to be let, for the heir—another John—was but 8 years old.

The Mercers were now visiting their estate less infrequently than in the immediate past to hold manor courts and record their quit-rents. Although the tenants had become more and more reluctant to pay these trifling sums the Mercers, as trustees were loth to forego them because a freeholder dying without heirs would leave an estate that escheated to the Trust and not to the Crown. At this period the steward of the manor had no difficulty in obtaining the information he needed, for by custom those who attended the court were invited to a beanfeast afterwards, and the Mercers usually allowed as much as £4 for the purpose. Barnaby Backwell's steward George Pitt Hurst held a court of the principal manor in 1751, and the bill for this particular beanfeast is fortunately preserved.[3] With ale at not more than 2*d.* a gallon and meat at less than 3*d.* a pound there must have been ample fare for all. When the Mercers held their court on 22 July 1783 the quit-rents payable came to £2 9*s.* 2*d.* per annum

[1] The Chester Account Books suggest that enclosed pasture was being let at 24*s.* and open-field arable land at about 5–6*s.* per acre respectively.

[2] He was the grandson and heir of Sir William Tyringham (p. 206), and purchased the manorial rights from Thomas, the son of Roger Chapman in 1750 (D/Ch/129/1–4).

[3] D/Ch/misc/27. Charges at the Court held at Sherrington on Friday 19 April 1751 for Barnaby Backwell Esq.

		£	*s.*	*d.*
	Meat	0	13	6
Received the contents by Mr Hurst	Flower and Plumbs	0	3	4
(signed) John Fountaine (Lessee of the Catherine	Bread and Cooking	0	5	0
Wheel Inn, no. 19)	Ale	1	6	0
		2	7	10

and the arrears £168 7*s*. 2½*d*. They collected two rents of 1½*d*. each and one relief of a like amount, a grand total of 4½*d*.![1]

It was in this same year, 1783, that John Chibnall, the last of the family to farm in Sherington, came of age. Except for a brief period when his father had been in control the estate had been neglected for nearly half a century, and some idea of how the agricultural economy of the village had been running down during this period can be gathered from comments by James and Malcolm in their *General View of the Agriculture of Buckinghamshire*, published in 1794.

They remark that the land in the northern part of the county, unlike that down south, had a general appearance of bad management. Many of the villages in the Newport Pagnell area, especially those bordering on the Ouse, were still tied to common field husbandry and they complained that the farmers there, though in possession of as fine a loamy soil as was to be found anywhere in the kingdom, ploughed their lands to a serpentine form with high ridges, and neglected their drainage, so that the wetness of the soil, occasioned by its tenacity, produced very serious losses by the rot. The cow-commons also, although on good soil, were overrun with rushes[2] and very apt to rot the sheep. They mention that Thomas Hooton of Tickford Park, who farmed in the common fields of Newport Pagnell, had lost on the average 70 sheep per annum from the rot between 1785 and 1793. Their most caustic comments, however, were reserved for those places where, by custom or terms of lease, green crops were not grown, and the rotation was two crops and a fallow; wheat or barley, beans, then fallow. They were informed

> that the farmers had continued to sow the same kinds of grain for so many years, without having it in their power to procure a sufficiency of manure, and by being restricted from sowing clovers, etc. to enable them to keep sheep to fold their land, that they were reduced from a state, which among them might be called opulence, to absolute penury; the land, though good in itself, being worn out, and incapable of bearing grain any longer.

Although it is probably true to say that the various agricultural authorities cited above were strongly prejudiced against the continuation of open-field husbandry there is no doubt that this last quotation epitomizes the situation in Sherington in the decades before the Enclosure Act of 1796. John Chibnall could have had but

[1] MAC, 1781–6, 3 Sept. 1783. The only remaining copyhold rent was one of 2*d*. payable by John Chibnall for a plot of enclosed waste. It was in arrear to a total of 12*s*. 1*d*.

[2] The families of Finnemore, Umney and Line had been mat makers for generations.

little experience outside his own rather backward home area, but he realized that the predicament to which they were all reduced called for a break-through of some sort and though still a very young man he took the lead himself. Under the date March 1787 the account book of his solicitor George Pitt Hurst[1] contains the entry 'Attending you and taking instructions to draw an agreement between the proprietors and occupiers of land in Sherington for a stint of common in the open fields: expenses etc. £3 15*s.* 2*d.*' No copy of this agreement appears to have survived, and so we do not know if John was seeking to apply changes more drastic than those set out in the earlier one of 1722, but the effect in any case was not lasting and in 1796 the main proprietors petitioned Parliament for powers to enclose. Meanwhile for John himself the situation had already become desperate and the shutters went up. Hurst records under the date January 1788 'Attending you several times and advising with respect to the sale of your estate at Sherrington and taking instructions to draw particulars thereof . . . 10*s.* 6*d.*' The sale to William Brooks of Clifton Reynes was completed late in 1789[2] and John left the village soon after.

[1] *Penes*, Messrs W. B. and W. R. Bull, Newport Pagnell.

[2] A fine was levied in Easter Term 1789 to break the entail and the sale by lease and release dated 9 and 10 Oct. 1789 was covered by a recovery suffered in Michaelmas Term in that year.

29

THE TURNPIKE TRUSTS

THE tortuous history of the toll gates in Sherington during the late eighteenth and early nineteenth centuries is an irrational story of how two vested interests, brought into being by Parliament to administer measures designed primarily for the public benefit, could nullify each other's efforts through sheer lack of co-operation and foresight.

Under the system known as Statute Labour, first put to use in 1555, the maintenance of a road had been made the responsibility of the village through which it passed[1] and where, as in Sherington, the traffic was heavier than that serving local needs the expense to the community there could be a grievous and indeed an unfair burden. Complaints about the state of the roads and especially of the bridge in Sherington[2] had been frequently laid before the justices and to alleviate the situation Parliament agreed in 1753 to the setting up of two turnpike trusts, one to deal with the road from Bedford and the other with that coming in from Kettering via Olney.[3] The toll gates were to be erected at positions not more than a furlong to the east and north respectively of the waypost at the junction of the two roads (Map 7) and to ensure that traffic should not circumvent them by using a side track the trustees were empowered to close Blackbird lane, as the former Monchlade was then called (Map 1).[4] The trusts were to operate for the usual period of 21 years, with a further five years under the General Act of 1755,[5] and between them they were to share the cost of maintaining the fabric of the bridge. The village was to gain, in that henceforth Statute Labour was limited to the Olney road.

For some time before then the Bedford road had been notoriously one of the worst for wheeled traffic in the county and the trust, which had come into being with only a small financial backing, found itself unable to maintain the road in a

[1] 2 and 3 P. and M. c. 8.

[2] Cf. pp. 216–17.

[3] 27 Geo. 2, c. 31 and 34.

[4] The windmill alongside the lane thereby became inaccessible and was pulled down. This is probably the reason why a new one was built to the W of the road junction in Sherington soon after the Enclosure of 1797.

[5] 28 Geo. 2, c. 17.

reasonable condition. The amount of traffic did not increase, as had been confidently expected, and the trustees, faced with dwindling resources, were eventually forced to suspend operations a year or so before 1770.[1] By default the Kettering trustees had now to bear the whole cost of repairing Sherington bridge, even though the removal of the Bedford gate meant that the Olney traffic could proceed along Gun lane to the top of Chicheley hill and hence to the bridge without paying any toll at all! Under the act which governed their own operations the trustees could take no remedial action until it came up for renewal in 1781, when they applied for and were granted permission to move their gate to a new position just north of the bridge, the keeper's lodge being erected on the site where Bridge House stands today.[2]

During the intervening years the fabric of the bridge deteriorated and now that the Kettering trustees had a monopoly of the tolls they tried their best to bring about some improvement, but in spite of an expenditure of over £400 during the first fourteen years of the new century no effective progress was made. By 1814, moreover, the Bedford road had once more become well-nigh impassable for wheeled traffic[3] and Parliament decided that it must become the object of a new trust.[4] The bridge, of course, remained the crucial issue and in 1815 the two trusts agreed to a joint campaign for it to be taken over by the county. A bill of indictment was accordingly brought before the justices at the Aylesbury Assizes in that year[5] and an appeal to have the bridge rebuilt at the public expense was successful.

The new bridge was formally opened in 1818, but many of the local people were still disgruntled, for the Bedford trustees had erected their gate at the top of Chicheley hill (Map 7) which meant in effect that Newport traffic from the east was having to pay toll there and again at the foot of the bridge, a double imposition that was naturally resented. When the Kettering trustees applied for the usual renewal in 1823 Charles Pinfold of Chicheley and other interested parties petitioned to have the bridge gate returned to its former position just north of the waypost so that they could have access to Newport on payment of only one toll.[6] In spite of strenuous opposition from the trustees, who foresaw a sharp drop in revenue and offered a ticket system that would avoid the payment of double fees, Parliament agreed to

[1] Thomas Jeffery's map of 1770 shows only the Olney road gate.

[2] 21 Geo. 3, c. 3.

[3] Lyson's, *Bedfordshire*, p. 23.

[4] 55 Geo. 3, c. 47.

[5] Buckinghamshire Record Office, Q/AB/35/1–161.

[6] Flysheet of April 1823 among the trust papers at the Northamptonshire Record Office.

the change and in order to prevent south-bound traffic from once more making use of Gun lane the gate was moved a little later to a new position north of the lane junction with the Olney road on Emberton hill.[1]

In retrospect it may seem strange that the original trustees should not have agreed at the outset to place their gates at the crests of the two hills, for there would then have been no need to bother about Gun lane. To argue thus presupposes perhaps that they would all approach the problem from the same point of view and this was clearly not the case. The two groups of men concerned—landowners and clergy from Bedfordshire and Northamptonshire respectively—would have had no previous experience in the running of a turnpike trust and, when a stretch of road common to the two trusts had to be dealt with, county prejudices came to the fore. It was not until the bridge gate had gone up the hill that better counsels prevailed. The two trusts then jogged along fairly happily together until they were forced by railroad competition to wind up in 1870 and 1878 respectively.[2]

[1] 4 Geo. 4, c. 64.

[2] I wish to thank Miss Joan Chibnall and her supervisor Prof. W. R. Mead for permission to make use of the turnpike data discussed in her thesis on 'The Roads of Buckinghamshire' (London University, 1964).

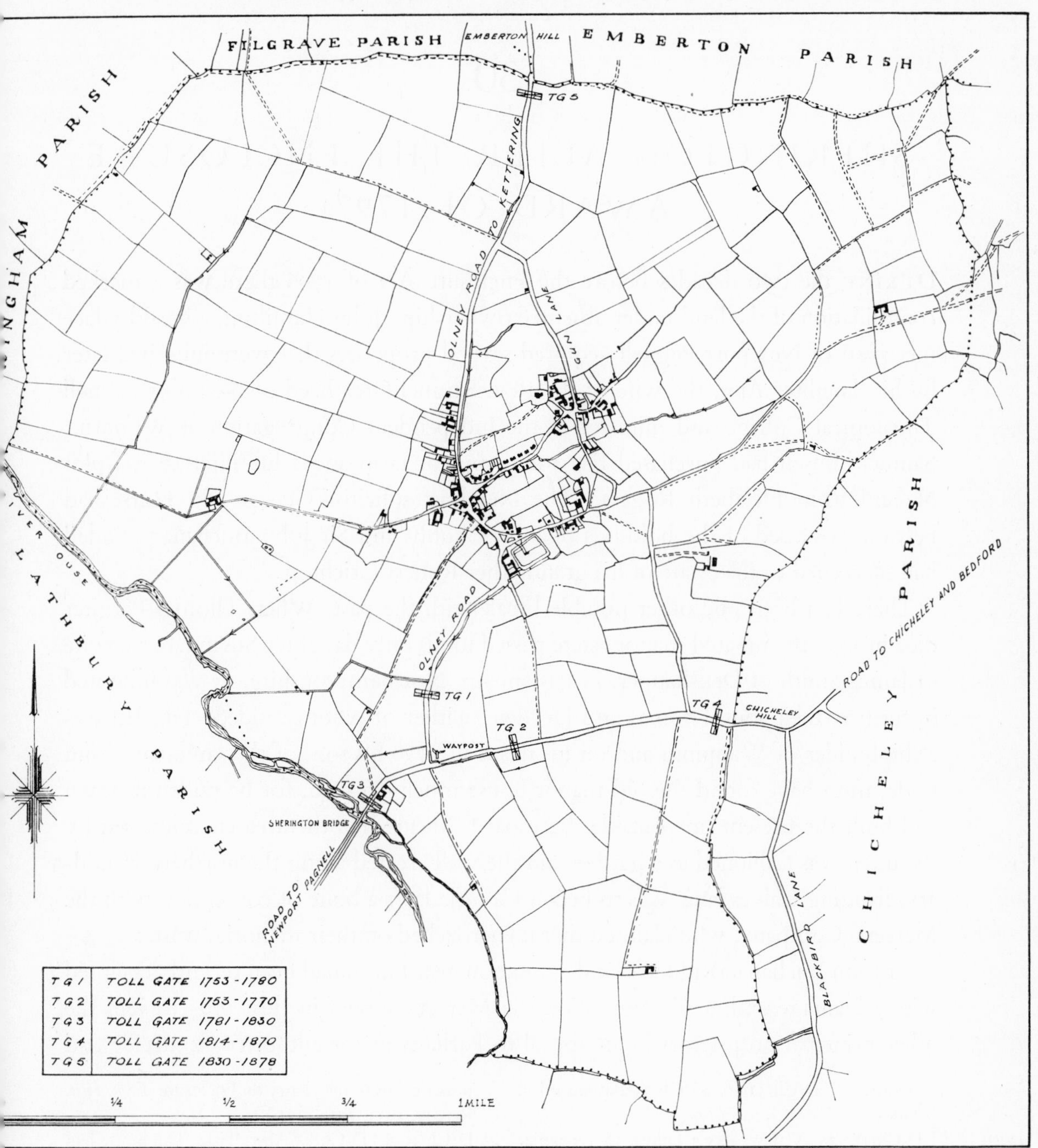

Map 7. Toll gates.

30

SHERINGTON AFTER THE ENCLOSURE AWARD OF 1797

DURING the two decades before the Enclosure Act of 1796 there was a marked consolidation of the land under absentee ownership. John Hamilton, a wealthy lace merchant of Newport Pagnell acquired several properties that were inherited later by his daughter Ann, the wife of the Rev. Samuel Greatheed of Newport Pagnell Theological College and minister of the Independent Congregation at Woburn.[1] Samuel himself had purchased Fitz John's manor farm and a life interest in a plot of land from Elizabeth Rogers.[2] The Newport solicitor George Pitt Hurst had become possessed of the holdings of John Chubb[3] and Sir John Buchanan Riddell had succeeded to the estate of his grandfather Robert Crichton.

There had been one other notable break with the past. When Thomas Pargiter died in 1712 the moated manor estate passed to his only daughter Susannah, the wife of James Smith of Denshanger, in Passenham, Northamptonshire. It was inherited in turn by their sons Thomas and Dryden, neither of whom resided. Dryden was a shipbuilder of Wapping, and on his death in 1770 his son, of the same name and trade, must have found the old manor house much decayed, for he pulled it down and built the present one outside the moat.[4] Meanwhile the area encompassed by the moat was fashioned as a garden and the wall erected along the northern boundary, fronting Calves lane, was to become a little later a bone of contention with the Mercers' Company, who claimed that it encroached on their manorial waste.

Sir John Buchanan Riddell's land at Sundon near Luton had been recently enclosed with advantage and at his suggestion the Mercers agreed in July 1795 to join the other principal proprietors in an appeal to Parliament for authority 'to divide and

[1] D/Ch/15/8. D/Ch/54/16. D/Ch/33/Battans Abst. Title.

[2] D/Ch/182/15. V. Lavrosky's failure to recognize that Greatheed was technically a lay proprietor and not an established clergyman has led him to make exaggerated claims about the amount of land the peasants lost to the clergy on Enclosure (*Econ. Hist. Rev.* IV, 1933, 273).

[3] D/Ch/19/8. D/Ch/53/Abst. Title. The house had been pulled down and the home close absorbed into no. 53.

[4] D/Ch/89/59.

inclose the Common Fields of Sherrington'.[1] The necessary act was passed the following year.[2]

The Enclosure commissioners made a detailed valuation of every holding, but the re-allocation of the land required special treatment because the tithe was computed for a corn rent issuing from certain specified allotments instead of being passed on proportionately with the new holdings or abolished altogether by grant to the rector of so much extra land. This rent, at a rate fixed at intervals of not less than 21 years, was based on the average price of a bushel of wheat in the 21-year period preceding the date of fixing. In 1798 the rate was 5*s.* 6½*d.* per bushel, and the corn rent attached to the special allotments was adjusted to bring in a total of £342 6*s.* 4½*d.*, a sum the commissioners considered the rector would have received as tithe that year if the enclosure had not been pending. These special allotments were annexed to properties whose owners were willing to receive them and those—like the Mercers and Sir John Buchanan Riddell—who preferred not to take on any such commitment, were called upon to accept a proportionately smaller allocation of land in lieu of their common rights (Table 43). The arrangement at the time seemed equable to all concerned, for no one could then foresee that the abnormally high price of wheat in the war years just ahead would lead to severe hardship in the hungry thirties and forties of the coming century.

The Enclosure Award was dated 4 July 1797.[3] The resetting of the old common fields seems to have been done effectively, the strong wheat lands to the south being consolidated with a few essentially arable farms and the drier lands to the north distributed with the meadows among a number of dairy farms.

As was apparent from earlier evidence[4] few of the cottagers could show the commissioners a valid title to common rights and only four smallholders were given allotments. Forty-five cottagers retained the garden within which their dwelling was built, but this seldom extended to more than half a rood, while 25 others—representing the old squatters on the waste—were allowed no more than the few poles of land upon which their mean cottage stood. All the amenities that might have been available to these folk in the old open fields were thus withdrawn without any attempt being made to give them satisfaction in other ways. The

[1] MAC, 1791–7, 31 July 1795.

[2] 36 Geo. III, no. 160.

[3] CP 43/861/103. The map accompanying the award, now filed as MPL 38, has inscribed on it tables giving full details of acreage and value of every plot of land.

[4] See pp. 230–1.

TABLE 43

Holders of land in Sherington after the Enclosure Award of 1797

No. on Map 8	Owner	Tenant	Home closes (a.)	Allotment for land and commons (a.)	Allotment for tithe (a.)	Total land (a.)
179	Rector	—	7½	11	—	18½
89	Dryden Smith	William Barker, George Griggs	64	55	—	119
188	Charles Chester	William Field	66¾	64	52¼	183
162, 178[a]	Mercers' Company	Benjamin Griggs	19½	109¼	—	128¾
138	Sir John Riddell	William Pyke }	24¾	71¾	—	96½
33[a]	Sir John Riddell	Thomas Harding }				
19	George Pitt Hurst	James Nicholls	6	102½	28¾	137¼
54	Rev. Samuel	Robert King }	16¾	162	37	215¾
15	Greatheed and Ann, his wife	Richard Shrieve }				
182	Rev. Samuel Greatheed	Thomas Davison	22½	55¼	87½	165¼
—	Rev. Samuel Greatheed (lifehold)	Thomas Rogers	—	23¼	4¾	28
52	Thomas Battans }	Thomas Harding	31	43¼	14	88¼
46	Thomas Battans }					
157	William Brooks	—	8¾	109¾	23¾	142¼
177	John Clayton	—	4½	78	19	101½
143, 139[a]	Samuel Boddington	—	28½	59½	—	88
16	Richard Higgins	Thomas Baker	50	—	6½	56½
18	John and Richard Hale	—	2½	38¼	—	40¾
—	William Praed	—	20¾	5	26¼	52
201	Thomas Odell	—	3¾	14	3	20¾
186	William Field	—	6½	4¼	—	10¾
—	Six miscellaneous small allotments	—	—	—	—	25½
—	Cottages	—	—	—	—	20¼
—	Stone pit	—	—	—	—	2¾
—	Roads	—	—	—	—	21¾
						1762½

[a] Farmhouse no longer in use.

re-arrangement of the fields, moreover, made for more efficient farming and in time there was a reduced demand for labour so that many of the hands became redundant and were forced to seek help through the parish rates. This failure to protect the poorest section of the community was indeed one of the grave disadvantages of the whole enclosure movement. In Sherington itself during the early years of change the situation was aggravated because the national economy was upset by the war with France. For several generations past many of the local families had been engaged in village industries like mat making and basket making, while their womenfolk had found gainful employment in lacemaking for the dealers and factors in Newport Pagnell. As conditions became more stringent some of these began to feel the pinch and in their turn were forced to seek parish relief. The local parish register provides poignant evidence of the changed conditions in the village during this period. Comparison of the occupations of the local men married in the church during the decades, 1796–1805 and 1762–71, indicates that by the turn of the century there had been a sharp contraction in the mat-making industry and a distressing increase in the number of those described as labourers. Meanwhile, as one would have anticipated, the smallholder and small tenant farmer had become a rarity.[1] By 1810 poverty there had increased to such an extent that 23 of those who owned their own cottage at the time of the enclosure had been forced to sell out to James Smith of Cave's manor house.[2]

At the time the commissioners were surveying the land in 1796 the Mercers were fortunate enough to acquire a substantial house which had just been built in the smallholding no. 161 that lay to the west of the cottage replacing the old manor house no. 159 in Calves lane.[3] The land duly allotted to them was let on lease for 21 years with this house, as Mercers' manor farm, to Benjamin Griggs at a rent of £175 per annum, free of land tax, a sum in keeping with the commissioners valuation and £70 more than the old scattered property had returned before the enclosure. The rent of the main Chester holding, no. 188, on lease to William Field, was also increased proportionately from £93 free of land tax to £160 10*s.* 0*d.* per annum.

[1] In the decade 1796–1805 (1762–71 in brackets) 47 (46) local men were married, including 22 (13) labourers, 4 (12) mat makers, 11 (6) tradesmen and 0 (6) husbandmen.

[2] A man was ineligible for parish relief if he owned property.

[3] See p. 240. Farm no. 178, in the tenure of Thomas Platt had been designated the manor farm before the Enclosure. It was pulled down later and the materials used to fence and improve no. 161.

While hostilities in France maintained a keen demand for agricultural produce the farmers could afford these inflated rents, but the year 1813 heralded a succession of blighted crops during which the price of wheat fell rapidly from about fourteen shillings to eight shillings per bushel. The Mercers visited Sherington in 1816 and found Benjamin Griggs' farm in good condition; he was, however, in arrear with his rent and when challenged about this replied forcibly that he was battling not only against adverse weather but also against a poor rate that had soared during the past few years from 4*s.* to 16*s.* in the pound, an impost three times as great as any that the tenants in south Buckinghamshire had to contend with.[1] He also pointed out that he was burdened with a heavy toll each time he took his produce over Sherington bridge to market it in Newport Pagnell.[2] Conditions did not improve as the years passed; his debts accumulated, and he was eventually forced to sell out in 1822. When the matter came up before the Court of Assistants the members were sympathetic and spontaneously voted him a pension of £50 a year,[3] but their colleague Charles Lane expressed the considered opinion that the Trust could not legally do this and the Mercers presumably provided the money out of their own funds until Griggs' death seven years later. The reports of the Mercers' land agent during this period enlarge on the tenants difficulties and year by year he put in a strong plea for some amelioration in rent. He was merely echoing here a nation-wide call from the farming community for a reduction of both rent and tithe. In Sherington the latter was in certain instances particularly onerous.

The rectors who followed Ignatius Fuller owed their preferment to family connexion. John Barton (1711–43), who was also rector of Great Brickhill in succession to his father Samuel, greatly improved the parsonage house in 1718 and was given leave to move the pulpit from its original position against the second pillar on the north side to the upper end of the nave.[4] He resigned Sherington in 1743 in favour of his son Philip, who was a great friend of the Buckinghamshire antiquary William Cole. Alexander Cromleholme (1781–1811) who also held Beachampton, arranged for the erection of the church pews in 1804. He had meanwhile negotiated the corn rent agreement with the commissioners, but it was under his successor John Pretyman (1811–42) that its provisions were brought into

[1] MAC, 1815–16, 12 Sept. 1816.

[2] A drawing horse paid 4½*d.* and a non-drawing one 1½*d.*

[3] Mercers' Company muniments 4/9/1313, 1318.

[4] Lincoln Episcopal Act Book 1715–23, f. 69.

sharp relief. John took his master's degree at the age of 25 in 1811, but before then his uncle the bishop of Lincoln had already collated him to the prebend of Aylesbury (value £62) and the rectory of Winwick (value £567) as well as the rectory of Sherington. Because of scarcity during the war years the average price of wheat on which the corn rents for the period 1819–40 were based jumped from 5*s.* 6½*d.* to 10*s.* 5½*d.* per bushel. This produced £646 per annum for the rector (Table 44) and as he was also entitled to Easter offerings, surplice fees and mortuaries he was able to return a gross income in 1822 from Sherington alone of £674 8*s.* 10*d.*[1] His curate F. A. Grace was paid £100 per annum and presumably his deputy at Winwick a like sum, so that during a long period of agricultural depression, with the poor people well-nigh starving, John was drawing a net income of about £1100 a year from clerical sources. Inequalities such as this were rife in the church of those days but they decreased as the century advanced and at the beginning of the new one the corn rents payable to R. F. Malham provided an income unworthy of his office.[2]

TABLE 44

Sherington corn rents

Period	Average price of a bushel of wheat during previous period *s. d.*	Examples of corn rents, to the nearest £: Shrieve's farm no. 15	King's farm no. 54	Fitz John manor farm no. 182	Total sum payable to the rector
1796–1818	5 6½	32	16	98	342
1819–40	10 5½	60	30	187	646
1841–62	7 1¾	42	21	128	441
1863–97	6 6½	38	19	117	403
1897–1922	4 4¾	26	13	78	271
1922–52	5 7⅓	30	15	90	311
1953–	6 7¾	—	—	—	—

The farm vacated by Griggs in 1822 was let to Edward Jefferson at a rent of £200 per annum, the Mercers agreeing to renovate the premises and to allow him the same rebate of 25 per cent that they had conceded to their tenants in south Bucking-

[1] Lincoln Record Office, terrier exhibited 1 July 1822.

[2] The successors of Pretyman were J. C. William (1842–8), Alexander King (1848–84), Edward Elton (1884–98), R. F. Malham (1898–1903), J. M. Geden (1903–12), H. A. G. Blomefield (1912–43), D. G. Gordon (1943–50), Hugh I. K. Jones (1950–61) and L. R. L. Bearman (1961–).

hamshire.[1] Conditions remained unfavourable throughout the decade that followed and in the years 1828–30 the rain was so prolonged that the farmers throughout the county lost most of their crops and had their sheep decimated by rot. Jefferson's farm, fortunately, had been made tithe free at the Enclosure and so he was in a better position to meet these troubles than, for instance, his neighbour Edward Caporn, the tenant of Fitz John's manor farm no. 182 of about the same overall size. In addition to the usual tenant's outgoings Edward had to find the exorbitant corn rent of £187 per annum payable to the rector (Table 44). The stultifying effect of this fickle tribute on the value of the farm was all too clear: in 1813 it had been worth £2000, but Samuel Griggs' executors could not obtain more than £1740 for it in 1847.[2] By contrast Shrieve's farm, no. 15, which had been assigned a more reasonable corn rent, was purchased by Michael Smith for £5100 in 1808 and sold by his executors for £8000 in 1862 to William Backwell Tyringham.[3]

James Smith of Aldenham, Hertfordshire, who had succeeded his father Dryden in 1810,[4] sold the Cave manor estate, including the 23 newly acquired cottages, in 1828 to Dr John Cheney, physician general to the army in Ireland.[5] Cheney resided in the manor house until his death eight years later,[6] when his property, which included two substantial farms,[7] went into the hands of trustees for the benefit of his widow Sarah, who lived in Ireland. The manor house was meanwhile let to John Bell.

During the middle decades of the last century many of the farms in Sherington changed ownership and—as mentioned in the Introduction—they became re-grouped in a way that effectively disguised their descent from the old manorial estates (Table 45). A London solicitor Alfred Umney, whose father William Umney came of a long line of Sherington mat makers, acquired two farms in 1847–8[8] and the whole of the Cheney estate except a few acres in 1856.[9] On the death of his widow Georgeana some 30 years later the property passed to the son-in-law George Nelson and from him to Col. Owen Williams, whose trustees

[1] MAC, 1823–4, 9 July 1824. The renovations cost £811.

[2] D/Ch/182/19.

[3] D/Ch/15/9, 10.

[4] D/Ch/89/54.

[5] For £4500, D/Ch/89/56.

[6] He was buried in the south-west corner of the old churchyard under a square pedestal which carries upon its eastern face a long exhortation from the scriptures. It does not record his name or date of death.

[7] In 1828 he purchased Harding's farm no. 52 and King's farm no. 54 from Amos Westaby for £4000.

[8] No. 19 for £3950, D/Ch/19/12; Water Lane farm no. 46 for £3279, D/Ch/46/21.

[9] For £4500, D/Ch/89/54.

TABLE 45

Holders of land in Sherington in 1862 and 1962

No. on Map 8	1862 Owner	1862 Tenant	1862 Acreage	1962[a] Owner	1962[a] Name of farm or tenant
179	Rector	—	18½	Rev. H. Sparling	Bancroft manor (so called)
19	Alfred Umney	Job Nicholls	137	R. Lane	Home farm
46	Alfred Umney	Samuel Bennett	72	Dudley Gardner	Water Lane farm
52	Alfred Umney	William Makeham	93½	M. G. Hicks	The Lodge (no farm land)
54	Alfred Umeny				
89	Alfred Umney	John Bass	76¾	P. Perrottet	Manor House
				J. Cook	Manor farm
182	W. B. Tyringham	—	130	J. T. Burgess	Griggs or Fitz John Manor farm
15	W. B. Tyringham	Job Smeeton	149	A. Rosenplatt	Church End farm
16	W. B. Tyringham	—	56		M. Cook
188	Rev. Anthony Chester	William Field	183	Chester estate	Church farm F. J. Field
157	Rev. Anthony Chester	William Field, Farside farm	95	J. Cook	Farside farm (disused)
157	Thomas Borton	—	33	Dr R. C. L. Griffiths	The Old House (no farm land)
138	Thomas Borton	—	96	J. Robinson	Yew Tree farm
143	Thomas Borton	—	87		
177	—	—	101	J. T. Burgess	No farm land
18	Thomas Hale	—	41	George Fleet	Village farm
162	Mercers' Company	George Jefferson	129	Lord Hesketh	J. Cook

[a] Information kindly supplied by Mr A. G. Hickson.

disposed of it piecemeal soon after 1945. William Backwell Tyringham (p. 206), who had inherited the Linford manorial rights with a few acres of land and wood,[1] purchased four farms between 1851 and 1872.[2] F. A. König acquired the whole Tyringham estate in 1908 and his trustees sold the Sherington farms at various times *c.* 1950. In both of these estates there had been interchange of fields among the various farms, and redundant farmhouses had been put to other uses. The Brooks, formerly Chibnall, estate was dispersed in 1842,[3] the land lying to the south of the

[1] *VCH Bucks*, IV, 305.

[2] Shrieve's farm no. 15; Baker's farm no. 16 consolidated with Hale's farm no. 18, Fitz John manor farm (Grigg's) no. 182.

[3] D/A/GT/8(Sher) 4, dealing with the division of the corn rent.

Bedford road (95 acres), known later as Far Side farm, becoming part of the Chester estate and all but a few acres of the rest going to Thomas Borton of Yew Tree farm. Col. F. E. Allfrey purchased the house, which he called the Laurels, for use as a private residence in 1900[1] and it is now under the more appropriate name of the Old House in the possession of Dr R. C. L. Griffiths.

The Jefferson family remained tenants of Mercers' farm until it was sold, with the reputed manorial rights, to Mrs Mary E. Jefferson in 1919.[2] This brought to a close a long association that for the most part had been beneficial to the village. The property yielded such a small fraction of the Colet Trust income that the Mercers tended to deal with the tenants in an easy-going way and their officials' complaisance often verged on indolence. The Trust Account Books show that the Sherington tenants were generally treated with more consideration than a private owner would have found economically possible and in times of agricultural depression or of personal hardship rents were often allowed to remain unpaid for years on end. Then, as like as not, the arrears would be waived and the tenant encouraged to make a fresh start. The Court of Assistants Minute Books tell the same benevolent story and often record gifts for parochial or church purposes that would have been much appreciated in a village where until recent times a modicum of poverty had been endemic since the early days of the enclosure movement.

The author has taken delight over many years in trying to unravel the feudal and economic history of the village from a study of documents left derelict in solicitors offices or forming part of various archive collections. With few exceptions, however, these sources have provided little if any information about what happened in the village during the past century or so. Yet contemporary newspapers show, for example, that the foundation of the Independent Chapel in 1828,[3] the rebuilding of the Wesleyan Chapel in 1864,[4] the opening of the school house in 1870 and the restoration of the church in the same year[5]—with the concomitant destruction of its old monuments—were events that loomed large to those concerned. The story of that period nevertheless brings us down to modern times and it should be told by one who knows the village as intimately as did Parson Fuller or Parson Gervase, and who has a real understanding of what the village means to the community

[1] He enlarged the Elizabethan house by building additions to the north.

[2] MAC, 3 Oct. 1919.

[3] D/Ch/misc/21. C54/10361.

[4] Bucks. Arch, Soc. Gough MSS. C54/16166.

[5] MAC, 17 Sept. 1869; 7 Oct. 1870. The Mercers subscribed 25 guineas towards each project.

TABLE 46

Rent of Mercers' farm after the Enclosure Award[a]

Period	Rent per annum (£)	Rebate allowed: Period	Amount per annum £	s.	d.
1798–1819	175				
1820–21	200				
1822–43	200	1822–31	50	0	0
		1832–8	20	0	0
		1839–43	40	0	0
1844–57	180				
1858–70	205				
1871–84	250	1879	40	0	0
		1880	20	0	0
		1882	10	0	0
		1883	40	0	0
		1884	50	0	0
1885–98	165	1886	15	0	0
		1889	7	10	0
		1893	37	10	0
		1897	27	10	0
		1898	20	12	6
1899–1919	130	1899–	41	5	0

[a] MAC, 1798–1919, *passim*.

living there today. In our changing world the present is more important than the past, and while many may appreciate that the old rectory has passed into lay hands or that the new one houses the incumbent of Sherington *cum* Chicheley, few will recognize that the Mercers withdrawal in 1919 broke an association that had existed for more than 400 years. Their manor, it is true, had been no more than a subsidiary one, but they had continued to exercise their manorial rights until well nigh the end of the nineteenth century whereas the last court of Cave's manor had been held in 1811 and of the principal manor as far back as 1751.

At a Mercers' court held in Sherington on 21 January 1817 James Smith, the owner of Cave's manor was presented for having built along the northern border of his garden a wall 90 yards long which encroached on the highway to a depth of 2 yards. He was also presented for having enclosed with a post and rail fence a plot of 20 perches on Calves Green, opposite the manor house, which he had planted with trees. The jury certified that Calves Green was the waste of the Mercers' manor and that the king's lieges had always had right of access. No action was taken at the time and the presentments were repeated at subsequent courts until 1859, when the Mercers decided to take legal action against the then owner, Alfred Umney.[1] After an exchange of letters, however, the Mercers were advised to withdraw, their representative pointing out that as no manorial map was in existence they would have difficulty in substantiating their claim.

The Mercers' main object in continuing to hold these courts nevertheless was to keep alive their quit-rents, for, as mentioned earlier, they never lost sight of the fact that they held as guardians of a trust. John (afterwards Sir John) Watney, the Clerk of the Company, was appointed steward of the Buckinghamshire manors in 1876 and four years later he held a court in Sherington. In his report to the Court of Assistants[2] he mentioned that Purefoy Fitz Gerald (who had married into the Chester family) was now paying a quit-rent of £1 per annum for Far Side farm (an allocation of the Chibnall quit-rent of *29s. 4½d.*) but that four other tenants, who between them owed *10s. 6d.* per annum, were in arrear since 1872. He then goes on 'Most of these quit rents were received by Mr Jefferson, the Company's tenant at Sherington and he tells me that as the amounts were small he used very often to pay out of his own pocket... I cannot recommend the Company to endeavour to enforce payment—if they were unsuccessful Mr Fitz Gerald might dispute the payment of the comparatively large sum that he now pays without demur.'

Ten years later local opinion had become set against any further legal tomfoolery. 'I beg leave to report that on 4 November 1890 I attended at Sherington for the purpose of holding a Court of the Manor, having previously summoned the tenants to attend, but as no tenant attended it was not possible to hold a Court.'[3] It is doubtful if John Watney, as he drove back to Newport Pagnell after this rebuff, was aware that his tenants had unwittingly buried the last remnant of those two knights' fees William, son of Ralph, had held of Henry II in 1166.

[1] MAC, 14 Jan. 1859.
[2] MAC, 4 June 1880.
[3] MAC, 7 Nov. 1890.

APPENDIX 1

RECONSTRUCTION OF THE FIELD MAPS FOR 1580 AND 1300

As mentioned in the Introduction, the interpretation of many of the older deeds and evidences that could provide information about the agrarian development of the village called for a map which would give the lay-out of the open fields, the furlongs and the meadows as they existed prior to the Enclosure Act of 1796, when most of the old boundaries were effectively swept away. If such a map had ever been in existence it had not come to hand, and when the idea of attempting to reconstruct one was first mooted a cursory glance through the relevant material suggested that 1770 would be a suitable date because two conveyances of that year had attached to them terriers of arable land totalling 108 acres in which each selion (strip, rood, ridge, land)[1] was described in more detail than was customary. It was identified as usual by the names of the owners of the selions on either side of it, but in addition the names of the furlongs against which it abutted were given, e.g. 'On Foxenhill Furlong one rood lying between the land of Archibald Buchanan on or towards the East and the land of John Glassbrook on or towards the West and abutting upon Waldecote Furlong on or towards the North and upon Rye Slade on or towards the South'. In the event experience was to show that without this latter information, which definitely linked one furlong with another without equivocation, the first general outline of the common fields and their constituent furlongs would have been difficult if not impossible of achievement. As the Enclosure Award of 1797 did not change the main features of the village—the sites of the houses, the home closes and the roads—an outline of these could be taken direct from the map attached to the original Award preserved in the Public Record Office.[2] A close study was then made of thirteen open-field terriers, including the two just mentioned, which showed that the three great common fields, known from the sixteenth to the eighteenth centuries as Marehill or Dropwell, Middle or Little, and Windmill Field respectively lay almost exclusively in the south, south-west,

[1] In Sherington this could be ½ rood, 1 rood, ⅓ acre—called a thirdendale, ½ acre or 1 acre.

[2] MPL, 38.

west and north-west sectors of the village, and that the meadow was a strip of land lying alongside the north bank of the river between Sherington bridge and the Tyringham boundary.

The majority of the furlongs could be readily assigned a tentative place in the field mentioned in the terriers, but a few of them, judging by the bounds recorded, were just as clearly a misfit. It was noticeable that in the former cases the selions of each particular holding in the furlong concerned were scattered, as one would expect to find in normal champion country, whereas in the latter they were often in compacted blocks extending to several acres. Such consolidation was indicative of demesne, and it seemed a fair surmise that if this had been located elsewhere than in the three open fields it must have been in the vacant north-east, east and south-east sectors of the map, the finer details of which could not be filled in because the terriers under review did not provide enough essential information. The only documentary material known for certain to deal with the manorial demesne was of Elizabethan date, and a detailed study of eight relevant terriers made it clear that in 1580 most if not all of the land in the three sectors just mentioned, which formed a compact quarter-circle bounded by the Olney road to the west and the Bedford road to the south, was indeed demesne. It was therefore decided to scrap the incomplete map for 1770 and start afresh on one for 1580.

The new map was drawn to the same scale as that attached to the Enclosure Award, 6 chains to the inch, and the main features copied in as before. To reconstruct the demesne area the various furlongs, closes and 'pieces' listed in Tables 47 and 48 were assigned squares of paper of a realistic scale size, and on these were written the names of the lands known from the terriers to be lying alongside them, the four sides of the square representing the four points of the compass. The squares were then played with as though they were parts of a jigsaw puzzle and by working from known boundaries such as Mercers' Wood, Olney road, Bedford road, Mill lane and the Chicheley border it was possible ultimately to integrate them so as to show the probable position on the map of the furlong, close or piece concerned. As the work progressed there were difficulties and inconsistences to be smoothed out, especially those arising from the alleged compass position of the neighbouring lands. It is to be remembered that when the Elizabethan attorney or his clerk was drawing up these terriers he would have had to visit the property with the owner, and as they wandered from track to track through the open fields it would have been easy for

TABLE 47

Distribution of the demesne area closes of pasture in 1580

Linford manor[b, c]	Acres	Cave and Fitz John manors[d, g]	Acres	Mercers' Company[a]	Acres	Thomas Tyringham and Lord Mordaunt[h]	Acres	Total in demesne area (a.)
Far Coneygre	5	Cow Close	20	Bancroft Close	8	Close N of Great Stocking, known later as Briant's Green	10	—
Nether Coneygre	6	New or Hay Close	20	Fullows Close	4			
Leasows, New Orchard and Home Close	8	Winyards Close	2					
		Mr Mountgomery's Grove Close	6½	Marshall's Close	1½	Tyringham Close to north-east of above	16	—
Bury Close	5½	Park Gate Close	2	Manor and Home Closes	4½	Duke's Dry Bank	11	—
Great Stockings	23	Church Yard Close	1¾	Sims Heynes Close	2	Duke's Wood Close	7	—
Two Little Stockings	12	Church End Close	3	Spicer's Mead	2½			—
Gowles Close	16			Church End Close	1¼			—
Close behind wood	12			Course's Close	1¼			—
Jaggins Close	2							—
Mowell's Close	3							—
New Diggins	2							—
	94½		55¼		25		44	218¾

[a] RCL, 143–164.
[b] D/C/1/1.
[c] D/C/1/2.
[d] D/Ch/89/5; Mountgomery to Mountgomery, 1601.
[e] D/Ch/89/15; Mountgomery to Halford, 1622.
[f] D/Ch/182/5; Babington *et al.* to Rogers, 1761.
[g] D/Ch/182/8; same parties, 1763.
(f and g) Both derived from a fine of Fitz John's manor dated 1600 between Wm. Mountgomery and his brother Theophilus.
[h] D/Ch/120/1 and Chester deeds.

TABLE 48

Distribution of the demesne arable land in 1580

Field	Linford Manor[c]	Acres	Mercers' manor[a]	Acres	Cave and Fitz John manors[d, e, f, g]	Acres	Total of demesne area (a.)
Windmill	Nether Berrye piece	18	—		Mercers' wood piece	11	—
	Upper Berrye piece	24	Park Gate furlong	1	Furlong abutting on Fullows Close	3	—
	Gore Leys piece	20	—	—	Furlong abutting on Gore Leys	1	—
	Sims Heynes piece	1	—	—	Sims Heynes piece	9	—
	Dawes Gap furlong	2	Crow's nest or Dawes Gap furlong	2	Dawes Gap furlong	6	—
	Gowles Corner piece	8	—	—	Gowles nether piece	11	—
	—	—	Furlong under Mr Catesby's Wood	9	Under wood furlong	2	—
	Burnt Leys piece	12	—	—	Gore piece	5	—
		85		12		48	145
Middle	Piece abutting on Winyards slade	6	—	—	Winyards furlong	12	—
	Piece abutting on Winyards slade	8	—	—	Mr Mountgomery's Dean	12	—
	Furlong abutting on Olney Way	4	—	—	Furlong abutting on Olney Way	8	—
	Long Doles furlong	12	—	—	Long Doles furlong	6	—
	Crabbe's piece	11	—	—	—	—	—
	Little Hill piece	12	—	—	—	—	—
	Piece shooting east to Little Hill	2	—	—	—	—	—
	Piece abutting east of Mercers' wood	8	—	—	—	—	—
	Spiney bushes piece	7	—	—	Spiney piece	6	—
		70		—		44	114
Marehill	Mr Ardes's Dean	27	—	—	Mr Mountgomery's Dean	20	—
	Willow bed furlong	2	—	—	Willow bed furlong	3	—
		29		—		23	52
	Hazlemead furlong*	10	Hazlemead furlong	6	Hazlemead furlong	7	23
Total (excluding Hazlemead furlong*)		184		12		115	311

For references see Table 47.

* Hazlemead furlong was not in the demesne area.

them to lose their keen sense of direction and unwittingly describe a boundary as lying, e.g. north instead of north-east or even east.[1]

As shown in Map 3, the reconstructed demesne sector includes all the holdings set out in Tables 47 and 48 as well as the four woods. There are no apparent gaps. According to the terriers the total acreage concerned was 611 acres, whereas the value computed from the Award map is 607 acres.[2] The agreement is remarkably close and affords good proof that the area in question has been correctly interpreted. It also provides a striking testimony of the accuracy with which Elizabethan attorneys and their clerks could measure land in the open fields.

The reconstruction of the three great open fields was based on the earlier study of the position in 1770, which showed that Marehill Field, Middle Field, the meadow and the cowpasture were all located in the large area to the north-west, west and south-west of the village and that Windmill Field lay to the south of the demesne in the sector bounded on the west by the old road to Newport. This information had been gleaned from valuable terriers drawn up in the eighteenth century and these fortunately could be used in the present instance because the individuality of many of the parcels of land concerned can be traced back to late Elizabethan times. All the terriers available, including those just mentioned, are set out in Tables 49–51. When making use of these data to prepare a final draft of the map it was necessary to proceed in such a way that a reasonable estimate of the extent of the cowpasture, hitherto an unknown quantity, was ultimately obtained.

Windmill Field had none of the cowpasture dispersed among its furlongs and the compact section of it lying to the south of the Bedford road, containing 260 acres

[1] A citation from reference 6, Table 47 is a case in point. 'And also threescore selions or lands Conteyninge by estimation twelve acres lyinge or being within the Middle Field in acerten Place called or knowne by the name of the Deane next unto awood of the Mercers on the North.' Actually the wood lies to the north-east of the piece concerned. A knowledge of the land in question shows how easily such an error could have been made. The terrier dealt with four large parcels of land in the northern sector of the demesne and the attorney's clerk would probably have jotted down his field notes from some fairly central position within it. Crossalbans Wood lay on rising ground on the other side of the northern boundary with Emberton, while Mercers Wood merged into it imperceptibly from the north-east. The Dean Piece butted against the former wood on the north and possibly because the clerk could not see precisely where one wood ended and the other began he assigned the north boundary to Mercers Wood.

[2] The Award map has engrossed on it a series of tables setting out *inter alia* the area of every plot in the village, each of which is numbered. The summation given above includes 84, 85, 88, 97–9, 101–112, 114–132, 134–6, 158, 159, 164, 178, 189–92, 203–214, 224.

TABLE 49

Distribution of land in Marehill (West) Field, 1575–1792

Furlong	Acreage of holdings													Total accounted for (a.)
	a	**b**	**c**	**d**	**e**	**f**	**g**	**h**	**i**	**j**	**k**	**l**	**m**	
Barrend Hole	$\frac{1}{2}$	—	—	—	—	—	$1\frac{1}{4}$	—	—	1	$\frac{1}{4}$	—	—	3
Broadmoor	—	—	—	—	—	$\frac{2}{3}$	—	$\frac{1}{3}$	1	$2\frac{1}{2}$	—	—	$1\frac{7}{12}$	$6\frac{1}{12}$
Bredonwell	$3\frac{1}{4}$	—	—	—	—	—	—	—	—	—	—	—	—	$3\frac{1}{4}$
Clay	$2\frac{1}{4}$	—	$\frac{1}{8}$	—	—	—	$\frac{3}{4}$	$2\frac{1}{4}$	$\frac{1}{4}$	1	$\frac{7}{12}$	—	$2\frac{1}{4}$	$9\frac{1}{4}$
Little furlong betweem Cowpasture and Clay	$\frac{1}{2}$	$\frac{1}{2}$	—	—	—	—	—	—	—	—	—	$\frac{1}{4}$	—	$1\frac{1}{4}$
Shotting to Cowmead	$1\frac{1}{4}$	—	—	1	—	—	—	—	—	$\frac{1}{2}$	—	—	$\frac{2}{3}$	$3\frac{5}{12}$
Under Down hedge or fence or Coppedmore	$1\frac{1}{2}$	$\frac{3}{4}$	$1\frac{1}{2}$	$\frac{1}{4}$	—	—	—	—	—	$\frac{1}{4}$	—	—	2	$6\frac{1}{4}$
Dowsdale	2	$1\frac{1}{2}$	—	$1\frac{1}{2}$	—	—	—	—	—	$\frac{1}{4}$	—	—	$\frac{1}{2}$	$5\frac{3}{4}$
Cross furlong above Dowsdale	—	$\frac{1}{4}$	—	—	—	—	—	—	—	—	—	—	$1\frac{1}{4}$	$1\frac{1}{2}$
Dropwell Leys	1	—	—	—	—	—	—	—	$1\frac{1}{4}$	—	—	$\frac{3}{4}$	$\frac{1}{2}$	$3\frac{1}{2}$
Foxenhill	$3\frac{1}{4}$	$\frac{1}{3}$	$\frac{1}{3}$	$3\frac{3}{4}$	1	—	—	—	$\frac{1}{4}$	1	—	—	$\frac{1}{4}$	$10\frac{1}{6}$
Cross furlong above Furmity Bush	—	—	—	$1\frac{7}{12}$	—	—	—	—	1	—	—	—	—	$2\frac{7}{12}$
Gore Broad	$\frac{1}{4}$	$\frac{1}{2}$	—	—	—	—	$1\frac{1}{6}$	$\frac{11}{12}$	—	—	$\frac{1}{4}$	—	$1\frac{2}{3}$	$4\frac{9}{12}$
Godescote	$1\frac{3}{4}$	$\frac{1}{2}$	$1\frac{1}{2}$	—	$\frac{1}{4}$	—	$1\frac{1}{6}$	$\frac{1}{4}$	$\frac{1}{2}$	$1\frac{1}{4}$	—	$\frac{1}{4}$	$1\frac{3}{4}$	$9\frac{1}{6}$
Furlong shooting above Godescote	—	—	—	—	—	—	—	—	—	—	—	$\frac{1}{4}$	—	$\frac{1}{4}$
Furlong under Godescote	2	—	—	$\frac{1}{2}$	—	—	—	—	—	$\frac{1}{3}$	—	—	—	$2\frac{5}{6}$

Upper furlong in Godescote	2	¾	—	2	—	—	¼	—	¼	¼	—	¼	—	5¾
Goldsworth	1¼	—	½	¼	—	—	—	1	—	¼	—	¼	4½	8
Long Greenditch	2¼	½	—	¼	—	½	—	—	1	1¼	½	½	1¾	8⅔
Short Greenditch	1	½	¼	½	¼	—	—	½	—	¾	⅔	—	1 7/12	6
Under Greenditch	—	—	—	¼	—	—	—	—	—	—	¼	—	¼	¾
One Hole (Deep furrow)	2	1 5/12	—	2½	—	¾	—	—	—	2	—	—	1	9⅔
Shooting to Filgrave hedge	¼	¼	—	—	¼	—	—	—	—	—	—	½	¾	2
Mare Hill	3¼	3	⅔	6	½	½	1	1	2½	4 5/12	1	—	6	29 5/6
Patch	—	—	—	1⅔	—	—	—	—	—	—	—	—	—	1⅔
Price (Breche)	3¾	¼	—	4¼	—	—	—	—	½	⅓	½	½	3⅓	13 5/12
Under Price	¼	—	—	—	—	—	—	—	—	—	—	—	—	¼
Little furlong above Price	—	—	—	—	—	—	—	—	1	1	—	—	—	2
Scragen Hill	¾	—	—	¼	—	1	—	—	—	1	—	—	1	4
Stoney Clay	½	¼	⅓	—	—	—	—	1	¼	—	—	¼	1	3 7/12
Stoney Clay shooting to Walcot	—	2¾	—	—	—	—	—	—	¾	—	—	¼	1½	5¼
Stuttels alias Dropwell	1	1	—	6	¾	—	—	—	—	½	—	¼	½	10
Below Stuttels	—	—	—	1	—	—	—	½	—	—	—	—	—	1½
Walcot	1½	1¼	½	2 5/12	—	¼	3	½	1	2⅓	¾	—	2 5/12	15 11/12
Cross Albans	1½	—	—	—	—	—	3¼	½	—	—	—	—	¼	5½
	40¾	16¼	5⅔	35 11/12	3	3⅔	11 11/12	8¾	11½	22⅙	4¾	4¼	38¼	206⅔

[a] RCL, 143–164.
[b] D/Ch/53/25, Lucas to Chubb, 1752.
[c] D/Ch/52/1, Lake to Cuningham, 1649.
[d] D/Ch/157/8, Chibnall marriage settlement, 1763.
[e] *BAS*, 413/44.
[f] D/Ch/20a/6, Hooton to Barton, 1771.
[g] D/Ch/182/2, Rogers to Babington, 1756.
[h] D/Ch/33/1, Chapman to Course, 1704.
[i, j] Tyr. D, 1712, Knight to Dewick, 1712.
[k] D/Ch/46/10, Brittain to Rogers, 1750.
[l] Glebe, Lincoln Terrier, 1707.
[m] D/Ch/138/1, Chibnall to Chibnall, 1714.

TABLE 50

Distribution of land in Windmill (South) Field, 1575–1792

Furlong	Acreage of holdings													Total accounted for (a.)
	a*	b	c	d	e	f	g	h	i	j	k	l	m	
Under the Ash	$1\frac{1}{2}$	$\frac{1}{2}$	$1\frac{1}{4}$	$\frac{1}{2}$	—	—	—	—	—	4	1	$\frac{1}{2}$	$1\frac{3}{4}$	11
Blackland	$\frac{3}{4}$	—	$1\frac{1}{3}$	$4\frac{1}{4}$	$\frac{3}{4}$	—	—	—	$\frac{1}{2}$	$2\frac{1}{3}$	$\frac{1}{2}$	—	$1\frac{5}{6}$	$12\frac{1}{4}$
Bullocks leys	—	$\frac{1}{2}$	—	$1\frac{1}{12}$	$\frac{1}{4}$	—	—	—	$\frac{1}{2}$	$1\frac{3}{4}$	$\frac{3}{4}$	$\frac{1}{2}$	3	$8\frac{7}{12}$
Denson alias Monchlade	$1\frac{1}{2}$	—	—	3	—	—	$1\frac{1}{4}$	—	—	1	$\frac{1}{2}$	$\frac{1}{2}$	$\frac{1}{4}$	8
Gomeshole	3	$\frac{1}{2}$	—	1	—	—	—	$\frac{1}{2}$	$\frac{1}{2}$	$\frac{7}{12}$	—	—	$2\frac{5}{12}$	$8\frac{1}{2}$
Holbrooke alias Dagger way	$\frac{1}{2}$	$2\frac{3}{4}$	—	—	—	—	—	—	—	$\frac{1}{4}$	$\frac{1}{4}$	$\frac{1}{4}$	$\frac{3}{4}$	$4\frac{3}{4}$
Little Furlong at Holbrook Hill	—	—	—	—	—	—	—	—	—	$\frac{1}{3}$	—	—	1	$1\frac{1}{3}$
Hollow Willow patch	—	$\frac{1}{2}$	—	—	—	—	—	—	—	—	—	—	6	$6\frac{1}{2}$
Beyond Hollow Willow Bush	$\frac{1}{4}$	—	—	1	—	$\frac{1}{3}$	—	—	$\frac{1}{4}$	—	—	—	—	$1\frac{5}{6}$
Homer Side of Hollow Willow Bush	1	—	—	$1\frac{1}{2}$	—	—	—	—	$1\frac{1}{2}$	1	—	—	—	5
Short furlong above Holloway	$\frac{1}{4}$	$\frac{3}{4}$	—	—	$\frac{1}{4}$	—	1	—	—	$\frac{1}{2}$	—	—	$1\frac{1}{2}$	$4\frac{1}{4}$
Holloway	—	—	—	—	$\frac{1}{4}$	—	$\frac{1}{2}$	1	—	—	$\frac{1}{4}$	—	$1\frac{3}{4}$	$3\frac{3}{4}$
Furlong beneath Holloway	$\frac{1}{2}$	—	—	—	—	—	—	—	—	—	$\frac{1}{2}$	—	—	1
Holloway Slade	—	—	—	—	—	$\frac{1}{2}$	—	—	—	—	—	$\frac{1}{4}$	—	$\frac{3}{4}$

Hunger Hill	1¼	—	—	1	—	—	—	¾	—	¾	—	¼	2½	6½
Short furlong under Hunger Hill	—	¾	—	—	—	—	—	—	½	1	—	—	1½	3¾
Bacon's womb or Miller's Knob	—	3	—	—	—	—	—	—	—	—	—	—	¾	3¾
Middle Malme	—	1	—	⅔	—	—	—	—	—	—	—	—	½	2⅙
Nether Malme	½	1	—	—	—	—	—	1	½	—	½	¼	1¾	5½
Upper Malme	1½	⅔	—	—	—	—	—	—	—	—	—	—	⅓	2½
Pinson Hill	2½	⅔	¾	—	—	—	—	—	—	½	—	—	2 5/12	6⅝
Raye	1	⅔	—	1¼	—	—	—	—	½	—	—	¼	¼	3 11/12
Rensfurrow	—	½	—	—	—	—	—	¼	—	—	—	—	1¾	2½
Above Rensfurrow	—	½	—	—	—	—	—	—	—	1	—	—	½	2
Ruden Hill	3	¼	—	3½	—	—	—	—	—	1¾	—	—	¾	9¼
Rye	¼	—	1⅙	½	—	—	—	1	¼	2	—	—	½	5⅔
Sim Shooters (to Wolfreycroft)	1¼	—	—	—	—	—	—	—	—	½	—	—	—	1¾
Standhill Marsh	1½	—	1⅓	—	¼	1	—	—	⅓	½	1⅙	⅓	1⅔	8 1/12
Staple Hill	3¼	⅔	⅔	3⅙	1 1/12	—	—	⅚	—	—	—	½	2	12⅓
Scardingswell	2¼	¼	—	—	½	—	—	—	—	½	—	¼	—	3¾
Townsend†	5¾	¼	—	4¼	—	4⅓	—	1	—	½	—	—	1¼	17⅓
Whitwell	¼	1 7/12	—	¾	—	—	—	1	—	1	—	¾	—	5⅓
Windmill	2¾	1	—	4¾	—	—	6	—	¼	2½	—	¼	3¾	21¼
Wolfreycroft	2½	½	—	½	—	—	—	—	—	—	—	—	1	4½
	38¾	18 9/12	6½	32⅔	3⅓	6⅙	8¾	7⅓	5 7/12	26¼	5⅓	4⅚	41⅚	206 1/16

* For references see Table 49.

† Includes furlongs named Upper Hay, under Burnt Leys, Hay, abutting down to New Close, abutting down to highway, Mr Catesby's Townsend.

TABLE 51

Distribution of land in Middle Field, 1575–1792

Furlong	Acreage of holdings													Total accounted for (a.)
	a*	**b**	**c**	**d**	**e**	**f**	**g**	**h**	**i**	**j**	**k**	**l**	**m**	
Backside	2	2/3	—	2	1/2	—	—	1/4	—	1/2	—	—	1/4	6 11/12
Cow Mead	1/2	—	—	—	—	—	—	—	—	—	—	—	—	1/2
Elderstub	3/4	—	—	—	1/2	—	—	—	—	—	—	—	—	1 1/4
Foxenhill	1	2 1/12	—	1/2	—	—	—	1	1/3	1	1	1/4	4 1/4	11 5/12
Fully Hill	2	1/3	—	3 1/6	1/4	1/4	1 1/2	—	—	3 1/6	2/3	1/4	1/2	12 1/12
Gusitslade	2 1/4	—	—	3	1/3	1 3/4	—	2 1/4	—	1	—	1/2	3 1/2	14 7/12
Ryeslade	1 3/4	1/2	1 1/2	2 5/8	7/12	—	—	—	—	1 3/4	—	1/4	3 1/8	12 1/12
Course's Townsend	2 3/4	—	—	—	—	—	—	—	—	1/4	—	—	1	4
Walcote	2 1/4	3/4	1	4 1/6	3/4	—	1 1/2	1 1/2	1/3	2	1	1/2	1 1/2	17 1/4
Yard's end	1/8	1/2	—	—	—	1	—	—	2	4	—	—	—	7 5/8
Total above Gutter	15 3/8	4 5/6	2 1/2	15 1/2	2 11/12	3	3	5	2 2/3	13 2/3	2 2/3	1 3/4	14 1/8	87
Alborough	2	2/3	—	6 1/4	1/2	—	—	1/4	—	1/2	—	3/4	1/4	11 1/6
Bridge Leys	2 1/4	2	2	—	—	—	—	—	—	1/2	—	—	—	6 3/4
North side of Clots or Tonditch	1 1/4	3/4	—	1 1/4	—	—	—	2	1 1/4	1 1/2	—	1/4	3 1/2	11 3/4

Clots	1	—	—	1	—	—	—	½	—	¼	—	¼	¾	3¾
Clots slade	—	—	—	¾	—	—	—	—	—	—	—	—	—	¾
Delves	—	¼	—	3	—	—	—	⅓	—	1	—	—	2¾	7⅓
England	—	—	1	—	—	—	—	—	—	—	—	¼	½	1¾
Farthingstile	½	—	¼	—	—	—	—	—	—	—	—	—	—	¾
Hareland	—	1	—	—	—	—	1¾	—	—	1¼	—	—	3¾	7¾
Longland	1¼	1	—	2¾	—	¼	—	—	½	1	—	¼	¾	7¾
Meadow without Lords	4	—	—	—	—	—	—	—	—	—	—	—	—	4
Millway	1½	1¾	1	1¼	—	—	—	—	½	1	—	¼	1	8¼
Pusty	1¾	—	1½	2	1	—	2½	—	—	½	¾	—	—	10
Little furlong above Pusty	—	—	—	1½	—	—	—	—	—	—	—	—	—	1½
Water Furrows	¾	¼	—	1¼	—	1½	—	—	¼	⅛	—	¼	½	4⅞
Water Swallows	½	—	—	—	—	—	—	—	—	—	—	—	—	½
Wetherhedge	1¾	—	½	—	—	—	—	—	—	—	—	1	—	3¼
Total below Gutter	18½	7⅔	6¼	21	1½	1¾	4¼	3 1/12	2½	7⅝	¾	3¼	13¾	91⅞
Total Middle Field	33⅞	12½	8¾	36½	4 5/12	4¾	7¼	8 1/12	5⅙	21 7/24	3 5/12	5	27⅞	178⅞
					Under a two-field system									
West Field	56⅛	21 1/12	8⅙	51¼	5 11/12	6⅔	14 11/12	13¾	14⅙	35⅚	7 5/12	5¾	52⅜	293¾
South Field	57¼	32 5/12	12¾	53⅔	9⅙	3 7/12	13	10 5/12	8 1/12	23⅞	6 1/12	8 1/12	55 7/12	304⅛
	113⅜	53½	20 11/12	105 1/12	15 1/12	10¼	27 11/12	24⅙	22¼	59¾	13½	13 11/12	108 23/24	597⅞

* For references see Table 49.

according to the Award map,[1] was a suitable area with which to start the task of reconstruction because the present-day Hollow Willow Close, which has been under permanent pasture since the time of enclosure, retains the headlands and ridges representing the five pre-enclosure furlongs called Under the Ash, beyond Hollow Willow Balk, on the homer side of Hollow Willow Balk, Blackland and Sim Shooters respectively. The terriers provided detail of only 183 acres of the 260 acres concerned. Bearing in mind that the motif of the present study was to produce a map that would illustrate the assemblage of fields and furlongs in the old days and not one that necessarily had any pretensions of being an accurate survey, it seemed plausible to assume that the holdings for which terriers were non-existent would collectively have had their land distributed among the furlongs in about the same proportions as those covered by the terriers. The total acreage recorded for each individual furlong was accordingly increased in the ratio of 260:183 or by a factor of 1·42. The sector map which emerged from this study seems to satisfy the evidence on which it is based: the various furlongs are in the right quarter and they butt against the lands indicated in the terriers. It is not suggested, however, that they are necessarily of the correct size or shape. The part of the field lying to the north of the Bedford road was revealed without difficulty and as, according to the Award map, it contained 36 acres the total area of Windmill Field must have been 296 acres.

The other two great open fields, with the meadow, the cowpasture and Hazlemead furlong (which was demesne in Elizabethan times) were in the west and north-west sectors of the village. This large area of 727 acres[2] could not be resolved in such a direct way as Windmill Field because the acreage of none of the components except Hazlemead furlong was known. Nevertheless, a close inspection of all the data set out in Tables 49–51 showed that in general there was a regularity in the distribution of the land between the three fields and, making the same assumption as before about the land not covered by the terriers, it seems reasonable to apply the correction factor that was permissive for Windmill Field to the other two common fields. The 206 acres assigned in the terriers to Marehill Field thereby became 293 acres and the 183½ acres in Middle Field 260 acres.

All the terriers under discussion, including those for the demesne area, mention strips in the meadow, the total for Lordsmead being 16½ acres and for Townsmead 21½ acres. If it be argued as before that the holdings for which terriers were not

[1] Award map, nos. 77–83.

[2] Award map, nos. 1–14, 34–38, 45, 58–68.

available contained their due proportion of meadow these values can be raised to $23\frac{1}{2}$ and $30\frac{1}{2}$ acres respectively, suggesting that the belt of meadow running from the bridge to the Tyringham fence contained 54 acres. This value, incidently, is in good agreement with that derived from the landholdings of the various owners in 1580, as set out in Table 30. Summarizing, we may say that the two fields, the meadow and Hazlemead furlong account for 630 acres out of the 727 acres in the north and north-west sectors of the village, leaving 97 acres for the cowpasture. In view of the various assumptions on which the correction factors have been based this estimate cannot be a precise one, but there is justification for believing that it is of the right order of magnitude.

I am confident that during the study of these common fields, in which many score of deeds besides those specifically mentioned have been consulted,[1] no furlong or close has been overlooked. Many of the perplexing problems encountered in the early stages were readily solved when it was realized that the names of certain of the furlongs and especially of the closes had been changed for one reason or another between 1580 and 1770. With all this information on hand the reconstruction of the north and north-west sectors of the map was accomplished without difficulty.[2] It will be realized of course that the dotted lines represent only a few of the selions known to have been present in each furlong.

The prime purpose behind the present study has already been explained, and when the project was started it was not anticipated that the various features of the map would be reproduced with any great degree of fidelity. There is, fortunately, evidence that this prognostication was too pessimistic. Three years after the new map was engrossed a terrier of the Sherington property drawn up by a qualified surveyor in 1753 was found among some miscellaneous papers of the Mercers' Company. All the ridges (selions) are described in detail and although the information supplied does not show the location of one furlong *vis-à-vis* another, the direction in which each furlong lies is stated, and the ridges are dealt with in turn as members of a numbered sequence. For example 'In Maire Hill Furlong shooting North West and

[1] Most of these deal with only a few selions, but even so a single entry can be profitable, e.g. '1 r. in the Lower Malme which is a headland against Rye furlong'.

[2] The location of the hedge dividing Marehill Field from Middle Field was not known. To ascertain this, full use was made of the knowledge that under the original two-field system of husbandry the dividing line between the two great fields was the town ditch, so that a furlong assigned in an early charter to North (East) Field and in a later terrier to Middle Field must have been located north of the ditch.

South East beginning at the North East side thereof. The 46th and 47th ridges land of Robert Chrichton lying on the North East part and of Mr. Wodell on the South West part thereof... 2 r. 32 p.' And so on for those numbered 59, 61, 82, 84, 93–5 and 109 respectively, the total area of the ten ridges being 4 acres 12 poles. Marehill furlong thus contained at least 110 ridges and its total area must have been of the order of 44 acres. The corrected value from Table 51 is 42½ acres. The agreement in this and all the other cases vetted, including Lordsmead and Townsmead,[1] is closer than might have been anticipated, a finding that increases one's confidence in the correction factors upon which Map 3 and the final data given in Table 52 are based. According to the Enclosure Award survey the total area of the village is 1763½ acres.

Evidence has been presented in earlier chapters and summarized in Tables 1, 17, 19 and 30 to show that no significant alteration in the overall land distribution took place between 1300 and 1580, the only effective incident being the superimposing on the arable expanse of three open fields instead of the original two pairs of two, in keeping with the development of a three-field system of tillage. It is clear from the Throckmorton charters that the dividing line between the old North (East) and South Fields was the town ditch, and on the assumption that the lay-out of the furlongs underwent no change in the meanwhile the furlong pattern in Map 3 has been used with only minor alterations in the drawing of Map 4. The names of the furlongs inscribed on the new map are those for which documentary evidence earlier than 1330 is available, and it will be noted that a fair proportion belong to furlongs on the periphery of the village, illustrating a point emphasized in Ch. 1 that most if not all of the village land had been opened out at an early date.

As mentioned above, the demesne lands of the four constituent squires and the holding of the Tyringham family in le Hoo Park underwent but little change between the two dates concerned. It has been assumed therefore that the general disposition of the demesne arable pieces and closes of pasture so successfully recreated in the map for 1580 would hold also for that of 1300, the only minor difference being the need to give more prominence to le Hoo Park. The Carun terrier for 1312 (Table 53) can be interpreted without difficulty in terms of the lay-out in Map 4, but the lands then in the hands of the escheator's official, John de Burgh, were not the whole of the Carun inheritance because Joan, mother of the heiress Sibyl Carun, was still holding one third of the manor in dower. Omitting the piece

[1] Cf. p. 112, Table 12.

TABLE 52

Computed distribution of land in Sherington in 1580

	Acres	Acres
Demesne		
Arable land (Table 47)	311	
Pasture (Table 48)	218	
Hazlemead	23	
	—	552
Woods		
How Wood	26	
Mercers' Wood	21	
Heyton Wood	18	
Linford Wood	17	
	—	82
Common fields		
Marehill	293	
Middle	260	
Windmill	296	
	—	849
Non-demesne closes[a]		22¾
Cowpasture		97
Meadows		54
Farms and home closes[b]		64
Cottages[c]		9¼
Roads[d]		22
		—
		1752

[a] Award map nos. 11, 13, 31–3, 41, 43, 56, 57, 75.

[b] *Ibid.* nos. 15–24, 28, 29, 40, 46, 52, 137–9, 147–52, 154–9, 163, 167, 176, 177, 179–82, 187, 188, 194, 195, 198, 202.

[c] *Ibid.* from table of cottagers.

[d] *Ibid.*

called le Stockyng, which did not become part of the Carun–Linford–Ardes estate until later, the 148 acres of Carun demesne arable and pasture land in 1312 was about two-thirds that owned by Richard Ardes a short while before 1580. For lack of contemporary evidence the sites of farmhouses entered on both of the reconstructed maps have been copied without alteration from the one which accompanies the Enclosure Award. The number of cottages has been reduced to 18 (Map 8).

In retrospect the most interesting outcome of the present study has been the clear demonstration that in late Tudor times the large sector of land to the north-east and east of the village, consisting of compacted furlongs of arable land and of

TABLE 53

Terrier of the arable land in the hands of the king's escheator on 21 September 1312[a]

To save space acr' and rod' have been abbreviated to a. and r. respectively. Throughout the list Arabic have been substituted for Roman numerals

'Numerus acrarum terre arabilis in manu Johannis de Burgo per J. Richer numeratus die Sancti Mathei apostoli anno regni regis Edwardi filii regis Edwardi sexto'

North Fild[b]	Idem habet in campo Boriali iuxta le Aubeles in una cultura 15 a. 3 r. Item apud le Hoveden 9 a. terre. Item apud Gotburyedole ½ a. Item ibidem 1½ a. Item super le Toftes 2½ a. Item super le Winlondes 1 a. Item ibidem 2 a. 3 r. Item apud le Longe dole 5 a. 1 r. Item ibidem 4 a. 3 r. Item ibidem 4½ a. Item apud le dedcroft 3 r. Item apud le Lytelhull 3 r. Item ibidem 4 a. Item apud le Tenacres 5 a. Item iuxta eundem locum 7 r. Item attelowe 3 r. Item apud le Wodeyhates 3 a.
	Summa ibidem 64 a. et 1 a. 3 r.
Est Fild	In campo orientali et contra portem Bosci 1 a. 1½ r. In eundem cultura 1 a. In Cockescroft 2 a. Item ibidem 1 a. Item ibidem 8 a. Item apud le Wodeyhate ½ r. Item apud le Salu 3 r. Item ex al (?) parti bosci 7 a. Item apud Audreuesmere 10 a. In le Stokyng 50 a.[c] Item super Heldebyry 10 a. Item ibidem 13 a. Item ibidem ½ a. Item in le Croftes 2 a.
	Summa 109 a. [except le Stokyng].
Sowth Fild	In campo Australi apud le Overestockynge 13 a. Item apud le Hoo (alf ?) 10½ a. et 2 partes 1 r. In [le Brendehoo 3 a.][d] In le Hay 7 a. Item [in Brendehoo 4 a.][d]
	Summa 31½ a. et 2 partes 1 r.
West Fild	In camp Occidentali iuxta le Aubeles 2 r. Item in le Pocpyt 2 a. ½ r. In Wellomed' 1 a. In Difford 3 a.
	Summa 6 a. 2½ r.
	Summa acc' 213 a. ½ r. [recte 210 a. 3 r.] Item 7½ a. prati.

[a] NRO, *Ecton*, 1190, m. 1. The land consisted of two thirds of the Carun estate and 50 acres (le Stockyng) recently sold by Margery de Carun to Ralph Basset of Drayton; cf. pp. 70, 132, 142.

[b] The field-names in the margin are in an early sixteenth-century hand.

[c] The statement is underlined in the text.

[d] Words in brackets have been cancelled.

enclosed pasture, was exclusively demesne.[1] The Carun terrier for 1312, although it concerns only a fraction of this land, tells the same story in a no less convincing way, while the hypothesis that the consolidation goes back to Domesday and the militant bishop of Coutances can be inferred from much good indirect evidence.[2] Land distribution on these lines is not entirely novel. In his study of twelfth-century charters for villages in the Danelaw, Stenton found that the lords demesnes were often composed in whole or in part of furlongs, but in these cases it would seem that the

[1] Cf. M. W. Beresford, *Econ. Hist. Rev.* 2nd series, I, 42, n. 2.

[2] P. 90.

TABLE 54

Compacted parcels of land in eighteenth-century deeds

Field	Furlong	Reference*... b	g	h	i	j	n
Windmill	Burnt Leys	18 ridges for 6 a.		13 ridges for 4 a.			—
	Wood	—	8 roods together 2 a.	—	15 roods together 3 a.	—	4 lands for $1\frac{1}{2}$ a.
	Gore Leys	—	—	—	—	15 roods for 3 a.	piece for 5 a.
	Shooting to Fullows Close	—	—	—	—	2 roods for $\frac{1}{2}$ a.	3 a. together
	Dawes Gap	—	—	—	—	—	17 ridges for 6 a. 17 ridges more for 6 a.
	Windmill†	—	14 selions for 5 a.	—	—	—	—
Middle	Mercers' Wood	28 ridges for 7 a.	—	—	—	—	—
	Winyards	—	—	—	—	—	33 ridges for 8 a. 8 lands together 4 a. $\frac{1}{2}$ a. more
	Olney Way	—	—	5 ridges for 2 a.	—	—	—
	Spiney Leys	—	—	4 a. piece	—	—	—
	Little Hill	—	—	11 ridges for 2 a.	—	—	—
Marehill	Hazlemead	14 ridges for 5 a.	—	10 one-third part together	—	—	—
	Cross Albans†	—	11 ridges for 3 a. 1 rood	—	—	—	4 roods together
	Foxenhill†	—	—	—	—	—	10 ridges for 4 a.
	Dowsdale†	—	—	—	—	—	9 ridges together 2 a.

* References **b–j**, see Table 49; **n**, Fitz John's manor farm in 1761–3; the holding also contained 19 acres in the open common fields.

† These furlongs are in the open common fields.

furlongs lay intermingled with the land of their men.[1] Whether the complete divorce between demesne and open-field land found in Sherington is in any way exceptional cannot be decided until more is known about the open fields in medieval and Tudor times. Such evidence is scarce and much of our present day knowledge of the disposition of the land under the open-field system has been based—unwittingly perhaps—on terriers and maps of a later period when the system itself might well have been already in decay. The ample Sherington data can be effectively used to illustrate the point.

Let us suppose that the terriers for the eighteenth century had been comprehensive enough for the completion of the projected map for 1770 and that no deeds earlier than about 1630 had survived. The inner history of the demesne being unknown, the map would have shown the whole of the village land parcelled out into three great common fields, and it will be instructive to ponder over the conclusion, if any, that could have been drawn from the disposition of the land in the north-east and east sectors recorded in the contemporary terriers.

At various times during the seventeenth century more than a half of the arable land and three-fifths of the enclosed pasture that we now recognize as having once been demesne became dispersed as arable land among a number of the farms, each of which had the rest of its holding scattered among the three great common fields. Terriers of the open-field lands of many of these farms are given in Tables 49–51, while the portions of the demesne that went with them are set out in Table 54. The latter table shows that most of the land concerned was in small compacted parcels that are well distributed over the north-east and east sectors of the village; it also shows a very few compacted parcels in the open fields. If no knowledge of the agricultural past had been available it would have been natural to deduce that these compacted parcels were evidence of consolidation to meet a rising standard of agriculture, as Tawney has suggested in another context.[2] While this was probably true of the open-field lands it would have been quite at variance with the real position in the demesne, for agricultural conditions in Sherington became progressively worse, not better, as the eighteenth century unfolded, and the compacted parcels of land there were symptomatic of a slow disintegration under a system of tillage that was already in decay and meet to be swept away on enclosure a few years later. There is a lesson to be learnt here that is worth recording.

[1] F. M. Stenton, *Documents Illustrative of the Social and Economic History of the Danelaw*, pp. lvi–lx.

[2] R. H. Tawney, *The Agrarian Problem in the Sixteenth Century*, p. 254.

APPENDIX 2

DRAFT OF A MERCERS' COURT ROLL FOR 1575

Paper draft of the proceedings at a Court Baron of the Mercers' Company held in Sherington on 16 September 1575. The preamble in Latin was apparently written out by the steward or his clerk while the jury was being sworn; the presentments, only a few of which are quoted below, were added later by the local bailiff Thomas Fisher. The final roll, engrossed on parchment as usual, is one of the series at Mercers' Hall.

Manerium de Sheryngton	Curia Baronis Custodii et Communitatis misterii mercerii Civitatis Londonii ibidem tenta 15 die Septembris anno 17 E. regine.
Libere tenentes	Thomas Tyrryngham armiger Edwardus Chybnall generosus Willelmus Mountgomery generosus Radulphus Hoton Antonius Smyth Johannes Spryngnell Thomas Mauncell generosus Katherine Ardes vidua pro termine vite sue Thomas Orpyn in iure uxoris suis sunt libere tenentes huius manerii
Tenentes per copiam	Thomas Fyssher Thomas Dycher Johannes Person Agnes Grome Radulphus Hoton Edwardus Chybnall generosus
Homagium Ibidem	Thomas Fyssher Johannes Person alias Pierson Radulphus Hoton Edwardus Chybnall generosus
Item	We doe present accordynge to the old customs Mystrys Ardes oethe sute And hathe made defaute Master Mungumbre oethe sute And hathe made defaute Master Turringgam oethe sute And hathe made defaute We present that Mystrys Ardes by loppyng of the ockes standynge of our Lordes frebourti Adjoynyng to the mounde hathe made defaute [in a different hand] mercy 6*s*. 8*d*. for lopping. We present that Mystrys Ardes shall deny us of our commins In the newe pasture called old Berryfurlonge cont. 25 acres and netherberryfurlonge[1] and denieth us of our waye from the mylle Lane and downe after Bancroft side leading to Parke Gappe into Wyndmill Feld and have daye till michailmas nexte to laye it abroad upon payne of 40*s*.

[1] No extent given.

[Item (*cont.*)] And that she denieth us of our comons in one close called Stocking cont. 20 acres and to Laye abroade the same by the feast of St Michael nexte comyng apon peine of 40*s*.

And that we have not our commons in on close called Gowles cont. 12 acres and yt she Laye it abroade before the said feast upon piene of 40*s*.

Item we present that the sayde Catherine hathe not layd abroade accordinge to the peyne of 40*s*. layd upon her one close called Leazowes containing 2 acres wherein the inhabitants of this towne should have commons from Lammas till ye Ladye daye in Lent and yt she Laye the abroade before the sayde feast of St Michael upon piene of 40*s*.

And that she denieth us of our commons in another close adjourning to the sayd Leasowes and abutting upon Willowbedd end containing 1 acre wherein we should have commons all the year in Fallowe time and the several time from Lammas to our Ladye daye and to be Layd abroade before the sayd feast upon piene of 40*s*.

And that William Moonegumberie gent denieth us of our commons in one close at Cross Awbells called the Deane close containing by estimation 15 acres wherein the tenants of this manor have had [commons] all the yeare in Fallowes times and he Laye abroade before the feast of St Michael next apon payne of 40*s*.

Item that whereas the tenants of thys lordshyp have had common of pasture in a piece of ground called Jacketes grene for all tymes of the yere they now present that they have the common aforesayd but from lamas untyll the Annuncyation of our Lady and so lose theire common for the rest of the yere.

[It will be noted that the season when commons could be taken varied from close to close, as it did in the middle ages; there is indeed a striking similarity between some of the above-mentioned complaints and those of Master William de la Mare in 1271–2, cf. pp. 109–10.]

Item that the tenants of this manor have had alwayes great timber allowed for their necessary reparations and desire to have the same still allowed

Imprimis For Thomas Fisher for reparations which he hath nowe in hand 4 trees.

Item Edward Chybnall for a baye that he hath nowe taken down 2 trees.

Item Agnes Grome widow one tree.

Item John Pearson one tree.

APPENDIX 3

COTTAGES IN SHERINGTON DURING THE PERIOD 1680–1710

Few relevant deeds earlier than the mid-eighteenth century have survived, but the ownership and descent of the cottages in existence during the period with which we deal can be deduced from entries in the court rolls of the three manors. Many of the cottages, or perhaps it would be more correct to say the site on which they were built, had their roots back in feudal times when the tenant owed service to the relevant lord of the manor. Such services would have long since been commuted for a small annual payment called later a quit-rent and according to the custom of the manor concerned, which happened to have been the same for all three of those in Sherington, a relief of a second quit-rent became due to the lord on change of ownership through death or alienation. The circumstances leading to the demand for payment of this relief, as it was called, are recorded on the court rolls, and by following the descent of any particular property through the succession of rolls[1] it is possible to deduce the name of the owner at the time of the enclosure in 1796 and hence to identify the cottage on the map attached to the award. The information thus culled is given in Table 55. Inspection of the lay-out of the cottages on Map 8 indicates that at some time prior to 1708 many had arisen by building a new cottage in the garden or home close of one already in existence, i.e. no. 197 out of no. 198, the new one being apportioned its share of the quit-rent at the relevant manor court —in the case mentioned that of the Mercers held in 1648. Rolls for Linford and Cave–Fitz John manors of date earlier than 1682, which could illustrate the point more extensively, have not, unfortunately, survived. As discussed fully on p. 201

[1] The following Court Rolls have come to notice: Northamptonshire Record Office (Carun, later Linford, manor): 21 Sept. 1312; 4 Oct. 1312.

Tyringham Estate (Linford manor) 1682, 1683, 1708, 1751; the quit-rents claimed totalled 15*s.* 1*d.*

Buckinghamshire Record Office (Cave–Fitz John manor): 1708, 1715, 1764, 1786, 1811; the quit-rents claimed totalled 17*s.* 7¼*d.*

Mercers' Hall (Mercers' manor): 1513, 1525, 1527, 1528, 1529, 1531, 1536, 1538, 1544, 1562, 1565, 1571, 1575, 1587, 1593, 1601, 1607, 1623, 1635, 1642, 1648, 1651, 1658, 1668, 1682, 1686, 1748, 1753, 1756, 1772, 1783, 1798, 1805, 1827, 1846, 1856, 1863, 1869, 1879. From 1562 the series is complete. The quit-rents claimed totalled £2 8*s.* 11½*d.* (Table 2).

TABLE 55

Owners of cottages paying quit-rents in Sherington

(compare Table 34)

No. on Map 8	Owner before 1708	Owner in 1708	Owner in 1796
16	William Scrivener	Thomas Richards	Richard Higgins
20	John Field	Robert Babington	Thomas Tandy
25	—	Edward Boddington	Thomas Odell
26	Thomas Chibnall	Richard Chibnall	James Cave
28	James Brierly	Thomas Osborne	William Umney
32	Richard Hunt	Ann Marshall	Friends Meeting House
40	Henry Newall	Robert Babington	John Underwood
42	Samuel Cunningham	Edward Cunningham	Rose's trustees
47	Mary Chapman	Edward Gant	William Davison
48	Henry Gravestock	Robert Field	Rose's trustees
49	Edward Finnemore	James Finnemore	William Davison
50	Bartholomew Course	Thomas Course, junior	Rose's trustees
51	Thomas Tyringham	Thomas Richards	Rose's trustees
55	Edward Britnell	Anne Lucas	William Warr
92	Bartholomew Finnemore	Thomas Clifton	Elizabeth Slater
93	Edward Fisher	John Fisher	Samuel Boddington
94	Thomas Umney	Thomas Umney	Thomas Umney
96	Edward Norman	Edward Norman	Richard Shrieve
141	John Knight	Mary Knight	William Thompson
144	Thomas Knight	Robert Knight	Thomas Talbot
145	Bartholomew Course	Thomas Course, junior	Rose's trustees
146	Christopher Wright	Thomas Marshall	Thomas Marshall
160	Joseph Tomalin	Robert Babington	Mercers' Company
161	Thomas Roughhead	William Roughhead	Mercers' Company
165	Robert Knight	Edward Hooton	Samuel Greathead
166	John Knight	Henry Knight	James Simcoe
183	Henry Gravestock	Robert Field	Rose's trustees
184	Andrew Clare	Francis Clare	Richard Clare
185	Edward Hooton	John Hooton	Thomas Platt
197	Thomas Harman	John Ruddy	— Hosea
199	William White	Thomas Clifton	Thomas Tandy
200	John Field	Robert Babington	John Brittain
201	Stephan Boswood	William Boswood	Thomas Odell

and set out in Table 34 the fusing of neighbouring cottages in this way suggests that at some earlier period the number of cottages paying quit-rent was eighteen.

In addition to the 35 cottages listed in Table 34 there were, during the period under review, 29 others standing upon manorial waste (Table 56). The Linford

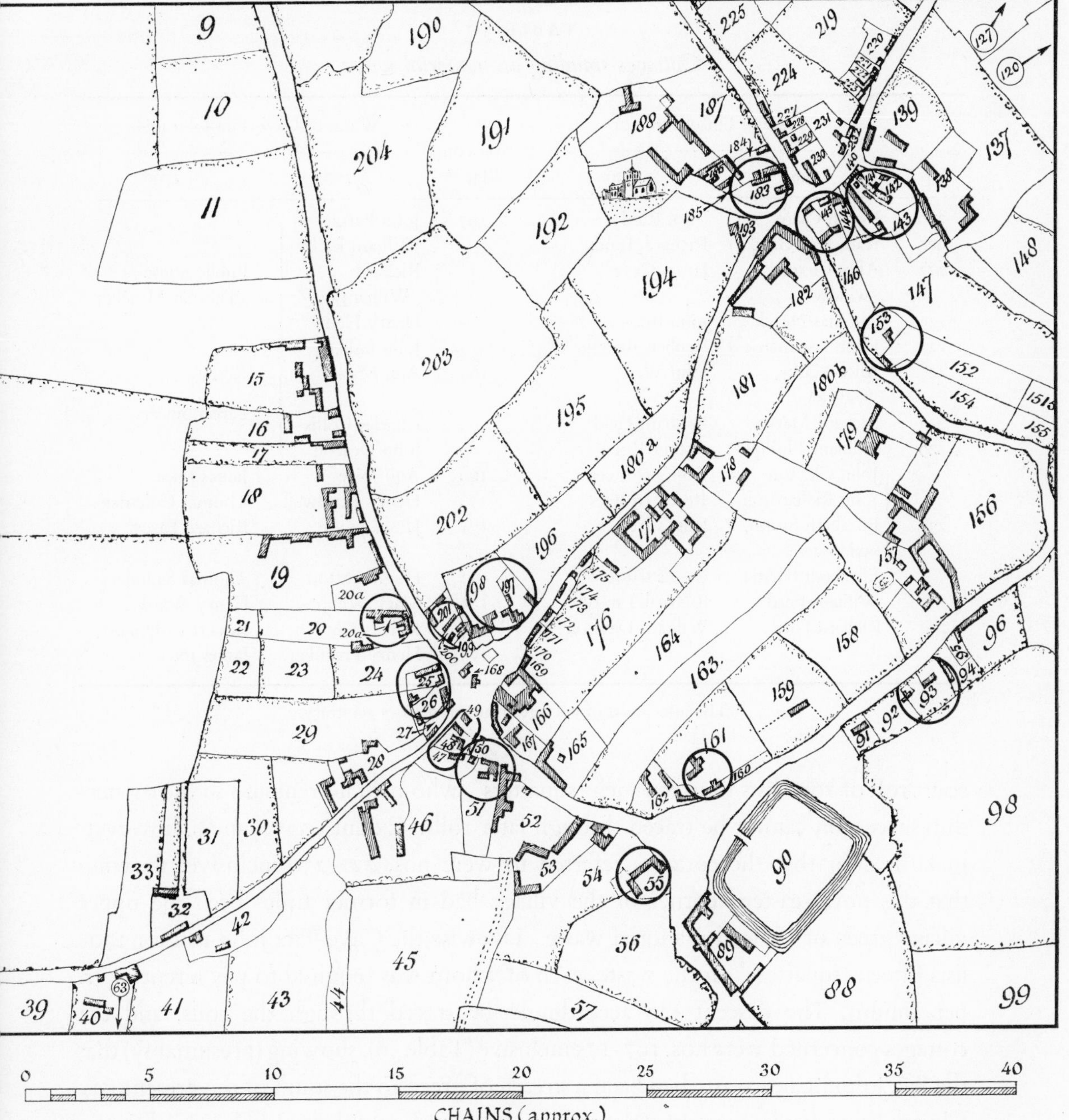

Map 8. Sherington village as depicted in the Enclosure Award map of 1797. The circles have been added by the author to show how two or more cottages were derived from one that formerly occupied the whole site concerned.

TABLE 56

Cottages standing on manorial waste

No. on Map 8	Waste of Linford manor 1682[a]	Waste of Linford manor 1796	No. on Map 8	Waste of Cave–Fitz John manor 1708	Waste of Cave–Fitz John manor 1796
220	Joseph Clare	Tho. Riddy	167	John Parratt	Public house of Thomas Meacher
221	Katherine Gant	Richard Tandy		William Earby	
222	Alice Caxon, widow	James Cave		Richard Williamson	
223	Thomas Neach	John Rose		Henry Hall	
226	Jacob Freeman	Reuben Brittain		John Fisher	
227	Alice Marks, widow	John West	168	Ann Marks	Parish officers
228	Richard Marks	William Field		Charles Collis	
229	William Phillips	Arthur Roe		John Deacon	
230	John Cleyton	Rose's trustees	169	Ann Joice	James Joice
	John Richardson	Rose's trustees	170	Henry Burdwell	Thomas Coleman
	Elizabeth Smith, widow	Rose's trustees	171	James Smith	Richard Fazey
	Elizabeth Forster	Rose's trustees	172	Hugh Clifton	Thomas Saunders
231	William Ford	Richard Tandy	173	Mary Webb	Henry Ward
232	Richard Ford	William Davison	174	Robert Church	Robert Coleman
			175	Henry Freeman	James Joice

[a] The allocation of cottages is in most cases arbitrary.

court roll of 1682 lists fourteen such 'squatters', who paid no rent and so the ownership succession cannot be traced through later rolls. Extant conveyances, however, make it clear that the cottages referred to were nos. 222–230 inclusive, showing that this north-eastern corner of the village had in former times been the upper village green or Linford manorial waste. Likewise the Cave–Fitz John roll for 1708 lists fifteen 'squatters' on the waste, each of whom was required to pay a rent of 1*s*. per annum. The descent can accordingly be traced through the rolls, and the cottages concerned were nos. 167–175 inclusive (Table 56), showing (presumably) that the Fitz John manor waste had been a stretch of green to the south of the present day Church lane where it meets the Newport–Olney road, together with the island site on which stood the three cottages numbered 168. As discussed on p. 257 the Mercers claimed that the strip of land to the north of the moat on Calves lane, together with the island site in front of the present-day manor house, was waste of their manor.

APPENDIX 4

MANOR COURT ORDERS, 1682

(D/Ch/misc/7)

		£	s.	d.
Manerium de Sherington in Com. Buck.	Orders made and agreed upon by ye Jury and other ye Inhabitants of Sherrington at ye Court Leet and Barron of Roger Chapman Gent there held for ye said Mannor ye tenth day of May 1682.	£	s.	d.

Imprimis It is ordered and agreed that no man shall put a Cow into ye Cow-pasture but upon a double Common and not to be put into ye said Cow-pasture untill ye tenth day of May upon pain to forfeit to ye Lord for every such offence — 0 10 0

2. It is agreed that every man shall give an account what Commons he hath and what Common he letteth or taketh by ye first day of May no man shall let a single Common but to make up a Common upon pain of forfeit etc. — 0 5 0

3. It is ordered and agreed that every man that hath threescore acres of Land and Leys may keep four horses or six Cowes and no more at Open-tide and so proportionably for a greater or lesser quantity of acres upon pain of forfeit etc. for every horse or Cow which shall be beyond this number — 0 10 0

4. It is ordered and agreed that no Cowes or Sheepe shall come into any of ye Several fields until such time as harvest be home in each field respectively nor ye Sheepe to come into ye Cowpasture until barley harvest be home upon pain etc. — 0 5 0

5. It is ordered and agreed that no Cow or Sheep shall be kept in ye several fields upon pain etc. — 0 5 0

6. It is ordered and agreed that every man shall keep his hogs and Piggs ringed after they are eight weekes old upon pain etc. — 0 2 6

7. It is ordered and agreed that no man shall let any Colt go loose in ye fields after it be four weekes old till harvest be home upon pain to forfeit to ye Lord for every colt so offending for every day — 0 10 0

		£	s.	d.
8.	It is ordered and agreed that every Lamb bred in ye fields shall be counted as a sheep at Martinmas: and if any be bought in Lambs they shall be esteemated sheep			
9.	It is ordered and agreed that no man shall bring any horse or Colt mare or gelding into ye Cowpasture or Meadow till harvest be fully home upon pain etc. for every time etc.	0	10	0
10.	It is ordered and agreed that no horse or sheep shall come into ye tilth field after ye first day of November till harvest be home subpona	0	10	0
11.	It is ordered and agreed that neither horse nor beast nor any great Cattle shall come into ye other fields which shall be sowen Cowpasture or Meadow after ye feast of St Andrew till ye tenth day of May except horses staked upon their own grounds after Lady day and that no horse nor Colt nor Cow shall come into ye fallow field after ye tenth of May, subpena for every head of such catell etc.	0	10	0
12.	It is ordered and agreed that every one shall keep for every acre of arable in ye fallow field two sheep and for every acre of Leys and Glades three sheep and no more and keep every year alike in ye fields proportionately subpeinâ for every offence etc.	0	2	6
13.	It is ordered and agreed that all ye lands that was counted Lammas grounds and now in tillage be laid down for sweard before ye first of November next and so kept, and none of ye formerly reputed Lammas ground to be plowed up subpoenâ to ye Lord	0	2	6
14.	It is ordered and agreed that no farmer shall give leave to any poor to break this order following under pain for every offence	0	5	0
15.	It is ordered and agreed that no Gleaner shall come into ye Pease Field till harvest be quite home except that owners after their own carts and that no person shall put any Catell into ye Pease field untill Harvest hath been ined four dayes subpoenâ etc.	0	5	0
16.	It is ordered and agreed that all Dung cart ways Lanes and harvest ways be laid open at convenient times subpoenâ etc.	0	10	0
17.	It is ordered and agreed that no Cowes nor horses be kept staked or led in ye high wayes except Clatts green only to ye herd subpoenâ for every horse or Cow kept staked or led	0	5	0
18.	It is ordered and agreed that after ye field tellers appointed have set and bounded out ye severall furlongs in ye fields of Sherington there			

	£	s.	d.
shall be allowed a pole consisting of sixteen feet and a half from ye meerstone in each furlong to be kept as headway to ye furlong and no man shall sow any part of it upon pain to forfeit etc.	0	5	0
19. It is ordered and agreed that every person shall give an account to ye fieldtellers of Sherrington what lands they occupy before ye twentieth day of March yearlie upon pain etc.	0	1	0
20. It is ordered and agreed that no man shall let a whole Common for horse or Cow after opentide subpoenâ etc.	0	5	0
21. It is ordered and agreed that Mr Chibnall, Thomas Knight, Thomas Marshall, Richard Knight, John Bull, Thomas Course, William Field and Christopher Right shall be fieldtellers for ye Cattle in ye fields and shall set out highways, head wayes and Lammas ground in ye fields of Sherrington at or before ye first of November next ensuing upon pain to forfeit for their respective neglects	1	0	0
22. It is ordered and agreed that ye fieldtellers shall be hereby impowered to take to their assistance such persons as they shall esteem convenient and ye forman to give three dayes public notice of their first going about it, to ye end as many of ye Jury as please may be with them			
23. It is ordered and agreed that ye Heyward do impound all Cattell as he shall find trespassing under ye penalty for every neglect	0	1	0
24. It is ordered and agreed that every person who hath enclosed any of ye field land do within two days after ye date of these orders lay open ye said Closes to ye fallow fields out of which they were taken and enclosed upon pain of forfeting for every acre and for proportionately	2	0	0
25. It is ordered and agreed that no man shall dig or cause to be digged any Morter in ye Cowpasture unless for ye use of ye husbandmen and farmers except one load in a year for a cottager's own use upon pain for every load digged otherwise	0	1	0
26. It is ordered and agreed that no man shall take above 4*d*. a load for digging ye said Morter upon pain for every load exceeding this rate	0	0	6

Thomas Osborn jury

Examined
N. M. Farrer
Senescal ibidem

APPENDIX 5

'A STATEMENT OF SHERRINGTON COMMONS, 1722'

(*BAS*, 414/44)

This agreement made concluded and agreed upon ye 20 March 8 George I (1722) between Sir John Chester of Chicheley Baronet, Tyrringham Backwell of Tyrringham Esq., . . . of Newport Pagnell gent, Nicholas Chibnall of Newport Pagnell gent, Anthony Chapman of ye same gent, Widdow Smith of Passenham in Co. Northants, Thomas Knight, Alden Fuller of Newport Pagnell gent, John Barton of Sherrington Clerk, John Chibnall of ye same, gent: John Knight of ye same yeoman, Robert Adams of ye same town and county yeoman, John Babington, Edward Hooton, John Course, Robert Brittain of Newport Pagnell, John Sharman, Thomas Umney, John Umney, Thomas Course, Edward Richards of Chicheley, Thomas Tebott, Ch. Brandun of ye same, John Merrill of Fillgrave, Joseph Brooks, James Brooks, William Freeman, John Olde labourer, William Goodride, Widdow Fountain, John Caves, Thomas Richards, John Marshall, John Rogers, Thomas Leaver, Daniel Broughton, William Jones, John Bull, Edward Lane, Richard Leapidge yeomen. Owners and occupiers of lands and tenements lying within ye said Parish of Sherrington of ye one part. And Robert Perrot of Newport Pagnell, William Chibnall of ye same town gent and John Cripps of ye same yeoman of ye other part.

Whereas there is not sufficient pasturage in ye Common Fields of Sherrington for so many sheep as are necessary to be kept and folded on ye arrable lands lying in ye same fields and by reason of ye want of Dung to supply ye defect thereof and also of ye small quantity of meadow and Inclosed pasture ground there is not a fitt quantity of grass to keep a sufficient stock of horses and cows as are necessary to be keept and feed upon ye several farms.

Imprimis it is agreed for ye plaintiffs above named their Heirs, Executors, Administrators etc. that there shall yearly at Easter be chosen by the major part of the owners and occupiers of the lands and tenements Field-tellers who shall forthwith set out ye several furlongs in all and every the common fields and ye bounds of the same furlongs and there shall be allowed and laid down for sward a peice of ground consisting of sixteen feet and a half in breadth between ye Mear-stones and marks of each of ye furlongs to be set out and kept as a head-way drift-way and cart-way to all the said furlongs which peice of ground between each shall not be ploughed up but continue laid down for ye space of one and twenty years from ye date above-mentioned.

Also it is agreed that at each of ye times and seasons when the furlongs of land in every of ye common fields shall next be respectively plowd up for the fallow there shall be laid down for sward and kept all ye said tearme of one and twenty years to be allowed as aforesaid of and from every half Acre of Areable Land lyeing within ye said common fields one foot in breadth from each side thereof and so proportionately of and from third parts and roods of Lands as they lye by estimation. And where two half Acres belong to ye same Person lyeing together there shall be laid down four feet that is to say two in breadth from ye outside of each half acre. And where three such half acres lye together there shall be laid down six foot from them in breadth that is to say three feet from each outside land. And when four half acres lye together there shall be laid down two foot from each outside land and four feet between ye two midlemost lands. And where any peice of land of any greater quantity doth or shall lye together there shall be laid down on ye outside of every two lands or ridges thereof so much as shall amount to ye proportion of four feet to every acre.

Also it is agreed that all the owners and occupiers of Areable Lands lying within ye Parish of Sherrington shall lay down for sward five acres out of every thirty that is to say every sixth acre as they lye by estimation if not allready laid down and so proportionable for a greater or lesser number of acres.

Also it is agreed that none of ye owners or occupiers of land lyeing in ye common feilds of Sherrington shall depasture or keep on ye sheep commons more than according to ye rate of one sheep for every acre of Arrable land which they possess during ye aforesaid tearm. And ye Lambs which are brede in ye said fields shall be accounted as sheep at Martimass. And ye Lambs which shall be bought and brought into or kept in ye said feilds from the Dams before Martimass unless their Dams die shall be accounted for skeep at their comeing in being kept in ye common feilds.

Provided always that ye said Sir John Chester his executors Administrators etc. and his and their tenants and occupyers of several parcells of land being about thirty two acres lying in a common feild called Windmill Field now occupyed by Edward Richards and Thomas Tebbot may keep one hundred sheep and no more in ye same feild which they usually kept sheep in but in no other of ye common feilds or commonable places of Sherrington.

Provided also that Tyrringham Backwell his heirs or assignes or the tenants of twelve acres of land lying in a common feild called Drappwell Feild may keep thirty six sheep and no more but in no other of ye common feilds or commonable places of Sherrington.

Also it is agreed that during the tearm of one and twenty years that no sheep shall be kept in ye common feilds when sowed with wheat or barley from ye first day of August untill the said grain be caryed off ye feilds. Nor shall any sheep be kept in ye feild when sowed with beans and pease from ye first day of August untill they are caryed out of ye field.

Provided allways the said Sir John Chester his assignes or their tenants may use certain peices of lands called Cowleys feilds now in ye occupation of Charles Brandon. And also that the said Sir John Chester his Heirs and assignes and his and their tenants may have liberty to inclose ye above mentioned peices called Cowleys feilds occupied by Ch. Brandum and also severall peices of land called dry bank, Gore leys and wood peice. And further it is agreed that Ch. Brandum or any other tenant shall have [no priveledge or right of common in any of ye feilds of Sherrington except before excepted or allowed to be inclosed] (parts between [ ] added later in a different hand) that ye said Sir John Chester his Heirs or Assignes or occupyers of a peice of land called Miller's Knobbs containing one acre and a half lying in a common feild called Windmill Feild in the Parish of Sherrington shall keep the same severaly to their own use dureing ye tearm of one and twenty years he or they paying ye sum of five shillings to ye overseers of ye poor of the parish of Sherrington the time being at Easter for ye use of the poor of ye said parish.

And it is also agreed that none of ye owners or occupyers of land in the said Parish of Sherrington shall keep above four horses or four cows after Open-tide in any of ye common feilds besides the commenalle Cows in ye Cowpasture for threescore acres of Areable land or ley ground and so proportionable for a greater or less number of acres.

Also the said Sir John Chester, Tyrringham Backwell and all other persons aforementioned their several Heirs Executors Administrators and Assignes shall and will from time to time at all times hereafter during ye space of one and twenty years to be accounted as aforesaid well and truly observe fullfill and keep all and every of ye Articles and Agreements above written on their respective parts to be observed kept and fullfilled according to ye true intent and meening of these presents.

Also it is agreed that if the said Sir John Chester Tyrringham Backwell or any other person aforesaid their several and respective Heirs Executors Administrators and Assignes at any time or times break any Artickle or Agreement above written shall pay the sum of five shillings and if not rectyfied in five days shall pay ye further sum of ten shillings and if any person or persons being found faulty shall refuse to pay the penalltyes aforesaid for such default or neglect shall lay himself or themselves lyable to be distrained by the Field-tellers that are lawfully chosen and appointed for such intents and purposes.

And also it is agreed by all and every ye said partys to these presents that any sum or sums of money that at any time or times during the space of one and twenty years shall be paid or recovered by or against any of ye said parties above named as herein concerned the then Lawfully chosen Feild-tellers haveing received or recovered such sum or sums shall dispose of the same to such poor people of the parish of Sherrington as they shall think fitt. Lastly it is agreed that if any Feild-tellers shall break any Artickle or Artickles aforesaid they shall also pay the sum of five shillings and if not rectyfied in five days shall pay ye further sum of ten shillings and if they or any of them refuse to pay ye penallty or penalltys aforesaid they do acknowledge themselves lyable to be distrained by the persons above named of ye other part (*viz*) Robert Parrot William Chibnall and John Cripps and that thay ye said Robert Parrot William Chibnall and John Cripps having received or recovered such sum or sums of money shall dispose of they shall think fitt to ye poore of Sherrington. In Witness whereof all the said parties to the said presents have interchangably set their hands and seals ye day and the year first above written. J. Chester, (mk) Edward Richards, Thomas Tebott, Charles Brandum, John Barton, (mk) Thomas Richards, John Chibnall, Richard Leapidge, Thomas Umney, Edward Hooton, Robert Adams, John Knight, Thomas Leaver, Susanna Fountain, John Marshall, Thomas Knight, Will Joanes, John Course, Daniel Broughton, (mark of) John Rogers, Edward Lane, Thomas Course, John Cave, John Bull.

[Underneath, is written:]

Item. It is agreed that whosoever soweth grass seeds or layeth down for sward any parcell or parcells of land that might have been sowed with grain shall have liberty to bait upon ye same untill harvest is ended in ye same feild.

Item, it is agreed that John Bull

APPENDIX 6

SHERINGTON FIELD-NAMES

The place-name elements of the furlongs and closes that form the boundaries between Sherington and its neighbours, but not those within the confines of the village itself, have been discussed in Ch. 1. A number of the names given in Maps 3 and 4 are self-explanatory and call for no comment, but others contribute in varying degree to the early history of the village and are set out in Table 57.

Charter T, A70, dated 1323, mentions 'a cultura next to Standeldig extending towards le rowehafdeues'. This last word contains ME *haft* or *haued*, 'head' and ME *eues*, 'edge or brow of a hill', and means rough headland or spur of a hill. At a later date the furlong was called Water Furrow and it extended from Stanidelf (Delves) furlong to the strips of cowpasture which butted up to the hillock upon which once stood the early medieval fort that gave name to Alborough Furlong.[1] Charter T, 210, dated 1317, provides confirming evidence, 'one head of pasture *viz* one half acre in the field of Schringtone at rowe Hauerdeus'. These comments, and those given in Table 57, column 4, are based on discussions with Prof. Ekwall.

[1] See p. 16 and Maps 3 and 4.

TABLE 57

A selection of Sherington field-names

The names refer to furlongs unless otherwise stated

Modern form, if applicable	1580	*c.* 1300[a]	Comment
		Attelowe	OE *hlāw*, at the 'mound'
Bancroft Close	Bancroft Close	Barounscroft	Presumably the croft retained for his own use by Lord Grey or Lord Bassett
Branch Green	Bryant's Green	Bryounscroft or Sampsonscroft	Derives from owner or tenant (T, 311, A87)
Broadmoor	Bredonwelle	Bredonwelle	OE *breden*, 'of boards', presumably was once a well lined with boards

[a] Based on the Throckmorton charters, fines quoted in *BASRB*, IV, and the terrier given in Table 53.

TABLE 57 (*cont.*)

Modern form, if applicable	1580	*c.* 1300	Comment
Burnt Hill	Burnt lees piece	le Brendeho	ME *brende*, 'burnt' ho
	Delves	Stanidelf	Stone pit or quarry
Calves End Lane	—	Cavysende (1410)	The lower end of the village, dominated by the Cave manor house
Drop Hill	Dropwell	—	No early form; presumably the same well as in Bredonwelle—'dripping well'
—	England	—	ME *eng*, 'meadow': it was land by the meadow
—	Fullows Hill	Fulewelle rithy Colewelle hegge	Alongside a brook running from a dirty well
Gooms Hole	Gomeshole	Cumbes	Hollow on flank of hill
	Gussocks Slade	Gosacreslade	Slade for geese
Clats Close	Gutter or town ditch	subtus Dys	Variant of OE *dīc*, 'ditch'
	Clot's slade	super caput de Dys	Head of the ditch, changed later by association with Clot's Close
—	—	Gotburyedole	Obscure
Hazlemead	Hazlemead	Wellemed	Meadow near the 'Fulewelle'
—	Hay	subtus le Hay	OE *hege*, 'enclosure'. It is below the large Cave manor enclosure
—	Holbrook Hill	Holebrochul	OE *broc*, 'badger'—Badger hill with holes in it
—	—	Hovedene or Honedene	OE *hōfe* 'possibly ground ivy'—valley where hofe grows
—	Furlong under Mr Mountgomery's Wood	le Hoo Alf	Presumably the scribe's rendering of le Hoo Half, containing OE *healf*, 'side', the side of the hill-top
—	Pery	Piri	Pear tree
—	Pusty	subter Quarreya	OE *Pytt-stig*, below, or on the way to the stone pit
Big Price	Upper Price	Rys	OE *hrīs*, 'brushwood', the later form apparently due to wrong division of up Ris
Staggering Close	Scragen Hill	Scregethornhul	Presumably connected with OE *scrag*, 'stump'
—	Staple Hill	Stapulhul	Hill with a post on it
—	—	Wartrou	OE *wearg*, 'felon', and OE *tréow*, 'tree': the furlong must have been alongside the village gallows[b]
—	Whitwell	Linolewelle	OE *līn*, 'flax', and *holh*, 'hollow': spring in the hollow where flax grows, changing later when flax was no longer grown
—	Willow Bed piece	le Salu	Place where sallows (scrubby willows) grow

[b] See p. 10.

INDEX